MW01027518

AT THE DAWN OF AIRPOWER

Titles in the Series

The History of Military Aviation

Paul J. Springer, editor

This series is designed to explore previously ignored facets of the history of airpower. It includes a wide variety of disciplinary approaches, scholarly perspectives, and argumentative styles. Its fundamental goal is to analyze the past, present, and potential future utility of airpower and to enhance our understanding of the changing roles played by aerial assets in the formulation and execution of national military strategies. It encompasses the incredibly diverse roles played by airpower, which include but are not limited to efforts to achieve air superiority; strategic attack; intelligence, surveillance, and reconnaissance missions; airlift operations; close-air support; and more. Of course, airpower does not exist in a vacuum. There are myriad terrestrial support operations required to make airpower functional, and examination of these missions is also a goal of this series.

In less than a century, airpower developed from flights measured in minutes to the ability to circumnavigate the globe without landing. Airpower has become the military tool of choice for rapid responses to enemy activity, the primary deterrent to aggression by peer competitors, and a key enabler to military missions on the land and sea. This series provides an opportunity to examine many of the key issues associated with its usage in the past and present, and to influence its development for the future.

AT THE DAWN OF AIRPOWER

THE U.S. ARMY, NAVY, AND MARINE CORPS'
APPROACH TO THE AIRPLANE, 1907–1917

BY LAURENCE M. BURKE II

Naval Institute Press • Annapolis, Maryland

Naval Institute Press
291 Wood Road
Annapolis, MD 21402

Library of Congress Cataloging-in-Publication Data

Names: Burke, Laurence M., II, 1969- author.
Title: At the dawn of airpower : the U.S Army, Navy, and Marine Corps' approach to the airplane, 1907-1917 / by Laurence Mitchell Burke II.
Other titles: U.S Army, Navy, and Marine Corps' approach to the airplane, 1907-1917
Description: Annapolis, Maryland : Naval Institute Press, [2022] | Series: The history of military aviation | Includes bibliographical references and index.
Identifiers: LCCN 2021059325 (print) | LCCN 2021059326 (ebook) | ISBN 9781682477298 (hardcover) | ISBN 9781682477502 (ebook)
Subjects: LCSH: Aeronautics, Military—United States—History—20th century. | Naval aviation—United States—History—20th century. | BISAC: HISTORY / Military / Aviation | HISTORY / Military / United States
Classification: LCC UG633 .B845 2022 (print) | LCC UG633 (ebook) | DDC 358.400973--dc23/eng/20220118
LC record available at https://lccn.loc.gov/2021059325
LC ebook record available at https://lccn.loc.gov/2021059326

♾ Print editions meet the requirements of ANSI/NISO z39.48-1992 (Permanence of Paper).

Printed in the United States of America.

30 29 28 27 26 25 24 23 22   9 8 7 6 5 4 3 2 1

First printing

This book is dedicated to the memory of my late wife,
who would have been thrilled that I have a book in print.

CONTENTS

ACKNOWLEDGMENTS

This book is based on part of my overly long dissertation. I thank my advisor, David Hounshell, and the other members of my committee, Steve Schlossman and Peter Karsten, for their aid and guidance in crafting the dissertation. Very little new research was done for the content of this book, aside from some minor research at the Library of Congress and the Air Force Historical Research Agency archives at Maxwell Air Force Base. In the interest of keeping this section brief, please see the acknowledgments in my dissertation for those who helped with and/or supported the research at the various archives cited herein.

Rearranging, revising, and editing down the text for this book (no small task), as well as writing new introductions and conclusions for the new chapters and the book as a whole, has been a very solitary task. Nevertheless, there are those who provided support and encouragement as I did the necessary work, advised on publication questions, helped me nail down things I was still unsure of, and let me bounce ideas and problems off them, occasionally reading snippets, while I tried to figure out what I wanted to say and how I wanted to say it. Most, if not all, of the task was completed while working at the National Air and Space Museum, and I greatly appreciate the contributions and support of my colleagues there. These are, in no particular order: Jeremy Kinney, Roger Connor, Bob van der Linden, Alex Spencer, Mike Hankins, Peter Jakab, Tom Crouch, Phil Edwards, Margaret Weitekamp, David DeVorkin, Matt Shindell, Paul Ceruzzi, Cathy Lewis, and the often-changing attendees at the office writers' group. Susan Englehardt at the Smithsonian's Office of Contracting worked very hard to synchronize the Smithsonian's interests with those of NIP to make this contract happen. Further afield, Frank Blazich, Colin Colbourn, Matthew Ford, Angel Callahan, Annette Amerman, Hal Friedman, and Ryan Wadle have each contributed in their own ways. Paul Springer, my acquiring editor, was invaluable in helping me with the proposal and preparing the manuscript for submission. I greatly appreciated Brian Laslie's very positive outside reader's review. I also want to thank the people at Naval Institute Press who helped get the contract finalized and have worked with me to help polish the book.

Finally, I am grateful for the help I got from the archivists at the Library of Congress (Jon Eaker), Air Force Historical Support Agency (David Bragg), and the NASM Archives staff (especially Brian Nicklas, Elizabeth Borja, and Melissa Keiser) in helping me identify photographs to consider for the book and supplying me with publication-quality copies.

Apologies to anyone I forgot to mention here!

ABBREVIATIONS

ACA	Aero Club of America (also just Aero Club)
AEA	Aerial Experiment Association
AFAL	Air Force Academy Library, Clark Special Collections Branch, Manuscript Collections, Colorado Springs, Colorado.
BEF	British Expeditionary Force
BOF	Board of Ordnance and Fortification (Army)
BOF Correspondence	RG165, Records of the War Department General and Special Staffs; Records of Discontinued Boards 1888–1922; Records of the Board of Ordnance and Fortification; General Correspondence, NACP
BOF Index Cards	RG165, Records of the War Department General and Special Staffs; Records of Discontinued Boards 1888–1922; Records of the Board of Ordnance and Fortification; Subject Card Index to Series 516 [Actions of the BOF], NACP
BOF Minutes	RG165, Records of the War Department General and Special Staffs; Records of Discontinued Boards 1888–1922; Records of the Board of Ordnance and Fortification; Minutes ("Proceedings") of Meetings of the Board, 1888–1918, NACP
Bristol Papers	Mark L. Bristol Papers, Naval Historical Collection, Manuscript Division, LC
BuAer	Bureau of Aeronautics (Navy)
BuC&R	Bureau of Construction & Repair (Navy)

BuEng	Bureau of Steam Engineering (Navy); after 1920, the Bureau of Engineering
BuEng Corresp.	RG72, Bureau of Aeronautics; Records of Predecessor Agencies; General Correspondence, Bureau of Steam Engineering; General Correspondence re: Aviation, NAB. (I have cited these as they appear on the documents: serial number first, then the -736 suffix indicating aviation subject matter. NARA has them filed as though 736 is a prefix.)
BuEquip	Bureau of Equipment (Navy)
BuNav	Bureau of Navigation (Navy)
BuOrd	Bureau of Ordnance (Navy)
CAC	Coast Artillery Corps (Army)
Chambers Papers	Washington Irving Chambers Papers, Naval Historical Collection, Manuscript Division, LC
CINCLANTFLT	commander in chief of the Atlantic Fleet
CNO	Chief of Naval Operations
CO	commanding officer
CSO	chief signal officer (Army), also called "chief of signal"
Cunningham Papers	A. A. Cunningham Papers, P.C. 459; Marine Corps Archives and Special Collections, Gray Research Center
DMA	Information Section—RG18, Records of the Army Air Forces; Division of Military Aeronautics, Records of the Information Section: Charts, Bulletins, Lecture, Memoranda, Syllabi, and other records relating to foreign and domestic air services, airplane construction and equipment, and flight training, 1917–1919: NACP
DMA-Letters	RG18, Records of the Army Air Forces; Division of Military Aeronautics Establishment and Organization, Letters and Memoranda, August 1907–June 1918; NACP
F.A.I.	*Federation Aeronautique International* (International Aviation Federation), based in Paris. For many years,

	this was the only formal licensing body for pilots, whether of balloons or airplanes
Foulois Papers–LC	Benjamin Delahauf Foulois Papers, Manuscript Division, LC
Foulois Papers–AFAL	MS 17, Foulois, Benjamin Delahauf Papers, AFAL
Foulois Thesis	Benjamin D. Foulois, "The Tactical and Strategical Value of Dirigible Balloons and Dynamical Flying Machines"
GB-XXX	refers to the appropriately numbered subject file in: RG80, Office of the Secretary of the Navy; Subject Files of the General Board, NAB
GC	general correspondence
HTA	heavier-than-air. Referring to airplanes, helicopters, and anything else that depends on movement to generate lift.
JAG	Judge Advocate General Corps
JMA	Junior Military Aviator (Army)
Lahm Papers	Lahm, Frank Purdy Papers (1894–1967), Document Collection, Air Force Historical Research Agency, Maxwell AFB, AL
LC	Library of Congress
LTA	lighter-than-air. Referring to balloons, airships, and anything else that relies on a low-density "lifting gas" to remain airborne.
MA	Military Aviator (Army)
MGC	major general commandant of the Marine Corps
Mustin Papers	Henry Croskey Mustin Papers, Naval Historical Collection, Manuscript Division, LC
MS	Manuscript Series
NAB	National Archives Building, Washington, DC
NACP	National Archives, College Park, MD
NAS	Naval Air Station. At Pensacola, this stood for Navy Aeronautic Station until December 7, 1917.

NASM	National Air and Space Museum, Washington, DC
[n.d.]	not dated. Where possible, I have given an estimated date based on information in the document and/or the dates of documents around the undated one where records are arranged chronologically.
ONA	Office of Naval Aeronautics. As a source: RG72, Bureau of Aeronautics; General Correspondence of the Office of Naval Aeronautics, 1914–1917; NAB
RFC	Royal Flying Corps (British Army)
RG	Record Group
RN	Royal Navy (British)
RNAS	Royal Naval Air Service (British)
SecNav	Secretary of the Navy
SecNavAC	RG72, Bureau of Aeronautics; Correspondence of the Secretary's Office Relating to Aviation; NAB. (These were originally part of the sequence in SecNavGC in RG80, but were transferred to BuAer shortly after its establishment.)
SecNavGC	RG80, Office of the Secretary of the Navy; General Correspondence; NAB
SecNavAR	Annual Report of the Secretary of the Navy
SecWar	secretary of war
SecWarAR	Annual Report of the Secretary of War
Squier Papers	Papers of George Owen Squier, MS-11, AFAL
Towers Papers	John H. Towers Papers, Naval Historical Collection, Manuscript Division, LC
T/O	Table of Organization
TO&E	Table of Organization and Equipment

Note on citations: many of the letters cited, especially the official letters, are sent by, and to, office titles. In the interest of brevity and clarity, these more lengthy titles have been changed to the names of the officeholders where known.

PROLOGUE

Modern flight research may be considered to have begun with the investigations of Sir George Cayley. Cayley was an English aristocrat and professional engineer, which allowed him both the time and resources to experiment. He also possessed the knowledge to make those experiments worthwhile. Born in 1773, Cayley began investigations into aeronautics in 1796, and, in 1809, built a successful unmanned glider. Between 1809 and 1813 he published three articles, each titled "On Aerial Navigation," in a prestigious British science journal. These articles summarized his research and laid out fundamental principles for subsequent investigators. Returning to aviation in 1849, Cayley built a tethered glider that successfully carried a small boy into the air, and in 1853, launched his coach driver into the air in a free-flying glider. The flight ended with a crash and the shaken coach driver tendered his resignation.

Others built on the foundation Cayley had established. In 1871, the French engineer Alphonse Pénaud demonstrated aeronautic stability with the eleven-second flight of a small, rubber band–powered airplane. Another French engineer, Clément Ader, demonstrated the first manned, powered aircraft in October 1890, though his craft was capable of neither sustained, nor controlled flight. In 1893, American inventor Hiram Maxim (of machine-gun fame) succeeded in operating a massive, three-man biplane powered by steam. This operated on a circular test track that prevented the craft from lifting more than two feet off the ground. French-born American civil engineer Octave Chanute came to aeronautics in the mid-1870s through his interest in the effects of high wind on structures, as well as the effects of air on increasingly faster locomotives. Chanute's reputation as a civil engineer brought a certain respectability to the research of heavier-than-air flight in the United States. He not only inspired many other U.S. investigators to begin work in the field, he also served as a common point of contact for the growing network of aeronautical experimenters who began working in the field in the 1880s. Among these were the respected scientist Samuel P. Langley, and the unknown brothers from Ohio, Orville and Wilbur Wright. Though they approached the problem of manned flight from different directions, their respective experiments eventually caught the interest of the U.S. military.[1]

It was within the context of increasing respectability for heavier-than-air manned flight (and the growing possibility of success by one or another of the many experimenters in the field) that the U.S. military made its first foray into heavier-than-air flight. This occurred in 1898 when the Army's Board of Ordnance and Fortification (BOF) agreed to support the aerial experiments of Samuel P. Langley, secretary of the Smithsonian Institution, ultimately giving Langley $50,000.[2] Langley had previously had some success with large, unmanned models in 1896 and believed that the BOF money would enable him to develop a larger version, capable of carrying a man. But what did the BOF expect of aviation such that it was willing to commit to spending the equivalent of one-quarter of its yearly testing budget in order to support the development of the airplane? In other words, how did the BOF conceptualize an airplane and envisage its role in warfare?

The secretary of war had created the Board of Ordnance and Fortification in 1888 at the direction of Congress. It consisted of five Army officers: a major general in charge of the board, officers from the Ordnance Department, artillery branch, and the Corps of Engineers, and a recorder. After 1891, the board also included one civilian member.[3] The original purpose of the board was to review the Army's coastal defense fortifications and "to make all needful and proper purchases, experiments, and tests to ascertain, with a view to their utilization by the government, the most effective guns, small arms, cartridges, projectiles, fuses, explosives, torpedoes, armor plates, and other implements and engines of war" with a view to upgrading those defenses.[4] However by 1898, helped by vague wording and a clear administrative need, the board had become the Army's evaluator of improvements and inventions of all types.[5] Since the Army was responsible for coastal defense within range of its guns, the board considered technologies like mines, torpedoes, and even floating batteries that might otherwise be seen as the province of the Navy Department. However, the board did recognize that there were some ideas that lay outside the Army's responsibility: the BOF occasionally forwarded letters to the Secretary of the Navy, who in turn occasionally referred letters received by the Navy Department to the BOF.

The board regularly received proposals from inventors (either directly or by referral from other Army departments and congressmen) describing ideas for potential use by the Army. Some of these ideas involved aircraft of various types. These correspondents proposed war balloons, dirigible balloons,[6] airships, and other "air-navigating machines," some of which were heavier-than-air craft. The board also received ideas for various "bomb-dropping devices" as well as special designs for bombs to be dropped from balloons. One inventor proposed a series of towers and overhead wires along the coast: bombs could be reeled out on the wires and dropped on attackers. The vast majority of these inventors were told that their ideas were "insufficiently developed," "impracticable," or, in a few cases, that their inventions did "not possess sufficient military merit." A very few letters did possess sufficient military merit to be passed on to the appropriate Army bureau chief for further evaluation.[7] For aviation matters, this was usually the Signal Corps, since that organization had experimented with tethered balloons for reconnaissance during the Civil War. As well, the Signal Corps was then reviving the idea of using balloons for military purposes.

Langley's interaction with the BOF, however, was different in almost every way. Above all, Langley was not an unknown with another crackpot idea, but a well-respected scientist who was head of the Smithsonian Institution. After establishing an excellent reputation as an astronomer and physicist with his pioneering studies of the sun, Langley turned his scientific attention to the question of artificial flight in 1887, shortly before he was selected to become secretary of the Smithsonian Institution.[8] Beginning with "whirling table" experiments of lift and drag, Langley then tested more than a hundred rubber band-powered models before declaring them inadequate for research and moving on to a series of larger models that he called "Aerodromes." In 1896, Langley succeeded in getting two of these larger models to fly. The steam-powered Aerodrome No. 5 and Aerodrome No. 6 made a total of three flights, each lasting from one minute, thirty seconds to one minute, forty-five seconds.[9] Alexander Graham Bell, a friend of Langley's and a supporter of his aerial experiments, witnessed the first two flights. Bell, aware of the power of good publicity, may have pushed Langley to invite Frank Carpenter, a reporter for the Washington *Evening Star*, to witness the third successful flight. Carpenter wrote a favorable account for his newspaper, stating, "The development of [the Aerodrome] will, in all probability, change the warfare of the world, and it may make war so terrible that the national troubles of the future will be settled by arbitration."[10] Publicly, Langley planned to stop his experiments at that point, leaving the construction of a man-carrying airplane to someone else.[11] Privately, however, Langley desired to continue his experiments and sought the $50,000 he estimated it would take to build a man-carrying aircraft.[12] Government funding was one possibility.

About this time, several bills were introduced in Congress that might have provided some of Langley's needed funds had they passed. A Senate bill (S.302, Dec. 4, 1895) proposed a cash prize to anyone who could demonstrate a successful flying machine before 1900 in or near Washington, DC, or before at least three members from the Department of War.[13] The following summer, identical bills were introduced in both houses of Congress proposing to pay one James Seldon Cowdon $15,000 to construct his airship design. Cowdon's offering was, in the words of the bill, "important, from a military point of view," though exactly why was left unsaid.[14] And in December 1896, after Carpenter's article about the flight of Langley's Aerodrome No. 6 came out, another Senate bill proposed to give $20,000 each to Cowdon and Langley to recognize (and presumably encourage) their experiments in aeronautics.[15] None of these bills passed. In fact, given the popular opinion of the time, that flying machines were an impossibility, the bills were probably voted down in committee without discussion.[16]

Langley does not seem to have been behind any of these bills, instead discussing possibilities for government funding with influential friends such as Bell, Cleveland Abbe (head of the U.S. Weather Bureau), Gen. Adolphus W. Greely (the Army's chief signal officer), and Charles Walcott (head of the U.S. Geological Survey, and, since 1897, acting assistant secretary of the Smithsonian).[17] Walcott succeeded in getting the attention of President William McKinley, arranging a meeting with him on March 24.[18] During the meeting, Walcott told the president about Langley's work in aeronautics, showed pictures of the successful Aerodrome flights, and suggested the military value of a manned aerodrome. McKinley was interested by this presentation and told Walcott to contact Assistant Secretary of War George de Rue Meiklejohn, and Assistant Secretary of the Navy Theodore Roosevelt.[19] Wasting no time, Walcott met separately with the two men the next day.[20] After meeting with Walcott, Roosevelt wrote to his boss, John D. Long, "[Langley's] machine has worked. It seems to me worth while [*sic*] for this government to try whether it will not work on a large enough scale to be of use in the event of war." Roosevelt recommended establishing a joint board with the secretary of war to "meet and examine into this flying machine, to inform us whether or not they think it could be duplicated on a large scale, to make recommendation as to its practicability and prepare estimates as to the cost."[21]

The two secretaries did create a joint board consisting of men with significant scientific training and technical experience: Cdr. C. H. Davis, USN (the superintendent of the Naval Observatory); S. J. Brown (professor of mathematics at the Naval Academy); Lt. Col. George W. Davis, USA (of the 14th Infantry Regiment—no relation to C. H. Davis); Maj. Robert Craig, Signal Corps; and Capt. William Crozier of the Ordnance Department (who had also spent five years as an instructor in mathematics at West

Point). The joint board's report, dated April 29, 1898, used Roosevelt's wording almost verbatim to describe its purpose. After consulting experts in aeronautics including Bell and Octave Chanute (who was independently corresponding with Langley regarding heavier-than-air flight), and visiting Langley's workshop at the Smithsonian, the board decided that Langley's Aerodromes could be scaled up to carry a man, and that Langley was the best person to do it. The board's report is probably the first documented explanation of why the military was interested in airplanes:

> The consideration of the subject by the board is necessarily confined to the practicability of the proposed construction on a large scale of the Langley machine, for useful service in war. Its first use in this direction would be limited by the size of the immediately proposed machine to three purposes:
>
> 1. As a means of reconnaissance, or scouting, with capacity to carry an observer.
> 2. As a means of communication between stations isolated from each other by the ordinary means of land or water communication.
> 3. As an engine of offense with the capacity of dropping from a great height, high explosives into a camp or fortification.[22]

As simple and concise as this statement appears, its phrasing raises additional questions. Note that these are only the uses of an airplane of the size proposed by Langley—a one-person craft. Nothing in the report indicates what uses the board might have considered for larger airplanes. Nor does it say whether the board envisaged the airplane as a decisive weapon, or simply another tool on the battlefield.

In the Navy, the report came directly to Secretary Long, who was out of the office when Walcott had met with Roosevelt. Commander Davis attached a cover letter that reiterated the joint board's recommendation to fund Langley. But Long wanted a second opinion and sent the report to the Navy's Board on Construction, an organization created to coordinate the work of (and avoid disputes between) the different Navy bureaus involved in designing and building new ships. When the president of the Board on Construction wrote back to Long, he as much as admitted that none of its members understood enough about aviation to evaluate the joint board's report. But this caveat was sandwiched between more confident statements that Langley's proposed aerodrome would be of no use to the Navy and so the Navy should not contribute to Langley's experiments.[23] Long chose not to fund Langley, though the Navy continued to keep an eye on his work.

In the Army, the joint board's report came to Langley's friend, Chief Signal Officer Greely, who gave a positive endorsement, concluding that "the great importance of such a machine for warfare, and the good that would result to the world at large should a flying machine be made practicable, are cogent reasons for favorable action by the various Departments of the Government and the Congress of the United States." Greely forwarded the report with his endorsement to Meiklejohn, who added his own endorsement. Meiklejohn then sent the whole package to the Army's Board of Ordnance and Fortification "for its consideration, with instructions to inform Prof. S. P. Langley, of the Smithsonian Institution . . . when he may appear before the Board for the purpose of making personal explanation of his invention and of his views as to what action he considers it advisable to take."[24]

Many referrals to the BOF were buck-passing by congressmen or other Army offices, letting the board do the dirty work of rejecting hopeful inventors. However, Meiklejohn's endorsement of the report was practically an order to give Langley a respectful hearing.[25] Langley attended the BOF's next meeting, six weeks later. Before calling on Langley, the board reviewed Greely's letter, as well as the report of the joint Army/Navy board. (In reviewing several years of BOF proceedings, this was the only instance I found of a proposal coming before the board having already been vetted by another branch of the Army, much less a joint Army/Navy board.) The board then interviewed Langley, who explained his experiments in some detail. The board concluded, "The further investigation of this subject along the lines indicated by Professor Langley gives promise of great military value in the perfected apparatus, and deems it worthy of special encouragement. It is therefore recommended that an allotment of $25,000 . . . be made . . . for the construction, development, and test of a flying machine under the supervision and direction of Professor Langley."[26] As for the balance of the $50,000 that Langley estimated he needed, the board decided it could give him additional money at a later date if his work showed sufficient progress.

Over the next several years, Langley spent this initial $25,000, plus a second $25,000 (which the BOF chose to give him), along with $23,000 in Smithsonian funding for developing the man-carrying "Great Aerodrome," or "Aerodrome A," as well as a new catapult to launch it.[27] Despite all this funding, by 1903 Langley had run out of money. He did not yet have a satisfactory aircraft, but he believed he could get more funding if he could demonstrate some success with his work to date. Despite his desire to keep his work quiet, word of his experiments (and funding) appeared in newspapers shortly after his first meeting with the BOF.[28] Thus, members of the government, press, and public were on hand to see the Great Aerodrome crash ignominiously into the Potomac River near Quantico, Virginia, on October 7, 1903, and again in the mouth of the Anacostia River (off the point of what is now Fort McNair) on December 8.[29]

In January 1904, several congressmen tried to open investigations of the actions of the Board of Ordnance and Fortification.[30] Congressman Gilbert Hitchcock (D-NE) expressed concern that the government was spending extravagantly and cited the BOF's funding of Langley's project as an example of "ridiculous and unwarranted expenditures" by the government. He derisively wondered, "If it is going to cost us $73,000 to construct a mud duck that will not fly 50 feet, how much is it going to cost to construct a real flying machine?" His colleague, James Robinson (D-IN), was of a similar mind. Robinson noted that Langley had caught up the members of the Board in his wild scheme, getting $50,000 in public funds, "only to have the venture fall flat and the money sunk at the first opportunity to test his apparatus. We should strike down such costly bubbles as Langley's

air ships and air castles and rescue the innocent public from such dreams."
Robinson called Langley's Aerodrome a "Don Quixote extravagance" and
said that his schemes made as much sense as a plan to build a house beginning with the roof. James Hemenway (R-IN), chairman of the Committee
on Appropriations, defended the actions of the board, however, citing the
immense advantage to the Army if a vehicle could fly over an enemy's
camp to see the number of men and type of fortifications. Hemenway recognized the BOF's funding of Langley as a calculated risk that had failed
rather than a misuse of public funds on pipe dreams, but he seems to have
been in the minority. The public shared the skepticism of Robinson and
Hitchcock.[31] With Congress' attention focused on the BOF and public
opinion running against such expenditures, there was no way the board
could provide Langley supplemental funds, even if it had wanted to. Nor
would Langley find the needed money elsewhere. His "Great Aerodrome"
languished in storage until after his death in 1906. He died believing that
the failure lay in the catapult design, not the aircraft itself, though modern
analysis has proven otherwise.[32] To the public, he was just one more crackpot inventor who believed he could fly.

Given Langley's failure and the political ill winds it stirred up, it is
surprising that the board did not turn its back on aeronautics entirely.
Following Langley's highly public failures and congressional threats to
remove the BOF's funding or even disband it, BOF members might very
well have vowed to stay away from airplanes altogether. While the BOF
did become more cautious about airplane proposals, it did not outright
refuse to consider them. The Wright brothers' first contact with the BOF
received the board's canned response that it "does not care to formulate
requirements . . . or to take any further action on the subject until a machine
is produced which by actual operation is shown to be able to produce horizontal flight and to carry an operator." Note that this is not a flat refusal
to consider airplanes: the board had simply set the bar a little higher.[33] Up
until Langley's failure, requests to fund experiments were met with the
pronouncement that a working model was needed before the board would
consider making allotments for development.[34] Langley's prior success

with the unmanned aerodrome models probably did as much to lead the board to support his efforts to develop a man-carrying airplane as did his scientific reputation and position as Smithsonian secretary. Unfortunately, Langley also proved that success with models did not guarantee success with larger aircraft. One wonders whether the BOF would not have subsequently demanded such proof of successful man-carrying flight regardless of the ridicule heaped on the board by the press and Congress following Langley's highly public failure. That the BOF funded Langley's project at an early stage suggests that the BOF was seriously interested in manned flight of a heavier-than-air craft.

Orville and Wilbur Wright, who had already made flights that would have satisfied the board, mistook the BOF's reply to mean that the government was not interested in airplanes. Had the board been less defensive, or had the Wrights included sufficient proof that they had successfully flown a man-carrying aircraft, the Army might have gotten its first airplane sooner than it did. The truth is that the various members of the Board of Ordnance and Fortification over time were in general agreement that a successful airplane (or dirigible balloon, airship, or any other device for aerial navigation) was of considerable interest to the Army. Indeed, when the board authorized payment to the winning bidders in the 1907 competition to supply airplanes to the government, they declared categorically, "The Board of Ordnance and Fortification has heretofore expressed its belief in the possibility of mechanical flight and in the value of a successful aeroplane flying machine to the military service."[35] But precisely what value did its members expect an airplane would have to the Army? Obviously, they thought that the benefits were great enough that they were willing to risk an outraged Congress once again in order to give the Wrights a chance to demonstrate their achievements in the air.

The BOF's support of Langley and subsequent willingness to set up the now-legendary Fort Myer trials of the Wright airplane demonstrates that the Army was extremely interested in heavier-than-air flight at a time when human flight was widely considered impossible. But planning for how to use a manned aircraft was, of necessity, theoretical. The formal acceptance of the Wright Military Flyer in 1909—and the beginning of flight training for the first Army aviators—marks the shift from just thinking about what the Army might do with an airplane to having to figure out what to do with this machine it had just purchased. Not only did the Army now have a tangible object to incorporate into its organization and warfighting doctrine, it also had, finally, the opportunity to gain much-needed experience from its operation: to try out ideas in practice, to probe the limits of the technology, and evaluate future progress in the art of flight. None who had witnessed the acceptance flights in 1908 and 1909 at Fort Myer would doubt that the Army's expenditure was worthwhile, though much work remained before the question of exactly why the airplane was useful to any branch of the military could be answered with any precision. The Navy and Marine Corps would soon develop their own interests in manned flight, leaving each service to search for its own answers to the question asked by Orville and Wilbur Wright: "What to do with the airplane?"[36]

INTRODUCTION

In 2006, I was attending the Society for the History of Technology's annual conference as a graduate student. Since my first idea for a dissertation topic had been shot down by my advisor, I was hoping something at the conference would spark a new idea. This happened during the meeting of the "Albatrosses," a special interest group dedicated to the history of aviation. The organizers asked us to start the meeting by going around the room, introducing ourselves and saying something about our current projects. When my turn came, I mentioned that I had no project, but was hoping to find a dissertation topic at the conference. Roger Launius later came up to me and suggested that no one had yet done a good multiservice history of military aviation. Looking back on the work I have done since then I can understand why: the cultural differences between the services create a significant barrier to researching and understanding—even just knowing where to find—primary sources. The difficulty of overcoming this barrier probably helps explain why the comparison of different air services tends to be in the same branch of the service compared across national lines, such as U.S. Army aviation versus U.K. army aviation, or naval aviation in the United States, United Kingdom, and Japan.[1] A rare exception to this pattern (besides my own work) is Carl John Horn's dissertation comparing U.S. Army and Marine Corps responses to the invention of the helicopter.[2]

Of course, that still left me with the issue of what, exactly, it meant to write such a history. Diving into the historiography, a couple of things jumped out at me. Foremost, that the period prior to World War I, and often the war itself, were treated superficially at best. Stephen Budiansky's survey of aviation history, *Air Power: The Men, Machines, and Ideas that Revolutionized War from Kitty Hawk to Gulf War II*, may be taken as representative of the type, despite his background as a journalist rather than a historian. Budiansky devotes roughly fifty pages each to the pre-war era and the World War I years out of a total of more than 440 pages, but more than half of the pre-war treatment is devoted to turn-of-the-century conjecture of future aerial war (such as H. G. Wells' 1908 novel, *The War in the Air*) and the Wright brothers' development of the first successful airplane.[3] This is not to argue that Budiansky and other survey authors *ought* to have written more about the pre–World War I era in their surveys of military aviation history; it is merely to note that surveys tend to give short shrift to the period. Books dedicated to the pre-war era of military aviation (U.S. or otherwise)—such as Herbert Johnson's 2001 monograph, *Wingless Eagle*—obviously cover the topic in greater depth but there are few such books out there.[4]

Further, my study of military aviation historiography showed that naval aviation generally remains invisible until World War II, and then appears only in the context of carrier aviation in the Pacific. Some of these broader histories say no more about naval aviation than that, while a few give a brief nod to the carriers' post-war importance before returning to the central (and apparently more significant) theme, the development of Army/Air Force aviation.[5] Those histories that concentrate on naval aviation (whether U.S. or global) tend to repeat the progressive nature of the general histories: brief mentions of the first experiments taking off from/landing on ships—Eugene Ely's flights for the United States, Royal Navy Squadron Commander E. H. Dunning's fatal experiments in 1917—followed by a quick treatment of the first experimental carriers after World War I, before digging into the story with the arrival of fleet carriers and the developments that would frame carrier aviation in World War II. Little to nothing is said of patrol aviation.[6] Another repeated pattern for the U.S.-centric histories: only brief mention (if at all) of U.S. Marine Corps aviation. And examining Marine Corps-specific aviation histories, we again see a certain presentism, with pre–World War I history skimmed over quickly.[7] Though, to be fair, there was not a lot of Marine-specific aviation activity prior to 1917.

All of this led me to a basic question: just what *was* happening during this period of roughly 1908–1917? While current doctrine may have its roots in later periods, these early aviators and administrators were not simply sitting around waiting for aviation doctrine to be invented. And so, this became the focus of my research: trying to find out what those involved with the very beginning of military aviation were pondering in the moment. How did they convince a skeptical Congress and their respective secretaries and uniformed leadership to spend the money to purchase and operate airplanes? And if their ideas indeed did not influence later developments in aviation funding, policy, or doctrine, why not?

This book concentrates on the period between the Army's test and acquisition of its first airplane in 1908–1909 and the United States' declaration of war against Germany on April 6, 1917. The prologue demonstrated (and chapter 1 will show) that the Army was considering the advantages of controlled flight—whether that involved an airplane or dirigible balloon—well in advance of anyone making a successful controlled flight. But thinking about the usefulness of a flying machine could be nothing but speculation until someone invented one that could test these ideas in the real world. Indeed, significant Navy interest in the airplane came only as a result of the Wright airplane's success in the 1908–1909 Army trials. Marine Corps interest was not directly related to the Wright trials, but the trials generated a surge in aeronautical interest that likely contributed to the Corps' curiosity. On the other end of this period, U.S. participation in World War I forced military leaders to recognize that whatever advances may have been made in technology and doctrine since acquiring the first airplane in 1909, neither American airplane technology nor American aviation doctrine was up to the challenges of aerial combat over the European battlefields in 1917. World War I would be a discontinuity for U.S. military aviation; a time when American aviation arms had to quickly adopt foreign aircraft and doctrine in order to hope to have an impact on the progress of the war.

That is not to say that the three U.S. air services did nothing to develop doctrine during this pre-war period. Still, it is surprising (in retrospect) that they were so unprepared in 1917, given all the lessons they could have learned from their observation of aviation progress in European military forces beginning in August 1914.

What were the three services doing with aviation during this period, and why were they not better prepared in 1917? That is the focus of this book. More specifically, it is about how each service brought on aviation in the years before the United States entered the war, and assessing these developments on their own terms, rather than assuming that the services *should* have been ready for the air war in 1917. While the creation of doctrine is central (who had the ideas, how were those ideas evaluated to become doctrine, and who decided what became doctrine), the improvement of aviation as a technology is also a critical component because the state of the technology is an important determinant in how, or even whether, these doctrinal theories were being tested in the real world. In turn, examining changes in technology, and who is driving that change, is evidence indicating whether or not the test results (where they existed) influenced doctrine.

But how to follow and analyze these developments? Many different theories about how militaries innovate have emerged since 1984, when political scientist Barry Posen published his book, *The Sources of Military Doctrine*.[8] I did not, however, find any of the proposed models compelling and have chosen a different approach: a methodology drawn from the history of technology known as Actor/Network Theory.[9] Briefly, Actor/Network Theory (ANT) presumes that change comes about through the creation of networks, and that these networks include both active actors (decision-makers, advocates, influencers) and more passive actors (supporters, converts to a new idea, or even nonhuman "actors" such as hardware that demonstrates or incorporates the new idea). However, as explained by one of its earliest proponents, Bruno Latour, ANT does not presume to predict what that network looks like. Instead, we must follow the actors and see what sort of network emerges from the patterns they make. Thus, ANT is perhaps less a "theory" than it is a "method," but I leave that argument to others.[10]

The "actor" in ANT is also problematic as it usually implies agency—the ability to make a decision—and includes hardware as an actor in a network, implying that technology has agency, that hardware progresses because of "what it wants" or that technology "causes" social change. This is an idea that the history of technology, as an academic field, has been fighting against from its beginnings. The "actor" in ANT, however, does not necessarily come with agency. It is anything that performs an action, whether that action is automatic or the result of conscious decision-making. To take an example from the topic of this book, a network around the acceptance of bombing as a valid and viable role for the airplane might include such nonhuman actors as the airplane, the bombsight, the bomb rack, and the bomb. If a human actor is going to convince another to join the network supporting the idea that airplanes are useful for bombing, that actor may need a bomb of sufficient size to accomplish the desired destruction, a plane with enough payload to lift both the bomb and the necessary aircrew, some method of aiming the bomb, and some method of releasing the bomb at the proper time. A failure by any one of these nonhuman actors during a demonstration of bombing will likely fail to convince the skeptic who will then not join the network supporting the idea.[11]

We can see an example of this in the prologue: Samuel Langley's desire was to secure funding that would allow him to continue his successes with model aircraft by constructing one that could carry a person. To do this, he created a network of people that he hoped would eventually lead to the necessary funding. To expand the network, he and his supporters relied heavily on the evidence of his prior success with Aerodrome No. 5 and Aerodrome No. 6 (photos of their flights and the models themselves). Indeed, it was a combination of the photos and the physical evidence in Langley's aeronautical workshop along with the word of reliable witnesses to the Aerodromes' flights and Langley's own reputation as a scientist that ultimately led the Army's Board of Ordnance and Fortification to give Langley the money he needed. Furthermore, it was the subsequent failure of the hardware to prove Langley's claims (that he could create an airplane capable of carrying a human) that led the board to cut off further funding and dissuaded others from taking up his petition to fund further efforts. The network had fallen apart.

Failure in the hardware, especially early airplanes' limited weight-carrying ability, is certainly one reason why air doctrine was not more advanced in 1917. But the failure of the hardware to perform as needed was not the only weak link in the network. There was also an inability to communicate effectively between the various managers at headquarters in Washington, and those actually flying the aircraft. This gap was partly geographic, but mostly intellectual: the two groups' knowledge about the airplane was fundamentally different. The difference is similar to that described by historian Monte Calvert in his examination of the emergence of the mechanical engineer in the United States in the nineteenth century, a difference he referred to as "shop culture" versus "school culture."

The notion of the "mechanical engineer," responsible for designing and building industrial machinery (as distinct from the "military engineer," focused on ordnance and its use, or the "civil engineer," who dealt with public works) arose about the same time as the growth of colleges in the United States. As the position of mechanical engineer became professionalized, there emerged a disagreement about how engineers would gain their professional knowledge: Should the engineer be a product of "shop culture" or "school culture"? Shop culture represented the older way of gaining knowledge: working your way up through a machine shop and learning through the accumulation of practical experience—an industrial-era version of the medieval apprenticeship. School culture was the new way: attending an academic institution and addressing engineering from the direction of theory. Shop culture was designing a part (its shape, thickness, type of metal) based on rule of thumb or even just an intuitive understanding of purpose, stresses, and strengths of materials, whereas school culture meant designing a part through such methods as calculation of stresses (often involving trigonometry and calculus) and tables of known values of material properties.[12] In short, it was the difference between knowledge gained by doing versus knowledge gained through classroom study.

The analogy is not perfect, but that difference between shop and school culture has echoes in the difference between the practical knowledge of the operators in the field versus the administrators in Washington who acquired knowledge primarily from reading articles and books about aviation. The problem was made worse by the fact that aeronautical engineering (not to mention flying itself) was in its infancy. Even the best writing about aviation during this era suffered from this weak foundation, with further problems arising from misunderstandings, overstated expertise, or even flat-out fabrication.[13] Furthermore, the senior officers were reading about aviation in an incidental way; they were certainly not engaged in a formal course of study on the subject. We can therefore see how the operators and the administrators approached problems from different directions, often with a significant gap between their respective understandings: the managers working from information that was sometimes wrong, and occasionally too far ahead of the state of the art, while the operators could filter such information through their own experience. This gap in understanding is perhaps clearest in the disagreements between field and headquarters over the safety of aircraft, especially the pusher designs of this era.

Through a longer period examined in my dissertation research (not all of which made it into the dissertation itself), I concluded that doctrine advanced best when each service's aviation networks included a link between a "technology advocate" and a "technology patron." I defined the advocate as an officer sufficiently junior to have extensive practical experience with aviation (i.e., a licensed military aviator), and the patron as an officer sufficiently senior (often, but not exclusively, flag rank) to have political and/or budgetary influence over aviation within the service. Numerous other contingencies could also affect the development of doctrine, but doctrine (as well as military aviation as a whole) could not meaningfully advance in the absence of such a relationship.

In fact, we seldom see such a relationship in the pre-war period covered in this book. In rare instances, patron and advocate are the same person, but mostly this part of the network just fails to develop in this period. Partly it is because the advocates and potential patrons were unable to permanently close the gap in perspective described above. But another problem, worse in the Navy than the Army, was turnover not merely of the administrators in Washington, but of the organization itself. The Army had an advantage in that the continued (albeit inconsistent) patronage of the Signal Corps offered organizational stability and, for the most part, predictable changes in leadership at both the Signal Corps and the aviation desk (by whatever title). In contrast, naval aviation experienced no such stability during this period, suffering numerous reorganizations due to insufficiently senior patrons, insufficiently engaged patrons, or occasionally a total lack of patronage. Naval aviation doctrine and technological development consequently faced greater challenges compared to Army aviation. Marine Corps aviation falls somewhere between the other two services, suffering from its small size (only five aviators by 1917, making it difficult to build momentum) as well as its dependency on the Navy's aviation program for aircraft and support, and yet Marine Corps aviation had a definite patron in the Marine Corps commandant.

For the most part, then, this book shows that advocates for military aviation within the services faced many difficulties in building a network with the necessary elements to advance aviation doctrine in significant ways. Advocates outside the military, such as the Aero Club of America, had little direct influence on military developments, but are mentioned on the rare occasion when their advocacy was significant. It is important, however, to recognize that there was not always consensus or unity within these designations (advocates and patrons, operators and administrators). We will see instances in which advocates disagreed with each other about the best course of action or even whether there was a problem that needed to be solved. For instance, the many disagreements between Army aviators Benjamin Foulois and Paul Beck: from the quality of Beck's aircraft repairs (and his culpability for a fatal crash in a repaired airplane) to their stances on congressional bills to give aviation independence from the Signal Corps. Disagreement among patrons was rarer, largely because there were fewer people (often only one) in that role at a given time. Actor/ Network Theory is useful here, because the slash is meant to indicate that something may be considered as both an actor *and* a network. In this case, advocates can be usefully treated as a single corporate actor when convenient but, when necessary, recognized as a subsidiary network of individuals who agree on some things but disagree on others. Conversely, every network (of advocates and patrons, for instance) may be consolidated as a singular actor in a larger network (that includes, for instance, the service secretary, the other services, Congress, and the president).

Because I am trying to trace doctrinal development, I delve more deeply into events that other histories cover only briefly or pass over altogether. This is because there were practically no formal expressions of aviation doctrine during this period. To the extent that doctrine could be said to exist at all, it was tacit, and perhaps not even recognized as such by the actors. Consequently, we must look at how aircraft were actually being used, what sort of training military aviators were being given (or that some thought ought to be given), and what features and/or performance the military wanted to get out of new aircraft purchases. We must make a deep dive into primary sources, reading closely to try to tease out the thoughts and attitudes of the various human actors in these budding networks.

And so, back to the question of why the military was interested in aviation and what it expected of the airplane in particular. The prologue showed us the first glimmerings of the Army's interest in airplanes, and, in the report of the ad hoc joint committee, the first suggestions for practical uses for the military airplane. From the acquisition of the first airplane through the American declaration of war against Germany in 1917, the Army struggled to turn those suggestions into reality. The Navy and Marine Corps would soon follow the Army's lead in aviation. Although their ideas for how to use the airplane were subtly different both from the Army and each other, they, too, struggled to translate ideas into accomplishments. Along the way, military aviation would be shaped by many factors: the basic function of the parent services, the underlying culture of the parent services (particularly in how they regarded technology), the makeup and form of the nascent networks that grew to advance each service's aviation doctrine and technology, and the innovation and drive of particular members of those networks.

One final note: while I have written here about wanting to track the efforts of the three U.S. military services at the time (Army, Navy, and Marine Corps), those examining the table of contents might wonder what happened to the Marines. There are two interrelated reasons for Marine Corps aviation not getting a chapter to itself. First, Marine Corps aviation in the pre-war period was exceedingly small, with the fifth Marine aviator qualified only just before the United States entered the war. There is simply not enough content for an entirely separate chapter devoted to Marine Corps aviation. Second, there is the Marine Corps' complicated relationship with the Navy: both function under the auspices of the Navy Department and their leaders report to the Navy secretary, but they are administratively separate entities. Nevertheless, operational command is integrated, with Marine officers reporting to Navy officers and vice-versa. Add to this that Marine Corps aircraft were (and still are) purchased out of Navy appropriations and the symbiotic relationship between Navy and Marine aviation becomes that much tighter. In short, Marine Corps aviation prior to 1917 had little opportunity to act independently of the Navy's plans, and this situation is better understood when presented alongside or as part of the Navy narrative.

1

ARMY 1907–1910

The Army Gets a Plane

Army interest in the potential usefulness of aircraft long pre-dated the Board of Ordnance and Fortification's interest in Langley's experiments. Within the Army Signal Corps, there had developed a broad aeronautical constituency around the proven technology of the hydrogen balloon, whether tethered or free. Chief of Signal Adolphus W. Greely, in particular, was a strong patron for military ballooning, but also saw its limitations. He had a strong interest in overcoming those limitations, and it was this that led to his support for Langley's experiments.

Along with Greely's patronage of ballooning, the BOF remained interested in aviation experiments despite the ridicule it received in the wake of the Langley debacle. The board did, however, become much more careful about awarding money, insisting that inventors had to prove they had a working aircraft before the board would disburse any funds. It was this new policy, combined with Orville and Wilbur Wright's desire for secrecy until they received a patent, that led to misunderstandings and delays in advancing what was, ultimately, a successful relationship.

This relationship between the Army and the Wrights came about with the assistance of James Allen, who had relieved Greely as chief of signal in 1906. Another aviation patron, Allen not only facilitated the agreement between the Wrights and the BOF, he also helped guide a similar arrangement for Thomas Baldwin and his dirigible balloon. Yet having acquired one airship and one airplane, Allen seemed to turn his attention (and patronage) elsewhere, leaving the Army's technology advocates in the lurch.

ARMY BALLOONS AND AN AIRPLANE

Army aviation began during the Civil War. On June 9, 1861, the U.S. (Union) Army conducted its first trial of a tethered balloon in Washington, DC. Following the ascent, the Army of the Potomac used (or attempted to use) balloons for reconnaissance several times throughout the war. In fact, the Union Army established a "Balloon Corps" (though the name was not official) in support of roughly a dozen aeronauts. The Balloon Corps even claimed the use of the "world's first aircraft carrier," the *George Washington Parke Custis*. A converted U.S. Navy coal barge operated by the Army, the makeshift vessel carried material and equipment for Army balloonists to stations along the Potomac River, and its flat deck provided a base for balloon operations as well. The contributions of the Balloon Corps were not so obvious to senior Army officers, and the corps was disbanded in June 1863, shortly after being transferred from the Army Corps of Engineers to the newly created Army Signal Corps. Subsequently, the U.S. Army ignored balloons for many years.[1]

In the 1880s, however, Chief Signal Officer Adolphus W. Greely drove a reawakening interest in the U.S. Army for military balloons. At that time, Europe was experiencing a great revival of military ballooning, and by 1884, many foreign armies had established sizeable balloon corps as part of their permanent forces. In 1890, Congress realigned the Signal Corps' duties, transferring responsibility for the weather service (which had developed within the Signal Corps) to the Agriculture Department, and refocusing the Signal Corps on its original tasks of collecting and transmitting information for the Army. Greely interpreted this mandate to include aerial navigation, since the Army had used (and would use) balloons to collect information. In 1891, he asked for appropriations to establish a new balloon corps and, the following year, reestablished a balloon section as part of the Signal Corps. Yet despite Greely's requests for increased funding in each subsequent year, by 1897—as war with Spain appeared ever more likely—the Signal Corps still owned only one balloon.[2]

To better prepare for war, Greely stepped up his efforts in 1898. Having followed Samuel Langley's heavier-than-air (HTA) experiments with interest, Greely helped to persuade the Board of Ordnance and Fortification to fund Langley's development of a manned "aerodrome." He also attempted to acquire more observation balloons. But most of Greely's attempts to prepare aviation for the coming war came too late: Congress declared war against Spain on April 25, four days before the joint Army/Navy board submitted its recommendations to support Langley. As related in the prologue, Langley's aircraft would not be ready for testing for another five years, whereas the Spanish-American War would last less than one.

Following the declaration of war, Greely had the Signal Corps' lone balloon sent to Santiago, Cuba, to assist the Army. With the aid of his assistant, Capt. George Owen Squier—a former artilleryman who had just transferred to the Signal Corps—Greely established a second balloon company and secured two more balloons. But the war was so brief that this new company and its balloons never left the United States. The lone Army balloon in Cuba suffered from inexperience on the part of the hastily assembled ground crew as well as among the Army officers responsible for its tactical employment. Figurative and literal mishandling led to the balloon being shot down by enemy fire on July 1. Though its pilot did make important observations during the Battle of San Juan Hill, soldiers stationed near the balloon condemned it for attracting enemy fire. The balloon's envelope was damaged beyond repair, thus ending aviation work during the brief war.[3]

The end of the Spanish-American War marked the beginning of a period of transformation for the U.S. Army as a whole, encompassing organizational change as well as adapting to new technologies.[4] Although aviation would be part of this new direction, Army ballooning remained small and underfunded in the years immediately following the war. Maj. Samuel Reber, for example, commanded a detachment from the balloon section that participated in Army-Navy maneuvers in 1903 (Reber himself did not secure a ballooning license until 1911), but a lack of personnel and difficulty securing adequate supplies of compressed hydrogen kept the balloons grounded for the next couple of years.[5]

Beginning about 1905, the Army again showed interest in ballooning when young officers Capt. Charles deForest Chandler and Lt. Frank Lahm, who had both received balloon training from foreign militaries while on assignments in Europe, helped revive the Army's program upon returning to the States.[6] Another part of this resurgence was the Army's establishment of the Signal Corps School at Fort Leavenworth, Kansas, already home to the Infantry and Cavalry School in addition to the Army Staff College. In 1905, Greely sent Squier to Leavenworth, where Squier developed a curriculum that included military aeronautics and recommended that the Army purchase balloon equipment for the school—a recommendation the Army rejected. Squier also instituted "journal meetings" in which students researched and discussed topics of interest to the chief signal officer, such as aeronautics and aviation. In line with his interest, Squier followed the growing number of newspaper articles on aviation and even discussed the Wright brothers' reported accomplishments with his friend Alexander Graham Bell while both were in New York City at the end of 1905. Following this meeting, Squier wrote to Greely that he hoped to stop in Dayton, Ohio, on his way back to Fort Leavenworth to learn firsthand what the Wrights were doing. Either Squier met with the Wrights, or else he received information from another firsthand observer of their Huffman Prairie flights, because he later described aspects of those flights not available from published sources at the time.[7]

Squier's desire to promote greater cooperation between the Signal Corps and the line undoubtedly contributed to a 1906 resolution of the combined Fort Leavenworth school faculties in support of establishing the Army's balloon school there. But on February 10, 1906, Brig. Gen. James Allen succeeded Greely as chief signal officer, and he chose to establish the balloon school and Army hydrogen generating plant at Fort Omaha, Nebraska. The combined Leavenworth faculties came together again in 1907 in protest, arguing that the balloon's tactical use with the combat arms—infantry, cavalry, and artillery—could only be studied at Leavenworth. Responding to the protest and to Squier's continued advocacy, Allen finally sent the Army's one balloon and its pilot, Frank Lahm (now back from Europe), to Fort Leavenworth. Though Squier had been involved in purchasing balloons while serving as Greely's assistant during the Spanish-American War, his association with aeronautics within the Army began in earnest at Fort Leavenworth.[8]

Allen had been Greely's assistant in Washington, so it is not surprising that he continued his former supervisors' pro-aviation policies when he succeeded Greely as chief.[9] He was particularly interested in the possibilities of "dirigible balloons," which were also experiencing a surge in development at that time, asking inventor Thomas S. Baldwin to provide a dirigible balloon (an airship) to the Army. Eventually, Allen convinced the Board of Ordnance and Fortification to allocate up to $25,000 from its budget to purchase Baldwin's experimental, nonrigid dirigible. Allen, planning an increase in the Army's aerial activities, established the "Aeronautical Division" on August 1, 1907. Created within the Office of the Chief Signal Officer, and directly under the command of the CSO with Captain Chandler in charge, the new division was responsible for "all matters pertaining to military ballooning, air machines, and all kindred subjects." This wording reflected Allen's (incorrect) expectations that Army aviation would soon include a large number of airships. Whether through serendipity or because Allen was also aware of Orville and Wilbur Wright's successes, the new Aeronautical Division, with its broad mandate for "air machines, and all kindred subjects," had been set up just in time to take charge of airplanes as well.[10]

THE ARMY AND THE WRIGHTS

The difficulties that Orville and Wilbur Wright faced in convincing the Army (through the Board of Ordnance and Fortification) that they did indeed have a working airplane were touched on in the prologue. The misunderstanding and miscommunication that caused these difficulties have been well described elsewhere, and it is unnecessary to go into detail here.

What is important to this narrative is that the Wright brothers' network of supporters eventually caught the ear of President Theodore Roosevelt, who, as Assistant Secretary of the Navy in 1898, had proposed supporting Langley's experiments. The president, it seems, was indirectly able to make the Board of Ordnance and Fortification pay serious attention to the Wrights' claims and break through the mutual misunderstandings.[11]

Roosevelt's intervention certainly helped move things along, but Allen and members of the Aeronautical Division were also quietly pursuing the issue. Squier, who was well acquainted with aviation developments as reported in the press, returned to Washington as Allen's assistant in July 1907. Almost immediately, Allen asked him to make a thorough investigation of aeronautics and temporarily attached him to the Army's Department of the East, headquartered in New York City, under George P. Scriven, chief signal officer of that department. There, Squier could easily consult with officials of the Aero Club of America (often shortened to "Aero Club" or ACA)[12] and many of the engineers investigating aeronautical problems. Meanwhile, Lahm was still in Europe but preparing to return to America as a balloon pilot with the new Aeronautical Division. Before leaving Europe, he arranged to meet Orville Wright, who was in negotiations to sell airplanes in France and Germany. After meeting Orville in Paris in late September 1907, Lahm recommended to Allen that the Army purchase a Wright airplane. Although the BOF minutes do not indicate whether Allen shared Lahm's report with the board, on October 3 members decided to send all of their correspondence with the Wrights to Allen for his evaluation of the Wrights' offer.[13]

The Signal Corps' response to the BOF is surprising, given that Squier was still working on his report in New York. In a letter prepared by Chandler, Allen suggested that improvements in both wired and wireless communication outclassed the airplane's ability to deliver messages, while the prone position of the pilot, and the inability to carry a second person who could concentrate on the task, rendered the airplane useless in reconnaissance. (In fact, the Wrights were already designing a new plane with upright seats, capable of carrying a passenger, to address these shortcomings.) The letter also expressed doubt that airplanes could bomb accurately, and cited other inadequacies in the current state of the art (so far as it was known in the Office of the Chief of Signal) before concluding that the airplane was unsuitable for Army service and recommending against congressional appropriations for purchase. Squier's biographer, Paul Clark, cites this recommendation as evidence of Allen's anti-airplane bias, showing that Allen preferred a helicopter-type aircraft and endorsed the use of dirigibles until a successful helicopter could be built. But note that the letter to the BOF was prepared for Allen's signature by Chandler, a balloonist, at a time when Squier, who was intrigued by airplanes, was out of the office.[14] This appears to be a power struggle between two competing technology advocates (Chandler and Squier) for the attention of a patron (Allen) with limited funds.

When the Board of Ordnance and Fortifications next met, on November 7, it considered the Signal Corps letter. Though the letter recommended against airplanes, the board created a committee to confer with Allen in order to draw up specifications for an airplane that would be "suitable for military uses," specifications that the BOF then sent to the Wrights for consideration. The meeting was a busy one for aviation, as the board also agreed to Allen's request for $25,000 to purchase and test a dirigible balloon. However, they rejected the request—endorsed by Allen—of W. E. P. French, a retired Army captain, for $5,000 to support his own aerial navigation experiments.[15]

In response to the board's specifications, Wilbur Wright met with General Allen and two BOF members (Gen. William Crozier, chief of ordnance—a member of the joint board that had evaluated Langley—and the board's secretary, Maj. Lawson Fuller) on November 25. At the board's next meeting on December 5, Allen was present when Wright told the board that he and his brother Orville were prepared to furnish an operating airplane capable of carrying two men sitting upright. As a result, the board directed Allen to prepare specifications for a military airplane and invite bids for board review. In response to this new directive, Allen assembled a committee consisting of himself, Fuller, Squier, and Chandler. Keeping in mind the information Wilbur Wright had provided during the meeting on November 25 and in his appearance before the BOF ten days later, Allen and the committee wrote the first Army specifications for a "heavier-than-air flying machine." The BOF approved the specifications on January 2, 1909, and Allen published them as "Signal Corps Specification, No. 486," inviting bids.[16]

Specification No. 486 called for an airplane capable of carrying two people with a combined weight of about 350 pounds and fuel for a 125-mile flight. It also called for an airspeed of 40 mph, with graded penalties and bonuses for top speeds between 36 and 44 mph. In addition to a test for airspeed, the airplane would also have to complete an endurance test of at least one hour in the air. Most likely, Allen's committee based these requirements on what Wilbur said that he and his brother could achieve; other requirements seem more likely to have originated with the committee since they address features that the Army would need to operate a plane in the field. For example, the specification required that the craft should be easily disassembled for shipment on Army wagons and be reassembled within about an hour. Further, the specifications called for an airplane that could "ascend in any country which may be encountered in field service." Although such military requirements may not have been discussed during the meetings with Wright, they certainly reflect the concerns in Allen's October letter recommending against the airplane.[17] Regardless, Specification No. 486 contained no requirements that Orville and Wilbur Wright could not meet.

Public reaction to the request for bids demonstrated the difference between what the Wrights could do and what the public thought was possible. The press was skeptical that anyone could build a plane that could meet the Army's specifications. The editor at the Aero Club's *American Magazine of Aeronautics*, for example, criticized the Army for publishing performance requirements that could not possibly be met given the current state of the art. He feared that such stringent requirements would only result in failure (assuming anyone even bothered to bid), setting back the cause of aviation rather than advancing it. Given the press' criticism, and the fact that Specification No. 486 had essentially been written around what Wilbur said he and Orville could deliver, the BOF was probably surprised when others also submitted bids. Perhaps more surprising, two of those bids also met all the preliminary requirements, including posting a bond of 10 percent of their bid, at a cost lower than that of the Wrights. Since the Board of Ordnance and Fortification had expected only the Wright proposal, it had only set aside the $25,000 Wilbur had told them he and his brother would charge for the plane. Consequently, the board was disconcerted to have to accept (by law) the two lowest bids, and to be unable to afford the one bid it was confident would actually meet the requirements.[18] General Allen immediately began a search for the additional funds.

Initially, he sought to use money that Congress had appropriated during the Spanish-American War but that the Army had not spent—a move that required only presidential authority, not congressional approval. Allen set up a meeting with President Roosevelt to seek the necessary approval. Concerned that Roosevelt might ask technical questions about airplanes, Allen brought along Chandler and Lahm. The president, however, did not ask questions and readily signed the request, thereby allowing the Army to contract with the Wright brothers. Even so, there seems to have been some hitch with this funding source: in October 1908, the board approved Allen's request to reassign money previously allotted for dirigible testing and use it instead to purchase the Wright brothers' plane. In the end, however, neither of the other two successful bidders was able to produce an airplane, let alone one that met Specification No. 486. Thus, when the Army accepted delivery of the Wright airplane, the original allotment was sufficient.[19]

If Allen was indeed hostile to the airplane, as Clark suggests, then why did he go to such effort to ensure the Army could contract with the Wrights? Without Allen's actions to secure additional funding, purchase of the first Army airplane would have been set back once more, and Orville and Wilbur Wright would probably have been even more reluctant to deal with the Army again. One possibility is that Allen changed his mind after Wilbur explained that the brothers' latest design would correct the shortcomings Allen expressed in his October letter. Another possibility is simply that Allen was a busy person, attempting to manage a Signal Corps that was tasked with too many responsibilities, too few men, and too little money: aviation was only a minor part of his responsibility, and so he likely relied on his subordinates for recommendations.[20] Since the letter to the BOF was prepared by Chandler (a balloonist) at a time when Squier was away in New York City, and Allen's more pro-airplane moves coincide with Squier's presence back in Washington as assistant CSO, it seems likely that Allen's actions were influenced by whichever of his subordinates had the most influence on him at any given time. Whatever the reasons for Allen's efforts, the result was that Orville Wright and the new "Military Flyer" arrived at Fort Myer, Virginia (on the western border of Arlington National Cemetery), on August 20, 1908, ready to begin acceptance trials.

When Orville arrived, the Army had just completed trials and acceptance of Baldwin's airship. The Signal Corps had issued Specification No. 483 for a "dirigible balloon" on January 21, 1908, and the Army signed a contract with Baldwin roughly a month later. On July 20, Baldwin began setting up his two-man airship at Fort Myer, and on July 27, Glenn Curtiss—Baldwin's engine manufacturer and friend—arrived to assist with assembly and testing.[21] On August 12, Baldwin and Curtiss were ready to begin the acceptance trials supervised by an aeronautical board designated by Allen. The board consisted of Squier, Maj. Charles Saltzman,[22] Capt. Charles Wallace, Lahm, and Lt. Benjamin Foulois. (Chandler was not a member because Allen had ordered him to Fort Omaha to supervise completion of the hydrogen plant and other structures to support ballooning there. Lahm had replaced him as head of the Aeronautical Division.)[23] Saltzman and Wallace were members of the Signal Corps, and Lahm was already a balloon pilot. Foulois was not merely another Signal Corps member—Allen had brought him to Washington and put him on the trial board because he was impressed with Foulois' thoughts on how the Army might use aviation.

BENJAMIN FOULOIS

Foulois had first enlisted in the Army during the Spanish-American War. Though he saw no combat during that conflict, he volunteered to deploy to the Philippines in 1899, where he served for several years, during which time he was commissioned as a second lieutenant. When Foulois returned in 1905 from his second tour in the Philippines, the Army accepted his request to attend the Infantry and Cavalry School at Fort Leavenworth. While there, he met many students from the Signal Corps School and became fascinated by their discussions of Squier's "journal problems," an experience that inspired him to transfer to the Signal Corps on a temporary basis. Newly promoted to first lieutenant, Foulois reported to the Signal Corps School in September 1907, where coursework required students to write a thesis on a topic of interest to the Signal Corps. Although Foulois had apparently never seen any sort of aircraft—not even a balloon[24]—he wrote his thesis on "The Tactical and Strategical Value of Dirigible Balloons and Dynamical Flying Machines." The work is a mix of prescience and ignorance that was typical for its day.[25]

On the one hand, Foulois accurately foresaw that army tactics would have to be revised to account for aerial reconnaissance. He predicted that future wars would feature aerial engagements between hostile air forces while ground forces were still maneuvering for position. He also hypothesized that the result of these aerial battles would affect the strategic movements of the ground forces, with the victor able to watch the movement and disposition of enemy armies. But Foulois also properly noted that the victor in the air battle would not be able to completely prevent aerial reconnaissance by the enemy unless he completely destroyed the weaker air force. Based on analogy with birds, he also predicted that the machine with greater altitude would have a significant advantage in aerial combat. He forecast a decreasing need for horse cavalry (since aviation could perform many of the same duties faster if not better), said it was "clearly evident" that wireless was the only way to communicate with aircraft, and that aviation's use with field artillery (for finding targets and observing gunfire) "will undoubtedly be of the greatest importance."[26]

On the other hand, portions of his work were based on the extremely limited and largely inaccurate knowledge of the time about aeronautical design. For instance, he believed that airplanes, being heavier than air, would be able to make headway against a wind blowing faster than the plane's top speed. He also believed that the lifting power of a balloon increased with its size, but that of an airplane decreased with greater size—a belief that later developments would invalidate. Given these faulty premises, Foulois therefore concluded that the airplane would only be used in messenger and reconnaissance roles, whereas the weight-carrying dirigible would be used in combat in addition to messenger and reconnaissance duties. Foulois was at least aware of the uncertain nature of his foundations, admitting in his paper that his predictions of usefulness for aviation, whether dirigible or airplane, were based on theoretical considerations and that future experiments could drastically change his conclusions.

Both the faults and the truths in Foulois' thesis were only revealed in hindsight: at the time, the substance of Foulois' thesis was enough for Allen to assign him to duty in Washington and to the board conducting the aeronautical acceptance trials.[27] Consequently, Foulois would soon have the opportunity to directly compare airships and airplanes, beginning a long association with Army aviation. Allen also made a late addition to the aeronautical board: Lt. Thomas Selfridge.

THOMAS SELFRIDGE AND THE AERIAL EXPERIMENT ASSOCIATION

By August 1908, when Baldwin and Curtiss were ready to begin the official airship trials, Allen had added Selfridge to the trial board. Selfridge had approached Bell in Washington in the spring of 1907 to discuss aeronautics and, according to Bell, had already devoted much attention to recent developments in heavier-than-air flight with the expectation that the Army would acquire such a machine eventually. Selfridge assumed that an officer with expert knowledge in aeronautics would be in great demand and thus sure of promotion. He wanted to be that officer. Bell granted Selfridge's request to join a group of aeronautical experimenters at Bell's estate in Nova Scotia that summer, going so far as to pen a letter to Roosevelt encouraging the president to approve Selfridge's request for temporary duty with Bell. Army approval in hand, Selfridge traveled to Nova Scotia to join Bell and two other men, J. A. D. McCurdy and Frederick Baldwin (no relation to Thomas Baldwin), to pursue Bell's aeronautical investigations; in July 1907, Glenn Curtiss joined the group.

Although they acknowledged the Wright brothers' success in heavier-than-air flight, these five men felt there was still much to do to improve the lift, propulsion, and control of such craft. With that work in mind, on September 30, 1907, the group, including Bell, formally organized as the Aerial Experiment Association (AEA). Each member would get a chance to design an airplane and the group would build and test it. The AEA successfully flew Selfridge's design, named the Red Wing, in March 1908. In July, the AEA captured public attention when Glenn Curtiss, flying his own design—the June Bug—won the *Scientific American* trophy. The magazine had donated the trophy, to be awarded annually for a significant achievement in mechanical flight (i.e., airplanes or other aircraft operating through dynamic lift rather than static lift such as balloons or dirigibles), to the Aero Club of America, which was responsible for adjudicating the contest and awarding the prize. Curtiss won the first trophy when he met the Aero Club's criteria for 1908: a successful straight-line flight of one kilometer in a heavier-than-air flying machine. (The low bar for winning the trophy reflects the Wright brothers' secrecy as to what they had accomplished to date and the consequent opinion—even among the well-informed—as to what goals would push airplane development, yet remain achievable within a relatively short timeframe.)[28]

The AEA's success and the associated publicity were the start of a feud between the Wrights and the AEA, especially Curtiss, that would escalate into a protracted court battle. As long as the Wrights thought the AEA was just experimenting, Orville and Wilbur were willing to give them information and advice. Selfridge had written to the Wrights in January 1908, and Wilbur had written back with answers to Selfridge's questions, suggesting he study the Wrights' patents and providing construction details.

However, with the AEA entering contests (and winning prizes), Orville and Wilbur began to see them as potential competitors who were making money by infringing on their intellectual property. When the Aero Club invited the Wrights to compete for the *Scientific American* trophy, for example, Orville and Wilbur declined, citing rules for the competition that prevented them from using their catapult. However, the real reason, as described by historian Tom Crouch, was that "the Wrights were simply not interested in competing with latecomers who were infringing on their patents."[29] In any event, they were too busy preparing for almost simultaneous demonstrations of their accomplishments in the United States (at the Fort Myer trials) and Europe. After learning of Curtiss' award-winning flight, Orville wrote to Curtiss warning him that all of the features of the June Bug were covered by the Wrights' patents and that the brothers had not intended to give permission to use their patents for exhibitions or commercial gain. Curtiss, in turn, responded that he and the AEA did not intend to participate in any exhibitions, and he would refer the question of patents to the AEA's secretary. As much as Orville and Wilbur Wright were convinced that the AEA's designs infringed their work, the AEA members were equally convinced that they had designed planes to avoid the Wrights' patent.[30] Such was the state of things when Curtiss and Selfridge set aside their AEA activities to participate in the trials at Fort Myer. AEA members were excited by their successes and eager to build on them, while the Wright brothers were increasingly wary and distrustful of the AEA and its members.

AIRCRAFT TRIALS AT FORT MYER

In mid-August 1908, Curtiss and Baldwin began putting Baldwin's airship through the Army's tests. The nonrigid airship consisted of a cylindrical balloon roughly twenty-three feet in diameter and a little more than eighty-eight feet long, pointed at both ends. An open-truss "car" hung below, with one operator sitting at the rear to control the rudder and another stationed near the front to adjust the elevator planes and to monitor the engine, which drove a single tractor propeller mounted at the front of the car. Despite a conflict of interest—Selfridge had designed the propeller on Baldwin's craft—Selfridge remained on the acceptance board. The Signal Corps had arrived at its specifications after consulting with Baldwin, in much the same way it had consulted with the Wrights on airplane performance. Therefore, while the airship was considerably larger than anything Baldwin had built to date, it passed the performance tests without surprise. Allen formally notified Baldwin on August 18 that the airship met each of the flight requirements. From then until August 22, Baldwin fulfilled the remaining part of his contract, which required him to instruct two officers in the airship's use at no additional cost. In fact, Baldwin willingly instructed three: Lahm, Foulois, and Selfridge. The Signal Corps formally accepted Signal Corps Dirigible No. 1 on August 22, and the three Army pilots continued making practice flights through Friday, August 28, weather permitting. Since weather prevented the final scheduled day of flying on Monday, August 31, the officers and enlisted ground crew began deflating and dismantling the dirigible and the hydrogen generating plant for shipment to St. Joseph, Missouri. On September 8, after Orville's test flights of the Wright airplane but before the official Army tests began, Foulois and the ground crew entrained with the airship for St. Joseph, where the Army wanted them to exhibit the new machine at a state fair and military tournament. Selfridge remained behind in Washington for the airplane tests but expected to join Foulois in time for the opening of the military tournament on September 21.[31]

Consequently, Baldwin's dirigible was quite active at Fort Myer between August 20 and 28, during the time when Orville Wright and his two mechanics were assembling the Military Flyer, designed and built for the Army. Foulois had a mechanical bent (he had trained as a plumber with his father and began his Army service with the Corps of Engineers) and he showed great interest in the dirigible's engine. He spent considerable time with Curtiss while at Fort Myer. But between dirigible training flights he gravitated to the shed where Orville Wright and his mechanics were assembling the Wright airplane. Foulois later recalled, "They paid no attention to anyone else, and shrugged off all questions from outsiders," but something about him must have gotten through this isolation. According to Wright biographer Tom Crouch, Foulois would become "a particular favorite of Orville's."

Foulois might have been welcomed, but both Orville and the absent Wilbur were considerably less sanguine about Selfridge's presence on the trial board. While they did not worry that he might deliberately fail their plane during the performance tests or turn fellow board members against the Wright airplane, they *did* worry that Selfridge was using the opportunity to glean more information on the Wrights' machine and their methods for the benefit of the Aerial Experiment Association. Orville wrote to Wilbur that he felt Selfridge was constantly trying to pump him for information at dinners and other social events, and that he was inquiring behind Orville's back for even more information. Interestingly, Orville Wright was less worried about Glenn Curtiss' presence. Curtiss had left Fort Myer following the dirigible's last acceptance test on the evening of August 15, but he returned on September 3 to help Baldwin troubleshoot the airship's engine before the dirigible was shipped to Missouri. Although Orville was still as wary of Curtiss as any other AEA member, their interactions during this period seem to have been more collegial than distant, perhaps because Orville did not feel that Curtiss was trying to dig out information the way Selfridge was.[32]

Whatever the personal dynamics, Orville still had to prove the Wright plane to the Army. The trial board was largely the same as that of the airship trials, except for the additions of Navy Lt. George C. Sweet, Naval Constructor William McEntee, and Marine Lt. Richard B. Creecy as official observers for their respective services. Of the three, only Creecy had been present for the dirigible tests.[33] Another change was that the board lost Foulois, who had to leave for Missouri before the airplane trials were complete.

Orville Wright flew the airplane for the first time on September 3, making an easy test flight. Over the next week and a half, as he grew more confident in both the conditions at Fort Myer and the plane's setup, he gradually explored its performance envelope. The airplane was so new that almost every flight set a new record. On September 9 in front of a large crowd,

Wright set an endurance record of fifty-seven minutes, thirteen seconds; he set another with his next flight, staying aloft for sixty-two minutes, fifteen seconds. Confident in his machine, he then made his first public flight with a passenger, taking Lahm up for a six-minute, twenty-four-second flight—an endurance record for a flight with a passenger. Following more record-setting solo endurance flights on September 10 and 11, Wright took Squier up on September 12, setting yet another endurance record with a passenger at just over nine minutes.[34] After several days when high winds and an engine overhaul kept the plane grounded, Wright was again ready to fly with a passenger, Thomas Selfridge. This flight, however, was disastrous: the plane crashed, killing Selfridge and sending Wright to the hospital for seven weeks with an even longer recovery time.[35] The trial board—without Squier, but with the assistance of Octave Chanute (who had been on hand to observe the trials)—investigated the accident and determined that a broken propeller had started the chain of events that led, unavoidably, to the crash, which effectively ended the trials.[36] In October, the trial board (now without Lahm as well, who had been sent to St. Joseph in place of Selfridge) agreed to let the Wright brothers undergo new trials the following summer.[37]

The Army's dirigible was in St. Joseph for just a few weeks, making eight flights before it and its crew returned to Washington.[38] Then in May 1909 the Army ordered Lahm and Foulois to take the airship to Fort Omaha, where they were to train other officers as dirigible pilots. Foulois remembered constant mishaps with the dirigible at Fort Omaha, yet he and Lahm were nevertheless able to train lieutenants John Winter, Raymond Bamberger, and Oliver Dickinson by mid-June. The three lieutenants and a ground crew of twelve enlisted men flew the dirigible at a military tournament in Toledo, Ohio, in July, and again, with the addition of Lahm as a fourth pilot, at another military tournament in Des Moines, Iowa, in September. Foulois remarked that his experiences that spring convinced him, in contrast to his thinking when he wrote his Signal Corps thesis, that there was no future in dirigibles. Thus, he was more than happy to leave the dirigible behind in mid-June 1909 when he and Lahm returned to Washington for the continuation of the Wright trials.[39]

Orville and Wilbur arrived in Washington on July 20 with a new, significantly remodeled airplane. First, they redesigned the propellers to overcome the weakness that had caused the 1908 propellers to split and modified the airplane itself to decrease the chances that a faulty propeller could cut a guy wire. Second, they changed the means of control. The 1908 aircraft used three fore-and-aft levers to control the plane: one each for the elevator, the wing warping, and the rudder. The wing warping and rudder controls were set next to each other so the pilot could easily grasp both and move them together for a coordinated turn. The 1909 aircraft replaced the two side-by-side levers with a single lever that moved fore-and-aft for wing warping and had a top "toggle" segment hinged to move left or right for rudder control. Finally, Orville and Wilbur added a foot pedal to retard engine spark, giving the pilot greater control over the engine speed beyond simply "on" and "off."[40]

Once the plane was assembled, Orville took a few days to familiarize himself with the new controls—his first opportunity to fly since the crash the previous fall. Though Wilbur was present at the tests, Orville did all the flying as a matter of principle. Following a few rough test flights, Orville began setting new flight endurance records with the plane in preparation for the official trials on July 27. The new trial board was much the same as the 1908 board: Squier, Saltzman, Chandler, Lahm, Foulois, and Navy Lieutenant Sweet returned, and 2nd Lt. Frederick Humphreys of the Corps of Engineers replaced the deceased Selfridge. Marine observer Richard Creecy apparently did not return for the 1909 tests; he seems to have been one of the few people involved with military aeronautics who was not taken with the idea of flight. (After his brief brush with aviation in 1908, he returned to the typical duties of a Marine officer and never again had anything to do with flying.) Despite Orville's rough start flying the new plane, he easily passed the Army's performance requirements, remaining aloft with Lahm for one hour, twelve minutes and completing a ten-mile round trip to Alexandria, Virginia, with Foulois for the speed trial. On August 2, the trial board submitted its report to the Board of Ordnance and Fortification, confirming that the Wright airplane had indeed met the performance requirements. All that remained for Orville and Wilbur Wright to do was teach two officers how to fly.[41]

For this training, Allen designated Lahm and Foulois, who were already dirigible pilots and had been involved in the flight tests of the Wright plane. Lahm was tasked with finding a better venue for training, since the Wrights deemed Fort Myer too small for new pilots to train safely and were unhappy with how easy it was for crowds to gather there. Because of his many free-balloon flights around Washington, DC, Lahm knew of several likely places and spent much of August inspecting them from the ground. Eventually the Signal Corps and the Wrights agreed on a site near the Maryland Agricultural College (now the University of Maryland) at College Park. It took some time for the Army to lease, clear, and pre-pare the field for flight operations, as well as erect a small hangar. With the new field at College Park ready for use, Wilbur Wright returned on October 6 from New York City, where he had made several public flights in connection with the Hudson-Fulton Celebration, to begin training the selected officers. (Orville had left for Europe on business shortly after the Fort Myer trials were completed.) However, instead of Lahm and Foulois, Wilbur Wright found he would be training Lahm and Humphreys.[42]

Shortly after the trials ended, Allen sent Foulois to the International Congress of Aeronautics at Nancy, France, as the American delegate. From there, he was to visit a major aeronautical exhibition in Frankfurt, Germany, and then report on it to the American military attaché in Paris, Col. T. Bentley Mott. Foulois later said that he had learned nothing new in Nancy and had arrived in Frankfurt after most of the exhibits had been taken down. Furthermore, when he reported to Mott, the attaché told him that others had already reported on the Nancy congress and the Frankfurt exhibition. In his memoirs, Foulois says that sometime after returning to the United States, he had an unofficial meeting with Major Saltzman, who told him that the trip was a reprimand for expressing opinions at odds with those of the senior staff of the Signal Corps, specifically, his testimony to the General Staff earlier that summer. In June 1909, after Foulois returned to Washington from training others to fly the dirigible, the General Staff had asked for his views on military aviation. Foulois gave them his honest opinion that dirigibles had no military future. He recommended that the Army not buy any more, but concentrate instead on airplanes. Saltzman, meeting with Foulois in October, told him that Allen—as well as unspecified members of his "nonflying but nevertheless expert staff"—believed that dirigibles were the future of Army aviation, and had sent Foulois on the useless trip as punishment for countering Signal Corps staff thinking.[43] Of course, the Signal Corps only had so many officers to send and even fewer who were knowledgeable about aviation. Furthermore, it seems unlikely that Allen (or, more likely, Chandler)[44] could have known in advance that the aviation conference would be a dud, or that he would have been able to control Foulois' travels to ensure that he arrived in Frankfurt *after* exhibitors began tearing down their displays. One way or another, however, Foulois' trip meant that he was not able to begin training at College Park with Lahm.

FLIGHT TRAINING

The Army's heavier-than-air flight training began at College Park on October 8, 1909. There is evidence to suggest that Wilbur Wright changed the airplane's controls to a system he had used in his 1908 flights in Europe. His system replaced the lever and toggle with something more like a joystick: moving it left and right rolled the airplane while fore-and-aft movements controlled the rudder. In both cases, a lever on the other side of the seat controlled the elevator. Wilbur Wright was there for about a month teaching Lahm and Humphreys to fly, with both men soloing on October 26. Allen had selected Humphreys, an Army engineer, to take Foulois' place, likely because he was the only other junior Army officer on the board that had judged the plane's acceptance tests. Though Wilbur Wright had fulfilled his and his brother's obligation to the Army once Lahm and Humphreys soloed, he was willing to remain at College Park to work with Foulois, who had returned to the United States on October 19 with hopes of training as an airplane pilot after all. Wilbur took Foulois on three training flights, first on October 23, and then twice more before all concerned agreed that Humphreys would take over Foulois' training. The pair went up together for the first time on October 30. On November 3, Lahm took Lieutenant Sweet for a flight—making Sweet the first Navy officer to fly. Then, on November 5, Lahm took Humphreys up as a passenger, but this first time the two officers flew together ended in a crash. Though both men were uninjured, the crash seriously damaged the plane, which could not be repaired with parts on hand and resulted in a training delay.[45] Foulois' switch in pilot instructor from Wilbur to Humphreys may have been because Wilbur Wright had completed his obligations by training Humphreys and Lahm and did not expect to stay in College Park much longer. Having Humphreys instruct Foulois may also have helped Humphreys to develop his own skills.

Instead of, or in addition to, Wright's imminent departure, there may have been technical reasons for the change in instructor. Although it was possible to fly the Army plane from either seat, the controls were mirrored, allowing both seats to share the complex warping/rudder lever between them, with separate but connected elevator controls on the outside of each seat. As such, early Wright pilots were either "left-seat" or "right-seat," since it would be too confusing to fly with the control levers reversed. The left-seat/right-seat identification of Wright pilots remained until 1912, when the Wrights devised a way to provide full duplicate controls to each seat.[46] The Wrights' original single-seat designs offset the engine to the right side of the plane, putting the pilot to the left of center as a counterbalance; to make their two-seat airplane for the Army, they added the second seat on the centerline. The left-seat trained pilot had an advantage in that he could fly without anyone in the right seat, but a right-seat pilot required either a passenger or equivalent ballast in the left seat to balance the plane against the weight of the engine.[47] This posed a problem, then, for a right-seat pilot as, generally speaking, a lighter plane maneuvers better than a heavily laden plane. Likewise, it can take off and climb faster, reach higher altitudes, and, depending on how the pilot manages the engine, achieve greater speed or greater endurance.

Since Wilbur Wright had taught himself to fly from what was now the left seat, both Lahm and Humphreys learned to fly from the right seat.

Thus, when they both went aloft on November 5, Lahm was clearly the pilot in the right seat. Humphreys, as passenger, was in the left seat and would have had difficulty taking over the controls if needed. Had Wright continued to instruct Foulois, all three Army pilots would have been right-seat and would not have been able to trade off flying duty in the air. Since Humphreys was a right-seat-trained pilot, Foulois would learn to be a left-seat pilot. Foulois, a small, lightly built man,[48] could fly the plane alone from the left seat, resulting in much lower total weight of the airplane, thus making the most of his physical advantages. The ability to have two flyers switch off flying duties in the air was probably the major reason to have Humphreys teach Foulois, though. Weight and balance considerations, if not simply serendipitous, probably played only a minor role in the decision.

That Foulois had received any flight training was either a lucky coincidence, or else it justified both Lahm's and Humphreys returning to other, non-aviation duties. As Humphreys had only been loaned to the Signal Corps for temporary duty with aviation, the Corps of Engineers recalled him shortly after he and Lahm crashed. As for Lahm, he was rapidly approaching four consecutive years on detached duty with the Signal Corps, which an Army regulation, widely referred to as the "Manchu Law," prohibited.[49] Consequently, Lahm had to return to his cavalry regiment at about the same time that Humphreys returned to the engineers. This left Foulois, at this point only partially trained, as the Army's sole officer on airplane duty, flying the original and only airplane in the Army inventory, from late November 1909 until 1911.[50]

In December 1909, Allen transferred Foulois, the Wright plane (Signal Corps Airplane No. 1), and a handful of enlisted men to Fort Sam Houston, near San Antonio, Texas, to take advantage of better weather. First, though, Allen ordered Foulois to display the Army's new airplane for much of January at the Chicago Electrical Trade Association's annual trade show, where it was suspended from the ceiling of the Chicago Coliseum. Foulois, with the help of a local amateur radio operator, rigged a radio-telegraph set in the suspended plane to demonstrate that it was possible both to send and receive messages from an airplane in the air. Of course, this test did not account for either sonic or electrical "noise" of an airplane in flight. In February, after the trade show closed, Foulois and his men shipped the plane to Texas.[51]

Though Foulois had been ready to solo in early November, he did not make his first solo flight until March 2, 1910. At that point, he was several months out of practice and without a "coach" in San Antonio to monitor his flying technique. In fact, his only feedback came from letters to and from the Wrights, leading to his oft-repeated claim to have learned to fly via correspondence course. As a result, Foulois' landings ranged from "very rough" to "near crashes," and the airplane section quickly burned through their $150 maintenance allowance and another $300 of its members' own pay—in addition, Foulois says, to "midnight requisitions" from Army stores—to keep the plane flying. (Although Allen had advised Foulois to bring plenty of spare parts, the first airplane contract made no provision for spares, and Allen had allotted only $150 for maintenance and supplies.) These personal expenditures, according to Foulois, resulted in another reprimand via distasteful orders: at Washington's direction, Foulois and his men spent a month (June 15 to July 16, 1910) installing an elaborate electrical signaling system at an Army target range twenty-five miles away from their flying field.

Following this "disciplinary" duty, Foulois and his men returned to the airplane, successfully installing wheels on the craft. Using wheels meant that the plane could be in the air faster since it no longer required the launching catapult (which had to be reoriented every time the wind shifted—a very long process) for takeoffs. After consultation with Wilbur Wright in October, Foulois and his crew further modified their plane to be more like the newer Wright B models.[52]

CONCLUSIONS

By late 1910, then, the Army had one airplane with one qualified pilot assigned to flying duties. It also had one dirigible, with three qualified pilots assigned. Yet despite all the effort made by the respective manufacturers and the Army itself to test, prove, and fulfill the contracts that resulted in this nascent air force, the Army apparently put these promising new technologies on a back burner. Perhaps having acquired an example of each of the competing technologies of manned flight, the Army (as an institution) was content to wait to see what developed before committing to any further expansion. But neither did the Army make any effort to rigorously evaluate or employ the new technologies. It left the officers in charge of each aircraft almost entirely on their own: the Army did not give any guidance regarding what it expected from either the aircraft or the officers in charge of them. Nor did the Army seem interested in ensuring that operational and maintenance funding were sufficient to keep the aircraft in operation. In short, the Army seemed to have lost interest in the technology after acquiring a sample of each. This was especially true of the dirigible: the Army would scrap it in 1912, and close Fort Omaha again in 1913, acquiring no more lighter-than-air (LTA) craft of any kind until World War I. The three airship pilots, Winter, Bamberger, and Dickinson, also disappear from Army aviation history. The Army would soon make additional investments in heavier-than-air flight, its revival of interest perhaps driven by the Navy's acquisition of its own airplanes. In the meantime, the nascent advocates seemed to have been cast adrift, their connections to the patronage of the apparently sympathetic chief of signal interrupted.

2

NAVY/MARINES 1909–1912

The Origins of Naval Aviation

Naval aviation had a rockier start than Army aviation, primarily due to the lack of any organizational clarity in the Navy regarding aviation.[1] The Army, at least, had a history of ballooning in the Signal Corps, so there was a certain logic in placing responsibility for airplanes in that organization. Even beyond that, the Signal Corps proactively sought out jurisdiction over all aircraft and faced no real opposition from other branches of the Army. There was no similar history of aviation in the Navy, making it far from clear just which part of the Navy's organization would, or should, be responsible for aviation. This led to an early competition between several of the Navy's semiautonomous bureaus for control of the new technology. On the other hand, whereas the Army was a manpower-intensive organization with relatively little money in equipment, the Navy relied upon complex, capital-intensive equipment operated by a considerably smaller number of personnel. To put it another way: "the Army equips the man, while the Navy mans the equipment."[2] So where the Army organized people by individual soldiers' tasks (e.g., infantry, artillery, cavalry, and communications, among others), the Navy organized personnel into bureaus responsible for jobs relating to the assembly, maintenance, and operation of its complex equipment (e.g., Construction & Repair [of ships], Steam Engineering [engines of all kinds], Equipment [everything from ship's boats to cooking gear], and Yards & Docks [shore-based infrastructure]—to name just the "material" bureaus). The Navy's single combat arm—ships—reported directly to the Secretary of the Navy, with no officer coordinator equivalent to the bureau chiefs until Congress created the Chief of Naval Operations in 1915. Given this organization, it was not obvious which bureau should control naval aviation; any bureau *could* claim naval aviation. After Langley's experiments, the next mention of airplanes in the Navy reflects both this uncertainty and this competition.

Despite the Board on Construction's clear rejection of Navy airplanes in 1898, official Navy observers (and many unofficial ones) were on hand in 1908 for the Wright Army trials. As already mentioned, Navy Lt. George Sweet was on the board that eventually accepted the Wright machine, giving up his seat to Selfridge on that fatal flight.[3] In addition to his input for the Army, Sweet prepared an enthusiastic report for his superior, the chief of the Bureau of Equipment (BuEquip), Rear Adm. William Cowles. Sweet's report, which Cowles forwarded to the Secretary of the Navy, outlined specifications for an airplane that would be useful to the Navy: long endurance with high rate of speed ("over 40 mph") as well as "the possibility of hovering, if such can be accomplished," able to carry more than one person, launch and alight on a ship's deck, carry a wireless telegraph set, operate "in weather other than a dead calm," be conveniently stowed on board the ship, take off without special launching apparatus (i.e., the launching rail used by the Wrights), and, if possible, capable of launching and landing on the water. Such a plane, he pointed out, could carry secure messages between ships or from ship to shore (with the added advantage that if shot down, the dispatches would sink with the wreck), could increase the search range of scouting vessels, and could reconnoiter enemy shore defenses or a blockaded fleet. He also made passing mention of spotting fire against targets. But the most valuable use of an airplane to the Navy, argued Sweet, would be in detecting and reporting submerged submarines and minefields.[4] Despite this positive report, and the proof of the Army trials that manned flight was a reality, the Navy secretary took no action on Sweet's report.

The secretary's inaction may have been a result of timing: First, Sweet's report came mere months after the crash that killed Selfridge, which cast a pall over the trials and left the Army's acceptance of the plane officially in doubt. Secretary of the Navy Victor Metcalf had been present to witness the crash, which may have been enough by itself to dissuade him from acquiring any planes for the Navy. Years later, Sweet recalled that Metcalf was "obdurate" in his belief that planes were not yet ready for Navy use. Prior to the Wright tests, Sweet had put in a requisition for four planes to train midshipmen at the Naval Academy, but after the Selfridge crash, Metcalf gave the requisition back to Sweet, saying that he "would have nothing to do with such flimsy, foolish playthings."[5] Second, by the time Cowles' letter reached the secretary's office, Metcalf had resigned. He was succeeded by Truman Newberry, who served the last few months of Roosevelt's administration. Cowles' letter may have been lost in the shuffle, or Newberry may have decided to leave it for the incoming Taft administration. Indeed, Newberry may have made a deliberate decision to do nothing.

Whatever the reason for inaction at the secretary's level, other naval officers showed plenty of interest in the airplane. After the Army's formal acceptance of the Wright Military Flyer in 1909, BuEquip (Cowles) requested authority to purchase two airplanes. The acting secretary's reply (likely Herbert Satterlee) probably reflected the consensus within the Office of the Secretary of the Navy: "The Department does not consider that the development of aeroplanes has progressed sufficiently to warrant their purchase at this time for use in the Navy."[6] A year later, Rear Adm. Hutch I. Cone, chief of the Bureau of Steam Engineering (BuEng), requested authority to purchase an airplane for the newest scout cruiser under construction: the USS Chester. To justify his request, Cone cited "the important role which [airplanes] will probably play . . . for scouting and signal purposes."[7] The chief of the Bureau of Construction and Repair (BuC&R), Richard Watt, made a similar request at about the same time. Their close timing suggests that these requests were probably competing attempts by the bureaus to claim responsibility for Navy aircraft without asking the secretary for an official assignment of authority. It is unlikely that the two men were attempting to collaborate to push the Navy into the field of aviation.

When George von Lengerke Meyer became Secretary of the Navy in 1909 he established four aides (more often spelled "aids" at the time): senior Navy officers with distinct portfolios to help him coordinate the bureaus' work.[8] Meyer circulated Cone's request (the first to arrive) among these men. The aide for personnel, Rear Adm. W. P. Potter, believed that the Navy should "defer action until a more perfect machine is developed."[9] The aide for operations, Rear Adm. Richard Wainwright, opined that the Navy should "enter actively into the subject of securing satisfactory aeroplanes or kites for observation purposes at sea," but he preferred the kite to "the present types of aeroplanes."[10] At least two of Meyer's aides recommended asking the Navy's General Board its opinion of Cone's request.[11] The board's president, Admiral of the Navy George Dewey, a proponent of aviation, responded: "The General Board believes that the value of aeroplanes for use in naval warfare should be investigated without delay and recommends that the Department approve the request of the Engineer-in-Chief [Cone]."[12] Acting on the somewhat mixed advice of the aides and the General Board, Assistant Secretary of the Navy Beekman Winthrop (acting in Meyer's absence) ordered BuEng and BuC&R to assign officers to coordinate with Capt. Washington Irving Chambers, recently tasked with handling the aviation-related mail for the secretary. These officers were to work *with* Chambers, not *for* him.[13] Nevertheless, this directive put Chambers in a leadership role, making him the first (if unofficial) "head" of naval aviation.

Washington Irving Chambers was a senior officer, well known and well-respected for his technical knowledge. The first aide for material, Rear Adm. William Swift, had been very impressed with Chambers' technical knowledge and felt he needed Chambers as an assistant to help establish the office. Swift convinced Chambers that his presence was so important that Chambers willingly gave up a battleship command after only six months in order to return to Washington.[14] (Chambers' decision would have important consequences a few years later.) In September 1910, about a month before Cone and Watt's requests, the Aero Club of America requested a contact within the Navy Department on aeronautical issues. Meyer asked his aides to assign someone to the task. By then, Admiral Swift had been forced to retire due to his health; his replacement, Capt. Frank F. Fletcher (not to be confused with his nephew of World War II fame, Frank Jack Fletcher), assigned Chambers the additional duty. As Fletcher's assistant, Chambers was already helping to coordinate the actions of the Navy's material bureaus—BuEng, BuC&R, BuEquip, and BuOrd (Bureau of Ordnance). Chambers also had a strong technical background: among other accomplishments, he had proposed several well-regarded warship designs and made several successful improvements to torpedo design during two tours at the Navy's Torpedo Experiment Station near Newport, Rhode Island.[15] Thus, when the General Board recommended that the Navy actively investigate aviation, the technically minded Chambers was a natural choice to coordinate.[16] Though given little authority, Chambers nevertheless had a great influence on naval aviation and was its first successful technology advocate. Other officers—such as Dewey, Cowles, and Sweet—were also aviation advocates, believing that aircraft could do great things for the Navy, but none of them had been able to accomplish anything as concrete or significant as Chambers would.

To perform his new duties more effectively, Chambers quickly read everything he could get his hands on about aviation, becoming an aviation enthusiast in the process.[17] Echoing one of the requirements in Cowles' 1908 memorandum, Chambers believed that a Navy airplane would have to operate from Navy ships, and he set out to prove that this was possible.

Stretching (if not actually overstepping) the bounds of whatever authority he had, Chambers organized Eugene Ely's November 14, 1910, flight, which marked the first ever takeoff from a ship. On that day, Ely flew a Curtiss aircraft from a specially built deck on the forecastle of the cruiser *Birmingham*, anchored in Hampton Roads, Virginia.[18] Two months later, on January 18, 1911, Ely landed on a similarly constructed deck (with ropes and sandbags to help him stop) on the stern of the battleship *Pennsylvania*, anchored in San Francisco's harbor—the world's first landing of an airplane on a ship. These events are typically cited as the experimental beginnings of the aircraft carrier. However, none of the participants had in mind the current notion of a dedicated aviation vessel with special decks and fittings to allow flight operations. These were simply proof-of-concept experiments to show that aircraft could operate with ships.

A third flight, almost forgotten in naval aviation histories—possibly because it does not advance the carrier paradigm—took place in San Diego harbor in February 1911: Glenn Curtiss himself demonstrated the possibilities of his new "hydroaeroplane" (a floatplane) by landing in the water next to the *Pennsylvania* and being hoisted aboard. After a brief visit on board the ship, Curtiss was hoisted out again and returned to his camp.[19] Chambers felt that the hydroaeroplane, or perhaps even a flying boat, would be most useful to the Navy. Operating from the surface of the sea, it would require no special modifications to its mother ship: it could be hoisted in and out like a ship's boat (using the same cranes) and disassembled for stowage below decks.[20] Chambers used these successful experiments to push for funding to permit the Navy to buy its own airplanes and not be dependent on the goodwill of manufacturers for further experiments.[21] (The three flights had been made with the enthusiastic cooperation of Glenn Curtiss, who no doubt saw them as a way to open a new market.)

The airplane was not the only aerial technology being considered to enhance the effectiveness of the fleet. The Navy was aware of the use of captive, spherical, hydrogen balloons from ships prior to 1910, but analysts saw numerous shortcomings and felt that man-carrying kites were the best solution to increasing the range of observation from ships.[22] Just a month before Ely landed on board, the *Pennsylvania* had experimented with such kites. Charles Pond, commanding officer of the *Pennsylvania*, was quite pleased with the results, as was his superior, Rear Adm. Chauncey Thomas Jr., commander in chief of the Pacific Fleet. After seeing a copy of Pond's report, the commander of the 5th Division of the Atlantic Fleet commented, "The carrying of an observer provided with a telescope and telephone communication at a height of 400 or 500 feet would have been of great value during the war with Spain and would probably have accelerated the result at Santiago" by allowing the battleships to use indirect fire against the anchored Spanish ships; "In the light of that experience," the commander concluded, "the most promising field for kite observation is the control of indirect fire." Though this generated excitement among some officers, others saw too many downsides to kites. The commander in chief of the Atlantic Fleet, Rear Adm. Seaton Schroeder, clearly saw problems with using kites in battle as well as the difficulties of getting accurate readings from such a platform.[23] But the three airplane flights had shown such promise that talk of kites and balloons died away. (Kite balloons, combining the benefits of both kites and balloons, would be developed during World War I and used both on land and on ships at sea.)

The period from mid-March to mid-April 1911 demonstrated the unstable position of aviation within the Navy's bureaucracy. Although he had been signing letters with the self-styled title, "Officer in Charge of Aviation," Chambers was nonetheless uncomfortable with his ambiguous position and authority. Secretary Meyer finally responded to Chambers' requests for clarification in mid-March, ordering him to "keep informed," advise, recommend, guide, and consult on aviation matters, but Meyer gave him no clear command authority.[24] Chambers' biographer, Stephen Stein, described Meyer's instructions as "an administrative arrangement guaranteed to magnify all the problems of bureau coordination" over aviation. In an effort to address these difficulties, Admiral Dewey (a potential patron) arranged to have Chambers transferred to the General Board on March 30, 1911, to provide him with some staff support and position him for a greater influence on policy.[25] In the meantime, the successful flights convinced Meyer to request money from Congress for naval aviation. Congress granted the request but placed the requested $25,000 in the budget of the Bureau of Navigation (BuNav). Thus, Chambers was shuttled again (as of April 14, 1911—the day President Howard Taft signed the budget), this time to BuNav so he could legally control and spend the money.[26] The chief of BuNav hardly welcomed Chambers, suggesting that he work from home rather than in its already crowded offices and ignoring Chambers' requests for office assistance. Chambers firmly believed he needed a physical presence in the bureau and finally found some office space in the basement of the State, War, and Navy building. He described the space as "objectionable in many ways" and "a good place to catch a cold."[27] This was only the first of many instances in which the embryonic naval aviation branch was bounced around by the Navy's bureaucracy, disrupting nascent networks of advocacy and patronage.

THE NAVY BUYS ITS FIRST PLANES

Chambers put organizational travails aside and purchased one airplane from the Wright Brothers and two from Curtiss. (The money could not be spent until the beginning of the fiscal year on July 1, but the date Chambers issued the requisition for the planes, May 8, 1911, is officially considered the birthday of U.S. naval aviation.) Like the first Army airplanes, the Navy planes were all "pushers," meaning that their engines were ahead of the propellers, and so the propellers "pushed" the planes forward. The tractor put the propeller ahead of the engine, so that the propeller "pulled" the plane forward. Curtiss had experimented with a tractor layout for his hydroaeroplane, probably in an attempt to avoid the damage caused when the propeller hit the spray kicked up by the float, but he found the tractor layout unsatisfactory (his design put the engine directly in front of the pilot at eye level) and returned to the pusher design. Curtiss' first Navy student, Lt. Theodore G. "Spuds" Ellyson, probably did not get to fly it as a tractor, but that did not stop him from asserting that "This machine will not be suitable for naval use owing to the fact that the propeller in front obstructs the vision."[28] Both Army and Navy planes remained almost exclusively pushers for some time.

The Wright aircraft (designated B-1 by the Navy) was a landplane, identical to the first Army plane. One Curtiss (the A-2) was also a landplane, essentially the same design that Eugene Ely had flown for the *Birmingham* and *Pennsylvania* tests. The other Curtiss plane (the A-1) was to be a "triad" design, so-called because it flew through the air, had a float to land on water, and employed retractable wheels for operating from land—what is now called an "amphibian." All three planes had the crew sitting out in the open (in front of the wing); they had an airspeed of about fifty miles per hour, and their endurance was more often limited by mechanical failure than by fuel capacity.[29] The single-seat A-2 was intended strictly as a trainer while the two-seat A-1 was to be more of a "service" aircraft, that is, one used "in service" rather than for training. The two-seat Wright B-1 served in both roles.

Chambers acquired these first planes with the intent that they would be used primarily for training pilots and secondarily in experiments to explore the airplane's potential. He knew that the airplane as a technology was not yet sufficiently advanced to be integrated fully into Navy operations. But Chambers expected someone would soon develop a plane capable of accompanying the fleet to sea and intended to have a nucleus of trained pilots by that time. Once the Navy had such a plane, all further training of aviators would take place in the fleet, where aviation would be used in scouting and reconnaissance, mine-hunting, and delivering confidential communications—much the same functions as enumerated by Sweet and Cowles in 1908.[30] Such integration, Chambers believed, would expose many more sailors to aviation—advancing its acceptance—than if airplanes were based ashore or in special-purpose ships.[31]

These simple plans did not prevent others from expecting even greater things from the airplane. In 1910, even before the Navy had its first plane, Chambers noted, "Many enthusiastic writers . . . are predicting all sorts of dire disaster to battleships from aerial warfare," but he pointed out that similar claims (that had not panned out) had been made for the torpedo boat when it was introduced. He also cited the present state of aeronautical development that limited the use of planes to reconnaissance or scouting due to their inability to carry much weight aloft.[32] Congressman Richmond Hobson (D-AL and a retired admiral) felt it necessary to make similar points to the House of Representatives in January 1911 to justify continued battleship spending.[33] Still, in April 1911 then-captain Bradley Fiske proposed to the General Board that "a hundred aeroplanes, costing about two hundred and fifty thousand dollars, would render the disembarkation and landing of a large number of troops an exceedingly difficult operation." Fiske's was one of the few voices within the Navy suggesting that airplanes could replace ships, but his enthusiasm and expectations were narrowly bounded. His proposed force was intended to defend the U.S. naval base in the Philippines—a distant location that the Navy could not quickly reinforce—and this would be accomplished not by sinking any ships, much less battleships, but rather by killing or destroying men and material on the decks of transports or sinking the small boats carrying them ashore.[34] A Mr. A. E. Baker wrote to Navy Secretary Josephus Daniels (who had succeeded Meyer in March 1913) in 1913 making arguments similar to those made by Billy Mitchell in the 1920s—that a fleet of airplanes could easily defend the country against enemy battleships and could be built for one-third the cost of a single battleship. Baker told Daniels to "quit building battleships and build a few aeroplanes instead."[35]

Chambers was quick to damp down such expectations. When BuC&R proposed bombing tests against the target ship *San Marcos* (ex-battleship *Texas*) in the fall of 1911, Chambers told his boss, the chief of BuNav, Rear Adm. Reginald Nicholson, "To utilize the few aeroplanes now owned by the Navy in bomb-dropping experiments . . . would, in my opinion, be a waste of valuable time." Chambers declared that bombing would not be useful against surface ships anyway, given that the first airplanes could only carry small bombs and would face great difficulty scoring a hit in the face of anti-aircraft fire and defensive airplanes (which did not yet exist). He did, however, believe that airplane bombs would eventually be useful in destroying enemy submarines and mines.[36] Chambers' response is interesting not only in that he did not foresee that airplanes might eventually be able to carry large enough bombs to threaten ships, but also in his assumption that airplanes would be deployed defensively. While Chambers may have had in mind something other than machine guns shooting down opposing aircraft, this may be the earliest written reference in any of the U.S. military services to the idea that airplanes might have an air-to-air role.

Training of the first naval aviators had started well before Congress approved the funding for the Navy planes. Taking advantage of an offer by Glenn Curtiss to train a Navy officer free of charge, Chambers arranged orders sending Ellyson to flight training. Ellyson transferred to aviation from submarines, a community that had much in common with aviation: both were in experimental stages (though submarines were more established); both were very small, technical communities whose "experts" were only slightly ahead of those they trained; both had problems with the reliability of their hardware (particularly engines); and both operated in a "test-fix-improve-repeat" routine. Ellyson had followed his friend, Kenneth Whiting, into submarines, and again followed his lead in applying for aviation. But Ellyson's application seems to have come at an opportune time, whereas Ken Whiting would have to wait until 1914 for aviation orders.[37]

Ellyson arrived at Curtiss' San Diego camp on December 23, 1910, where he eagerly began learning to fly and maintain Curtiss' airplanes. Because Curtiss had not yet built a two-seat airplane, instruction proceeded more slowly than in the Wright plane. The Curtiss method was to start his students in an underpowered plane, with the throttle restricted to prevent takeoff. With this craft, new students made numerous "ground runs" at increasing speeds to get a feel for how the plane responded to control inputs. Once Curtiss felt they were ready, students progressed to a more powerful plane. In this craft, they made longer and longer straight-line flights before attempting turns. In addition to flight training, Ellyson also helped Curtiss with his experiments, including working with Curtiss and Ely to plan and prepare for Ely's flight to the *Pennsylvania*. On the day of the flight, Ellyson expected to be in San Diego with Curtiss setting up the field there, but he reassured Chambers that his absence would not be a problem: "I went over the whole thing with [Ely] the night before I left San Francisco, and it was I who suggested the use of the sandbags and the spacing of the same."[38] Ellyson was also involved with Curtiss' development of the hydroaeroplane and appears to have been behind Curtiss' choice of the *Pennsylvania* as the destination of his demonstration flight with that craft. As Ellyson told Chambers, "The experiment was made at my request to determine the practical value of the hydro-aeroplane for ship's use."[39] Ellyson helped coordinate these tests and was undoubtedly useful as a liaison between Curtiss and the Navy.[40]

A few months after Ellyson began in aviation, the Wright brothers also extended an offer to train an officer free of charge, fully expecting that the Navy would soon purchase an airplane.[41] Lt. John Rodgers thus became the Navy's second aviator, reporting to Dayton, Ohio, for training on March 17, 1911. He had been assistant engineer on the *Pennsylvania* and had witnessed both Ely's and Curtiss' flights to and from the ship. Further, he had been one of the two officers hoisted aloft by the man-lifting kites in January.[42]

Lt. John Towers soon became the third naval aviator. Towers' previous job was as a ship's spotter[43] for the battleship *Michigan*. His desire to improve the accuracy of ships' fire led to his interest in aviation. As a spotter, he was positioned at the top of the ship's mast to increase his range of vision. Though he had never seen an airplane, he recognized that airplanes could fly even higher than a ship's mast and thus allow him to see targets and adjust fire at longer ranges. His November 2, 1910, request for aviation duty was actually the first received in the Bureau of Navigation (which controlled all personnel assignments), but was too early:[44] Ellyson and Rodgers' requests had come in much closer to when Chambers asked BuNav to assign officers for aviation, and Towers' ship was in Europe at that point. Nevertheless, the detailers remembered Towers' request when it became clear that Curtiss would accept another officer for pilot training.[45] Towers reported for training at Curtiss' plant in Hammondsport, New York, on June 27.[46]

These three pioneering naval aviators, all with technical backgrounds, would subsequently have great influence in this early period of Navy aviation. Not only would they always be the most experienced aviators (though not always the highest ranking) during a crucial period in naval aviation history, but they were the ones who trained the next group of naval aviators and established the regimen for flight training in the Navy.[47] Their approach to the work influenced all who came after them.

Even while in training with Curtiss, Ellyson was developing ideas for training future naval aviators. He felt that all pilots should be trained as aircraft mechanics before beginning flight training.[48] His ideas were clarified by the contrast he saw between himself and the Army officers who had started training with Curtiss the same time as Ellyson: "The three Army officers [Paul Beck, George Kelly, and John Walker] who are here are not doing the amount of work which they should. None of them have any idea of engineering or desire to learn the practical side of the care of the machine, which in my opinion are the most important. Their one and only idea seems to be to learn to fly."[49] His criticism of the Army officers suggests a disdain for anyone using equipment without fully understanding it, but it is also possible that Ellyson recognized that an aviator forced down at sea would be more helpless than one forced down on land, especially if he could not even do simple repairs to his airplane.

AIRCRAFT TRAINING AT ANNAPOLIS

Once Ellyson, Rodgers and Towers had their licenses,[50] the new pilots, with their planes, made their way to the Navy's first aeronautic station near the Naval Academy in Annapolis, Maryland. Earlier in the year, the Army had extended an offer to share its aviation facilities at College Park, Maryland, with the Navy, but Chambers (perhaps thinking of the need to operate hydros) felt the Navy could "find a more suitable location nearby."[51] In particular, Chambers wanted "some point on the Atlantic Coast accessible to Naval vessels" that would ease the expected transition of airplane operations from shore to ship. He selected Greenbury Point near the Navy's Engineering Experiment Station, across the Severn River from the Naval Academy in Annapolis. Not only did this provide the water access to operate the hydros, but it also allowed the aviators to take advantage of the resources and mechanical expertise of the nearby Engineering Experiment Station run by BuEng. Ellyson preferred the isolation of Annapolis, fearing that College Park was too open to distractions by the visiting general public.[52] The major downside to the site was that it placed the aviation camp in line with the academy's rifle range, but Chambers felt there would be "no need to use the aerodrome during rifle practice."[53] Apparently, he failed to consider that equipment left downrange might still be vulnerable!

Along with a small cadre of enlisted men to help with repairs and basic camp functions, Rodgers and Towers were at the new "aviation camp" by September 1911, though Rodgers did a lot of flying from the Army's College Park field while waiting for the Navy airfield to be prepared.[54] Ellyson remained in Hammondsport to help test an idea he had had for launching a plane from an inclined, taut wire slide that could be set up easily on almost any ship. Though the test was successful, Chambers recognized that there was a great difference between attempting the feat on land as opposed to a rolling, pitching ship, so he ordered this line of development abandoned. Ellyson relocated to Annapolis on October 3.[55] In their camp, the aviators began to familiarize themselves with the characteristics of the Navy's new planes, practice their flying, and plan future experiments with aircraft.

Many of these experiments had the goal of making airplanes safer to fly. The great need for improvements in aerial navigation and aircraft powerplants was illustrated by another little-recognized early flight. In January 1911, another Curtiss exhibition pilot, J. A. D. McCurdy, attempted to fly a Curtiss airplane more than a hundred miles from Key West, Florida, to Havana, Cuba, apparently to demonstrate the airplane's ability to traverse long distances over water. McCurdy had a compass to steer his straight-line course, but he also had the assistance of Cdr. Yates Stirling's squadron of four Navy destroyers. It was a simple straightaway course, and we may question just how much he relied on the compass for his navigation, given the presence of the destroyers spaced ten to fifteen miles apart along his intended course.[56] In addition to the compass, McCurdy planned on carrying an early wireless set, though the record is not clear regarding whether he did or not.[57] McCurdy's flight ended nineteen miles short of Havana, when his engine failed (due to a cracked oil line). He was forced to land on the water, damaging the plane, and was picked up by Stirling's destroyer.[58]

Beyond demonstrating the need for more reliable engines, McCurdy's failure to reach Cuba impressed upon Chambers that much work needed to be done in aerial navigation over the trackless ocean before planes could be allowed, with any degree of safety, to fly out of sight of either the land or their parent ship. By the fall of 1911, Chambers was working on an aeronautical compass—one that would not be influenced by the engine's electrical system or the vibration of the airframe.[59] Chambers also wanted the Navy flyers, in conjunction with BuEng's nearby Experiment Station, to run tests of aero motors in order to increase their reliability.[60] (Even on a short flight, it was not uncommon at this time to have it forcibly ended by engine failure—a more dangerous prospect over the ocean than over land.)[61] Finally, there was the question of whether airplanes could be equipped with wireless sets. If they could, their usefulness would be vastly greater, since scouting and reconnaissance reports would not have to wait until the plane returned to the ship.[62]

In addition to such tests, the three aviators were also expected to begin teaching other officers to fly. Their first student, Ens. Victor Herbster, was another aviation enthusiast. In 1910, he had visited the Antoinette Aeroplane Co. and the French army and navy pilot training field at Mourmelon-le-Grand (near Reims). His report assessed the suitability of the Antoinette airplane for Navy use, citing its likely ability to float and the "security and location of pilot [that] gives it superiority for scouting purposes."[63] When Herbster arrived in Annapolis in November 1911, Chambers assigned him to training in the Wright B-1, which highlighted two sources of tension already extant in this small community of naval aviators.[64]

The first source of tension was rooted in the legal feud between the Wrights and Curtiss regarding intellectual property. While the two sides wrangled over the issue in court, some of that animosity filtered down to the pilots they trained.[65] The separation into Wright and Curtiss "camps" could be quite literal at times: when the aviators moved to San Diego for the winter of 1912, the Curtiss and Wright camps were separated by about three-quarters of a mile over a "circuitous path through the cactus and brush." The reason for the separation was probably because the Curtiss camp was, at Glenn Curtiss' invitation, sharing space with Curtiss' own winter operations, and it would have been impolitic to have the Wright airplane there.[66] But the fact that the two manufacturers used entirely different designs for their flight controls reinforced the separation. As already described, the Wright airplane used two levers: one for elevator (pitch) control and the other for wing warping (roll) control with a hinged top for rudder (yaw) control. In contrast, Curtiss' planes used a wheel on a post: moving the wheel post forward and back controlled the elevators (pitch), while turning the wheel controlled the rudder (yaw). Curtiss believed that the Wright airplane patent only covered wing warping to make the plane roll, so instead used ailerons. These were connected to a frame around the pilot's seat that moved from side to side. Padded bars on either side sat at about shoulder level and, ideally, fitted tightly to the pilot's shoulders so that the frame would move when the pilot leaned in one direction or the other, thus rolling the plane in the corresponding direction. Due to the differences in control schemes, a pilot trained on one type could not fly the other, as the skill and muscle memory acquired on one control system did not transfer easily to the other, a discrepancy that divided Wright pilots and Curtiss pilots.[67] The differing systems made it neither easy, nor necessarily desirable, for an aviator to be trained in both, given that confusion at a critical time could be fatal. Thus, Herbster's assignment to the Wright B-1 meant that Rodgers had to be his instructor rather than Ellyson (who had been in aviation longest), since Ellyson was not trained in the Wright controls.

That Rodgers became instructor to the newly assigned Herbster also highlights the second source of tension, which stemmed from questions of seniority. Was seniority in rank or in assignment to aviation more important to command of aviation? Rodgers was senior in date of rank to Ellyson. But since Ellyson had started aviation training prior to Rodgers, Ellyson pushed the idea that he was "senior aviator" and should be in command of the camp. That Rodgers had charge of training Herbster did nothing to clarify the relative authority between Rodgers and Ellyson. According to Ellyson's biographer, Rodgers never made an issue of it, but the situation seems to have bothered Rodgers; at least once, he signed a letter as "senior aviator." Never officially settled, the matter caused tension within naval aviation while Rodgers and Ellyson were both flying.[68] As we shall see in chapter 4, the problem would soon arise again with a different pairing. The problem would mostly disappear once the naval aviation training pipeline became regularized after the United States' entry into World War I in 1917, effectively synchronizing the two measures of seniority. It would not fully be put to rest until 1921: the legislation establishing the Bureau of Aeronautics also addressed the rank/experience dilemma in favor of rank. But in 1911, the fact that Ellyson (the senior by date of assignment to aviation) and Rodgers (the senior by date of rank) were also on opposite sides of the Wright/Curtiss issue exacerbated both problems and hindered the development of a united front in support of naval aviation.

In addition to these problems, the aviators were occasionally frustrated by the nonflying Chambers. One disagreement concerned how best to advance naval aviation: the flyers wanted to make their existence known to the public and demonstrate their usefulness to the rest of the Navy through participation in air meets and by setting new aviation records. Chambers, on the other hand, was terribly concerned that fatal crashes would do lasting harm to the reputation of naval aviation in the rest of the Navy. Thus, he did all he could to emphasize safety, including preventing his aviators' attendance at aviation meets in an official capacity and warning against record-seeking for its own sake.[69] Another source of friction was that the flyers did not understand the difficulty Chambers, though a captain, faced in getting what he wanted from the admirals in charge of the various bureaus. Instead, they attributed any delay or disappointment in advancing their interests to Chambers' indifference. But the least tractable issues arose from the fact that Chambers was not a flyer.

Very much an engineer, and having no practical flying experience, Chambers based his understanding of aircraft design and operation on his understanding of the theory of flight and issued commands to the aviators accordingly. The aviators recognized that the theory of flight at the time was still a long way from describing what happened in the real world and harbored a certain resentment that Chambers could not (or would not) appreciate their problems.[70] For instance, Chambers wanted to

develop a standard control for aircraft, but when one flyer suggested trying the Deperdussin controls (the now familiar yoke-and-rudder pedals),
Chambers resisted. He felt that steering with the feet would be awkward
for a sailor and, in any case, was just a "European vogue" that would pass.
He believed that steering with a wheel (as on the Curtiss controls) would
be more natural to a Navy man.[71] The aviators also felt that Chambers
was ordering new planes without considering their opinions on what was
desirable in a new design. In one case, the flyers grew so frustrated that
they jumped the chain of command by writing directly to the secretary
and recommending that a flying officer be involved in selecting new aircraft designs. Chambers felt blindsided; he had no idea that the flyers
were unhappy with their planes, though it was really only one plane: the
O.W.L. (Over Water and Land). In any case, it was deemed too heavy and
with too short a float. Another attempt at an amphibious airplane, the
O.W.L. was Chambers' redesign of the A-2. When completed, it was designated the E-1.[72]

Events that occurred in San Diego during the winter of 1912 provide
another example of the gap between theory and experience that set the
flyers apart from nonflying officers who governed naval aviation: Naval
Constructor Holden C. Richardson, another engineer, had been working for some time on airplane floats. He joined the aviation camp in San
Diego to test his designs and train as a pilot himself. Although Richardson
had created his floats using the latest understanding of hull design and
tested them in the Navy's model basin, the floats were a complete disaster—an assessment made by Curtiss, Ellyson, and Towers (based solely on
appearance and the flyers' experience with Curtiss' various float designs)
before they were even installed on an aircraft. Though Richardson took
offense at what he considered a premature judgment, subsequent tests of
the floats on the airplanes were disastrous, quickly proving the aviators'
instincts correct.[73] Once Richardson learned to fly, he came around to
the aviators' way of thinking; he was the officer who proposed trying out
the Deperdussin controls in the first instance! There was a strong feeling
among the aviators that actual flying officers should have the final say over

issues connected with flying. They contended that there were too many intangibles that non-flyers would never understand.

SAN DIEGO

The aviation camp wintered over in San Diego because Annapolis was considered unsuitable for work during winter (Chambers wrote that there was "considerable risk of an aviator contracting bronchial diseases" after falling in the water in winter weather), and Guantanamo was deemed too far away from a supply of spare parts—a considerable need at this time. San Diego offered warmer weather and better access to supplies, especially since Glenn Curtiss had offered the Navy the use of his aeronautical facilities at North Island in San Diego Bay.[74] Chambers, through the chief of BuNav, ordered the flyers to San Diego on December 28, 1911. Though Curtiss' invitation specifically included the Wright airplane, Chambers' orders emphasized the two partisan "camps" and the unclear command relationship between them: Ellyson was "entrusted with the care and control of the Navy Curtiss machines, the Navy Wright machine being independently under control of Lt. John Rodgers." Rodgers' orders were similarly worded, but no reason was given for the separation.[75] The flyers remained in San Diego until May 1912, when they returned to Annapolis.[76]

In addition to the tests of different float designs (Richardson's were not the only floats tested), there were many other tests planned in San Diego. But other issues cut into the schedule. Shortly after arriving in San Diego, Herbster finished his training and qualified for his license.[77] In addition to seeing the floats tested, Richardson had come to California intent on becoming an aviator himself. That way, he would be able to conduct his own tests without having to wait for the aviation camp to fit such testing into the schedule. Richardson's flight training lasted until April 22.[78] Training Herbster and Richardson cut into the time the aircraft were available for experiments. In addition, despite the potential for confusion at a critical time, the flyers had begun cross-training in controls just before they left Annapolis, and this continued in San Diego as part of Chambers' plan to develop a standard control system for all planes.[79] On top of these training flights, the flyers also took interested Navy officers (from ships in the harbor) on "introductory flights" to give them a taste of aviation.[80] These all cut into the time the planes were available for experiments. Tests with radio, begun in Annapolis, were delayed first by the damage in transit of the only radio set, then by problems with the engines, and finally by crashes.[81] Though only one crash caused serious injury to the pilot (Ellyson), several resulted in having to rebuild the planes.[82] These setbacks further reduced the time for experimental flights.

Despite sharing space with Curtiss and his facilities, the Navy flyers rebuilt even the Curtiss planes themselves, adding their own modifications as they saw fit. Towers rebuilt the Curtiss A-2 after Ellyson's crash, changing it from a landplane to a floatplane.[83] Towers also claimed to have been the one to decide that the forward elevator in the Curtiss airplanes (Curtiss machines at the time had both a forward and rear elevator) might not be necessary, and found that the plane flew better without it. After that, no Navy Curtiss plane used the forward elevator (Curtiss himself began omitting the forward elevator on new builds) and the design became known as a "headless pusher."[84] Later that summer, once the aviators were back in Annapolis, Herbster even built an entirely new Wright airplane (designated B-2) out of spare parts and materials on hand![85] That the aviators could accomplish this work themselves stemmed from Ellyson's insistence in training each officer to be a mechanic as well as a pilot.

But if the aviators did not avail themselves of Curtiss' knowledge and equipment in rebuilding aircraft, the physical proximity to Curtiss had other benefits: Curtiss came over to watch when Richardson's floats were being tested, and the two discussed aircraft design.[86] While Navy planes were being repaired and rebuilt, Towers also did some experimental flying for Curtiss, thereby becoming familiar with (and influencing) Curtiss' newest design ideas, especially the flying boat, which floated directly on a hull-shaped fuselage.[87] This meant that the Curtiss flying boat, was both familiar to the naval aviators and also well suited to Navy needs when the Navy purchased its first one in December 1912.

CONCLUSIONS

The differences between the Army's beginnings with aviation and those of the Navy can be attributed to a number of different factors, primarily the interrelationship between the services' respective organizations and their culture. In its establishment, Army aviation benefitted from a certain degree of air-mindedness in its culture (having utilized balloons) as well as from having an existing "bureau" (the Signal Corps) with an active interest in controlling aviation. The Navy did not have a history of ballooning, and consequently had no air-minded culture to build on. The Navy actually suffered in having two different bureaus interested in taking control of aviation, in that the Navy secretary refused to make a choice between them, instead creating a situation where a captain of uncertain position on the organizational chart ended up with primary responsibility. This indecision on the secretary's part meant that Congress could weigh in on the issue, which it did by assigning funds to a third bureau (for reasons that are unclear) whose chief had no interest in controlling aviation.

Naval aviation did have an advantage, however, in that the Navy had both a culture and an organization steeped in acquiring and operating complex systems, particularly those with engines. Though it suffered from having responsibility for various subsystems distributed among several bureaus, at least the Navy could easily incorporate appropriate parts of the airplane into the work of those existing bureaus. Perhaps it was the culture and experience with mechanical systems that led the Navy to make an initial purchase of three airplanes (from two different manufacturers), as opposed to the Army's initial buy of only one airplane. To be fair, though, there *was* only one manufacturer in existence when the Army bought its first airplane. Furthermore, while the origins of naval aviation parallel those in the first chapter thematically, they happened concurrently with the Army events addressed in the next chapter.

In contrast to the multiple complex systems that made up even the smallest Navy ship, the most complex mechanical systems in the Army at the introduction of the airplane were small arms and artillery (technologies that were only a part of what the Navy dealt with). Trucks and other motor-ized vehicles were still in the Army's future. Consequently, Army aviation could get little assistance for its aircraft (particularly their engines) from other parts of the Army and had to become self-sufficient. In fact, as we will see in a later chapter, Army aviation's experience with internal com-bustion engines meant that it led the way in adopting internal combustion land vehicles as well.

3

ARMY 1911–1912

More Pilots, More Planes

While the Navy had made a larger initial purchase of airplanes than the Army (three to the Army's one) and assigned a larger number of personnel to aviation training (again, three to one), the Navy's actions actually coincided with a similar increase in Army aviation. Despite the Army's longer experience with the airplane, it was equally unprepared for the problems the Navy faced as described in the previous chapter (but occurring at about the same time): issues with training new aviators, operating and maintaining multiple aircraft from different manufacturers, and uncertainty as to whether rank or flying experience determined superior/subordinate relationships.

In early 1911, even as Ely's landing on the USS *Pennsylvania* was making headlines, Robert J. Collier, owner and publisher of *Collier's Weekly* and an aviation enthusiast, decided to loan his new Wright Model B to the Army until the Army could secure funding for more planes. Collier's plane arrived in Texas in February, along with a Wright pilot, Philip Parmelee, whose presence meant that Foulois finally had an opportunity to receive real-time professional coaching on his flying. Foulois said later that Parmelee was also there to instruct him on the use of a "new and different control mechanism." If Wilbur Wright had indeed instructed the

Army officers in his preferred system of using the joystick for roll and yaw, then the "new" control was Orville's preferred lever and toggle, which was rapidly becoming standard on the Wright aircraft.[1]

While learning to fly by himself, Foulois had often engaged in what he called "indoctrination flights": flying low over the tents and picket lines of the Maneuver Division assembling at Fort Sam Houston, partly in response to the beginnings of the Mexican Revolution, partly as a training exercise.[2] While Foulois asserted that his flights were "psychological warfare" in retaliation for their dismissal of his airplane and its capabilities, they may have been effective in getting both men and animals accustomed to working around airplanes. With Parmelee and the new Wright B, however, Foulois was able to make proper military flights: performing reconnaissance and delivering messages. One such flight on March 3 marked a turning point for military aviation: it was the first official military reconnaissance flight, the first use of radio (radiotelegraph) on a military flight, and it set American records for weight carried (1,400 lbs.) and distance covered (106 miles).[3]

The Army did not have to rely on Collier's loaned airplane for very long. Since Congress had rejected Allen's earlier requests for aviation funding ($200,000 in FY 1908 and $500,000 in FY 1909), the new secretary of war, Jacob Dickinson (who had only taken office on March 12, 1909), assumed that the War Department needed to reduce expenses, and so, as he explained in his report at the end of FY 1909, he had not bothered to request any aviation funding for FY 1911.[4] An unidentified congressman was supposedly overheard saying (in response to one of Allen's requests), "Why all this fuss about airplanes for the Army? I thought we already had one!" The story may be apocryphal, but it does seem to capture the perception of Congress' attitude toward aviation at the time. Nevertheless, in March 1911 Congress voted its first appropriation for Army aviation: $125,000 for FY 1912, with the first $25,000 immediately available. With funds in hand ahead of the July 1 beginning of the fiscal year,[5] the Army immediately ordered three Wright Model Bs. By this time, Glenn Curtiss had been selling his own airplanes for several years. Despite ongoing intellectual property litigation between Curtiss and the Wrights, the Army also purchased two Curtiss Model Ds.[6] Soon after the delivery of the first of these orders, the Army retired Signal Corps No. 1 and donated it to the U.S. National Museum of the Smithsonian Institution.[7]

Prior to the increased funding for airplanes, the Army had already assigned more officers to aviation. Following Eugene Ely's successful take-off from a ship in November 1910, Curtiss offered free flight training to both Army and Navy officers at his new winter flying camp on North Island in the San Diego Bay. In response, the Army sent three officers, each of whom had already flown as passengers before beginning formal flight training: Lt. Paul W. Beck, Signal Corps, 2nd Lt. George E. M. Kelly, and 2nd Lt. John C. Walker, the latter two both from the infantry. Beck, on orders from Allen, had met Curtiss the previous year at the International Aviation Contest in Los Angeles in January 1910. Although Curtiss had requested Squier, Allen sent Beck, who was on duty at the Presidio in San Francisco. As it happened, Beck had designed an aerial bombsight and tested it during flights with Curtiss in a Curtiss plane and with French pilot Louis Paulhan in Paulhan's Farman airplane. In January 1911, at another air meet in San Francisco, Beck continued his bombing experiments and also operated a radio transmitter of his own design from a plane flown by the Wright Company's Parmelee. Walker and Kelly also attended the 1911 meet, during which Walker flew as a passenger with Walter Brookins in a Wright plane, taking aerial photographs of a nearby airfield. The next day, Kelly went up with Brookins on a photoreconnaissance flight, but they did not sight the marching cavalry troops and field artillery battery that was their objective.[8] (It is not clear whether these officers attended the meet before or after reporting to Curtiss as students. Navy student Ellyson had already reported to Curtiss and attended this meet in his company.[9]) Little came of these tests, however, as far as Army development was concerned: there was no rush to acquire bombsights, cameras, or lightweight radios, nor was any official testing initiated at this time.

After the meet, the three Army officers traveled to Curtiss' North Island camp where they began training in February in a class that included the

Navy's Ellyson and three civilians. Curtiss reported at the end of February that the Army officers were progressing satisfactorily, but in April, before their training was complete, he shifted operations back to his home of Hammondsport, New York, for the summer. Unlike Ellyson, the Army officers did not follow Curtiss back to New York to finish training. Instead, Allen ordered them to Fort Sam Houston, where they could complete their training under one of Curtiss' other instructors.[10]

The first two of the new airplanes were delivered to Fort Sam Houston in late April 1911: one Curtiss Model D (Signal Corps plane No. 2) and one Wright Model B (S.C. No. 3). The Wright and Curtiss companies had sent civilian pilot instructors to Fort Sam Houston to oversee delivery and assembly of their respective aircraft—Frank Coffyn for the Wrights and Eugene Ely for Curtiss. Once the planes were ready to fly, Coffyn and Ely began instructing the existing flyers (Beck, Walker, and Kelly needed to finish their instruction in the Curtiss plane, while Coffyn helped Foulois greatly improve his landings) as well as interested officers from the fort. According to Arnold, eighteen officers from Fort Sam Houston requested flying duty as a result of the aviators' presence there.

The presence of four flying officers necessitated some sort of organization. Consequently, Squier, who was now assigned to Fort Sam Houston as the divisional signal officer of the Maneuver Division, established a "Provisional Aero Company" on April 5—the first Army field command for airplanes. Beck, the senior officer by rank, was placed in command. But since Foulois had more flying time, Squier ordered him to write up the "Provisional Aeroplane Regulations for the Signal Corps." The regulations set brief rules for routine handling, operation, and maintenance of airplanes, and the responsibilities of the pilots and ground crews, but did not address how the Army might use airplanes.[11]

For perhaps the first time, Army flyers had a chance to freely compare the Wright and Curtiss products side by side; the Army even planned a flying competition between the two airplanes, but called it off for unknown reasons.[12] Judging from Foulois' memoirs, the rivalry between the Wright faction (Foulois) and the Curtiss faction (Beck, Walker, and

Kelly) remained friendly for the time the Provisional Aero Company operated at Fort Sam Houston. Chandler and Lahm recorded that Curtiss' Ely took the Wrights' Coffyn for a ride in the Curtiss plane—it was a one-man plane, but a passenger could be carried on a seat behind the pilot's seat—and Coffyn returned the favor.[13] Squier's creation of the Provisional Aero Company and his explicit designation of Beck as its commanding officer, as well as his presence on-site as Beck's superior officer, may also have kept any budding animosity in check. This was a very different dynamic than that of the Navy aviators in Annapolis, where Chambers was not on-site, nor did he establish any formal command structure.

While the simple fact of whether one flew a Wright or a Curtiss was apparently not enough to create bad blood between the two groups at this time, Foulois felt that the Curtiss training left much to be desired, based on what he saw in the flying abilities of Beck, Kelly, and Walker. He said, "They did many things [while flying] that I had learned not to do, and practiced their mistakes time and time again." On May 2, Walker's limited training apparently contributed to a bad landing that scared him so much he requested reassignment away from aviation.[14]

In addition to doubts about their flying skills, Foulois also doubted the others' knowledge of airplane construction and repair, echoing Ellyson's observation (while they trained together at North Island) that the three Army officers appeared to have no interest in learning such things. Foulois' doubts crystallized following events that culminated in a fatal crash.

The day after Walker's poor landing, Beck crashed No. 2 (the Curtiss), badly damaging the plane and losing consciousness. He awoke to find himself wandering around with the control wheel still in his hands but luckily suffered no permanent injury. Over the next few days, Foulois watched while Beck directed the repairs. Foulois observed that some repairs were made with inferior, knotty wood and another piece had an extra hole drilled in it, probably, according to Foulois, because the mechanics had measured incorrectly and simply redrilled the hole in the proper place rather than starting over with a new piece. Knotty wood is weaker than straight-grained wood and the extra hole would also result in a weaker structural member. Foulois called these problems to Beck's attention, but Beck "shrugged it off." Foulois was also disconcerted that Beck, the most experienced of the Curtiss flyers, did not see the need to test-fly the plane himself after the repairs were complete. Instead, on May 10, Kelly, whom Foulois felt "hadn't had much training" and was "the least experienced of the three [Curtiss] pilots," took No. 2 to the air. On his first landing attempt, Kelly bounced the plane hard off the ground. His second attempt was not much better, and Foulois remembered hearing "a sickening, wrenching sound on impact and I thought the plane would disintegrate right there." The plane bounced into the air again and either Kelly intentionally attempted a turn to avoid some tents, or else his controls failed and induced a turn. Either way, when the plane crashed, Kelly was ejected, landing on his head and fracturing his skull. He died a few hours later.[15]

Kelly's death seems to have cemented in Foulois a personal dislike of Beck. Foulois believed Beck was negligent both in ignoring the potential dangers of the substandard repairs and in not taking the plane up himself to test the repairs he had supervised. When Squier approached Foulois about serving on the board of investigation, Foulois refused and recommended that the board not call him to testify, "because if I do, I'll find Captain Beck negligent in the death of Kelly." He also told Squier, "in view of my three years' practical air experience as compared to Beck's five months, I had lost all confidence in his qualifications to be commanding officer" and suggested that either he (Foulois) or Beck should be relieved. Although Foulois later claimed he had neither served on the board nor was called as a witness, he is indeed listed as a board member. Whether Foulois was a member or not, the board's report assigned the probable cause of the accident to Kelly's poor judgment in selecting an "unsuitable" landing place. Following the crash, Gen. William H. Carter, commanding the Maneuver Division, ordered a halt to all flying at the fort. Toward the end of June, Beck supervised the movement of the planes and men back to College Park, while on July 11, Foulois was reassigned to the Division of Militia Affairs in the War Department in Washington.[16] Here we see the beginning of another competition between two technology advocates

(Beck and Foulois) with different visions for how the technology should be used. At this point, the differences were minor, but the two would soon grow further apart.

About the same time that Allen ordered Beck, Walker, and Kelly to San Antonio, the Army also took further actions to expand Army aviation. On March 28, 1911, it ordered Lt. Roy C. Kirtland to College Park, where he was to oversee construction of four hangars to prepare for renewed flying operations. In April, the Army selected two officers from a list of applications for aviation duty on file in the War Department—Henry H. "Hap" Arnold and Thomas DeWitt Milling, both second lieutenants—and sent them to the Wright School in Dayton, Ohio. As with other officers assigned to flight training, Kirtland, Arnold, and Milling had put in requests for aviation some time earlier.[17]

Arriving in Dayton at the end of April, Arnold and Milling trained alongside Navy Lt. John Rodgers, who had almost finished the training he began in March.[18] Though this was another opportunity for Army and Navy flyers to get to know one another, Arnold and Milling probably saw less of Rodgers (since he had started well before they did) than Beck, Walker, and Kelly saw of Ellyson in San Diego, where all were in the same "class." While Arnold and Milling had both Orville and Wilbur Wright as instructors for parts of the ground school, they had other Wright Company employees for their "in the air" training. The two soloed by mid-May, though they continued flying and practicing under the eyes of Wright Company instructors at Dayton until the Army's next Wright plane, S.C. No. 4 (another model B), was ready for delivery in early June. At that point, the two pilots, and the plane, traveled by train to College Park.[19]

RETURN TO COLLEGE PARK

Army aviation now began to coalesce at College Park. Kirtland had the field ready for use, and Arnold and Milling joined him there on June 15—the same day that Beck received orders to transfer the men and equipment from Fort Sam Houston. On June 20, Captain Chandler, who had spent the last year as a student at the service schools in Fort Leavenworth (during which time Capt. Arthur S. Cowan was chief of the Aeronautical Division), returned to Washington to resume the position of Aeronautical Division chief as well as commanding officer of the Signal Corps Aviation School at College Park. Airplanes, too, soon arrived at the reactivated airfield: first the Wright S.C. No. 3 from Texas, then the new S.C. No. 4 from Dayton.[20] With the funds granted in March, the Army also ordered a Burgess-Wright airplane, a Wright design built under license by the Burgess Company in Marblehead, Massachusetts. It first flew at College Park on July 8, crashing when the motor stalled out. Though neither Milling (flying as observer) nor the pilot, W. Starling Burgess, was injured, the plane was a complete loss. Its replacement did not arrive until August 10. Later in July, Beck arrived with the Army's Curtiss plane (S.C. No. 2) only partially rebuilt following Kelly's crash.[21]

With the arrival of the first Wright plane, Arnold began Chandler's flight instruction, while Milling instructed Kirtland. In addition to flight training at College Park, the four officers also had duty in the Signal Corps office in Washington, duties that they could combine with flight training because of College Park's proximity to Washington and the practice of making instructional flights in the early morning and late afternoon, when the air is calmer. On August 3, they were joined by 2nd Lt. Frank Kennedy, who began training in the Curtiss plane under Beck.[22]

While fulfilling their duties as instructors, Arnold, Milling, and Beck also began thinking seriously about how the airplane could be used in war. At Curtiss' request, Beck addressed the issue in a chapter, "The Aeroplane as Applied to the Army," for the *Curtiss Aviation Book* published in 1912. Beck reduced the issue to two questions that the Army applied to all new technologies: First, "whether or not it can be used to kill the other fellow and, second, . . . whether or not it can be used to prevent the other fellow from killing us." Regarding the airplane, he answered both questions in the affirmative. Airplanes could kill the enemy on the ground, he reasoned, by dropping bombs against strong points and large troop formations, while "some small machine-gun or rifle" would be needed to "brush [the enemy airplane] aside and allow our own information-gathering aeroplanes to perform their function unmolested." In other words, these planes would need to be armed for self-defense. These "information-gathering" planes were his answer to the question of how the airplane could be used "to prevent the other fellow from killing us." Airplanes, said Beck, could "find out where [the enemy] is, what he is doing, and how he proposes to accomplish his . . . object." In addition to the airplane's bomber and fighter roles (though the terms were not yet in use) and its usefulness in reconnaissance, Beck explained that the airplane would be useful for "speedy messenger service between detached bodies of troops" (the liaison role) and in delivering ammunition or food to besieged forces (the transport role).[23] Some of the examples he mentions in the chapter undoubtedly came from the flyers' experiments that had begun in autumn 1911 and continued into the following year.

Once training was complete, and the officers had passed their F.A.I. tests (except for Kennedy, who had started later), work in the air turned to investigating practical uses of the airplane for the Army. The flyers tested aerial photography and attempted to send messages to the ground with Morse code-like smoke signals. In October, Riley E. Scott, a former Coast Artillery Corps (CAC) officer, arrived with a combination bombsight and bomb-dropping apparatus of his own design. With Milling piloting, Scott made several bomb runs at four hundred feet, eventually striking within ten feet of a four-by-five-foot target. Sgt. Stephen J. Idzorek, one of the ground crew at College Park, also made a single bomb run because Scott wanted to see how someone else would do with his apparatus; Idzorek (chosen for his light weight) came within eleven feet of the target. Although Scott had planned to test the bombsight from three thousand feet, he postponed further testing so that he could leave for a bombing competition in France, where he would place first.[24]

Between experiments, the flyers continued to practice their skills, pushing their own limits as well as those of their planes. Almost every flight was a "first" of some sort—or at least they were reported as such by the newspaper reporters assigned to cover the activity at College Park. One example of pushing the limits was the increasingly longer "cross-country" flights, which meant a flight landing somewhere other than College Park, as opposed to just circling over the airfield. On July 7, Milling and Kirtland flew roughly eight miles from College Park to Washington Barracks (now Fort Lesley J. McNair); on August 7, Beck, in the Curtiss, and Arnold and Chandler in a Wright B, flew a slightly longer course from College Park to Fort Myer; and on August 21, Arnold and Chandler flew the Burgess-Wright (S.C. No. 5) forty-two miles to the DC National Guard encampment at Frederick, Maryland. Of course, these flights were not without risk: Milling and Kirtland, in a Wright B, were also to have flown to Frederick, but engine failure forced them down early. Nor was Arnold and Chandler's return flight without incident: they landed in a field along the way to get directions (dusk and haze hid their landmarks), but Arnold's aborted takeoff (to avoid trees and telephone lines around the field) damaged the plane's skids. Since the plane could not take off again, the two officers had to take the railway back to College Park.

When not making cross-country flights, Arnold sought to fly higher, setting several successive altitude records. The Army also gave the flyers permission to attend various air meets that fall and even to fly manufacturer's machines (i.e., not Army planes) in those meets. In this way, Milling, Arnold, and Beck separately attended several meets, stretching their abilities in air races and other competitions, and winning extra money for themselves as well. Chandler, meanwhile, had gone to Dayton to study airplane construction firsthand and to receive additional flight training from Orville Wright as a sort of "master class."[25]

As the year wound down, the flyers at College Park faced the same problem Foulois had experienced in 1909: the weather. Whether because of Foulois' reports of turbulent air currents at Fort Sam Houston or because General Carter's prohibition against flying still stood, CSO Allen chose not to send the aviators back to Texas. Instead, he tasked Chandler with finding a new winter location for the Aviation School. Chandler reported on several potential sites, including a farm to the east of Augusta, Georgia, that the Army soon leased. The men and equipment left College Park on November 28, and, once they had assembled the first plane in Augusta

(S.C. No. 5), the four Wright pilots made their first flights at the new field on December 7. The two Curtiss pilots, Beck and Kennedy, were delayed and did not arrive in Augusta until January.[26]

Though an uncharacteristically cold and wet winter limited flying time in Georgia, the aviators continued activities they had pursued at College Park as best they could, and training remained an important element. Kennedy, who was not yet fully trained when the group left Maryland, passed his F.A.I. exam in Georgia. Beck and Milling both elected to cross-train in the other aircraft's control system: Arnold instructed Beck in the Wright controls, while Beck coached Milling in the single-seat Curtiss. Additionally, as spring approached, new students began to report to the school for flight training, including 2nd Lt. Leighton Hazelhurst Jr. (Infantry), Lt. Col. Charles B. Winder (Ohio National Guard), and Lt. Harry Graham (Infantry). Graham arrived just before the school moved back to College Park at the beginning of April 1912, but the other two made numerous training flights in Georgia. In addition to training, the pilots continued experiments, most notably testing a new aircraft radio transmitter designed by Benjamin Foulois. Though Foulois was no longer assigned to flying duties, his interest in aviation continued unabated. All trained pilots continued to practice cross-country flying, while Arnold sought to push the planes to ever-greater altitudes.[27]

Their combined experience led the flyers to conclude that existing Army planes were good for little beyond flight instruction. For instance, the Wright B's lack of power, and thus weight-carrying capacity, had severely limited tests of Scott's bombsight and bomb-dropping device. With the added weight of Scott and his equipment, the plane could only get off the ground with the lightweight Milling as pilot. Similarly, Sergeant Idzorek had been selected as the "untrained" bombardier almost solely because of his light weight. The flyers realized that airplane performance would need to greatly improve if the airplane were to prove useful to the Army. Moreover, they realized that the Army would need different types of airplanes for different missions. In the fall of 1911, Arnold expressed to the Wrights the need for planes that could carry more weight and climb faster.

He also queried them about ways in which the powertrain of the Army's existing planes might be modified in order to get more performance while waiting for new, more powerful planes to be developed and delivered. By the spring of 1912, the chief signal officer had issued specifications for two new types of airplane: the "Scout" and the "Speed Scout."[28]

On February 8, 1912, Allen released the "Requirements for Weight Carrying Military Aeroplane" (the "Scout"), which called for a two-person plane with dual controls and fields of view such that piloting or observation were equally possible from either seat. In terms of performance, the plane had to climb to 2,000 feet in less than ten minutes while carrying 450 pounds and enough fuel for a four-hour flight with a top speed of at least 45 mph, although the requirements would be reduced if the plane could carry 600 pounds. The specifications also called for a two-hour endurance test of the engine in flight and at least a 6:1 glide ratio (meaning the plane travels forward 6 feet for every 1 foot of altitude lost). The glide ratio was to be tested by climbing to 1,000 feet before turning off the engine, then measuring the horizontal distance traveled to landing; the requirement was clearly intended to give pilots the best possible chance at finding somewhere to land safely when the engine inevitably cut out mid-flight. Further, the plane had to be able to take off and land from plowed fields, and though newer Wright designs had dispensed with the starting catapult, the Signal Corps rejected any revival, stating that "the starting and landing devices must be part of the machine itself, and it must be able to start without outside assistance." Finally, the document included wording about transportability and easy setup reminiscent of Specification No. 486 (the original airplane specification).[29]

"Specifications for a Light Scouting Machine" (the "Speed Scout") followed a month later, on March 9. While it set forth the same requirements as the "Scout" for self-contained "starting and landing devices," operation, endurance, transportability, and setup, the "Speed Scout" was intended to be a one-person plane "with the seat so arranged as to permit of the largest field of observation." It would have to have a three-hour endurance, though for a test where it would have to climb to 1,800 feet in three minutes, it would only need to carry the pilot and enough fuel for one hour. Finally, the airplane required a top speed of at least 65 mph, though at 5.28:1, the glide ratio was slightly less than that for the two-person Scout.[30]

The Signal Corps expected the two-person Scout to perform reconnaissance some distance ahead of ground forces. Although the specifications set weight-carrying requirements, the Army did not contemplate using the Scout offensively. Rather, the extra capacity was intended to accommodate cameras and/or radio gear. The flyers had already concluded that it was best to train pilots also to be observers, and the ability to switch off flight duties while in the air would mean that the two crewmembers could spell each other on long flights to relieve the "mental and physical strain connected with long-[duration] flight." The one-person Speed Scout, on the other hand, was expected to perform short-range reconnaissance for only the most immediate threats. Its quick-climbing ability would let it rapidly ascend for observation, and then quickly descend so that the pilot/observer could immediately report his observations. The immediacy would be necessary since the flyers had already discovered that the pilot of a one-man airplane had limited ability to observe the ground and no real way to record observations in notes or maps. This expectation of a quick "up and down" mission profile also explains why the climb rate was to be tested with less than a full tank of gas—the three-hour endurance was likely intended for ferrying flights.[31]

Although the Army did not approve the specifications for the two new types until February and March 1912, it *was* able to place orders for them in December 1911 and January 1912, because the flyers and the Signal Corps frequently communicated with the three manufacturers who had already supplied Army planes: Wright, Curtiss, and Burgess. Consequently, the manufacturers were aware of the broad requirements, even if the final specifications had not yet been approved. Arnold's request that the Wrights make a plane with more power, for instance, crossed in the mail with Orville Wright's letter to Arnold explaining plans for a new plane (eventually designated Model C) with a more powerful engine. Curtiss was already building two-seat planes for the Navy that could be flown from either seat and boasted a more powerful engine than the Curtiss Model D (S.C. No. 2) the Army was then using. Curtiss believed his new plane would also meet the Scout specifications, and the Army ordered a Curtiss "Scout" (a Model E) on December 1, 1911. In January, the Army also ordered five planes—three Scouts and two Speed Scouts—from the Wright Company and one Scout from the firm of Burgess and Curtis. This last plane would be the Army's first tractor aircraft. The Curtiss Scout was the first to be ordered and the first delivered, arriving in Augusta March 12. However, it did not complete acceptance testing until after the flying school had returned to College Park.[32]

Once again, the Aviation School entrained at the end of March to move back to College Park, arriving on April 2. More new students began arriving shortly thereafter: Lt. Harold Geiger (Coast Artillery Corps), Capt. Frederick B. Hennessy (Field Artillery), and 2nd Lt. Lewis C. Rockwell (Infantry) reported in April and May. Lt. Samuel H. McLeary (Coast Artillery Corps) reported in July. September saw a relative rush of students, all lieutenants: Lewis E. Goodier Jr., Lewis H. Brereton, and Loren H. Call (all from the Coast Artillery Corps), William Sherman (Corps of Engineers), and Joseph D. Park, and Eric L. Ellington (both of the Cavalry branch). The Army had assigned Sherman in relief of Second Lieutenant Kennedy, who had seriously injured his back in two crashes, which led the Army to reassign him away from aviation in October 1912. The new students, as part of a new Army training policy, took both a shop course and a flying course with an airplane manufacturer. The newcomers were distributed between the Wright Company at Dayton and the Curtiss factory at Hammondsport, though Call and Ellington were assigned to the Burgess and Curtis plant in Marblehead late in the year. In January 1913, the Burgess Company sent Call and Ellington to Palm Beach, Florida, to finish their training, along with Frank Coffyn (Burgess' flight instructor) and two planes.[33]

New airplanes designed to meet the Scout and Speed Scout specifications soon began arriving in College Park.[34] In May, the Wright Company delivered a Model C, the first of its scout designs. Tragically, on June 11, 1912, civilian test pilot Arthur L. "Al" Welsh and his passenger, Lieutenant

Hazelhurst (who had only joined the aviators a few months earlier), died when their plane crashed while attempting to meet the requirement to climb to 2,000 feet with 450 pounds of weight in less than ten minutes. The crash shocked military aviators because Hazelhurst was the first military fatality from an airplane crash since Kelly's death in 1911. It also followed closely on Wilbur Wright's death from typhoid fever on May 30, an event that had affected all of the aviators, most of whom knew him personally. Shocking as the crash may have been, it was chalked up as an unfortunate accident due to Welsh's unfamiliarity with the slow handling of such a heavily laden airplane, though the Model C would soon acquire a reputation as a dangerous design. Since the Army had not accepted delivery before the crash, the Wright Company delivered a replacement Model C later that summer, which passed its acceptance tests on October 3.[35]

The nature of flight training changed slightly that spring when the Army introduced its own flying test. Over the winter the flyers realized that just as the Army's current aircraft inventory comprised planes that were inappropriate for field work, so too was the F.A.I. test insufficient for examining the skills needed by an Army aviator. As a result, the Signal Corps introduced the "military aviator" qualification that summer. The Army continued to use the F.A.I. test as a preliminary qualification that showed the trainee could safely fly an airplane, but the military aviator designation was intended to show that the aviator could fly a plane in a *militarily useful* way. The new test required that an aviator reach an altitude of at least twenty-five hundred feet—a height deemed necessary to get above most ground fire in battle—and fly for at least five minutes in a wind of at least fifteen miles per hour to prove he could fly in less than perfect conditions. The aviator would also have to demonstrate skill and accuracy in flying and landing with a passenger, as well as in a "dead stick" landing with the engine off—both abilities that would be required of a working reconnaissance pilot. Finally, the aviator would have to make a "military reconnaissance flight," covering a distance of at least twenty miles at an average altitude of fifteen hundred feet, with instructions given beforehand on things to observe during the flight for report upon landing.[36]

While the new students went off to the airplane manufacturers for initial training, the senior flyers remained at College Park to prepare and take the tests for the new designation. Among those who passed the Army test that summer was Benjamin Foulois. Though still assigned to nonflying duty in the Division of Militia Affairs, Foulois capitalized on the proximity of College Park to his office in Washington to take up flying again in the summer of 1912 in order to test airplane radio generators that he had designed.[37] This put him in a position to earn the Army's new qualification.

The Army also made its first tests of firing a machine gun from a plane that summer. Two years earlier, Army Lt. Jacob Fickel had fired a rifle at ground targets from a plane flown by Glenn Curtiss at a 1910 air meet in Sheepshead Bay, Long Island, a stunt that proved that a gun could be fired accurately during flight without interfering with the plane. In the fall of 1911, the previous year's stunt had become a competition, albeit a small one with only two teams. This time, at the Nassau Boulevard air meet, on Long Island, Arnold was Fickel's pilot; the two had served together in the 29th Infantry Regiment. Despite the participation of Army officers, these flights were not conducted at the Army's request, nor did the Army take much interest in them. As such, the aerial rifle competitions remained little more than stunts. Only in the summer of 1912 did the Army take up such experiments, albeit still very informally. Army Col. Isaac Newton Lewis, an artilleryman who had become an ordnance expert, wanted to test-fire his new lightweight, air-cooled machine gun from a plane. Chandler agreed to Lewis' request and even served as gunner for the tests, with Milling as his pilot. Only two tests were flown, one at 250 feet and the second at 550 feet. Like Fickel's rifle demonstration, this was not an especially rigorous test of an armed airplane; it showed little more than that the Lewis machine gun could be fired from an airplane without endangering the plane or its occupants. As with the rifle competition, all targets were on the ground, and the airplanes stayed low.

The flyers wanted to explore the potential of an armed airplane and requested ten Lewis guns for further testing. However, although CSO Allen approved the request, the Army did not purchase the Lewis guns.

Instead, the Ordnance Department supplied the flying school with several light machine guns of the type the Army had just adopted as its standard: the Benet-Mercié (also known as "Benet-Mercier" or "Hotchkiss"), which carried the ammunition on the underside of a long metal tray. This tray stuck out one side of the gun, feeding through the breech to stick out of the other side when empty, rather like a typewriter carriage. However, the tray would interfere with the Wright control levers on each side of the seat, and so the flyers declared it could not be used from a plane. (The gun itself soon proved notoriously finicky.) Thus, the machine-gun experiments, while generating some interest within the Army, had no more immediate result on embryonic Army aerial doctrine than did Fickel's rifle feats. The ever-present newspaper reporters printed stories of the Lewis gun experiments along with comments from the aviators on the future possibility of air-to-air combat, but the War Department insisted that the only foreseeable use of aircraft was in reconnaissance.[38]

THE DEVELOPMENT OF AERIAL RECONNAISSANCE

Though Foulois, in flights with Wright instructors Parmelee and Coffyn, had demonstrated the possibilities of aerial reconnaissance in connection with ground troops in early 1911, the Army did not prepare more extensive tests until mid-1912. In August, it began maneuvers in Connecticut incorporating organized militia units from New York, New Jersey, Connecticut, Massachusetts, Maine, and Vermont. To take part, the Army sent experienced aviators from the flying school: Hennessy, Kirtland, Arnold, Graham, Geiger, and Milling. Foulois, though technically still on nonflying duty, arranged orders to participate as well. From his position in Militia Affairs, he had encouraged the Army to begin accepting aviation units in the National Guard. Even though New York's aviation battalion was still provisional and unofficial, it contributed a single aviator along with his plane. Beckwith Havens, though an established civilian aviator, had only recently joined the National Guard and held the military rank of private first class.[39]

The flyers were handicapped by the fact that by the time of the maneuvers, the Army had accepted only two of the new airplanes based on the

Scout/Speed Scout requirements. The second of these, a Burgess and Curtis Model H, broke new ground for the service. First, it was a seaplane. Although seaplanes had been developed at the Navy's request, the Army had decided that they would be useful in coastal and island defense, assisting the Coast Artillery Corps. (This was an exception to the general rule that landplanes were for the Army, and seaplanes for the Navy.) Second, it was the Army's first tractor airplane, though still built around Wright wings. Finally, it was the Army's first plane to feature a cockpit within an enclosed fuselage. Unfortunately, Arnold and Kirtland crashed this plane (S.C. No. 9) while trying to fly it from the Burgess factory in Salem, Massachusetts, to the maneuvers near Bridgeport, Connecticut; this left the Curtiss E (S.C. No. 6) as the only "high-powered" plane at the maneuvers. The other Army plane in Connecticut was the Burgess-Wright (S.C. No. 5) that Foulois had been using for radiotelegraph tests. Of course, the Army also had the use of Havens' Curtiss, but that was only a single-seat plane, probably a Model D like S.C. No. 2. While the Army's planes were two-seaters, they seldom carried a dedicated observer during these maneuvers. The engine in S.C. No. 5 was old and in need of an overhaul and produced insufficient power to carry two people. S.C. No. 6 had a new engine with plenty of power, but the plane often operated from fields too small to permit takeoff with a passenger. No. 5 had Foulois' radio installed, which could have sped delivery of aerial information, but Foulois had only marginal success sending messages and usually had to land and deliver his observations in person, just like the other planes' pilots.[40]

Despite these difficulties, the aviators proved the airplane's usefulness to ground troops. Initially, the flyers were assigned as a group to the umpires—the men who ruled on the outcome of the mock battles—but were soon reassigned to first the Red (attacking) and then the Blue (defending) forces. The aviators were instructed to conduct reconnaissance at no less than two thousand feet, and higher than that over enemy lines, thereby avoiding mock ground fire. Shortly after the maneuvers ended, Chief Allen wrote that "the results obtained [by the aviators] . . . proved to be of considerable value," despite using "inferior equipment":

With newer planes, he expected their performance to be even better.[41] Similarly, the officers conducting the maneuvers agreed that the airplanes had given a decided advantage to whichever side they were assigned. The following year, with more time to digest the lessons of Connecticut, Allen's successor as CSO, George Scriven, reported that, though small in number and despite restrictions imposed by the maneuver rules and their hardware problems, "troops were located very easily and accurately by all the aeroplanes at the Connecticut maneuvers." Scriven continued: "The results were good; the information obtained was accurate and covered the whole field of operations."[42]

Beckwith Havens' presence at these maneuvers was instructive by contrast. An expert flyer, yet without military training, his performance during the maneuvers bolstered the notion embodied in the military aviator qualification test that there was more to being an Army aviator than just flying the plane. Testifying before Congress in 1913, Samuel Reber, a Signal Corps officer assigned to the Connecticut maneuvers, pointed to Havens as proof that civilian flyers had neither the knowledge nor experience needed by Army aviators. "[Havens] was given the same problems that were given the military aviators and was asked to submit his report in the same way that they did. He went up and came down and came to me—I happened to be in charge at the time—and he said, 'I went up all right and I saw something, but I have not the faintest idea of what it was. I do not know the difference between a wagon and a tent when I get up at that height.'" In addition, Reber pointed out that few civilian aviators had experience with cross-country flights. Most were exhibition pilots who would take off, fly over, and land at the same airfield (where the paying crowd was), then have their plane shipped to the next event.[43] Arnold agreed with Reber, telling Congress, "As a rule these men fly around a field, but they do no military work. They can not read a map, and half of them if attempting cross-country flights will get lost. Finding the way through the air across country is one-half of the game." At the maneuvers in Bridgeport, he found the "civilian flyers," meaning Havens, "absolutely useless."[44] Havens' poor performance made him an excellent foil for the

Army's aviators to prove that they were something more than merely air-plane pilots.

In October, Arnold and Milling competed for the Mackay Trophy, named in honor of Clarence H. Mackay, a member of the Aero Club of America who had bestowed the cup on the War Department as a prize for an annual competition among Army aviators. Mackay left the specif-ics up to the Army, though he felt that the tasks should be made increas-ingly difficult each year as airplane performance improved. For this first competition, the Signal Office proposed a reconnaissance flight: the com-petitors would fly twenty miles cross-country and reconnoiter a triangular area ten miles on a side for a body of troops; on finding their objective, the aviators would then return to the starting field, land accurately, and report on the location and composition of the troops. Both the War Department and the Board of Governors of the Aero Club approved the plan, and on October 9, the two competitors took off from College Park. Arnold suc-cessfully located and reported on the troops but Milling fell ill soon after the start and withdrew from the competition. Despite Milling's with-drawal, the judges considered the competition valid and declared Arnold the winner.[45] The significance of this contest is not who won, but rather in the nature of the competition itself: another opportunity for aviators to demonstrate the airplane's usefulness to the Army. As well, the fact that the competition was one of reconnaissance and not simply speed, altitude, navigational accuracy, or even bombing, shows that the Army, and per-haps especially the Signal Corps, wanted to emphasize the airplane's prac-tical value in relation to a recognized and accepted mission.

At the end of October, the Army began exploring another mission for airplanes: artillery observation. While still in the early stages of developing methods of indirect fire (where the gunners themselves cannot see the tar-get, but must rely on a "forward observer"), the Field Artillery Board at Fort Riley, Kansas, requested an airplane for experiments in observing (correct-ing) shellfire from the air. The board undoubtedly recognized that a forward observer based in an airplane would have a better chance to find targets and could more accurately determine the distance of shells striking long or short of a target than could a ground-based observer.[46] So the question was: could it be done? In response to the Field Artillery Board's request, the Signal Corps sent Hennessy, Arnold, Milling, eight enlisted men, and two Wright C airplanes (S.C. Nos. 10 and 11) to Fort Riley. Hennessy had passed his F.A.I. test but had not yet qualified as a military aviator. Nevertheless, the Signal Corps selected him specifically because he was a field artillery-man and could presumably help coordinate the work. Unfortunately, he was forced to return to Washington, DC, almost immediately to care for his ailing wife and so had little influence on the experiments.

The Fort Riley experiments tested various methods of reporting information from the air to the ground and used nonflying officers of the Field Artillery as aerial observers. At first they tried dropping weighted messages to the battery, but since the planes needed to fly over the target for the best view, this meant time lost as the plane flew back to the battery position to drop its message and then returned to the target for the next shot. (The weighted messages tended to get caught in the airplane's structure until the aviators repurposed a section of stovepipe as a chute to guide the messages through the tangle of wires.) The group also experimented with blowing lampblack into the air (much like skywriting) to form Morse code dots and dashes, but the plane's turbulent wake too quickly dispersed the message. The most successful method attempted was radiotelegraphy. Using a new sending set, the flyers sent signals at distances up to fifteen miles. However, this radio only *sent* communications, it could not receive them; receivers at this time were too heavy, delicate, and prone to noise both electrical (from the plane's unshielded ignition system) and audible (from the motor and air flow) to function in airplanes. Messages from the ground required a system of cloth panels laid out in shapes, which limited the type of messages that the battery could send back to the plane and, as with the weighted cards, required the plane to fly back to the battery in order to see the panels. These experiments revealed both the promise and the problems of aerial observation for artillery fire.[47]

During these tests, Arnold lost control near the ground, narrowly avoiding a violent crash. The experience so unnerved him that he requested temporary relief from flying duty.[48] He returned to Washington, where Allen reassigned him as assistant to the officer in charge of aviation in the Signal Corps office. Although Arnold's respite from flying was originally intended to be temporary, he later requested permanent reassignment away from aviation duty due to his impending marriage. While there was not yet an official regulation prohibiting married men from flying, there was a general sense among the aviators that due to the dangers of flying, aviators should be bachelors. Arnold's (apparently permanent) departure from aviation, in addition to the deaths of Hazelhurst and civilian test pilot Al Welsh, capped a number of losses of trained Army aviators during 1912. A second fatal crash at College Park on September 28 killed Lieutenant Rockwell, who had passed the F.A.I. test, but crashed while practicing for his military aviator qualification test. Cpl. Frank Scott also died in the crash; he had been the passenger required by some of the military aviator qualification tests. This second crash led acting CSO Scriven to ban pilots from carrying passengers until they had qualified as military aviators; aviators would have to practice and take their tests with sandbags or other additional ballast in lieu of a passenger.[49] Other aviators' departures were less final, though this was not apparent at the time. Kennedy, who had requested relief from flying due to back injuries sustained in bad landings, would return to what would then be known as the Aviation Section in 1917, though in balloons, not airplanes. Beck, too, remained out of aviation for many years after the secretary of war ordered him back to infantry duty on May 1 under the "Manchu Law." He remained quite interested in aviation, as we shall see in a later chapter. He returned to flying status in 1920; however, he died soon after under scandalous circumstances.[50]

Foulois, though he had orders to fly at the Connecticut maneuvers, was still technically not on flying duty. After the maneuvers, while recovering in the hospital from a hernia, he requested a return to aviation work. Chandler and Reber backed his request, but Army Chief of Staff Leonard Wood and acting CSO Scriven both opposed it. Wood explained, "All these youngsters [assigned to aviation] must go back to troops for a time, and then can be detailed again" to aviation, emphasizing that Foulois "must put in his period with troops," suggesting that Wood was probably just following the "Manchu Law." Scriven's response is more enlightening: he recommended against Foulois' request because "it is the present policy of the War Department to establish . . . a reserve in all branches of the Army." Aviators returned to their parent service would form just such a reserve, he explained, "but with duties much wider in scope than is now possible at the College Park station, as, for instance, the establishment of aeronautical centers for the organized militia or at regular Army centers, such as in the Philippines or at Fort Leavenworth." This last sentence is particularly interesting because, although Scriven said the Signal Corps was too small to take on such a plan for expansion for at least another year, Allen had already ordered Frank Lahm to establish a station in the Philippines and would soon order Foulois to do the same at Fort Leavenworth.[51]

Lahm, of course, had been ordered to rejoin his parent unit, the 7th Cavalry Regiment, shortly after completing his flight training in 1909. As part of normal unit rotation, the Army sent the 7th Cavalry to the Philippines in early 1911, though Lahm remained behind, finishing up a course at the Cavalry School at Fort Riley that would keep him there until November. In August 1911, a few months after the 7th Cavalry's departure, Allen recommended establishing an air station in the Philippines. Lt. Col. William A. Glassford, chief signal officer of the Philippines Department, then requested that Allen dispatch airplanes and aviators to the islands to participate in maneuvers planned for 1912, to which Allen replied that he had no aviators to send. (Glassford was an early proponent of military aviation, having written an article exploring the potential of manned flight for a military journal in 1898.)[52] However, in November, with Lahm about to take ship for the Philippines to rejoin his unit, Allen saw a chance. He sent a telegram asking Lahm if he would be willing to fly airplanes again at his new station. Lahm agreed, and Allen arranged for a Wright B (S.C. No. 7) to be shipped directly from Dayton to Manila, where Lahm opened the Philippine Air School on March 12, 1912, at Fort William McKinley.[53]

On March 21, Lahm and his enlisted mechanics completed assembly of the float-equipped S.C. No. 7, and Lahm made the first flight the same day. At Fort McKinley, Lahm instructed two students: Lt. Moss L. Love and Cpl. Vernon Burge. Burge had been a member of the Balloon Detachment in 1907 and had been a mechanic at Fort Sam Houston with Foulois. Allen ordered him and another airplane mechanic from Fort Sam Houston to Fort McKinley in December 1911 as Lahm's ground crew along with five additional enlisted men from other Signal Corps units in Manila. Once in Manila, Burge asked for flight lessons. Since no other officers were interested or available for instruction, Lahm accepted Burge's request. Both Burge and Love passed their F.A.I. tests in June 1912, though news of Burge's accomplishment brought a reply from the CSO's office that Glassford, who had approved Burge's training, had violated (apparently unwritten) War Department policy against training enlisted men as pilots.[54] (Despite this "policy," the chief signal officer approved other applications from select enlisted men for flight training in the years before World War I.) By July, the Philippine rainy season had rendered the flying field unusable, and the plane was put in storage until the following year.[55]

Similarly, when Foulois left the hospital in November 1912, the Army sent him back to his infantry unit, the 7th Infantry Regiment, at Fort Leavenworth with orders to establish an aviation center in addition to his regular duties. Despite Scriven's concerns that there were not yet enough officers to man an aviation center, the Signal Corps shipped S.C. No. 10—the Wright C in which Arnold had his near-crash—from Fort Riley to Fort Leavenworth, accompanied by two enlisted men. When the plane arrived, Foulois had already laid out a flying field and the post quartermaster had supplied him with a hangar. Since Foulois had not yet flown a Model C, he wrote to Orville Wright for advice on flying it. In the meantime, he and the two enlisted men began assembling the plane. Despite his preparation and persistence, Foulois never made it into the air at Leavenworth. First, the plane needed repairs that took until early 1913 to complete; second, events conspired to keep him busy elsewhere.[56]

CONCLUSIONS

The Army, having moved slowly on the issue of aviation from 1908–1910, began moving more quickly to establish the possibilities in the Army airplane as well as greatly increase the numbers of both pilots and planes in the service in 1911 and 1912. More pilots and planes meant more opportunities to experiment with ways in which the airplane could be useful to the Army, even if, as happened with the machine-gun tests, the Army seemingly ignored the results. On the other hand, the success of the plane in the reconnaissance role and its promise in the correction of artillery drove greater demand for airplanes and influenced the service to begin "pushing" planes into field service, establishing aviation centers at Fort Leavenworth and Fort McKinley. Of course, the Army would need to train the new pilots needed for these centers, which would take time. Likewise, time spent training new pilots was time that senior pilots did not have for practical work or even experiments. Training also meant that the senior pilots were not getting their own flying time to gain experience. Both the Army and the Navy would have problems balancing these conflicting needs until they reached some minimum, as-yet unknown size.

4

NAVY/MARINES 1912–1913

Return to Annapolis and the Beginnings of Marine Corps Aviation

In the spring of 1912, even as the Army aviators were returning to College Park from their winter in Georgia, naval aviation ended its own wintering-over in San Diego and returned to Annapolis, where three more officers reported for flight training: Lt. Alfred Austell Cunningham, the first Marine Corps aviator, arrived on May 22 with Navy lieutenants Isaac Dortch and Laurence McNair reporting in June.[1]

Before reporting to Annapolis, Cunningham had been assigned to the Marines' Advance Base School in Philadelphia. In the event of another conflict like the Spanish-American War, where Dewey's Asiatic Squadron battled the Spanish in far-off Manila Bay, the steam-powered Navy would need some sort of forward location in a harbor where they could conduct minor repairs, refuel, and rearm the ships of the fleet. The Marine Corps' Advance Base Force was expected to make a landing to take such a harbor (in an unoccupied or undefended location, not the opposed assaults of World War II) and then defend it from attack. This was still a relatively new idea, with the Corps only having gotten primary authority for planning such a force in 1910 and the Advance Base School that was established in 1911. In 1912, officers at the Advance Base School were still considering what such a force should include and what kind of equipment it must have.[2] By then, Cunningham was already an aviation enthusiast. A member of the Aero Club of Philadelphia, he was also trying to teach himself to fly using an underpowered airplane, nicknamed "Noisy Nan," on loan from its builder.[3]

Cunningham envisioned the airplane as a substitute for cavalry (which the Marine Corps did not have) to reconnoiter nearby ground and scout enemy forces for the relatively small Advance Base organization; in modern parlance, this would be called a "force multiplier." On February 12, 1912, he suggested to his commander that a small aviation force be added to the Table of Organization and Equipment (TO&E) of the Advance Base Force. His recommendation was forwarded to Major General Commandant of the Marine Corps (MGC) William Biddle, who noted that the Marines had no appropriation for purchasing airplanes. Yet Biddle recognized that airplanes would greatly improve the defense of an Advance Base and recommended that Marine officers should be trained to fly "so that a sufficient number of expert aviators . . . may be available" to conduct reconnaissance for the Advance Base Force in anticipation of the Marine Corps eventually getting its own airplanes.[4]

Ultimately, the Navy's officer in charge of aviation, Captain Chambers, was consulted on the issue. In a memo to the Navy's aide for personnel, he agreed with Biddle's proposal and recommended that the Marines send as many officers "as can be spared from their other duties" (but not more than two at a time) to train at the Navy's aviation camp. Acting Secretary Winthrop quickly approved the flight training of Marines on Navy airplanes at Annapolis.[5] Consequently, Biddle ordered Cunningham and 1st Lt. Bernard Smith to aviation training. Cunningham reported on May 22 and Smith on September 18, 1912.[6] Thus a new tension was introduced to aviation, one that largely continues to this day: while the Marine aviators thought of themselves as doing Corps-specific tasks, naval aviation leadership (and perhaps the Navy aviators themselves) viewed the Marines as additional resources for Navy missions.[7]

In addition to new students, the flyers at Annapolis also had the promise of new aircraft. With the beginning of the new fiscal year in July, Chambers had money for three new planes.[8] Chambers, however, hoped to free up money for more, telling both the Navigation Bureau chief and Congress that "the three machines we have now are worn out and not up to date. We will need others to replace them for the purposes of instruction at least."[9] Glenn Curtiss tried to help Chambers, telling his congressman, Edwin Underhill, "I believe that the Navy are more in need of aeroplanes—one for each battleship and cruiser—than the Army, and I am certain that aeroplanes will become as useful to warships as the wireless is to-day," and that "it is no idle dream that future battles will be fought in the air." Congress, however, refused to lift the limit on naval aeronautical expenditures, and the flyers had to settle for just three new aircraft: Another Curtiss like the A-1 (designated A-3), Curtiss' flying boat (the C-1), and a flying boat from a Wright licensee, Burgess and Curtis (designated D-1). Furthermore, they had to wait several months before the planes were delivered.

TOWARD A MISSION FOR NAVAL AVIATION

Once resettled in Annapolis, the Navy flyers resumed the testing that had been disrupted by training flights and crashes while in San Diego. Ellyson, leaving the West Coast, detoured to Hammondsport, where he spent much of the summer flight testing and refining Curtiss' flying boat. In Annapolis, Rodgers, Herbster, and Towers continued work on the radio installations. With a new antenna design (stretched across the top wing rather than the earlier weighted, trailing line, which often broke), they successfully sent messages up to six miles away, though they continued to have problems with the generator and the engines.[10] Ensign Maddox, the radio specialist working with them on and off since 1911, also attempted to receive radio transmissions in the air, but between the electrical interference from the engine and the noise and vibration of flying (the latter playing havoc with the physically delicate receiver), his efforts failed.[11]

The aviators had more time for experiments since there were no students to teach for a few months. Though Alfred Cunningham reported in May, he was given little instruction at that time because the planes still needed to be uncrated, repaired, and reassembled. Instead, he was sent to the Burgess factory, in Marblehead, Massachusetts, to inspect (and learn about) the new D-1 flying boat being built there. He came back to Annapolis briefly in July and then returned to Marblehead for preliminary flight training from the company.[12] Cunningham's assignment as an inspector was part of Ellyson's plan to train flyers in the construction and maintenance of the planes they flew. Pre-war Navy and Marine officers assigned to aviation often spent time as inspectors at plants building government planes before beginning flight training. Many also received primary flight training from the manufacturers. Both practices would be standard through at least 1915.[13] Cunningham returned to Annapolis late in August, having soloed at Marblehead. After Dortch and McNair, the next officer assigned for training, Bernard Smith (the second Marine), did not report until September. Thus, for several months in 1912, the unit's planes could be devoted entirely to testing.

Rodgers left aviation late that summer, receiving orders to sea duty in August 1912. Though he had earlier written to Chambers that "I do not care to leave the aviation [sic] until it is well under way," the orders to sea came at his own request, apparently to keep his mother from worrying about his safety after his cousin, civilian aviator Calbraith Perry Rodgers, died in an airplane crash.[14] Another factor that may have influenced his departure, however, was that the new Navy secretary, Josephus Daniels, refused to promote anyone without the required time at sea. At the time, Chambers, as well as many other officers (including the aviators), saw aviation as just another assignment for a naval officer; after serving actively with aviation, officers would return to the fleet, where they would be a reserve of aviators to be called upon if needed.[15] No one yet understood that flying was a perishable skill that needed constant practice to maintain; they thought that trained officers could pick up flying again at any time.[16]

Thus, Rodgers' return to the fleet was seen as neither unusual nor a particular setback to naval aviation.

In June the General Board expressed "the desirability of testing and developing the tactics of the aeroplane" once aviators developed the necessary proficiency in flying. While it recognized that manufacturers would continue to improve airplane hardware and performance, particularly with respect to improving safety, the board felt that "the tactical development should proceed with the mechanical." Consequently, the board presented several issues that would need to be addressed in order to assess the airplane's usefulness, such as:

- whether airplanes could be carried by a battleship or cruiser, or whether they would need a dedicated auxiliary craft instead
- how far from the ship an airplane could scout
- the range of wireless communication from planes to ships and from plane to plane
- whether pilots could detect submarines underwater
- the effects of wind and sea conditions on airplane use
- whether an airplane could detect an enemy and successfully shadow it while reporting the enemy's movements back to the fleet[17]

The flyers were already working on the wireless issue. They were also pushing the limits of wind, sea, and weather conditions in which they could operate airplanes as they gained more experience (and, eventually, stronger planes with engines of greater power). As for the rest of the questions posed by the board, Chambers was already thinking about them.

Responding to the board only a few days later, Chambers highlighted the special problems involved in flight over the open ocean, especially in regard to scouting: "It will not be discreet to permit aeroplanes to lose sight of the base ship before the 'air compass' has been completed and tested, and before aeroplane motors have been improved with respect to reliability." (Chambers' "air compass" referred to an instrument that would not be affected by the airplane's vibration and relatively rapid movements about the roll, pitch, and yaw axes, and insulated from the passive magnetism of the engine block and the dynamic magnetism of its ignition system.) This restriction on the plane's radius of action hindered the naval aviators from discovering the limits to airborne wireless sets, but Chambers reassured the board that "we are not behind others in any respect," in their development. These restrictions also limited the plane's ability to find and shadow an enemy while reporting its movements, but Chambers felt sure that these limitations to aerial navigation over open water would soon be overcome.[18]

CATAPULTS AND OTHER TRIALS

Chambers had been thinking for some time about how to launch a plane from a ship. Floatplanes and flying boats could, of course, be put over the side and take off from the water, but that meant stopping the ship. (Chambers also hoped, eventually, to find a way to recover planes without having to stop the ship, but he considered the takeoff-while-moving more important.) Ely had demonstrated the use of platforms, but they interfered with the ship's guns, and Chambers dismissed them as too cumbersome for regular use. Ellyson's taut-wire slide provided yet another approach to the problem, but it was clearly unsuited to a pitching and rolling ship. Chambers therefore began developing his idea for a catapult, consulting with Ellyson, Richardson, and Lt. Cdr. G. L. Smith, an officer at the Washington Navy Yard. Together, they built a catapult out of some old parts available at the yard. Their design used a high-pressure air piston, working through cables and pulleys, to drive a cart down a rail. The airplane, resting on the cart, would achieve flying speed and fly off the cart. Using high-pressure air as the motive force took advantage of the fact that many Navy ships at the time already had air compressors to supply the high-pressure air needed to launch their torpedoes. This catapult would, therefore, require little additional equipment installed on the ship.[19]

When completed, the experimental catapult was sent to Annapolis and installed on a dock there. Chambers thought that the catapult needed hold-downs to keep the car on the rail and the plane on the car until achieving flying speed. All others involved, however, believed that the weight of the plane would keep everything in place until the plane lifted off. Since Ellyson was in the latter group, he volunteered to be the first pilot launched from the catapult. However, when the test was made on July 31, Chambers was proven correct: the plane (the A-1) reared up before reaching flying speed and crashed into the river. (Ellyson was unhurt.) The catapult was shipped back to the Washington Navy Yard where Richardson redesigned it, incorporating the necessary hold-down devices and modifying the air valve so that it opened gradually instead of all at once (smoothing out the acceleration). Richardson acquired a barge on which to mount the improved catapult, and Ellyson successfully launched from it twice in Washington: first in the newly accepted Curtiss A-3 on November 12, 1912, and then in the recently delivered Curtiss flying boat (the C-1) on December 17. Richardson made further refinements in the design and worked to build a completely new catapult, but two years would elapse before anyone could try it out.[20]

The Navy also began testing the proposition that airplanes could spot submerged submarines. Sweet had mentioned this in his report on the 1908 Wright trials, where he called the possibility "perhaps the most valuable use to which the flying machine can be put."[21] Ellyson had wanted to work on spotting submarines from the air as early as February 1911, when the former submariner told Chambers, "I hope to be able to work with Crittenden, who is in charge of the submarines here [in San Diego] and attempt to pick up the submarines when they are totally submerged."[22] But actual trials of spotting submarines from the air did not occur until late in 1912, when the commander of the Atlantic Submarine Flotilla, Chester Nimitz, proposed "a series of joint maneuvers" between subs and planes to thoroughly test the ability of planes to spot submarines.[23] Nimitz's subs pulled into Annapolis late in October, and the joint maneuvers went on through early December. Towers' report on the exercises detailed the many conditions under which they ran the tests: varying the plane's altitude, the sub's depth and speed, time of day, and weather conditions. Towers concluded that the tests were only of limited value, due to the muddiness of the water in the Chesapeake Bay where the tests were conducted. The problem was exacerbated by oyster tongers nearby, whose work stirred up more mud. He recommended repeating the experiments off Guantanamo Bay during the annual winter fleet exercises there.[24] This was just the first of many practical trials of aircraft with units of the fleet.

Meanwhile, the number of aviators began growing at a faster rate. Beginning with Bernard Smith in September 1912, a new officer reported for flight training each month through the end of the year. On October 25, the ninth officer assigned to naval aviation, Ens. Godfrey Chevalier, reported for duty. On the next day, Lt. (jg) Patrick N. L. Bellinger came to the aviation camp, but not yet for flight training. A commander of one of Nimitz's subs, Bellinger had asked for orders to aviation well before the subs arrived in Annapolis, and he did not understand why he had not heard anything further about his request. It turned out that a detailer had confused his name and ordered Ens. William Billingsley to the camp instead. Bellinger got things straightened out and officially reported to the flying camp as a student aviator on November 26. Though Billingsley had gotten orders earlier, he was finishing his previous assignment and did not report to camp until December 2. Interestingly, Billingsley may be the only officer in *any* U.S. service to be assigned to aviation without volunteering first (the Army's Humphreys is another possibility), though when the mistake was discovered, Billingsley chose to keep his aviation orders rather than take an alternative assignment.[25]

Early in 1913, the aviation camp packed off to join the Atlantic Fleet in its annual winter maneuvers at Guantanamo, Cuba. Since Ellyson had broken a leg, he remained in Washington, helping Chambers. Towers was put in charge and was instructed (probably by Chambers) to sell the aviation concept to the rest of the Navy. While in Guantanamo, the seven officers of the camp (including the two Marines) flew their five aircraft as much as possible (A-1, A-2, B-1, B-2 and, after late January, Curtiss' first flying boat, the C-1). Flying instruction was given to those officers not yet qualified as aviators. The aviators practiced further with submarines, continuing the work done the previous fall in Chesapeake Bay, and participated in a scouting exercise to find a "hostile" fleet approaching Guantanamo Bay.[26]

Their most important role, however, may have been that from Towers' instructions: "selling" aviation by giving rides to officers of the fleet.

With such flights, Navy officers gained a sense of what could be seen from the air, and many returned to the ground vowing to become aviators. Lt. Cdr. Henry Mustin was among the latter. For some time, he had been interested in the possibilities of using airplanes for extending naval gunfire and had aided Cunningham in his attempts to fly in Philadelphia. Mustin pursued the opportunities for instruction diligently, and soloed before the aviators left Cuba.[27] Though not officially assigned to aviation until late in 1913, he continued, in the interim, to be an active thinker on the topic of naval aviation (e.g., developing plans for putting planes on cruisers).[28] Other passengers in Cuba included two future commanders of naval aviation (Cdr. Noble E. Irwin and Lt. Cdr. Thomas Tingey Craven) and a future Marine Corps commandant (Lt. Col. John Lejeune).[29] The most senior Navy officer to fly at Guantanamo was probably Rear Adm. C. McR. Winslow, who commanded the Atlantic Fleet's First Division, but even more important may have been Congressmen Lemuel P. Padgett and E. R. Bathrick, chair and member, respectively, of the House Naval Affairs Committee, which controlled the Navy's budget.[30]

Naval aviation also made an impression on the commander of the Atlantic Fleet, Rear Adm. Charles Badger, even though he did not ride in an airplane. When word arrived in Cuba that Gen. Victoriano Huerta had overthrown Mexican President Francisco Madero, Badger fully expected that the fleet would be ordered to Veracruz to protect American interests and debated whether to take the airplanes with him in such an event. Badger summoned Towers to a conference, and Towers later reported that, after an hour and a half, he had "persuaded [Badger] that we were absolutely indispensable."[31] Anticipating that the planes would be flying over land, Towers requested that landing gear be sent to the camp, but Chambers soon quashed that idea: he did not want Navy planes being used far inshore for "Army work," because they were not designed for that.[32] In any case, the fleet was not ordered to Mexico, so the aviation camp returned to Annapolis in mid-March, where it spent the rest of 1913 performing more experiments and training new aviators.[33]

That spring, Ellyson became the second officer to leave naval aviation voluntarily, following a drift away from the "action" of the aviation camp to the politics and paperwork of the Navy Department in Washington. Ellyson was away from the aviation camp for much of 1912 and early 1913, testing the new Curtiss flying boat at Hammondsport, testing the first aircraft catapult, and then working as Chambers' assistant in Washington while his leg healed. In mid-March 1913, Ellyson, apparently frustrated with Chambers' leadership of naval aviation and, like Rodgers the year before, cognizant of the need for sea time, requested orders to sea duty and left aviation on April 29.[34]

One important nonflying assignment to aviation duty occurred that summer. Responding to a request from the president of the Massachusetts Institute of Technology, Secretary of the Navy Daniels ordered Assistant Naval Constructor Jerome Hunsaker back to MIT to develop a course in aerodynamics akin to the MIT naval architecture degree that Hunsaker had just completed. Hunsaker toured the aviation centers of Europe in company with Albert Zahm, a pioneering aeronautical engineer, until 1914. When he returned to MIT, he established the first doctoral program in aeronautical engineering in America, which he ran until 1916 when he returned to duty in Washington. Hunsaker was not a flyer, and played little direct role in developing aviation doctrine, but he was responsible for designing airplanes and airships to meet the specifications desired by those who did make policy.[35]

Naval aviation experienced its first fatal crash that summer. On June 20, the C-1 flying boat and the Wright B-2 took off from Annapolis for a flight across the Chesapeake Bay to St. Michaels, Maryland. The flight was intended to give Chevalier (in the C-1) and Billingsley (in the B-2) more experience in long-distance flying with passengers and to test some instruments. Herbster was to be Billingsley's passenger in the B-2, but he had missed the boat from the academy to the camp, so Towers was a last second substitution. On the return flight to Annapolis at about sixteen hundred feet, a gust caught the B-2 from behind, pitching the plane forward, and throwing both Towers and Billingsley from their seats, since they were not wearing seatbelts. Billingsley cleared the plane and fell to his death. Towers managed to hold onto the plane as it pitched down and crashed into the water. He was rescued but seriously injured. He remained on convalescent leave until September 30. In the meantime, the camp was under command of Lt. (jg) James Murray as "senior officer present." Murray had only reported to aviation in January 1913 and had been detailed to the Burgess factory to learn to fly until ordered back to take over the camp. The wrecked B-2 was written off, though parts would be used to build the B-3. The short-term effect was that naval aviation practically stopped until Towers' return.[36] It permanently removed a promising flyer (Billingsley) from the roster, temporarily removed the senior aviator (Towers), and reduced the number of available aircraft by one.[37]

The crash also led to a change in regulations and equipment. The Wright plane did have seatbelts, but the naval aviators were used to flying at lower altitudes and were more worried about the difficulty of undoing the belt in the event of a water crash (and being held under by the belt) than they were about falling out of the plane. The aviators had decided just days before that the belt should be worn on high-altitude flights such as this one, but habit seems to have been too strong: neither Towers nor Billingsley was wearing theirs. Curtiss planes had shoulder straps to keep flyers connected to the shoulder yokes, which also served to keep the pilots in the plane. They were considered easier to slip out of in the event of a crash than a seatbelt. Consequently, they were worn more often. After the accident, however, the Navy mandated the use of proper seatbelts on all future flights. The accident also resulted in the design of a quick-release buckle that could easily be undone regardless of the amount of tension in the belt.[38]

That summer saw another "departure" (of sorts) of a technology advocate who had had a significant impact on the development of naval aviation. On June 30, a special board forcibly retired a number of captains, including Chambers. In the service vernacular of the time, he was "plucked," ostensibly for lack of sea time as a captain—the fate feared by Ellyson and Rodgers if they remained with aviation too long. Chambers' willingness to place the good of the Navy over his own—giving up his battleship command after only six months to lend his technical expertise to the new aide for material—had come back to bite him. Chambers had wanted to go back to sea and was looking forward to commanding a battleship, but he delayed because the Navy had not assigned his relief as head of aviation. He feared what could happen to naval aviation without a senior officer in charge or, perhaps worse, one who did not understand the problems and issues peculiar to the job.[39] He tried to groom first Ellyson and then Mustin as his replacements, but Ellyson did not want the job and needed sea time. Mustin was interested in the job, but apparently others in the Navy administration did not favor him in the role.[40] Chambers was aware of the potential danger to his own career, but he felt he was protected by friends and by his important role in managing naval aviation. What he might not have realized was that many of his friends in Washington had suddenly left for sea tours, lest they themselves be plucked, and were thus no longer in positions to protect him. However, the real reason behind his plucking was likely the manipulation of a superior, Rear Adm. Bradley Fiske (aide for operations since January 1913), who felt that Chambers was retarding naval aviation.[41]

As noted earlier, though a "radical" in that he supported aviation, Chambers was very conservative in his development of naval aviation. Among other things, Chambers recognized the limitations of the machines. He knew that these early aircraft could carry little weight aside from a pilot and passenger. He firmly believed that improvements in propulsion and navigation (both of which contributed to improved safety, another of his goals) took precedence over tests of bombs and bombing equipment.[42] In any case, Chambers continued to believe that bombing was one of the less important uses of naval aviation. Navy planes, he thought, would be much more useful in scouting and reconnaissance, though he admitted that the airplane could also assist the fleet through locating and, using light bombs, destroying shore batteries, mines, and submarines.[43]

Fiske, on the other hand, had grand ideas for advancing naval aviation. He envisaged waves of Navy bombers repulsing a landing force and torpedo planes sinking transport ships. Fiske even patented the basic idea of a torpedo plane in 1912.[44] Although Chambers had logical reasons for his policies, his pragmatism seemed more like unfounded conservatism to his aviators and outright opposition to Fiske.[45] Ironically, though Fiske may have wanted Chambers gone to put his own man in place, no one else was available. Once Chambers had been officially retired, Rear Adm. Victor Blue, chief of BuNav and Chambers' boss, asked Chambers to remain on active duty as the head of naval aviation until a replacement could be detailed. In fact, Chambers would remain on active duty with naval aviation through October 31, 1919, but his significance as a technology advocate began to wane with his plucking and mostly disappeared when he was formally replaced as the head of naval aviation in January 1914.[46]

In August, naval aviation lost yet another flyer when Alfred Cunningham requested orders away from aviation. Unlike Rodgers and Ellyson, Cunningham's exit from naval aviation was not his own idea; Cunningham's fiancée forced him to choose between flying or marrying her.[47] Unlike Rodgers or Ellyson, however, Cunningham continued to be an advocate for aviation from his subsequent post, coordinating Marine aviation from the major general commandant's office. Cunningham also served as the Marine representative on the Chambers Board and, later, helped Richardson with experimental flights of a new flying boat at the Washington Navy Yard. Cunningham would eventually overcome his wife's objections, returning to active flight status in 1915 and remaining on aviation duty through 1922.[48]

Officially named the "Board on Aeronautics" but better known as the "Chambers Board" (temporary military boards such as this tended to be referred to by the name of their senior member or officially named chairman), this was the Navy's first effort to formalize just what naval aviation was expected to do for the Navy, and the resources it would need to fulfill those expectations. It convened in October 1913, on the orders of Assistant Secretary of the Navy Franklin D. Roosevelt. Consisting of Richardson,

Towers, Cunningham, one nonflying officer each from BuNav, BuEng, and BuOrd, and the recently plucked Chambers as the senior member, Roosevelt charged them with "drawing up a comprehensive plan for the organization of a Naval Aeronautic Service." The board was to consider airplanes, of course, but also dirigibles, shore stations, mobile equipment, schools, personnel, and estimated appropriations necessary for the proposed organization.[49] This exercise was Chambers' last big influence on naval aviation. Under his leadership, the board sought to define an "adequate Naval Aeronautic Service" in relation to the needs and characteristics of the fleet and of overall naval policy, while avoiding unnecessary expenditures.[50]

Completed on November 25, 1913, the board's report opened with a discussion of shore stations. Although "certain foreign powers" (probably Great Britain and France) were building multiple shore stations for aerial defense, the board declared that such construction was based on improper analogy with surface forces. Unlike ships or armies, airplanes could not effectively defend an area by establishing a line in the sky. Instead, said the board, the only way to neutralize enemy airpower is to seek out and destroy the enemy's aircraft bases, destroying aircraft on the ground as well as the resources and facilities necessary to keep the enemy's aircraft operating. (This notion of "offensive defense," or defending against the enemy's air forces by attacking them at the source, was an idea that would reappear during both World Wars.) Given this, the board declared that building multiple shore stations for coastal defense against aircraft would be useless and a waste of resources. Apparently, the board did not consider the idea that multiple shore stations might be useful to patrol against surface or subsurface coastal threats. The only use for shore stations, said the board, was for instruction and experimentation and, therefore, recommended only one. The board proposed the Pensacola Navy Yard (recently shuttered as an active Navy base) as the location for its one prescribed aeronautical center, though laboratory and design work would continue at the Washington Navy Yard.[51]

Regarding aircraft, the board said that at least one airplane should be assigned to *all* combat ships of the fleet, especially battleships. Auxiliary vessels should be designated to carry stores, supplies, spare parts, reserve planes, and hangar tents for expeditionary service. The board also conceded that some auxiliary vessels might be fitted out to carry planes but suggested that, if needed, those should be "*special ships*" (emphasis in original) whose design would "require special study by those who are to be responsible for carrying out the details." The board believed the Navy should develop a single kind of plane, using a standard control, to "meet all of the general requirements of both the Navy and the Marine Corps, without impairing the efficiency of either." To meet the needs of the Navy, it recommended the purchase of fifty planes for the fleet, and six for the Advance Base Force.[52] Curiously, the report failed to address explicitly the need for training planes.

The Chambers Board also considered that an "adequate" aeronautic service for the Navy might mean more than just airplanes when it declared: "Adequate sea power cannot be maintained by force of arms unless adequate superiority is maintained over the whole sphere of aerial development." The board was not convinced of the need for Navy dirigibles (either rigid or nonrigid) but, noting the importance given to them in European navies, recommended purchasing "at least one suitable dirigible at the earliest practicable date" to be used initially with the fleet and later transferred to the Advance Base Force. Though recommending the purchase of only one dirigible, "It is assumed that others will be required after experience [is gained] with the first." The board also recognized the need for a balloon capable of both free and captive flight for instruction of dirigible pilots and recommended that the Navy purchase just one: "Our experience with it will determine the value of simple balloons for fleet service." The balloon should be hydrogen-filled, though the board admitted that experimenting with hot-air balloons would be worthwhile. As for observer-carrying kites, the board recommended simply that "standard plans for building kites be furnished to all flagships," without any discussion of their recommended use.[53] These weak recommendations for dirigibles and balloons, and the even weaker recommendation regarding kites, probably indicate that the board did not think they would be important, but wanted to hedge its bets.

Roosevelt created the Board on Aeronautics to recommend what was needed to establish an "adequate air service." "Air service," however, was merely a descriptive term. What Roosevelt was really asking was *What planes, equipment, and manpower are needed in the Navy?* without necessarily giving any thought to establishing a new organization. Nevertheless, the board provided Chambers with another opportunity to call for the formal creation of an Air Department (led by a director of Naval Aviation) in the Division of Operations. Such a department would overcome the instability and bureaucratic inefficiency that Chambers saw in the current organization. However, the report emphasized that an entirely separate (i.e., independent) department or bureau was neither intended nor necessary; the present bureau system coordinated by the Navy secretary was adequate, though in need of refinement. The proposed Air Department would merely be an office under the aide for operations, concentrating on aviation issues and helping to resolve the existing problems of coordinating aeronautical work among the different bureaus. Each of the bureaus responsible for some piece of aviation work would have an officer assigned to this new department as a liaison, representing the bureau in Air Department discussions and the Air Department in bureau discussions. The proposed department would collect the strands of responsibility under the director of Naval Aviation, whose sole responsibility would be naval aviation. This would be a great improvement over the existing situation where lack of any such clear authority meant that recommendations for aviation might come directly to the secretary (bypassing Chambers) from any of the bureaus having responsibility for some part of naval aviation. The proposed director, however, would still have only advisory authority, making recommendations to the aide for operations, who would, in turn, advise the secretary. Still, the creation of such a post would codify and strengthen the weak position Chambers currently attempted to hold, and would, Chambers hoped, put an end to the inter-bureau rivalries that made it difficult for him to get anything accomplished.[54]

The Chambers Board recommended further that the Navy assign a ship to Pensacola to help develop equipment and techniques for handling and

operating airplanes with ships, particularly the development of the catapult, in order to speed the use of airplanes with the fleet. After aircraft had
become a regular part of the fleet, the aeronautic ship could continue to
assist in the service tests of aeronautical equipment at sea (basic research
and "bench tests" would continue to be conducted at the Washington
Navy Yard) and also provide advanced instruction to pilots fresh out of
the training school based ashore.[55]

Finally, the board made numerous recommendations concerning the
officer personnel both as students at the school and in the fleet (whether as
aviators or on other duty). Perhaps the most important recommendation
made about personnel was that "The duty of officers and men on this service should not operate to prejudice their advancement, and their service
in aeronautical work, whether on shore or at sea, should be regarded as sea
service as far as it is requisite for promotion." Such a provision would have
allowed Ellyson and Rodgers to remain with aviation and would, perhaps,
have prevented Chambers' plucking.[56] But while many other recommendations in the Chambers Board report would soon come to fruition, this
one would not be enacted for many years. As in the Army, the notion that
Navy officers might be damaging their chances for promotion through
their work in aviation led to various proposals for special status or consideration for aviators, which senior officers tended to interpret as greedy
junior officers trying to get a jump on promotions.

The work of the Chambers Board was complete with the final report.
After individual review of the final document, the board members signed
the report, which was then submitted to the Navy Department.[57] Secretary
Daniels got a copy and submitted it to Congress in 1914 as a supporting
document in his testimony before the House Naval Affairs Committee.[58]
Presumably the General Board got a copy, and Roosevelt would probably at least have read the report, even if he did not get his own copy. Soon
after the report came out, the opinionated and strong-willed Bradley Fiske
would seize control of naval aviation in January 1914. Certainly Fiske saw
a copy of the report eventually, though whether and to what extent it influenced his actions is unclear.

CONCLUSIONS

Over the course of 1912 and 1913, naval aviation finally made some progress toward establishing just what it would be doing for the Navy. Experiments were conducted with radio in airplanes and spotting submarines from the air. Airplanes also began working with the fleet (albeit only experimentally) during the 1913 annual fleet maneuvers. Finally, the Chambers Board delivered its recommendations for an "adequate air service" for the Navy. These included not merely how many airplanes and personnel were needed and for what purpose, but also issues of organization, both those internal to aviation as well as how the aeronautical organization should fit into the Navy as a whole.

Marine Corps aviation also got its start in 1912, with an advantage of sorts over both Navy and Army aviation in that it started with a clearer mission statement than the other two. Cunningham's proposal clearly stated that a small aviation unit should be attached to the Advance Base Force for reconnaissance and scouting purposes. It was a mission statement for Marine aviation that did not waver until the eve of U.S. entry into World War I in 1917. Likewise, Marine aviation had an advantage of support from its senior leadership that Navy aviation lacked. The Marines' officer corps was small and tight-knit, and this likely contributed to the first Marine aviators receiving more support from the major general commandant than did either the Navy or Army aviators from their respective service heads (though it was similar to what the Army aviators got from the chief of signal). The relatively speedy action of the Marine Corps in moving from proposal to action (compared to the Army and Navy) may have come from the major general commandant having a sense of who Cunningham was as an officer (whether he was a solid thinker or prone to crackpot ideas), but was also likely a function of the Corps' culture of flexibility: a certain practicality in considering unconventional solutions to accomplish whatever task needed to be done.

The unique relationship between Navy and Marine aviation under the umbrella term "naval aviation" led to its own tensions, though these did not come to a head until U.S. entry into World War I. In particular, even though Cunningham had his own clearly established ideas for the "proper" employment of Marine aviators, Navy leadership tended to view the Marine aviators merely as additional trained bodies for the Navy's purposes. The special relationship also meant that the Marines were entirely reliant on the Navy for airplanes and related material, and so had to suffer from the same benefits and flaws of the bureau system that affected the Navy aviators. Thus, while the Marine aviators may have had the support of their commandant as a strong patron, they still suffered from the Navy's somewhat absentminded neglect of its own aviation—something Washington Chambers hoped the Chambers Board's recommendations might fix.

5

INTERSERVICE ORGANIZATION I
Finding Common Interests

Most single-service histories of aviation ignore what was going on in the other services unless it is impossible to explain events or decisions within one service without reference to the others. This leads to a perception that aviation in the War Department and the Navy Department developed without reference or connection to each other. This was far from the case. Good reasons for ignoring such links do exist: with a few exceptions, interservice connections do not seem to have played a major role in shaping the development of aviation in either the Army or the Navy. Further, single-service developments can usually be explained without tracing interservice threads that add another layer of complexity to an already complex story. It is also necessary to bound the narrative somewhere, and a single service makes a convenient boundary. These reasons have contributed to the single-service chapters offered thus far.

Interservice connections were present, however, and the services did not (and do not) exist in a vacuum but are intimately associated with the wider world. Links between services exerted both positive and negative influence on events, though that influence was often subtle or obscured. This chapter looks at the casual, informal connections that grew. (Chapter 9 will address the growth of more formal structures in which interservice connections could be regularized.) Many of the connections discussed in this chapter persisted throughout later eras, indirectly influencing later developments. These connections may seem minor within the scope of this book. While their greater importance emerges much later in history (particularly the evolution of the friendship between Arnold and Towers), it is important to document these beginnings here.

In order to understand the significance of interservice associations, one must understand events in both services and how the points of contact affected each. One possibility is to thoroughly integrate the narratives of the separate services as much as possible.[1] Another approach is either to foreshadow events in the other service while writing about the first or to interrupt the narrative of the second service by flashing back to a previous point. Instead, I have chosen to follow the "warp" threads in the single-service chapters, and, in these two interservice chapters, to go back to the beginning of the narrative "cloth" to point out how the "weft" of interservice relations connects the services.

In the pre-war period of aviation development (up to April 1917), interservice relations, like the air services themselves, were nascent and evolutionary. The pre-war years offer no dominant interaction between the services that can stand as a representative case study. Indeed, prior to the advent of the airplane, the Army and Navy had few reasons either to cooperate or to oppose each other directly.[2] As historian Samuel Huntington noted, the War Department and the Navy Department received appropriations from different committees in the House and Senate at this time, so political and budgetary conflicts were more often between military and civilian groups rather than between Army and Navy.[3] Consequently, when the airplane offered possibilities for interservice connections, few examples of such coordination existed to guide officers in either service. The lack of examples probably also explains why most interservice interaction in the pre-war era was informal and is thus difficult to find evidence for. Broadly speaking, the examples given below have a unifying theme in that they reflect the intermittent and unfocused growth of military aviation. Just as the air services needed to learn how to interact with their parent services (and vice-versa), so too did the air services need to learn how to interact with their counterparts in the other military branches.

RIVALRIES—FRIENDLY AND NOT SO FRIENDLY

In many ways, the story of interservice connections begins with individuals. Many early aviators met their counterparts in other services while training with the aircraft manufacturers. While Army officers Frank Lahm, Frederick Humphreys, and Benjamin Foulois had trained before the Navy got into aviation, the Army's Paul Beck, G. E. M. Kelly, and John Walker learned to fly from Curtiss alongside Navy man Theodore Ellyson. Beck was also in Hammondsport while Ellyson was training John Towers there. Army students Thomas Milling and H. H. Arnold were at Dayton at the same time as the Navy's John Rodgers, though Rodgers was well ahead of them in his own training.

Furthermore, the Army and Navy summer flying camps were located relatively close to each other, at College Park and Annapolis, Maryland, respectively. Beck attempted at least one flight to Annapolis (presumably to visit the Navy's aeronautical camp there), and other flights were made in both directions.[4] John Rodgers, for instance, seems to have made many flights at College Park in August and September 1911 because the Navy's landplane field was not yet ready and the Navy's Wright did not yet have floats. Even after the Annapolis field opened, Rodgers continued to make flights to and from College Park.[5] The following summer, the naval aviators invited their Army counterparts to fly to Annapolis to watch the annual Army-Navy baseball game, but only the Army commander, Charles Chandler, was free to make the flight on June 1, 1912. When Chandler experienced problems with his engine before the return flight, Ellyson directed the mechanics to replace the ignition wires on the Army plane with a set of Navy spares.[6] "Hap" Arnold and John Towers met for the first time at the 1911 Chicago air meet and had occasional contact while the Army flyers were at College Park and the Navy flyers were in Annapolis. Their friendship deepened in 1913 when Arnold was assigned to desk duty in Washington. One of his responsibilities was aero-engine inspection, which frequently brought him to the

Navy's Engineering Experiment Station in Annapolis (next to the naval aviators' camp) to observe aviation engine tests.[7] Undoubtedly, he took the opportunity to wander over to where the naval aviators were operating; in a letter to Chambers, Cunningham mentions Arnold's inspection of the B-1.[8] At least one interservice pair was friends first, before getting into aviation: Marc Mitscher and John Edgerly became friends while students at the Naval Academy. Edgerly left the Navy to join Army aviation (though he did not earn his license until World War I, and so has not been mentioned elsewhere in this book), while Mitscher remained in the Navy and later went into naval aviation. These friendships were such that historian George Van Deurs says both the Army and Navy aviators "swapped parts, parties, information, and other help in greater quantities than the surviving records show."[9]

Not all interservice contact was friendly, of course; some rivalries emerged. Ellyson, for instance, did not think much of the attitudes toward flying exhibited by the Army officers he was training with in 1911. He accused them of being reluctant to do the hard work of learning the mechanical aspects of flying: airplane construction and repair. Indeed, the Army pilots ended up having to rely on Eugene Ely to set up the Army's new Curtiss Model D when it arrived in San Antonio. Both Ellyson and Chambers expressed hopes that the Army pilots would not come back to Hammondsport when Curtiss returned there in the summer of 1911, with Ellyson hoping "that we do get ahead of the Army both [in] regard to getting a machine and the work done."[10] Yet later that summer, Ellyson expressed dismay that "the Wright machines are the only ones that are given a fair chance in the Army" and wanted to help Beck, in charge of the Army's Curtiss machines, to change that. Ellyson asked Chambers to try to get CSO James Allen to Hammondsport where "Beck and myself will show you the real possibilities" of the Navy's two-person Curtiss with dual controls.[11]

Ellyson, in particular, seemed touchy about Navy aviation being compared to its Army counterpart. In 1911, he worried that the Navy Department might think he was taking too long to qualify as an aviator, especially compared to Army flyers. Having been with Curtiss for close to three months (and intending to stay with him longer), he wrote to

Chambers, "The Army [presumably the three officers also in San Diego with Curtiss] are continually referring to the fact that the Wrights only took three weeks to instruct Lieutenant Fulois [sic], but he was the only one under instruction."[12] The Army trainees seemed unaware of just how much Foulois had to learn after his three weeks' instruction in College Park in 1909. Ellyson was still sensitive to the issue a year later when he wrote to Chambers that he was proud of what the Navy had accomplished, "considering the difficulties that we have been up against." Ellyson admitted that the Army record looked "much better," but pointed out that the Army had seven planes at that point to "our two" (it was actually three at that point) and that landplanes were easier to take care of than hydros. Furthermore, he noted that the Navy was "constantly shifting base, and that instead of having permanent hangars we worked in tents." The Navy's enlisted men also had to take care of the tents, camp, and the motor boats, whereas the Army had "one entire company of the Signal Corps for the cooking detail, police work, and sentry and yeoman duty" at College Park, allowing the Army men (aviators and mechanics alike) to concentrate solely on keeping their machines in the air.[13] Navy Capt. Mark Bristol, who would succeed Chambers as director of naval aviation at the start of 1914, was likewise unimpressed with the work of the Army aviators: "The officers who fly have little or nothing to do with their machines. They are more like chauffers [sic] than anything else."[14]

Interservice connections were not limited to the aviators, but existed higher up the chain of command as well. Asked in August 1913 to comment on cooperation between the Army and Navy air services, Chambers wrote back to the Secretary of the Navy:

The Army is having troubles of its own, peculiar to the Army organization, very much the same as we would have if the air service of the Navy were all under one Bureau. It has learned much from contact with the Navy air service and the Navy has profited exceedingly from intercourse with the Army organization. Information is freely exchanged. The natural spirit of rivalry has been avoided by the Navy for obvious

reasons and with good results. I do not care to enlarge upon the defi-
cencies [*sic*] of either service, but there has been no effort at cooperation for certain good reasons.

Those reasons were the very different natures of land and seaplanes.
Chambers believed that the kinds of planes required by the services, as well
as the kinds of missions flown, were so different that there was no point of
commonality on which Army and Navy could cooperate. But Chambers
may also have been thinking in purely operational terms when he wrote,
"There has been no effort at cooperation," since in the same letter, he noted
that the Langley Advisory Committee (described in chapter 9) "provides
excellent cooperation between Army and Navy in development."[15]

Further belying Chambers' claim of "no cooperation" between the services, there was plenty of informal cooperation going on. Chambers, for
instance, had received copies of letters sent by Army aviator Milling to
his superior, Samuel Reber, reporting on foreign aviation schools during
Milling's 1913 inspection tour.[16] At about the same time (August–November
1913), the Navy Bureau of Engineering was arranging to purchase, through
the Army Signal Corps, an aeronautical radio set being tested by the Army
aviators. But Reber warned Chambers that "the whole thing was still in the
experimental stage, and unsatisfactory," and advised him against spending the money.[17] In September, Chambers reported that Reber "would be
very glad to see the Navy do something with dirigibles," perhaps because
the Army chief of staff had just rejected Reber's recommendation that the
Army purchase two airships.[18]

This interservice aid extended to the highest levels. In October 1914,
the assistant secretary of war, Henry Breckinridge, wrote to Secretary of the
Navy Josephus Daniels to inform the Navy of a competition the Army was
holding to determine which airplanes to buy—in modern terms, a "fly-off."
He invited Daniels to send someone to observe the contest, "as I think the
information that he could obtain will be of value to your aviation service."
Daniels warmly replied, "I have felt for some time that it would be a great
advantage to both the Army and Navy to have close co-operation between

the two Aviation Services." Not only did Daniels accept the Army's offer, but he reciprocated by inviting the Army to send officers to Pensacola "to observe tests or gain any other information. When any important tests or experiments take place I will take occasion to especially notify you."[19] Responding to a query in early 1915, Daniels informed Albert B. Lambert, a wealthy businessman and aviation enthusiast who wished to know more about aviation in the Navy, that "in an unofficial way the Aeronautic Service of the Army . . . and the Aeronautic Service of the Navy keep in close touch."[20] Indeed, Bristol and Reber, while each was in charge of their own service's aviation, were in close contact with each other, sharing information received from their respective attachés observing the "Great War."[21]

In light of all this knowledge, information, and even equipment sharing, when Chambers asserted that there was "no cooperation" between the services, he likely meant that the air services of the Army and Navy were not operating together and did not plan to. In fact, any such combined operations would have been difficult to organize because the land/sea boundary that separated the Army from the Navy extended to their aircraft. Since unexpected landings were common in the pre–World War I era, the nature of the terrain flown over dictated the landing gear used: generally speaking, landplanes were the preserve of the Army, and seaplanes were reserved for the Navy. In 1913, Chambers made clear that, in his mind, the term "aeroplane" was not (and should not be) an umbrella term for any flying machine. Responding to a query about the number of airplanes in the Navy, he wrote: "There are no 'aeroplanes' [in the Navy,] although the wheel attachment for hydroaeroplanes permits of their descending on land and of rising from smooth ground." [22] Likewise, Daniels asserted that "the Navy deals in aeroplanes for sea service, which requires either hydroaeroplanes or boat-aeroplanes."[23] Though Daniels' correspondence muddied the terminology, he confirmed that the Navy used only seaplanes. (Bristol officially retired "hydroaeroplane" as a term in 1916, telling the secretary of the Naval War College that all heavier-than-air craft would thenceforth be known as "airplanes.")[24]

Chambers clearly wanted to emphasize to anyone concerned that Army and Navy aviation were quite different, possibly to prevent any idea that they should be merged. In the same letter in which he explained that the Navy had no landplanes, he also stated: "The Army does not require the same class of machines as the Navy. They require several classes, but it is desirable for the Navy to adhere to one class that all can fly." In other words, the Army might need different designs for different tasks, but Chambers was adamant that the Navy only needed a single design, and it would be a seaplane. Though Chambers acknowledged that the Marines might need landplanes, he also viewed Marine aviation as a necessary evil, one that would always threaten to move Navy aviation away from its "proper role," stating that "In time of war there will be no difficulty in the way of each service doing its proper part, but there will naturally be some desire on the part of the Marine Corps aviators to distinguish themselves as flyers for both Army and Navy."[25] In 1917, though no longer in charge of aviation, Chambers was still concerned that the Navy and Army remain separate: "The rivalry between Navy Aviators and Marine Corps Aviators is bound to be a disturbing factor and he who has to bear the brunt of responsibility for seeing that the [combined naval] Aeronautic Service is organized to do Navy work and not Army work will always have a perplexing problem to face."[26] Still, he recognized that the Navy would occasionally need to fly over the land, particularly in advanced base work, though he preferred amphibious aircraft rather than dedicated landplanes.

Yet the separation of seaplanes for the Navy and landplanes for the Army was not absolute; one issue that drove Chambers to push for seaplanes of whatever type—safety in overwater flights—drove the Army to purchase a few seaplanes in the pre-war era. As early as 1912, the Army had decided that seaplanes could be useful for coastal and island defense. Also, Army pilots often flew over rivers, lakes, and other watery terrain that, in the era before airfields in every small town, might offer better opportunities for emergency landing than the surrounding landscape. At some point in 1912, the Army had equipped its single-seat Curtiss D (S.C. No. 2) with a pontoon. Since there was no significant body of water at College Park, the Army sent the seaplane to the Army War College, which was then on the riverfront in Washington. From there, the plane could operate in either the Potomac River or Anacostia River, according to conditions. Once Burgess finished repairing S.C. No. 9 (after its August 1912 crash on the way to the Connecticut maneuvers), the Army stationed it at the War College as well. The Army Corps of Engineers built a floating hangar in the Anacostia for the two seaplanes.[27] The nearby Washington Navy Yard assisted Army operations of these seaplanes by supplying a motor launch and crew for general utility and as an emergency "crash boat."[28] In October 1913, Chambers predicted, "The Army will be clamoring for [amphibious aircraft] sooner or later."[29]

In December 1913, naval aviators Victor Herbster and Melvin Stolz sent a report to Reber, the Army's chief of aviation, on their inspection of a float-equipped Burgess and Curtis H-40 airplane, apparently as part of the Army's acceptance of the machine. The Army had waived flight testing of three Burgess Hs (S.C. Nos. 24–26) if the company tested the planes before delivery, but it is not clear whether Burgess (as part of the testing) or the Army (as a condition of the waiver) asked the Navy officers to file this report. Since Herbster and Stolz were already at the Marblehead, Massachusetts, factory (Stolz was putting in his time with a manufacturer prior to flying lessons while Herbster may have been inspecting new construction), it was certainly convenient for either party to have them inspect and report on this Army plane. Interestingly, while both signed the report, only Herbster flew in the plane and only as a passenger. Why the Army waived flight testing is unclear; perhaps the Army considered that it still had no seaplane pilots qualified to run the tests, or it could be that the Army had no pilots to spare for these tests. A third possibility is that, with all the Army aviators on the West Coast, the Army thought to save the costs of a cross-country trip for such a short period of time.[30] Whatever the reason, Herbster and Stolz's report seems to be an isolated incident of interservice cooperation on this level prior to U.S. entry into World War I; it was the only instance found of such cross-service acceptance testing.

Soon after Herbster and Stolz completed their report on the Army's plane, Army aviators on the West Coast conducted experiments with the Navy. In January 1914, Army aviators from San Diego participated in experiments with the Coast Artillery Corps and the Navy to see whether underwater mines could be detected from the air. On January 6, Lt. Joseph Carberry flew over the CAC minefield with Lt. Townsend Dodd (detailed to aviation from the CAC) as observer. Though they flew at an altitude between eighteen hundred and twenty-four hundred feet, Dodd was able to make a map showing three of the mines guarding San Diego Bay and many of the wires for controlled detonation. Around January 20, one of the Army aviators took up Maj. William C. Davis, who commanded the coast defenses at San Diego. Davis noted that he was able to see kelp on the bottom of the bay and that newly planted mines showed up clearly from the air, although marine growth on older mines thoroughly camouflaged them against aerial spotting.[31] The experiment indicates that not all information was shared between services, since the naval aviators had carried out mine-spotting tests while with the fleet in Guantanamo the previous year.[32]

In the summer of 1915, the Army requested two hydroaeroplanes (with pilots and crews) from the Navy to assist the Army's Coast Artillery Corps in some tests at Fort Monroe, Virginia.[33] The Navy ordered Patrick Bellinger to the fort early in August, along with a floatplane (the AH-10, a tailless Burgess-Dunne) and a small detachment of men.[34] Flying over the approaches to Hampton Roads, Bellinger spotted the fire of the fort's mortar, signaling his "spots" with different colored flares from a Very pistol (a signal gun named for its inventor, Navy Lt. Edward W. Very).[35] The record is not clear as to why the Army asked the Navy to assist, though it was likely a lack of seaplanes in the Army. In the summer of 1915, the Army had only one seaplane in its inventory: a Curtiss Model F flying boat at San Diego. The Army needed that plane in San Diego to instruct new pilots in overwater flight. Consequently, the Army could spare neither the plane nor qualified Army seaplane pilots for the exercises. The test is interesting not only because the Navy spotted Army fire, but also because this was the first time that the Navy actually attempted spotting from the air, despite much discussion of the possibility and despite the personal interests of some of the naval aviators (particularly Mustin and Towers) in doing so. Furthermore, this spotting was in support of, and at the request of, the

Army, though the Navy began its own experiments with spotting ships' fire later that winter. Despite a demonstrated need for seaplanes, however, the Army never developed more than a minor interest in them, though it did maintain that interest through World War II.

While the Army would have occasional need to fly over water, the Marines would have an even greater need to fly over land. This generated concern among Chambers, Bristol, and Mustin. Nevertheless, in October 1915 Lt. William M. McIlvain (USMC), at his request, was ordered to the Army school at San Diego for a course in "land flying." At the time, he was a Navy inspector at the Curtiss factory, and he had to wait until December for Louis Maxfield to relieve him of that duty before he could join the Army course.[36] McIlvain was only the first of many Marine aviators to train with the Army.[37]

For all the overlap such examples highlight, however, there was still a sense, at least on the Navy's side, that there were essential differences between Army flying and Navy flying. In 1915, for instance, Glenn Curtiss proposed to donate a trophy and cash purse to establish a race between Army and Navy pilots, flying American planes "capable of starting from and alighting on the water" in order to "further the interests of American Aeronautics." While Daniels appreciated the public spirit behind the offer, he told the president of the Aero Club of America (who would administer the race and award the prize), "The types of machines used by the Army and Navy are, and perhaps always will be, different, so that it does not seem practicable to have a competition between the aviators of the two services," and he declined the invitation to compete.[38] Mustin thought that the Navy should not be doing any work at all with either land flying or dirigibles, "because I think they both belong to the Army, although our marines [sic] should be able to operate land machines." He wanted the Marines to get *all* their aviation training from the Army "and confine ourselves to purely naval aeronautics."[39] Bristol likewise wanted to keep Navy and Marine aviation separated, telling the Advance Base School in Philadelphia, "The land defenses [of an Advance Base] should be supplied by Marines and the sea defense should be handled by the Navy. There should be land aeroplanes for the land defenses and water aeroplanes for the sea defenses." He also wanted dirigibles for the seaward defenses, presumably crewed by the Navy as well. But while Bristol advocated that the Marines should use Army aircraft and train with the Army, he stated that Marines would continue to be trained in both land and water flying. What is more, he also suggested that some number of Navy officers also receive training with the Army so as to better coordinate with the Marine flyers in advanced base operations.[40] Thus, the policy in this era remained that Marines learned to fly seaplanes with the Navy at Pensacola first before some learned to fly landplanes with the Army.

CONCLUSIONS

Although interservice rivalry existed in the period prior to U.S. entry in World War I, it tended more toward friendly competition than animosity. There is considerable evidence for personal friendships between Army and Navy/Marine flyers, who may have found more in common with their fellows in the other service than they did with their own nonflying superiors. There is also plenty of evidence of formal (and more often informal) communication between the heads of Army aviation and Navy aviation. However, there was concern in the Navy that the Army would try to take over all aviation if the Navy were not diligent. Chambers, Mustin, and Bristol felt that the land flying of Marine aviation would create a "slippery slope" leading to the loss of naval aviation to the Army and sought to differentiate between Navy and Marine aviation. Marine flyer Alfred Cunningham also supported the idea that Navy and Marine Corps missions were very different; thus, in his opinion, the Marines should have as little to do with Navy flying as possible.[41] This attitude may explain why tensions between the Marine and Navy flyers seemed to be stronger than those between either service and the Army in this period.

6

ARMY 1912–1914

A Permanent School and a Move Toward Operational Status

WRIGHT AND CURTISS CONTINGENTS

In October 1912, the Army's experiments at Fort Riley were winding down, as were the operations of the flying school at College Park. Once again, winter weather caused the Signal Corps to seek warmer climes, and the school closed on November 18. This time, however, its aviators split up for the winter, with the Curtiss flyers going to California and the Wright flyers returning to Georgia. Glenn Curtiss had again offered to share space with the Army in San Diego, so the Signal Corps leased land next to his winter school on North Island. When College Park closed, Harold Geiger (of the Curtiss contingent) was ordered to California to set up a flying school on the newly leased land. At the same time, under Charles Chandler's command, the Wright pilots and planes entrained for the field at Augusta, Georgia. Thus, for the first time in its short history, Army aviation was physically split into Wright and Curtiss contingents—a physical separation (even greater than the Navy's two camps at the beginning of 1912) that stepped up the rivalry between the two groups.[1]

The Wright contingent arrived in Augusta in November. While they were in Georgia, engine problems and weather, though not as bad as the previous year, limited training opportunities. Still, on January 17 Kirtland earned the military aviator rating, and on February 25, Chandler made the first cross-country flight from Augusta, landing twenty-eight miles away from the airfield to spend the night with a friend. The school also began acceptance testing for the new Wright Model D, which was built to Speed Scout specifications. But before testing could be completed, Scriven, as acting CSO, ordered the school to move to Texas City, Texas, twenty miles from Galveston.[2] Ironically, the orders arrived the same night that Chandler flew to his friend's house. The school called him that night to alert him of the move, but it was too late for him to fly back. Chandler returned early the next morning to supervise two days of hasty preparations for the move.[3]

Increasing tensions with Mexico had prompted the relocation. In Mexico, General Victoriano Huerta had seized power on February 22, 1912, overthrowing President Francisco Madero. The Army quickly began concentrating troops in Texas, including the fledgling aviation corps, just as in 1911.[4] Later that year, Scriven explained to Congress that it was "obvious" to him that the Augusta school should be transferred to Texas "in order to take part in field operations." But he also suggested that the move would allow application of "a cardinal principle heretofore not fully realized[:] that aviation should be carried on in the presence of troops in order that the Army, and especially commanding officers, may learn something of the use of the aeroplane under actual field conditions." Likewise, the aviators would become accustomed to working with the line units of the Army, "for whose advantage they are being trained."[5] Though the 1911 maneuver camp had introduced aviation to the ground troops, any experience gained that year had been limited by the fact that the Army really had only one pilot (Benjamin Foulois, since the three Curtiss pilots were still in training) and one plane capable of conducting field operations (Collier's Wright B, followed by S.C. No. 3, the Army's first B). By 1913, the Wright B planes had been relegated to primary training duty; the Signal Corps now had a half-dozen next-generation planes to put in the field with as many pilots, though many of the latter were still in training.[6] In addition to the Augusta contingent, the Signal Corps also ordered two lieutenants,

Call and Ellington, from Palm Beach, Florida, to Texas City, along with the new high-powered Burgess I seaplane (S.C. No. 17) they were learning to fly.[7] Scriven suggested that the organization should be designated the "1st Aero Squadron," but since the Army never made this designation official, the unit is generally referred to as the "1st Provisional Aero Squadron."[8]

Among the units assembled in Texas was Foulois' 7th Infantry, assigned to Fort Crockett in Galveston. As he had in Washington, Foulois took advantage of his proximity to the aviation unit, securing permission from his commanding officer to spend his free time in Texas City. Though not officially assigned to aviation work, Foulois nevertheless put in enough time with the aviators to keep up his flying skills and become familiar both with the new equipment and the new personnel. His responsibilities with the 7th, however, meant he had little chance to assist in the squadron's work.[9]

Flying in Texas City began March 5, but flyers found the conditions there difficult. Turbulent winds and a constricted field meant that only the most experienced aviators did much flying. In addition, high temperatures and humidity made the air much less dense (though this was not well understood at the time), reducing the airplanes' lift. Milling, along with Lt. William Sherman (who had passed his F.A.I. test and was working toward his military aviator rating) as reconnaissance officer, made two significant flights during this time: on March 12 they flew cross-country to Houston and back (a round-trip distance of eighty miles), and on March 28 they flew to San Antonio, 240 miles away. On the return trip from San Antonio, Sherman sketched the terrain under the plane every ten minutes on a continuous roll of paper, effectively creating a rolling map. More aerial maps soon followed. On May 1, during a maneuver problem with the ground forces of the 2nd Division, Milling and Sherman flew from the division headquarters (at either Fort Crockett or Texas City) northwesterly to the town of Webster, then south to Algoa, mapping and taking aerial photos while seeking to locate the "enemy" forces. A second plane, with Kirtland piloting and Ellington as reconnaissance officer, flew directly to Algoa and back, mapping the locations of both "enemy" and friendly defensive forces. Milling also made another flight by himself to locate the 6th Cavalry. General Carter, who had commanded the Maneuver Division in 1911 and was now in command of the 2nd Division, commended the aviators' excellent work in this maneuver problem.[10]

There were a few personnel changes while the squadron was in Texas. On March 6, Scriven ordered Samuel Reber to Galveston on temporary duty. Though his assignment did not involve aviation directly, it did put him near the squadron. Fred Seydel, Ralph Jones, and Hugh Kelly (all second lieutenants) were detailed to aviation in March, though Jones was soon sent back to his parent unit for ineptitude. On April 1, Capt. Arthur S. Cowan, chief signal officer of the 2nd Division, took over as squadron commander when Chandler left Texas under orders to the Philippines. In May, three more officers reported to the squadron. Moss Love had earned his F.A.I. qualification under Lahm in the Philippines, but the other two, Lt. Townsend Dodd and 2nd Lt. Joseph Morrow Jr., were novices.[11]

Toward the end of the squadron's time in Texas, an incident occurred that gave the aviators a reputation for insubordination: as a group, they circumvented the chain of command and wrote directly to Scriven. The flyers shared their concerns about both the current state of affairs in aviation and the likelihood of more problems in the future if the Army did not make immediate corrections. First, they felt that the new planes were unsafe, with numerous nonfatal crashes in addition to the fatal ones cited in this book. Second, they complained about a lack of airplane-qualified aviators in the command structure and demanded changes not only in Texas City (where the nonflying Cowan had replaced Chandler and was likely one reason for the aviators' going outside normal channels), but in Washington and San Diego as well. As we shall see shortly, the San Diego school had experienced two fatal crashes and numerous nonfatal crashes and seen the resignation of two of its assigned flyers. In Washington, command of the Aeronautical Division had fallen to Maj. Edgar Russel in November 1912 when Chandler left for Georgia with the Wright contingent.[12] Though Russel had been involved with balloons and had even served on the trial board for the Baldwin airship in 1908, he had never flown in a balloon, even as a passenger, much less in an air-plane. Arnold's request to be relieved of flying duties had led to his being assigned as Russel's assistant, but by May, Arnold was working directly under Scriven, which meant that the Aeronautical Division in Washington was officially without an aviator. Arnold, however, *was* still in Washington and working for the CSO; he was thus able to mediate between Scriven and the low-ranking flyers who had signed the letter.[13] Though the problems were smoothed over, the lack of flying officers in the aviation chain of command was a complaint that would resurface many times in the future (in naval aviation as well as in the Army).

In June, when it became clear that there would be no military action against Mexico, Scriven ordered the squadron to join the other aviators in San Diego. The Signal Corps Aeronautical Board, which consisted of Cowan, Hennessy, Kirtland, Graham, and Milling, had met on May 23 and recommended transferring all students and most of the experienced flyers to California to expedite training and qualification of both new students and older students who had not yet qualified as military aviators. The board chose San Diego rather than returning them to Maryland because the Army's lease at College Park was set to expire on June 30, 1913. Scriven recommended against renewing the lease because winter weather made College Park unusable for much of the year and shifting the ever-grow-ing aviation school from summer to winter locations and back was both time consuming and expensive. Though bills were introduced in Congress to enable the Army to buy the land outright, they did not pass, and the Army allowed the lease to lapse. Following a search for acceptable sites for year-round training, a commission had recommended San Diego. Since the Army already had an inexpensive lease there next to Curtiss' winter camp, it was probably an easy decision: Scriven issued movement orders to the Texas City group on June 6, and they began the transfer to San Diego on the fifteenth. Meanwhile, Scriven shipped the equipment remaining at College Park to California on June 14.[14]

When Cowan and the rest of the squadron departed for San Diego, Kirtland, Graham, and Call remained in Texas and continued to operate as the 1st Provisional Aero Squadron, with Kirtland in command. The reduced squadron consisted of these three pilots, twenty-six enlisted men, and two airplanes: a Wright C (S.C. No. 11) and a Wright D (S.C. No. 19 or 20), which the Signal Corps had finally accepted. None of the pilots flew the Wright D, though, because it was considered terribly difficult to handle and restricted to use by only the most experienced pilots. This meant that the squadron effectively had only one plane.[15] The three-flyer "squadron" quickly took up where they left off as Kirtland and Call flew No. 11 in a maneuver problem on June 26, quickly locating the "enemy" force and reporting its location, status, and march route to headquarters. But the already-reduced squadron lost two more pilots in quick succession. On June 30, Graham injured himself in a motorcycle accident, and his recovery was so slow that the Signal Corps relieved him of aviation duty and returned him to his infantry regiment. Then, on July 8, as Call was flying No. 11 by himself while attempting the precision landing requirement of the military aviator rating, he banked into a turn at two or three hundred feet, lost control of the plane, and crashed. Witnesses heard a loud crack and reported seeing the wing or some part of it separate from the plane in the air. Call did not survive. These unfortunate events left only Kirtland in Texas with the Model D that no one wanted to fly. Because Scriven lacked enough trained flyers to send any more to Texas, he eventually ordered Kirtland to join the school in San Diego on November 28, 1913, bringing an end to the 1st Provisional Aero Squadron.[16]

THE AVIATION SCHOOL AT SAN DIEGO

In November 1912, as the Wright contingent under Chandler left for Georgia, the Curtiss contingent, under Geiger's command, packed up for San Diego, arriving in December. Lieutenants Goodier, McLeary, Brereton, and Park soon followed, having finished basic flight training at Curtiss' plant in Hammondsport, New York. The San Diego school had four Curtiss planes for these students to practice in: the three Curtiss planes from College Park (Nos. 2, 6, and 8), as well as the Army's first flying boat, a Curtiss Model F (S.C. No. 15) shipped directly from Hammondsport in

December. Although the four students had completed basic flight training at Hammondsport, they had not yet passed their F.A.I. tests. Geiger worked with the students toward that end, and then guided them toward their military aviator ratings.[17]

At the end of February, when the Army began forming the 2nd Division in Texas, it made sense for Scriven to send the Wright contingent to become the division's operational squadron; not only did Augusta have more pilots than San Diego, it had a greater number of qualified flyers. San Diego had just two, Geiger and Goodier, and since Goodier had only qualified as a military aviator in mid-February, he had very little experience. Thus, it made sense to leave the Curtiss contingent in San Diego to continue training uninterrupted instead of consolidating all flyers in Texas City. McLeary qualified as a military aviator in March, Brereton in April, and Park in May. At that time, the Army considered a military aviator qualified to instruct new pilots. Therefore, with more instructors available, including unofficial access to the Curtiss instructors nearby,[18] the Signal Corps began sending more students to San Diego. On March 15, the Signal Corps assigned three new second lieutenants (Rex Chandler, Walter Taliaferro, and Joseph Carberry) to San Diego, and they reported to the school soon afterward. Taliaferro and Carberry had completed basic flight training with the Curtiss school in Hammondsport in December and remained there, practicing, until ordered to San Diego. Rex Chandler, however, was a new student.[19]

Despite these new additions, the number of aviators in San Diego was soon whittled down. On April 8, as Brereton was giving Rex Chandler his first flights, their Curtiss flying boat caught a wingtip on the water and crashed. Brereton survived, but the motor struck Chandler in the back of the head. He drowned before he could be removed from the wreckage. This was not only the first Army death in San Diego, but also the first Army death clearly attributable to the pusher design, with the engine behind the aviators. Brereton crashed again in May, this time as a passenger with one of Curtiss' civilian instructors. He survived but requested relief from aviation duty shortly thereafter. His request was, apparently,

motivated more by his impending wedding and his father's objections
to the risks flying entailed rather than any personal fears he might have
developed from his narrow escapes. The Signal Corps granted Brereton's
request, and he left aviation in June, though the Army would recall him to
aviation during World War I.[20] On April 17, McLeary, at his own request,
also left aviation.[21] Then on May 9, Park became the San Diego school's
second fatality. Two days after earning his military aviator qualification,
he set off on a cross-country flight to Los Angeles. Fog forced him down to
ask for directions. Though he landed safely, the barley in his landing field
lengthened his takeoff roll, causing Park to hit a tree with a wing, tearing
the plane apart. His body was found beneath the engine, and while it was
unclear whether he was dead before the engine landed on him, the incident marked another strike against the pusher design.[22]

Reassignment of the Texas City aviators to San Diego in June added
significantly to the Army's presence on North Island. Prior to their arrival,
flying personnel had dropped to only Geiger, Goodier, and two advanced
students, Taliaferro and Carberry. Cowan brought to North Island nine
additional flyers, a mix of experienced aviators and basic students.
Furthermore, the Signal Corps ordered two additional officers to North
Island for instruction: Lt. Virginius Clark and 2nd Lt. Henry Post.[23]

Upon Captain Cowan's arrival, he relieved Lieutenant Geiger of command of the school, per orders. The change of command coincided with
other changes at the school. Since December, the Signal Corps had been
leasing space from, and sharing facilities with, Curtiss' school, but the
additional planes and personnel from Texas made this policy imprac-
tical.[24] To remedy this problem, Cowan ordered construction of a new
camp, separate from Curtiss' field. But Curtiss was himself renting from
the land's actual owners, a development company.[25] Therefore, the Army
entered negotiations with North Island's owners in the fall of 1913 to purchase the land now occupied by the aviation school. The owners refused
to sell but did give permission for the Army to use the land without cost,
with the proviso that the Army would vacate when asked. Given this
uncertain tenancy, the Army preferred not to spend too much money

upgrading the field, and those improvements it did make were of a temporary nature.[26]

Concurrent with the orders for Cowan to take command in San Diego, Scriven ordered Geiger, twelve enlisted men, and a civilian engine expert to Hawaii to establish a new aviation school. Geiger, his men, and their equipment arrived in Honolulu mid-July and made their first flight on August 8. Their airplanes were S.C. Nos. 8 and 21—the latter a new Curtiss Model G, a tractor design with enclosed fuselage and side-by-side seating for the crew. However, poor flying conditions combined with design problems in the Model G meant that very little flying was done. (No. 21 was Curtiss' first attempt at a landplane tractor design and was essentially an experimental plane.) Given so many obstacles, Geiger recommended against attempting to continue the school in Hawaii. The personnel packed the two planes for storage on November 25, 1913. Over the winter, Geiger and his men addressed the problems with S.C. No. 21 and had it back in operation by June 1914 when the weather improved. The Hawaii Department commander, however, refused to allow any instruction, nor did he want the airplanes participating in maneuvers. With the detachment having little purpose, flying stopped again soon afterward. The Army shipped the planes' engines back to the mainland and sold the airframes in Hawaii during November 1914. Geiger and almost all of the enlisted detachment returned to the United States in August, having never had any students assigned to the school during the roughly twelve months they were in Hawaii.[27]

Scriven had also directed the reopening of the flying school in Manila. On March 10, 1913, Lahm was once again placed on temporary aviation duty as instructor to three new students from Philippine-based units: 2nd Lts. Herbert Dargue, Perry Rich, and Carleton Chapman. S.C. No. 7 (a Wright Model B with floats) was removed from storage in Manila and refurbished, and Lahm began instructing his students. By early May, all three students had passed their F.A.I. qualifications, though their certificates are all dated July 16, 1913—perhaps a result of the mail delay to the continental United States. About the same time the students passed their tests, a float-equipped Wright Model C that Scriven had ordered sent to the Philippine school arrived at Fort McKinley. Upon inspection, school personnel found that the plane (S.C. No. 13) had been damaged in shipping. Though they completed its assembly and repair on May 16 as a landplane, No. 13 was not flown until May 21, when Dargue, Rich, and Chapman began flying it in preparation for their military aviator tests. Along with Lahm, they also participated in reconnaissance flights during maneuvers in May and June. Chandler arrived in Manila in early June, assigned to flying duty in addition to his main responsibility: preparing to relieve Glassford as chief signal officer for the Philippines on March 15, 1914. Lahm remained in charge of the aviation school, however, as Chandler's primary duties kept him too busy to take over the school as well. But the orders meant that Chandler was able to keep his piloting skills fresh with frequent flights at Fort McKinley.[28]

In July, the summer rains again flooded the field at Fort McKinley, so the school relocated to a temporary base on Manila Bay (on the grounds of the Manila Polo Club, which at that time was located near the mouth of the Pasay River) and reinstalled pontoons on both of its airplanes. However, with the extra weight of the pontoon, No. 7's engine lacked the power to fly with a second person on board, so it had to be flown solo. During one such flight on August 28, Dargue was forced down by engine failure. As a crew from the school was towing the plane back to base with a rowboat, a squall came up and dashed the plane against the rocky shore, damaging it beyond repair. Just two weeks later, on September 12, Lahm was flight testing No. 13 as a seaplane when he crashed into the bay. Although he survived, the plane was a total loss. Another Wright C, S.C. No. 12, arrived from Texas City on October 2.[29] Using parts from No. 13, the school got No. 12 in the air six days later. However, this plane lasted only until November 14, when Rich crashed into Manila Bay. When the plane hit the water, the engine broke loose, fatally striking him in the head. This was the third fatal crash of a Wright C since Call's crash in Texas on July 8. Given these three fatalities, the two nonfatal Wright C crashes (Arnold's and Lahm's), and a general unhappiness with the design's flight characteristics, the Wright C was earning a bad reputation among the Army flyers. More immediately, the lack of planes also meant an effective end to the flying school in Manila. Chapman and Lahm had been ordered back to their units, and Chandler became increasingly busy as Glassford's assistant CSO. In any case, both Lahm and Chandler had been officially relieved of flying duties. Now–sergeant Vernon Burge, though qualified as an aviator, was not officially assigned to duty as a flyer—he remained part of the ground crew. By December, only Dargue remained flying.[30]

In light of the dwindling numbers of airplanes, Scriven sent S.C. No. 17 (a Burgess Model I) to Corregidor Island as an operational airplane. It arrived at Fort Mills in early September, but was so badly damaged that it needed replacement wings. On October 18, Dargue, Sergeant Burge, and two enlisted mechanics reported to Fort Mills and built a hangar on the beach, where they completed the necessary repairs to the plane on November 6. As with so many other planes sent to the Philippines, No. 17 lacked enough power to lift two people and the pontoons (again, probably the combined effects of heat and humidity on air density). The aviators were nonetheless able to use it in numerous reconnaissance and observation flights, spotting the fire of both siege guns and large mortars based on Corregidor. By January, the detachment had installed lighter pontoons, which allowed the plane to carry two people.[31]

With Burge now able to assist Dargue in the air, the two continued to work with the forces stationed on Corregidor. In 1914 they began practicing photoreconnaissance and worked more with the Corregidor artillery. Following a break for the rainy season—which lasted from June to November that year—Burge began testing an aerial radiotelegraph set designed by Lt. J. O. Mauborgne, head of the radio station at Fort Mills. Mauborgne had directed the radio experiments during the tests of airplane-spotted artillery fire at Fort Riley in 1912. Two years later, Mauborgne had designed not only a new aerial transmitter, but also an airborne receiver that could withstand the physical vibration of the plane and the electromagnetic interference of the unshielded engine ignition system. With

Dargue flying and Mauborgne as radio operator, the two successfully conducted two-way Morse Code conversations with Corregidor at distances
of up to seven-and-a-half miles. Flying in the Philippines finally came to
an end on January 12, 1915, when Dargue survived a crash into San Jose
Bay on the southern coast of Corregidor. The plane was damaged beyond
repair, and Dargue, the last flying officer in the Philippines, was ordered to
the flight school at North Island, San Diego.[32]

Chandler and Lahm's book says that Dargue had been returned to
his parent unit on Corregidor, though no other sources consulted mention this.[33] Since Dargue was a member of the Coast Artillery Corps, it
is entirely possible that he could have been stationed on Corregidor. If
true, then Dargue was not simply an example of how trained aviators
would form a reserve when returned to their units (as Scriven described
in 1912 when he denied Foulois' request to return to aviation). If he had
been returned to his CAC unit *in a flying capacity*, then perhaps he might
have served as a model of how aviation could have developed further in
the Army: men could be assigned to the Signal Corps to train and to gain
experience in flying, then returned to their parent branch to work on integrating aircraft into the combat forces. However, if anyone in the Army
saw this possibility, no one seems to have said or done anything about it. In
any case, Dargue's 1915 reassignment to the school at North Island ended
the Army's attempt to establish aviation in the Pacific, on both an instructional and operational basis, until after World War I.

CONGRESSIONAL HEARINGS

In February 1913, Representative James Hay (D-VA), chair of the House
Military Affairs Committee, introduced a bill that proposed to separate
aviation from the Signal Corps. The War Department opposed the legislation. Scriven sought opinions on the proposed legislation from the experienced flyers, including Arnold and Foulois, neither of whom was on flying
duty at the time. All stood in opposition to the bill.[34]

Writing from Fort Leavenworth, Foulois encapsulated the general response.
He allowed that "legislation is absolutely necessary for the future development

of aviation," but lambasted Hay's bill as "hasty and ill-considered." Having read the bill, Foulois said it was clear that the author had considered neither the opinions of the aviators themselves ("the best judges, in the United States Army, as to their present and future needs") nor the then-current policy guiding the reorganization of the Army. While the bill provided for permanent assignment to the proposed Aviation Corps, it limited the number of officers assigned to thirty lieutenants, with a major as commandant of the new corps and only two captains under him. While thirty-three officers would be an increase over the current officer personnel assigned to aviation, it would not allow much room for growth. Furthermore, Foulois pointed out that there were currently three captains available in the Army with aviation experience (Beck, Chandler, and Hennessy). One could be promoted to major, and the other two would occupy the captain slots allotted in this bill. But that would leave no place for lieutenants like Foulois and Lahm, who could expect promotion to captain in the next few years. Since the bill provided for only two captains, such wording would force them out of aviation altogether following their promotions. "This one fact," wrote Foulois, "makes this bill stand out clearly as a personal measure, solely for the benefit of some particular officer or officers," and not something geared toward the future efficiency of Army aviation. Though Foulois avoided naming names in his letter, he and many of the other aviators believed Paul Beck was behind Hay's bill.[35] If Beck was indeed the instigator, then the proposed bill represented a new stage in the competing visions of Beck on the one hand, and Foulois (and the apparent majority of aviators) on the other.

Foulois had other complaints as well. For instance, the bill limited command of the Aviation Corps to officers who had "displayed especial skill and ability as a military aviator." Foulois felt that *none* of the officers so far assigned to aviation (including himself) had yet displayed such skill and ability. He further opined that *all* Army aviators had but limited experience in flying, and that they still had years of study and practice ahead of them before they could begin to devote any time to the organizational duties required of a corps commandant. For this reason, Foulois stated that "the head of the aviation service, for some time to come, should be an experienced executive and administrative officer" from the Signal Corps. Foulois concluded by noting that aviation might be sufficiently developed in another year or so to consider making it independent, but until then, it was better off under the Signal Corps.[36]

Foulois' letter is evidence that the provisions of Hay's bill greatly agitated him. In his correspondence with Russel and Scriven, Foulois also sensed their concerns. Eventually, he felt compelled to take personal leave in order to return to Washington and do what he could to help block the bill, a trip that kept him from flying S.C. No. 10 at Leavenworth as soon as it had been repaired. Just how much influence Foulois' lobbying had is uncertain, given that the War Department itself officially opposed the bill. Regardless, the bill died in committee, and the danger seemed to be averted.[37]

However, a new Congress was installed on March 4, and Hay introduced a new bill quite similar to the original, despite suggestions from the War Department and a panel of flying officers (organized by Scriven) on more appropriate and acceptable legislation.[38] This time, the House Committee held several days of hearings (August 12 and 14–16, 1913) in which it called a variety of Army officers to testify, including Assistant Secretary of War Henry Breckinridge, Chief Signal Officer Scriven, Lieutenant Colonel Reber, Major Russel, and the flyers themselves: Beck, Foulois, Arnold, Milling, and Hennessy. The Committee even called ex-Army officer (and bombsight developer) Riley Scott, as well as Army Capt. William "Billy" Mitchell.[39]

Mitchell had been called to give the General Staff's opinion of aviation. Although he had had no personal experience with aviation to date, it was a Signal Corps responsibility, and Mitchell was the only Signal Corps officer then serving with the General Staff. Mitchell had not yet developed the ideas about aviation that would underlie his later reputation as a maverick willing to do anything to advance the creation of an independent air force. Instead, at this hearing, he followed the official line of the General Staff by opposing separation of aviation from the Signal Corps. He stated that airplanes would be used for reconnaissance, but only for "getting information about large units and not little details about small detachments. We have troops for that [latter] purpose." He informed the committee of the significant advances that the French army had made in aerial observation of artillery fire, stating, "We would [also] need a unit for that purpose." As to offensive uses of the airplane—the argument that he would eventually use to justify aviation's independence—Mitchell told the committee, "The offensive value of [the airplane] has not been proved." Although he acknowledged successful experiments in dropping bombs and firing machine guns from planes, he explained to the congressmen, "there is nothing to it so far except in an experimental way."[40]

Mitchell was not alone in opposing separation during these hearings. Scriven, too, fought against taking aviation away from the Signal Corps. Scriven began his testimony by discussing aviation developments in foreign countries (especially expenditures), describing the present numbers of airplanes, dirigibles, pilots, along with the respective 1913 aviation appropriations in France, Germany, England, Italy, Russia, and Japan. Even Mexico, he reported, had seven planes and five pilots at the time, compared to the U.S. Army's seventeen planes and nineteen officers on aviation duty (though only seven U.S. Army officers had qualified as military aviators to date). Yet Mexico had allocated $400,000 to aviation in 1913—more, Scriven pointed out, than the total that the U.S. Congress had appropriated to Army aviation since 1909.

This argument led Chairman Hay to ask about the European practice of making aviation a separate arm of the Army. Scriven admitted that that was, indeed, the practice in Europe, but pointed out that none of the armies in question had a technical organization equivalent to the U.S. Signal Corps. The Signal Corps, he explained, contained men of "undoubted scientific ability" in electricity, materials, physics (specifically, "the action of natural forces"), and internal combustion research. In short, "men of the kind that it is absolutely essential to have in an aviation corps, as the staff and the directing heads of the corps and its scientific departments." The aviators might gain such knowledge themselves in time, he reasoned, but for the moment, the actual flyers were young men who had not yet had time to acquire the necessary knowledge and experience. Scriven allowed that aviation might become independent in the future, but for the present, keeping it as part of the Signal Corps would allow it to be managed by experienced administrators with technical backgrounds unparalleled elsewhere in the Army.[41]

Historian Herbert Johnson implies that the Signal Corps as an institution, and Scriven as its chief, emphasized the reconnaissance aspects of aviation and downplayed the offensive uses in order to maintain control over it. A hint of this accusation emerged during Arnold's testimony, though it was directed at Scriven's predecessor rather than Scriven himself. Arnold told the Committee that one reason that things were getting better for aviation—that the Signal Corps was doing more for aviation than it had been—was that Scriven had demonstrated a real interest in aviation. (Apparently he had gone as far as taking a few flying lessons to better understand the aviators' problems, though he never soloed.)[42] Scriven, said Arnold, had "shown that he wants to do all he can for the aviators." In contrast, Arnold said that General Allen, Scriven's predecessor, "did not have an especial interest in it." Hay responded that in his experience, Allen "was very much interested in aviation; at least, he was very much interested in getting appropriations for aviation." Arnold responded, "Yes, sir; in that way he was." Hay undoubtedly offered Allen's efforts to secure funding as evidence that he did care about aviation. But while the transcript does not register tone of voice, it is likely that Arnold gave his response sarcastically, implying that Allen's interest was less in aviation itself than in the power and prestige of controlling a larger appropriation.[43]

Whether the Signal Corps really was more concerned with controlling aviation than advancing it, even the flyers were against separation from the Signal Corps, at least at that time. Foulois, Arnold, Milling, and Hennessy all sided with Scriven, the War Department (represented by Assistant Secretary Breckinridge) and the General Staff (represented by Mitchell). Interestingly, at the time of the hearings, Milling was the only aviator called before the committee who was still assigned to aviation.[44] Nevertheless, all were considered experts in Army aviation and all agreed that aviation was better off within the Signal Corps than as an independent part of the line. The aviators opposed the bill on many of the same grounds that Foulois had laid out in his letter about the previous bill: aviation was not sufficiently developed or of a sufficient size to be on its own yet. They felt that the Signal Corps was the best organization in the Army to manage aviation until it was ready for independence. As for the proposed independent organization: the bill's grand total of thirty-three officers was too small; the specified ranks for those officers were too limiting; and, at least for the moment, there was no one who was both a flyer and a good organizer capable of leading the proposed aviation corps. All agreed that any problems in pushing the development of aviation stemmed from a lack of personnel and funding, not poor management by the Signal Corps (barring Arnold's comments on Allen).[45]

Of all the witnesses before the committee, only Beck spoke in favor of separation. He believed the Signal Corps was mismanaging aviation, insisting that "there is no certainty that [aviation] will ever attain any size or importance under the Signal Corps. They have been handling it now for five years with no appreciable results." Beck was perfectly clear that aviation "should be taken away from the Signal Corps for the simple reason that it does not logically belong to the Signal Corps." In support of this assertion, he cited Army regulations that explicitly stated the duties and functions of the Signal Corps, which, he emphasized, said nothing about aviation: "There has never been any specific provision giving aviation to the Signal Corps; they just reached out and took it. Nobody awakened to the fact; nobody realized the condition that they had allowed it to be done. Nobody in the War Department seemed to care one way or the other, and no one outside seems to have investigated, and there is no reason why we should continue to permit it."

Moreover, he derided Scriven's claim of Signal Corps men with aviation experience as "a gigantic bluff." According to Beck, no one currently in the Signal Corps was "thoroughly competent in aviation matters," though he allowed that there were many competent officers who *had been* part of the Corps but had returned to the line.[46]

Beyond the Signal Corps' incompetence in managing aviation, Beck felt that it was actively holding back aviation development. He complained that the existing chain of command was too complex and included too many non-flyers to manage aviation efficiently. He pointed out to the committee that the Signal Corps had never presented any plan for the ultimate organization of aviation, and had ignored international demonstrations of the uses of military aviation because the non-flyers running the Signal Corps "had failed to grasp the situation." In response to Hay's query about other witnesses' suggestion that separation from the Signal Corps should wait until aviation had grown larger, Beck replied, "there is no certainty that it will ever attain any size or importance under the Signal Corps."[47]

Although Beck favored the separation of aviation from the Signal Corps, he was less certain that it should be organized into a new corps. Instead, he argued that the responsibility for aviation should be distributed among existing Army organizations so as to prevent duplication of effort and align aviation with existing strengths. That is, since the airplane is a method of transport, he said, it should fall under the Quartermaster Corps, leaving only the wireless equipment to the Signal Corps. Beck explained that bomb releases, once developed, would fall under the Ordnance Department, and any special device for fire control of artillery, whether field or coastal, should be developed by the artillery. Actual flying should be done by line officers since the line, not the Signal Corps, was responsible for reconnaissance: "It is a line function because a man in order to perform the reconnoissance [sic] duty must know his military art; he must be a topographer," and, Beck claimed, permanent Signal Corps officers did not have that training.[48] Beck does not seem to have been aware that he was proposing the same distributed organizational structure the Navy was using to manage aviation, nor the troubles it was causing them.

Everyone who testified after Beck—even Mitchell—rebutted each of Beck's claims, reiterating that aviation was better off (or at least no worse off) remaining part of the Signal Corps for now. If Beck had support from other aviators for the earlier bill, his network seems to have fallen apart by this point. Immediately following Beck's testimony, Scriven told the committee that Beck's view of the Signal Corps was incomplete, because he had only been in the field and had not been involved with its administration in Washington. Furthermore, the Signal Corps *did* have a plan for aviation, Scriven told the congressmen. During his earlier testimony he had touched lightly on these plans, but the full details were in supplementary documents, which the committee included in the record.[49] These documents laid out what was, effectively, a table of organization (T/O) for a squadron and most of a table of equipment, though these types of documents were not yet in use.[50]

Scriven planned to establish a permanent aviation school along with several "aeronautical centers" around the country that would provide a home and support base for operational aviation squadrons of the regular Army and the reserves. The centers would be located near established Army camps so that aviators and ground forces could get used to working with each other; some of the centers would also host aviation supply warehouses. Scriven eventually wanted six operational squadrons in addition to the students at the school. Each squadron would consist of eight planes and sixteen flying officers (two for each plane), a couple of nonflying staff officers, and the necessary enlisted ranks for support: a total of twenty officers and eighty-eight enlisted men. One squadron was to be located near the headquarters of each of the Army's four geographic department headquarters, one squadron was to be located in the Philippines, and companies (half-squadrons) were to be located in Hawaii and the Panama Canal Zone. The document also laid out a plan for the Signal Corps to resume operating dirigible balloons as part of a "well-balanced system of aerial defense." An appendix contained a suggested organization and equipment list for the operational squadrons in the field. During Mitchell's testimony, he specified that each squadron would have two airplanes for strategic reconnaissance, four for tactical reconnaissance, and two for observing artillery fire. Since these missions are not specified in Scriven's documents, it seems likely that this distribution of planes came out of the General Staff's thinking.[51] Regardless, these were the first official indications that either the Signal Corps or the General Staff had any long-term goals for aviation.

The hearings revealed that the biggest thing holding back aviation was not mismanagement by the Signal Corps, but rather lack of funding, followed closely by lack of personnel. U.S. Army aviation was woefully underfunded compared to Japan and the European powers, and even Mexico's annual budget for aviation in 1913 was almost four times that of the Army's. Foulois also told the committee that any lack of attention from the Signal Corps was because that organization had been thinly stretched in its duties, which included the development of wireless as well as aviation. Although earlier legislation had exempted those officers assigned to aviation from the limits of the Manchu Law, the provision provided only limited relief to the Corps.[52] The Signal Corps needed more men for aviation as well as its other duties, but was hobbled by the statutory limit on its personnel. Scriven explained that existing legislation allowed for 30 officers in the Aviation Section, but that the Army chief of staff had authorized only 20.[53] In any case, this allowance had to come out of the Signal Corps' statutory cap on total personnel. Scriven explained to the committee that the Signal Corps presently had 17 permanent officers and 29 detailed temporarily from other branches—this was for *all* Signal Corps duties, he explained, not just aviation. Thus, even if the chief of staff authorized the full 30 officers permitted by law for aviation, a mere 16 officers would be available for other Signal Corps responsibilities. Against this limited number of officers, Mitchell proposed establishing two squadrons immediately, which, along with those officers assigned to the flying school, would require a total of 62 officers assigned to aviation. Scriven's plan called for immediately establishing four squadrons, requiring 80 officers, plus those staffing the school. Eventually, Scriven's full six squadrons would require a minimum of 120 flying officers in addition to school personnel. With the entire Signal Corps limited to 46 officers, Congress would need to act to commit more men and money to Army aviation if it was going to grow much beyond its present status.[54]

Following the hearings, Hay rewrote his bill to address both the Army criticisms of the original bill and the additional issues raised in the testimony. Mitchell claimed that Hay let him redraft the bill, later known simply as the "Act of July 18, 1914," for the date it passed. The act formally renamed the Aeronautical Division, promoting it to a full section and establishing the newly designated "Aviation Section" by law as part of the Signal Corps. It provided for up to 60 officers and 260 enlisted men to be assigned to aviation in addition to the existing allowed strength of the Signal Corps. Further, the bill declared that all new aviation students would be selected from unmarried lieutenants of the line, no older than thirty. This last detail would seem to corroborate Mitchell's claim to have written the bill, since Mitchell had specifically suggested these limitations in his testimony. Although Scriven and Russel had both referenced the notion that men past a certain age were no longer suited to learning how to fly, neither specified what that age might be, and no one else even mentioned the idea that someone might be too old to learn to fly. Likewise, though both Arnold and McLeary had requested relief from flying duty due (at least in part) to their anticipated nuptials, nothing was said of this during the testimony, and only Mitchell discussed whether marriage was or should be an issue in assigning men to flying duty.[55] Once signed into law, the bill relieved the strain on the Signal Corps for personnel, since the aviation personnel no longer counted against the authorized strength of that organization. It also put to rest, for the moment, any attempt to remove aviation from Signal Corps control. The limitations on age, rank, and marital status, however, created new pressures that would soon be challenged.

The act also established new classes of flight certification. An aviation student would now have to pass his tests for a junior military aviator certificate within one year from reporting to the Aviation Section. (The F.A.I. still seemed to be required as an initial certification.)[56] Congress left the details of the test up to the secretary of war but specified that the examining board must consist of 3 officers "of experience in the aviation service" and two medical officers. After no less than three years as a junior military aviator (JMA), a flyer could elect to go before a similar board to be passed as a military aviator (MA), though the bill permitted no more than 15 officers with the military aviator qualification on active flying service at any one time. Thus, not every flyer would be able to advance to the MA rating even if they could meet the qualifications. As with the JMA, the qualifications for the MA rating were left up to the secretary of war. The bill also established the enlisted rating of "aviation mechanician" and allowed for up to twelve enlisted men at a time to be trained as pilots. Congress further authorized pay bonuses for men holding each of these qualifications while detailed to flying duty and also directed that the widow of any officer or enlisted man killed in an aviation accident would receive a death benefit equal to one year's pay.[57] Passage of this act meant a rejection of Beck's view of how Army aviation should be organized, and marked the end of Beck's chances to be *the* technology advocate for Army aviation.

Shortly after the congressional hearings, Milling left on a six-month tour of the aircraft factories and flying schools of France, England, Germany, and Austria. Scriven, late in the summer of 1913, had decided that the Army needed more information on foreign aviation developments, in both airplane design and production, and in foreign military aviation training. Military attachés in Europe were beginning to include such information in their reports, but aside from Squier, whom the Army had sent to London as attaché in June 1912, none had sufficient technical knowledge—much less specific knowledge of aviation—to report on aviation developments in any detail.[58] Even if attachés could have provided useful reports, Scriven felt it was important for at least one Army aviator to have firsthand knowledge of state-of-the-art aviation in Europe. Milling, who departed the United States on September 9, 1913, was undoubtedly the best officer to send. He was both an experienced pilot and still assigned to flying duty in the Signal Corps. His selection for this task, however, deprived the San Diego school of its most experienced pilot and best instructor for several months. Milling would complete his tour and return to the United States in the early spring of 1914.[59]

Samuel Reber officially took over what was still designated the Aeronautical Division (it would not become the Aviation Section until the bill became law on July 18, 1914) from Chandler on September 10, 1913. Shortly after the congressional hearings, Reber took advantage of Foulois' presence in Washington to discuss the possibility of Foulois' return to aviation. With Milling detailed to Europe and so many other experienced flyers leaving (or preparing to leave) aviation for one reason or another, Reber was concerned that the nonflying head of the San Diego school, Cowan, would be left without an experienced aviator officer to advise him. Foulois was more than willing to return to aviation as the senior aviator at the school, for which he received orders on December 5, 1913, arriving in San Diego shortly after Christmas.[60]

On October 27, 1913, Scriven issued stringent requirements for the new military aviator rating, which were to take effect on January 1, 1914. The new standard called for several cross-country flights, one over a triangular course of at least one hundred miles with two intermediate stops, which was to be completed within forty-eight hours using the same airplane throughout, and a second flight over a designated straightaway course of sixty miles without intermediate stops. The pilot would have to submit military observation reports for both flights. In addition, the pilot would have to maintain an altitude of twenty-five hundred to three thousand feet for at least thirty minutes, which could be done separately or as part of the cross-country flights, and would have to make a dead-stick landing starting from an altitude of fifteen hundred feet, stopping within three hundred feet of a previously designated point. Scriven also introduced a written knowledge test on an aviator's knowledge of map reading, the use and limitations of the magnetic compass, the theory of flight, the theory of internal combustion, and troubleshooting and repair of both airframes and engines. Anyone on aviation duty who had qualified under the previous requirements before the new ones took effect could gain the new qualification by making flights equal to or better than those required and demonstrating a general knowledge of engines and airframes and their repair. However, if they did not meet these lesser requirements, or failed to do so before July 1, 1914, they would have to sit for the formal exam, meet the practical requirements, and be passed by an exam board.[61] The apparent lack of published/disseminated standards for the JMA rating suggests that the difference between the two ratings was rank/seniority rather than a difference in required skills; something the wording of the bill permitted. Another possibility is that the old, less stringent military aviator requirements became the new JMA requirements.

CHANGES AT SAN DIEGO

Since the new military aviator standards required extensive theoretical knowledge, not just practical skills, Scriven also instituted an academic ground school at San Diego, with hired civilian experts as instructors. The winter course, beginning on December 8, 1913, offered lectures from visiting experts on aerodynamics and airplane design (Dr. Albert Zahm, of the Smithsonian Institution), propellers (Professor W. F. Durand, Stanford University), atmospheric and meteorological physics (Dr. W. J. Humphreys, U.S. Weather Bureau), and internal combustion engines (Dr. F. R. Hutton, American Society of Mechanical Engineers). Other course topics included the strength of materials used in airplane construction, topography, photography, aerial reconnaissance, and radiotelegraphy. In addition to the formal coursework, the Army hired a civilian, Oscar Brindley, as a dedicated flight instructor for the Wright planes. He began teaching at the school on December 12, 1913. This new concentration on theoretical instruction, in addition to the existing practical course, coincided with the school's formal inclusion in the Army educational system as the Signal Corps Aviation School. Given the instructional improvements, the Signal Corps did not expect student pilots to have trouble passing the updated military aviator examination after nine to twelve months. However, the newly reorganized Aviation School curriculum could not solve all the Army's problems.[62]

The congressional hearings had touched on the many fatalities suffered by Army aviation. Since Selfridge's death in 1908, seven Army officers (including Selfridge), one enlisted man, and one civilian had died in Army airplane crashes. The last fatal crash had occurred just about a month before the hearings with Lt. Loren Call's accident in Texas on July 8. During the hearings, Arnold, Russel, and Milling explained the apparently large number of fatalities as the unfortunate consequence of having such a sizable percentage of officers still in the instructional stage—the most dangerous time. Russel pointed out that the Army's pilots were almost all students, since so many aviators to date had been returned to their parent units just about the time they qualified as expert pilots. The historical record shows that out of a total of forty-one Army officers assigned to flight training in airplanes by the beginning of the hearings, seven had died in crashes and another thirteen had been removed from flying duties. Of the twenty-one officers remaining on aviation duty by August 1, only eight held the (old) Military Aviator rating that these officers considered the end of training. Another seven had achieved the F.A.I. license, but all had only done so in June and July before the hearings.[63] Arnold pointed out that while the United States fared poorly when compared with foreign programs in terms of aviation deaths as a percentage of officers assigned to aviation, the Army was not so badly off when compared on the statistic of miles flown per death. Looked at that way, he told the committee, the U.S. military, with about thirty officers assigned to aviation, had one death per 12,800 miles flown, whereas Great Britain, with 140 aviators, was only marginally better with one death for every 13,000 miles flown. France, with nearly 600 aviators and one of the lowest percentage of deaths among officers assigned, averaged one death for every 54,000 miles flown. Of course, Arnold explained, the vast majority of French aviators had already passed the initial training stage. And Milling reassured the congressmen that accidents would decrease now that the Army had found and was using what he declared "the best instructional method" at San Diego.[64]

Despite Milling, Russel, and Arnold's confident statements, several fatal crashes occurred in close succession in the months following the hearings, all in Wright Model Cs. Lt. Moss Love died in a Burgess-built Wright Model C (S.C. No. 18) in San Diego on September 4, 1913. On November 14, Lieutenant Rich fatally crashed S.C. No. 12 in the Philippines. Then, ten days later in San Diego, S.C. No. 14 dove into the ground while approaching a landing, killing the chief instructor, Lt. Eric Ellington, and his student, Lt. Hugh Kelly. The report on this last crash blamed an inherent tendency in the Wright C to plunge downward when power was suddenly applied in a glide.[65] Once Foulois took over as senior aviator at the Signal Corps Aviation School, he issued two general orders for the school that were intended to prevent further fatalities. First, he believed that some crashes had occurred because aviators had pushed the boundaries of their own experience in order to get their names in the newspapers or, conversely, took such media praise to heart and so believed that their skills were greater than they actually were. Consequently, Foulois' first general order prevented anyone but the school's commanding officer from discussing events at the school with reporters. Second, to help flyers survive crashes, he directed them to wear flying helmets at all times and either leather jackets when flying over land or life jackets when flying over water. The helmets, leather jackets, and life vests were expected to help aviators survive injury from the terrain, rather than protect from the crash itself.[66]

Henry Post's fatal crash on February 9, 1914, proved that Foulois' orders did not fully address the underlying causes of such accidents. The investigating board determined that, although Post had been attempting to set a new solo altitude record, he was not at fault for the accident. Post met his end in a Wright C (S.C. No. 10: the same airplane that had given Arnold such a scare at Fort Riley in 1913), which led Scriven to order the Wright B and C model planes grounded until further notice. He further asked Cowan to report on their safety and suitability for continued use in the Army. In response, Cowan assembled a board of aviators consisting of Foulois, Dodd, Taliaferro, Chapman, and Carberry to investigate the issue. On February 24, the board condemned all pusher designs as unsafe due to their tendency to stall, as well as for the location of the engine behind the pilot, where it was likely to break loose and crush him in an otherwise survivable crash. The series of fatal crashes also led the inspector general's office to send an officer, Col. John Chamberlain, to examine the situation at the school. While his report addressed more than just the airplanes then in use by the Army, he agreed with the findings of the board of aviators. As a result of these investigations, the Signal Corps permanently grounded all pushers. From February 1914 until at least the United States' participation in World War I, the Army would purchase and use only tractor landplanes (Curtiss' pusher flying boats remained in use, however).[67] The Navy did not permanently ground its own pushers (for similar reasons) until the summer of 1916.

Grounding the pushers left the Signal Corps Aviation School with only five planes in the inventory: one Curtiss G tractor and four Burgess H-model aircraft (one of which was being rebuilt at the factory when the pushers were grounded). Not only did this limit the number of planes in San Diego, but since the remaining planes were classed as high-performance service airplanes, few aviators were qualified to fly them. The lack of available airplanes and qualified aviators caused a bottleneck since both current students and several who had already qualified to fly solo had to compete for instruction time in the few planes available. In the meantime, from March 11 to 13, the Signal Corps convened a board at the school to draw up specifications for a new airplane to be used for training. This board, comprised of the same men as the February board, decided that primary flight students needed a plane that was lightweight yet strong. It needed to be maneuverable at all speeds, but especially at slow speeds. The board also specified that the plane should have a tachometer, an airspeed indicator, gas and oil gauges, an aneroid barometer (used as an altimeter), and a clock. The Signal Corps placed orders for more training tractors with Burgess, Curtiss, and Glenn Martin, but none of these would be delivered before the end of June.[68]

Another problem facing the San Diego school was that the tractor planes now being used for instruction were intended for the 1st Aero Squadron rather than the school itself. On December 4, 1913, the War Department had issued General Order No. 75, which outlined a provisional organization for an aero squadron. As a general order, the issuance was automatically part of the Army's *Field Service Regulations*, thereby designating aviation as a standard part of the field army for the first time. The provisional organization called for a total of twenty officers, ninety enlisted men, eight planes, sixteen trucks, and six motorcycles distributed between a squadron headquarters and two aero companies. Subsequently, on January 7, 1914, Scriven approved the formal organization of the 1st Aero Squadron at San Diego, with Cowan in command of the squadron and Foulois and Taliaferro in charge of the two companies. Meanwhile, the Army had ordered the tractors as service planes to equip this new squadron. However, during Chamberlain's inspection of the school in February, he found that the squadron existed primarily on paper and reported that there was very little difference between the squadron and the school. He suggested that these shortcomings were not intentional, but simply the result of insufficient personnel to adequately populate both organizations. The need to use the service planes as training machines further blurred the line between squadron and school.[69]

The 1st Aero Squadron, such as it was, conducted several experiments and practiced cross-country flying in the first few months of 1914. Between January 6 and 20, Army pilots made several attempts to locate submerged mines that had been planted in San Diego Bay as part of the Army's port defenses, and at the end of February the San Diego flyers watched a parachute demonstration by Glenn Martin. Though this static-line parachute generated such initial interest that the Army eventually purchased two, the aviators never used or even tested them. Indeed, airplane parachutes would not come into use in the Army until the 1920s.[70] In early 1914, Aero Squadron pilots also set new Army and American flight records for speed, distance, duration, and altitude in the course of their cross-country flights. By April 1914, Riley Scott had returned from France, and the Squadron resumed testing Scott's bombsight. Such noninstructional flying practically ended on April 26, when most of the experienced flyers, and the three best of the five available planes, left under Army orders for Texas. Dodd attempted to continue the tests with S.C. No. 9, the Army's first Burgess H tractor, but this plane could not lift the added weight of the bombsight and bombs.[71]

Once again, deteriorating relations with Mexico spurred an aviation deployment. This time the U.S. military did see action, though Army aviators did not. On the morning of April 21, President Wilson ordered the

Navy and the Marine Corps to occupy the port of Veracruz[72] on the Gulf of Mexico to prevent a German merchant ship from delivering weapons, though this was just a convenient excuse—the United States had been planning to capture Veracruz for some time as part of a larger plan to intervene in the Mexican Revolution. The Army and Navy had coordinated plans in place for just such an occupation, whereby the Army would arrive to replace Navy and Marine forces once the sea services had occupied the city.[73] With Navy and Marine forces ashore in Mexico (their actions are described in the next chapter), the Army quickly ordered troops to assemble in Galveston for transport to Veracruz. It also ordered the Signal Corps Aviation School to send five qualified aviators, thirty enlisted men, and three airplanes to Galveston. With Foulois in command, the detachment left for Texas on April 26. Milling (back from his European inspection tour), Taliaferro, Carberry, and Dodd, along with a medical officer, made up the rest of the officer personnel. They took three Burgess tractors with them (S.C. Nos. 24, 25, and 26). However, when they arrived in Galveston, they discovered that their transport had sailed a few hours earlier. According to Foulois, "We arrived . . . just in time to see the last ship loaded with American troops disappear over the horizon. For the next six weeks [we] literally sat on the sea wall at Galveston waiting for whatever the fates decided." Technically, the detachment left the 1st Aero Squadron back in San Diego; when the orders came through, Foulois was squadron commander, but when he decided to command the detachment, he relinquished command of the squadron to Capt. William Lay Patterson. But on May 2, the Army officially designated the Galveston detachment as the 1st Company, 1st Aero Squadron, while the qualified flyers in San Diego were designated the 2nd Company, with Patterson in command. The order named Cowan as squadron commander. Four days later, the Army sent Morrow to join the 1st Company in Galveston. But the fighting in Veracruz had largely ceased by the time the Army troops arrived there, and President Wilson decided that the Army would *not* advance inland as originally planned. With the fighting in Veracruz effectively halted, the

Army ordered the aviators, who had never even unpacked their planes, back to San Diego in mid-July. Upon their return, the 1st Aero Squadron was reorganized. Cowan published Signal Corps Aviation School General Order No. 10 on August 5, explicitly naming the staff of the school and the personnel of the 1st Aero Squadron. This order once again put Foulois in charge of the squadron with Geiger and Goodier commanding the 1st Company and 2nd Company, respectively.[74]

Before the detachment left for Galveston, the flyers had outlined specifications for new service aircraft. The proposed requirements worked their way up the chain of command, and on July 1, Scriven announced that the Signal Corps would hold a contest in October to select a new, two-seat reconnaissance plane. Manufacturers' entries would have to meet certain minimum requirements based on the aviators' recommendations, including a certified bench test of the engine, a nonstop flight of four hours, and a climb to four thousand feet in ten minutes while carrying full load. Once the minimum requirements were met, the planes would be awarded points based on other desired attributes. The Signal Corps would then purchase (for stated amounts) those planes finishing in the top half of all planes meeting the minimum qualifications: if five or more planes qualified, the Signal Corps would buy the top three scoring aircraft; if three or four qualified, they would purchase the top two; and if only two qualified, they would buy the better of those.[75]

Scriven had high hopes that the competition would prompt manufacturers to develop a new standard service plane that the Army could purchase in significant numbers. Twelve airplane manufacturers expressed intent to enter the competition, but when the competition began on October 20, only Curtiss and Martin were ready. As a result of the poor turnout, Reber, as head of the Aviation Section, called off the competition. At the request of the Curtiss and Martin representatives, however, the Aviation Section allowed the two manufacturers to demonstrate their planes under competition conditions with the understanding that the Army was under no obligation to purchase either plane. As it turned out, only the Curtiss plane, likely a Model N prototype, met all the minimum requirements, and *Aeronautics* magazine called the event "more or less of a farce."[76]

Although the competition fell short of expectations, the Signal Corps still purchased new airplanes. About the time the Army grounded all pushers, it had ordered two planes each from Curtiss and Burgess. Intended as reconnaissance planes for the 1st Squadron, they were also used as trainers, thanks to the ongoing aircraft shortage at the school. In May, the Army accepted delivery of the two new Burgess H tractors at Fort Wood, New York. The first of the new orders to be delivered, S.C. Nos. 27 and 28 arrived in San Diego at the end of July. The planes were identical to S.C. No 26, which had been delivered in January, except that they were equipped with a new type of control that the Wright Company had begun using in February. This new control combined roll, pitch, and yaw in a single wheel that also included throttle control on the hub.[77] The two Curtiss planes were of a new type: the Model J; Signal Corps Nos. 29 and 30 arrived in San Diego on June 24 and September 15, respectively. In addition to these new acquisitions from both Curtiss and Burgess, the Signal Corps also purchased a Martin T trainer, S.C. No. 31, on June 20, which Martin delivered on July 2. Since Martin's factory was located just up the coast from San Diego, it was easy for Martin to bring down the plane and demonstrate it for the Army. The Army soon purchased two more Martin trainers, S.C. Nos. 32 and 33, for which they accepted delivery, respectively, on August 26 and September 11, 1914. At least one of these newer trainers was a Martin TT, a variant of the original T design.[78] Finally, on September 21, the school accepted delivery of S.C. No. 34, a Curtiss F flying boat—the first flying boat, in fact, on the school's inventory since the April 1913 crash of S.C. No 15, which Brereton survived but Rex Chandler did not.[79] Although the Curtiss F was a pusher design, it seems to have been exempt from the decision to ground all pushers. This may have been because the Curtiss F was considered the best seaplane design at the time. The Army not only continued to use them for overwater flights, but also purchased more "F-boats" from Curtiss, though only a few and those one at a time.

The shift from pushers to tractors and the influx of new designs were not the only changes during 1914. The way those planes were purchased also changed. In Chamberlain's wide-ranging inspector general's report on his February 1914 visit to the school, he recommended that the Army hire a qualified aeronautical engineer to help evaluate the safety of both new and repaired airplanes. Part of the reason the Army had purchased designs that proved so unsafe, he felt, was because it had no one who could evaluate aircraft on a scientific basis. Thus, on July 15, the Signal Corps hired Grover C. Loening, who had previously worked as an engineer and general manager at the Wright Company. Loening was put in charge of the newly established Experimental and Repair Department at the school, with Milling serving as his assistant. The pair immediately went to work. First, they began addressing the shortcomings of existing planes. In particular, the school considered the Burgess H models, as delivered, too fast for beginners but underpowered for service use. Thus, Loening and Milling began rebuilding the Burgess H aircraft as advanced trainers. Second, they helped convince Glenn Martin to build and demonstrate his Model T trainer to the Signal Corps without a contract. Finally, toward the end of 1914 they collaborated on the design of a new trainer, which they then had Curtiss build in his North Island shops. Though it was completed on December 30, 1914, the collaborative design proved to be something of a step backward, and the Signal Corps found it unacceptable.[80]

Late in the fall of 1914, the Signal Corps Aviation School hired another civilian flight instructor. On October 5, Francis "Doc" Wildman, formerly of the Curtiss Company, joined Oscar Brindley in giving basic flight instruction to student pilots. Scriven, in his annual report, explained the new policy of hiring expert civilian instructors instead of relying on officers who had qualified as junior military aviators or even full-fledged military aviators: "There are now a number of expert aviators in the service, but expert aviators are not necessarily competent instructors. Instructors must have special qualifications in addition to being expert aviators. Teaching men to fly is probably the most dangerous occupation in the world, and men who can do this work and do it well are very rare." Wildman became the chief instructor for overwater flying, and he and Brindley shared other basic instruction duties.[81] The Signal Corps recognized that training others to fly required special skills; hiring Wildman and Brindley ensured that the school had personnel with those special skills without having to worry that they might be ordered elsewhere, as with officer-instructors. At the same time, it freed up two flying officers for assignment to field squadrons. With the passage of Hay's act, Congress had authorized up to sixty officers on flight duty, but the Army had not yet assigned new officers to flight training, and the Aviation School was limited in how many new students it could accept. As a practical matter, then, the Aviation Section would remain undermanned for some time.

Though the Army had ordered many new planes at various times in 1914, most deliveries occurred toward the end of the year. Consequently, when Loening and Milling remodeled some of the Burgesses for training, they effectively deprived the 1st Aero Squadron of that many service planes, even though the Burgesses were only marginally suitable for field service. This juggling act slowed aerial work by the squadron pilots for much of the latter half of the year but did not stop it altogether.

The squadron's work that fall included testing various airplane armaments. In August, it resumed testing Scott's bombsight and bomb racks using one of the new Martin trainers. The Army's Ordnance Department had manufactured 15-lb and 50-lb live and dummy bombs for the tests and also sent an Ordnance Corps colonel to observe the tests. These tests were primarily designed to test the detonation and fragmentation of the bombs, which performed well, but the colonel was so astonished at the accuracy of the drops that Capt. Hollis Muller, the Aviation Section's official observer for the tests, recommended purchasing several Scott bombsights and giving specialized bombardier training to a few officers. Cowan endorsed the plan, but Scriven blocked it, arguing that airplanes were primarily for reconnaissance. Despite this attitude, Scriven investigated a recoilless gun design (the Davis gun) in September, but concluded that it was too heavy to mount on airplanes.[82] In November, Chief of Ordnance General Crozier suggested to Scriven that the Signal Corps make further

tests with machine guns and offered to design aircraft mounts. The aviators in San Diego conducted these tests soon afterward but without lasting
results since Army planes continued to be unarmed.[83]

The squadron finished out the year by competing among themselves
for the Mackay trophy, which Foulois believed would sharpen the skills of
his squadron. The plan was to have the two-man crews fly their planes to a
field in Los Angeles. From there, they would attempt to find and reconnoiter
troops located somewhere in a large swath of land around San Diego, before
landing at North Island. Six planes left San Diego, but only two reached
Los Angeles safely. The team of Taliaferro and Foulois (with Foulois as the
observer) actually lost two planes trying to make the flight. Their first plane
suffered an engine failure, but they landed safely; though the school sent
a replacement plane, the team was again forced down while attempting to
complete the flight when Taliaferro's goggles broke. Due to his limited vision,
Taliaferro landed on rough ground, and the plane turned over. On the day of
the competition flight, one of the two planes that had successfully made the
flight to Los Angeles suffered a fuel line break and was severely damaged in
the subsequent emergency landing. Only one plane successfully completed
both flights. Fortunately, none of the crashes was fatal, though one plane had
been forced down at sea, and Lt. Frederick J. Gerstner drowned while trying to swim to shore for help. The planes themselves fared less well: of the six
planes that crashed, half of them were declared total losses. While the high
number of crashes and the permanent loss of three planes was cause for concern, there was room for some optimism since the losses did not result from
either poor equipment or untrained pilots. Instead, the crashes were seen as
a learning opportunity resulting from Army aviation's attempts to push the
boundaries of airplane operations. In all, the competition taught the Signal
Corps that circumstances beyond human control could still put numerous
planes out of action in a short time. Consequently, the Army would have to
maintain a large reserve of airplanes to ensure that squadrons in the field
would not be grounded due to a similar string of accidents.[84]

Despite the results of the Mackay competition (considered a temporary
setback), the aviators, at the beginning of 1915, felt that Army aviation was

finally on a path of steady progress. Airplane inventory was set to increase, and the newer airplanes promised to better suit either training or field operations. Moreover, while the Signal Corps Aviation School was learning how best to train new personnel, the Aviation Section had room to add more officers. Still, Army aviation faced several problems.

The biggest threat to the growing organization was probably its lack of a permanent location. As with College Park, the Army did not own the land on North Island occupied by the Aviation School, which made the Army reluctant to commit to further development of the site. The Army recognized its need for a permanent home and again entered negotiations to buy the land. However, the Coronado Beach Company still did not want to sell. Though it still had no immediate need for the land, the company was worried that the Aviation School seemed to be increasingly permanent. Consequently, before the end of 1915 it would ask the Signal Corps to vacate the land before it became too difficult to remove the school. Scriven had reminded the Army of this danger in his FY 1914 annual report to the secretary of war, endorsing Cowan's recommendation either to purchase the North Island plot or purchase land nearby to which the school could move. When the inspector general's office made its second annual inspection of the Aviation School and the Aero Squadron in January 1915, the lack of a permanent site was the first criticism listed in the report. In the FY 1915 Army appropriations bill, passed March 4, 1915, Congress authorized the secretary of war to establish a commission to search out potential sites for purchase that would provide a permanent location for the Aviation School. Secretary Lindley Garrison ordered Reber and an officer from the Quartermaster Corps to investigate sites near San Diego, San Francisco, Portland, and Seattle.[85] On December 29, 1915, they submitted their final report recommending a site in Coronado Heights, San Diego, but the land was never purchased.[86]

Scriven himself made an inspection tour in the spring of 1915 to see the Aviation School in person and to initiate construction of a new aviation center. Beginning on March 6, he observed the operations of the Aviation School and reviewed the facilities and personnel. While at the school he took at least two flights, one in the flying boat with Wildman, the civilian instructor, and another in a Martin tractor with Taliaferro. From San Diego, Scriven left for Texas. On March 11, accompanied by Foulois, Scriven inspected a site near Fort Sam Houston where he wanted to establish the first of the aeronautical centers he had proposed in the congressional hearings. The FY 1915 Army appropriation bill had granted $48,200 to begin construction at San Antonio, and Scriven was eager to get started. Though the money was insufficient for completing all necessary improvements, those structures that could be completed with the allotted funds were ready to receive the 1st Aero Squadron when it arrived in San Antonio later that year. These were sufficient to house the Squadron and its equipment, though much remained to be done to turn the space into an airfield. But while San Antonio offered plenty of space, Scriven's intent was not to move the school there, even after the Coronado Beach Company asked the Army to vacate North Island as soon as possible after March 31, 1916. (The school was still well ensconced there, with no plans to relocate, a year after this deadline, when the United States joined World War I.) Scriven wanted the Aviation School to be isolated from other flying activities to conduct primary and advanced aviator training (through junior military aviator status) without distractions. The aeronautical centers would only conduct third-stage training (what would today be called specialty training), where aviators and ground troops would learn to work together, integrating aviation into the field army. It was here, assigned to field squadrons at the aeronautical centers, that aviators would acquire the knowledge and skill to try for the military aviator rating (vacancies permitting). As it turned out this third stage was never put into practice before the United States' entry into the war changed everything.[87]

CONCLUSIONS

Over the course of 1913, Army aviation faced several challenges, surviving some and overcoming others, emerging shaken, but stronger than it started the year. Army aviation left College Park forever at the end of 1912, physically separated into Wright and Curtiss contingents, the former soon sent into the field on an emergency basis, while the latter began establishing a permanent school, albeit on borrowed land. The two rejoined by the middle of the year, but the aviators were dispersed again in premature efforts to establish a new aviation school in Hawaii and reestablish the one in the Philippines. Both were plagued by problems keeping their few aircraft operational in tropical conditions, but the bigger problem was simply a lack of students. Without enough would-be aviators drawn from the local garrisons, it was difficult to justify the effort and resources necessary to keep the aircraft in flying condition. The San Diego school, on the other hand, finally reached a size where it not only could become solidly self-sustaining but could even afford to have experienced flyers (and their airplanes) concentrating on making the airplane useful to the Army without the distraction of instructing the next class of students. Both the school and the nascent 1st Aero Squadron, however, still faced the same uncertainty over their tenancy of rented land that had contributed to the Army's abandoning College Park in the first place. The direct effect of this was the Army's unwillingness to make capital improvements to the site, which made life (and work) in San Diego more challenging than it might have been.

Army aviation also spent much of the year under legislative uncertainty, as Congress introduced several bills aimed at "improving" the development of Army aviation in various ways, most of which both the aviators and the Army's senior leadership opposed. Congressional hearings in August 1913 put the Army's treatment of aviation under a microscope (with a particular focus on the Signal Corps), forcing Signal Chief Scriven to make explicit his long-term ideas and plans for the Aeronautical Division. The final bill, passed in June 1914, relieved some of the pressures on the Signal Corps (especially the number of personnel it could assign to aviation) and took the first steps toward professionalization with the statutory establishment of the junior military aviator and military aviator ratings, though the qualifications for those ratings were left to the Signal Corps to determine.

The Inspector General's February 1914 report on Army aviation in San Diego further contributed to the professionalization of the Aeronautical

Division (called the Aviation Section after June 1914). The report forced the Army to recognize that it had provided aviation with insufficient resources, and that this had resulted in overwork of both personnel (who often had multiple, blurred responsibilities) and equipment. While the Army could address the equipment problems itself (especially replacing the pusher designs the IG report declared unsafe), solving the personnel issues required congressional action, such as the June 1914 legislation, which authorized an increase in the personnel assigned to aviation. The Army also did what it could to reduce the workload of its aviators by hiring a civilian aeronautical engineer to evaluate new airplane designs and two dedicated civilian flight instructors. This freed Army aviators from those responsibilities, allowing them to concentrate on further developing their own flying skills so that they could begin molding the airplane into a practical tool for the Army as part of the 1st Aero Squadron, itself now considerably less intertwined with the school.

The 1st Aero Squadron's efforts yielded mixed results at the end of 1914 due to the technological immaturity of the airplane on the one hand, and the signal chief's rejection of developing airplane ordnance on the basis that airplanes were primarily for reconnaissance. Ironically, this latter issue—the Signal Corps' apparent determination to block airplane development that was outside of its interests—was the main reason behind the various 1913 efforts to separate aviation from the Signal Corps!

7

NAVY/MARINES 1914–1917

Reorganization and Disruption in Naval Aviation

While Army aviation faced many challenges in 1913 and 1914, it could be considered to have been in good shape by the end of 1914. Organizationally sound, it had grown past the point where all the senior aviators' efforts had to go into training the next generation, thus permitting the most experienced aviators to turn their attention to developing the airplane as a military tool. At the same time, the material condition of Army aviation was also improving, with pushers grounded (at least for training purposes) to be replaced by new tractor-engine designs. While Signal Corps leadership prevented the actual arming of aircraft, it was at least willing to support experiments in that line, and this restriction was but a minor mark against the Signal Corps' otherwise strong support for its Aviation Section.

As we shall see in this chapter, naval aviation also faced challenges beginning in 1913 and continuing through 1916. The year 1914 was particularly difficult, ending in arguably worse shape than when it started, with senior aviators scattered to nonflying duties, causing an almost complete curtailment of training. A potential, powerful patron would briefly take control of naval aviation, only to turn responsibility over to yet another officer who had not asked for the job and knew nothing of aviation. Only in finally having a permanent location for the school did the Navy and Marine aviators have things better than their Army brethren. Naval aviation faced additional setbacks in 1915 and 1916, though they were at least not as frequent as in 1914 and generally minor by comparison. At the start of 1917, naval aviation finally seemed to be on firm footing, ready to begin proving its worth operationally.

The series of events that began at the end of June 1913 with Chambers' plucking found their resolution during the winter of 1913–14, when Rear Adm. Bradley Fiske, the aide for operations, began making moves to take more direct control of naval aviation. In December 1913, he had Capt. Mark Bristol report to him for "special duties." Only after Bristol had reported did Fiske tell him he was to take charge of naval aviation. Because Fiske could not provide any office space for Bristol, he had Bristol work on the opposite side of his own desk.[1] Fiske's orders to Bristol were problematic since, officially, Chambers was still in charge of aviation in the Bureau of Navigation under its chief, Rear Adm. Victor Blue. But in January, Fiske succeeded in having Navy secretary Daniels transfer aviation (and Chambers) to the staff of the aide for operations. Fiske then named Bristol the head of what would on July 1, 1914, officially be called the Office of Naval Aviation (ONA).[2] Although Fiske's outspokenness would eventually cause problems, in the short term, his rank facilitated the coordination of the various, contentious Navy bureaus responsible for different aspects of aviation.[3]

This new regime immediately sprang into action, issuing a flurry of orders to implement the recommendations of the Chambers Board, though the changes may also have been ones Fiske had intended to make regardless. Fiske had earmarked the old battleship *Mississippi* as the new aviation ship and got orders cut for Lt. Cdr. Henry Mustin to take command. Mustin reported aboard *Mississippi* as executive officer and acting captain on December 31, 1913. Three days later, secretary Daniels ordered the aviation camp at Annapolis to move to Pensacola.[4] Shortly thereafter, Bristol ordered Mustin to take his ship to Pensacola, where it would become the station ship of the new Pensacola Naval Aeronautic Station.[5]

Mustin's assignment as acting captain of the *Mississippi* likely had many causes. One was the fact that he had already soloed and was the most senior naval officer to have done so at that time. (He would earn his Navy license in June 1914.) Fiske or Bristol probably thought Mustin's higher rank would help settle down the younger officers assigned to aviation and set at ease those in the Navy's administration, though as a lieutenant commander, he was too junior to be named the actual captain of a battleship, even an outdated one like the *Mississippi*. Another reason was surely his proposal, submitted to the secretary in November 1913, to put airplanes on scout cruisers. His twelve-page "tentative outline" showed evidence of considerable thought as to the necessary changes in training of aviators as well as the physical changes to ships needed to accommodate airplanes and their supporting apparatus. As the commander of the *Mississippi*, Mustin was in a position to turn his proposals into reality.[6]

Continuing the flurry of orders, Bristol also ordered John Towers to establish the Navy Flying School ashore at Pensacola, but confused the issue of just who was in charge of the new station by noting that Mustin, as senior officer present, would decide exactly where the school would be established.[7] This arrangement reintroduced some of the problems that had existed between Ellyson and Rodgers: Mustin, a lieutenant commander, clearly outranked Towers, a lieutenant, but Towers was equally clearly the senior aviator, having taught Mustin to fly while in Cuba. The two were willing to work things out between themselves, though events would limit the amount of time Towers and Mustin were together in Pensacola in any case. More damaging over the long term would be the poor relationship that developed between Mustin and Bristol.[8]

Mustin and Bristol clashed almost from the beginning. Much like Chambers had been, Mustin was uncomfortable with the ambiguity of his position; he complained to his wife about the evasive answers he was getting from Bristol as to the exact nature of his (Mustin's) authority, but Mustin expressed the hope that it would all be cleared up when Bristol came to

Pensacola to inspect the work.[9] In fact, Bristol's arrival made things worse. Bristol spent much of February 1914 in Pensacola, negating Mustin's already vague status as "senior officer present" while he was there, and making decisions that might otherwise have been Mustin's.[10] One exception to Bristol's involvement was the investigation into naval aviation's second fatality. Though Bristol had witnessed the final flight of Lt. (jg) James Murray, he did not put himself on the board investigating the accident.[11] Other than that, Bristol remained very much in charge while in Florida. Even after Bristol returned to Washington, he continued to override Mustin, writing him, "I want you to do things my way with the proper allowance for that individuality which is required. . . . I do not consider I have any right to neglect or shirk any work necessary to have those under me do what I believe to be right."[12] For the good of the service, Mustin tried to ignore Bristol's micromanagement and second-guessing, but the tensions grew.

MARINES IN PUERTO RICO, THE NAVY IN VERACRUZ

While the rest of the aviators were preparing to move the camp from Annapolis to Pensacola, Bernard Smith and the newest Marine aviator, 2nd Lt. William McIlvain, had their own orders. They prepared two aircraft and ten enlisted Marine mechanics to join the Marine Corps' first Advance Base Maneuvers in Culebra, Puerto Rico, in January 1914 to do exactly what Alfred Cunningham had proposed in February 1912.[13] The "Marine Section of the Flying School" was more involved in practice maneuvers with the Advance Base Force than the whole Aviation Camp had been with the Atlantic Fleet's winter maneuvers the previous year, but Smith and McIlvain still found time for flying interested Marine officers over the practice area in order, in Smith's words, "to show the ease and speed of aerial reconnaissance and range of vision open to the eyes of an aerial scout." Smith expressed confidence that his unit had demonstrated "the possibility of aero planes for defence [sic] using bombs of high explosives" while circling above the attacking fleet.

Smith recommended that the Advance Base Force have an aeronautical section of five aviators, four aircraft, and twenty enlisted men (five for each aircraft). The planes, he said, should consist of two flying boats, one amphibian, and one landplane—the last for work over land, for when quick climbing was needed, and for when "a flying boat would be too slow." (The comments about quick climbing and speed show that Smith was already well aware that a landplane had inherent performance advantages over seaplanes and amphibians.) He also recommended that the force have canvas hangars to house the aircraft.[14] In their work at Culebra, the Marine aviators made favorable impressions on the commander of the Advance Base troops, Col. George Barnett (who was made major general commandant of the Marine Corps on his return to the States), as well as the Navy's Rear Adm. Charles Badger, still commander in chief of the Atlantic Fleet.[15]

The Marine Section returned to Pensacola in plenty of time for naval aviation's first real test, though the Marine flyers would be mostly left out of it. The Mexican Revolution was heating up again and Rear Admiral Badger once again expected to receive orders to intervene, as he had a year earlier. This time, the orders came: on April 21, 1914, a landing force of Navy and Marine personnel from the Atlantic Fleet occupied the Mexican port of Veracruz. Other ships of the fleet went north to Tampico and prepared to land forces there as well, if necessary. Naval aviation was not with the fleet when the forces landed, but arrived a few days later: Towers, Smith, Ens. Godfrey Chevalier, four airplanes (C-5 and A-4, along with the older C-4 and E-1 for spare parts), and ten mechanics reached Tampico on board the USS *Birmingham*, while the *Mississippi* (commanded by Mustin) sailed to Veracruz with Bellinger, three student aviators (Lt. Richard Saufley, Ens. Melvin Stolz, and Ens. Walter LaMont), and the remaining two planes (A-3 and C-3).

Bellinger and the *Mississippi*'s aircraft did the bulk of the flying: Towers' section was specifically ordered not to make any flights in Tampico. With the exception of searching for a mine reported in the Veracruz harbor (the rumor was proven false) and finding a sunken wreck whose location was marked incorrectly on the charts, the flights were all in support of the landing forces. The flights made over Veracruz were more in the nature of Advance Base work—the Navy pilots were even prepared to drop makeshift bombs if necessary—but the only Marine aviators were in Tampico (Smith) and back at Pensacola (McIlvain), so the experience went to Navy flyers who would never be part of the Advance Base Force.[16] The A-3, the plane flown most often, was reconfigured as a landplane since most flights were over the land. Within Towers' section, the A-4 was also converted to a landplane and also flew missions once the section was ordered to rejoin the *Mississippi* at Veracruz on May 24, though the tactical importance of such flights was much reduced by that time. Even so, the Navy never placed the planes under direct control of the Marine forces ashore, further limiting the useful experience that might have been gained from the episode, both by the flyers and by the Marine commanders.

In fact, Chambers and Bristol worked actively to prevent the Marines (or worse—in their eyes—the Army) from taking control of the planes. In 1913, when it had looked like the fleet might be sent from Guantanamo to Mexico, Towers had put in a request for land gear for the planes. The request made sense to Ellyson since the planes were expected to do much flying over land. But Chambers quickly countermanded the request when he returned to the office, because, as he later explained, he "did not believe in utilizing Navy Equipment for Army work far inshore, as it was not designed for that purpose."[17] Bristol may have had the same concerns in mind in 1914, when Badger wanted the Marine aviators sent ashore, since Bristol told Mustin, "I had hard work stopping that."[18] He may also have been concerned about giving the Army an excuse to appropriate the Navy's planes, pilots, and ground crew. When an Army brigade (without Army aviation, which had been left on the docks in Texas) arrived on April 30 to relieve the Navy landing parties, the Army did indeed attempt to commandeer the Navy's aviation sections. But the planes remained under Navy control, supporting the Marines (who stayed ashore when the sailors returned to their ships) and the Army, until the *Mississippi* returned to Pensacola in June, taking the airplanes with it.[19] Afterward, Badger praised the work of the airplanes in supporting Navy and Marine Corps forces as they defended the city against Mexican troops.[20]

Once it became clear that the excitement in Veracruz was over, Mustin was eager to get back to Pensacola. He worried about the delay in training and the wear and tear on his aircraft, but the experience with actual operations had also taught him several lessons that he wanted to put into practice. One was his assessment that the flying boat was unsuitable for Navy work: with their long hulls (having a waterline almost from nose to tail, unlike later designs), Curtiss' flying boats could not take off or land in heavy seas. Because of this, Mustin no longer believed the flying boat had any place in the Navy, and he wanted to see it phased out. The second lesson concerned the importance of developing the catapult. Operations at Veracruz had convinced him of the "absolute indispensability of the catapult for naval work."[21] Mustin looked forward to installing Richardson's new catapult on the *Mississippi* for testing. That would not happen, however.

THE "EUROPEAN WAR"

Instead, the outbreak of what became known as World War I would have major repercussions on naval aviation, even before the United States became a belligerent. On June 28, 1914, soon after the aviators had returned to Pensacola, Gavrilo Princip assassinated Archduke Franz Ferdinand of Austria in Sarajevo. By August 4, the major European powers had declared war on each other, and Germany had invaded Belgium. Towers had been in Hammondsport since shortly after returning from Mexico, consulting with Glenn Curtiss on plans for a transatlantic aircraft flight. On learning of the outbreak of war, he immediately requested to be sent to Europe as an observer and soon received orders to London as an assistant naval attaché.[22] Towers would spend the next two years in London, frustrated at times by his inability to get good information about the Royal Navy's (RN) progress in aviation, but in the end, he probably got more intelligence than anyone else due to his friendship with a lieutenant commander in the Royal Naval Air Service (RNAS), Cyril Porte. Porte and Towers had become acquainted while working on the transatlantic aircraft (eventually named "America") with Curtiss. The plan had been for Porte to pilot the plane with Towers as his copilot. When the war broke out, however, plans for the flight were canceled. Porte returned to England, where he was later able to provide Towers entrée to British naval aviation. Indeed, the friendship with Porte may have been responsible for Towers' assignment to London rather than Paris.[23]

In London, Towers made many additional personal connections with officers in the Royal Navy and the RNAS, as well as in the British aviation industry. Shortly after Towers' arrival in London at the end of August 1914, Porte took command of Hendon, an RNAS training aerodrome just north of London. For a few weeks, Towers was a frequent visitor to Hendon, even flying some of the planes available at the base. Officially, however, the Admiralty (the British counterpart to the U.S. Navy Department) was reluctant to provide such access to Towers and his superior, naval attaché Cdr. Powers "Pete" Symington. The Admiralty's reticence stemmed partly from British losses in the first few months of the war, and partly from the fear that anything known to the U.S. Navy would soon be printed in the American press for everyone to see. Despite the Admiralty's official reluctance to talk, Towers continued to befriend RN officers, among them Lt. Cdr. Spenser D. A. Grey. Grey commanded an RNAS squadron about to deploy to northern France and wanted Towers to accompany them, though nothing came of the request at this time.[24]

By mid-January 1915, however, the Admiralty was beginning to loosen up a bit. It permitted Symington to go out with the Grand Fleet as an observer, though this was kept secret even from the Office of Naval Intelligence in Washington for several months. In July 1915, Towers finally got permission from the British to visit Porte's new command, the flying boat patrol station at Felixstowe. This marked the beginning of an easing of restrictions on Towers' activities. The following summer, 1916, the Admiralty finally granted him permission to visit the RNAS stations around Dunkirk, France. These moves (putting Symington with the Grand Fleet and letting Towers visit various RNAS stations) may have been an extension of efforts by the British foreign secretary and the War Office to bring the United States into the war on the British side that resulted in Army attaché George Owen Squier's visit to the front lines in 1914.

However, while Squier's tour was sanctioned at the highest levels of the British Army, Towers' visit to the front lines was, in the end, only possible because of his friends' willingness to bend (or ignore) the rules. British authorities in Dunkirk initially prohibited Towers from going any farther than that town, but Grey, now stationed in nearby Coudekerque, learned of his presence there and arranged for Towers to spend two weeks with his naval fighter squadron. On Towers' last day with the squadron, Grey acceded to Towers' request to accompany a bombing raid into Belgium. Had Towers' presence as an observer/gunner in an escorting two-seat fighter been discovered by the Germans, it would likely have caused an international incident. But Towers and Grey were lucky, and Towers' plane returned safely and without incident to the Coudekerque aerodrome.[25]

Meanwhile, in the United States further development of naval aviation effectively halted for the remainder of 1914. On the day the Archduke was shot, the *Mississippi* was headed for Norfolk; Greece had purchased the ship, and the shipyard in Norfolk was to prepare the vessel for transfer. In Norfolk, Mustin and his skeleton crew of aviation personnel shifted the planes and all aviation equipment to the bigger and faster armored cruiser *North Carolina*, the new aviation station ship.[26] Almost as soon as the aviators were settled on board, the *North Carolina* was ordered to Boston, where they offloaded all airplanes and aviation stores in preparation for the next assignment: on August 7, the ship sailed to Europe in company with the *Tennessee* (on which Towers sailed to Europe) to provide relief to Americans trapped overseas by the outbreak of hostilities. Because the relief expedition was assembled in haste, the Navy conscripted the aviation officers—Mustin, Bellinger, Smith, Herbster, and flight students LaMont, Saufley, and Wadleigh Capehart—as ship's crew. Mustin remained as executive officer, but Capt. Joseph Oman took command just before the *North Carolina* sailed. McIlvain (the Marine) was the only flyer ordered off the ship, and that was so he could oversee shipment of the offloaded aviation gear back to Pensacola.[27] The aviators remained on duty on board

the *North Carolina* as watch-standers while the ship sailed to and around
Europe, and they were effectively away from aviation until their return to
the United States at the end of 1914.[28] (The ship itself would not return to
Pensacola until September 1915.)[29] The loss was not just of personnel—
Pensacola was effectively operating out of the station ship. All accounts
(including pay for the men left in Pensacola) and all official paperwork had
to go through the ship. Until the cruiser returned, or the problem was rectified some other way, the development of naval aviation was paralyzed.[30]
Therefore, between the disruptions caused by intervention in Mexico and
the U.S. reaction to the outbreak of World War I, almost no development
occurred in naval aviation in the final months of 1914.

The *North Carolina*'s engagement in Europe was not a complete blow to
naval aviation, however. Upon the ship's arrival in France in mid-August,
Mustin, Bellinger, and Smith went to Paris on an impromptu fact-finding
mission.[31] They toured several airplane factories, which led Mustin to
marvel at how much more advanced the French planes were than those
in the United States, declaring the U.S. Navy's planes "nothing but a lot of
junk in comparison." Mustin also rode in a Bleriot airplane with a tractor engine and an enclosed cockpit—Mustin's first experience with both
features and the first report on them by any U.S. naval aviator. In addition, the three were able to observe some of the operations of the local
French army aviation squadrons. Mustin lamented that he and his fellow
officers did not have more time in Paris. With a loosely worded pass from
Brig. Gen. Félix Paul Antoine Bernard (in charge of the French Office
of Aeronautics) giving them access to manufacturing plants and airfields
around Paris, hostilities barely getting started (and thus official channels still rather fluid), and a serendipitous meeting with an Australian
acquaintance who was flying for the French, Mustin believed he and his
colleagues had a unique opportunity to gather information.[32] But while
their trip to Paris was limited, their presence in Europe undoubtedly
made it easier for Bristol to have Smith and Herbster assigned as assistant
naval attachés in Paris and Berlin, respectively.[33] Over the next two years,
Towers, Smith, and Herbster gathered much information on European

aviation and its uses during what was then called "the European War," though as we shall see shortly, their intelligence produced little material change in U.S. naval aviation.

Though the *North Carolina*'s absence caused hardships for those left behind in Pensacola (left under the command of now Lieutenant [junior grade] Chevalier), they continued testing and development as best they could. Developing airplane wireless remained important, and new sets were being assembled for testing.[34] At the end of July, while the *Mississippi* was being exchanged for the *North Carolina*, Herbster and Smith piloted a flying boat to the Navy's proving grounds at Indian Head, Maryland, where they tested both bombs and a bombsight. The bombs were small and dropped by hand, with the bombardier leaning over the side of the fuselage, holding the bomb in an outstretched arm while looking through the bombsight mounted on the outside of the plane.[35] Some earlier, informal efforts had been made along this line, but this was the Navy's first formal evaluation of bombs or bombsight.[36] That fall, Admiral Fiske (in one of his rare direct actions concerning naval aviation) replied to a BuOrd query about allowed weight for ordnance. He had to admit that none of the airplanes in service had been designed to carry extra weight in the form of bombs, though he allowed that they could carry bombs if a passenger remained behind or they carried less fuel. He informed BuOrd that an allotment of 150 pounds for guns and/or bombs was being considered in future plane designs and invited it to design bombs "for the various purposes for which they might be used." Fiske believed these plans and designs for ordnance would in turn inform aircraft design.[37] As it happened, the first specification allotting weight for ordnance did not come out until the following summer when the Office of Naval Aviation specified that its newest airplanes should be able to carry eighty pounds of ordnance.[38]

The Navy also continued to evaluate new products from airplane manufacturers. The first of two Burgess-Dunne aircraft were delivered that summer. Built by Burgess (which had supplied the D-1 and D-2 flying boats), these were very futuristic-looking pusher floatplanes featuring swept-back wings and a tailless design. (Among other potential advantages for the Navy, the tailless design was shorter overall and promised to occupy less space on board ships.)[39] Fiske had also requested permission to buy some European planes, both to let the aviators experience for themselves what was being done abroad and to challenge domestic manufacturers.[40] Secretary Daniels approved the request, and orders were placed (one plane each from Germany and France). The outbreak of war, however, prevented their delivery. Bristol also took up the recommendations of the Chambers Board and began agitating in the fall of 1914 for a training dirigible.[41]

Officers continued to be assigned to naval aviation, despite the absence of most of the qualified aviators needed both for instruction and to judge the licensing tests. Lt. (jg) Clarence Bronson arrived in Pensacola while the *Mississippi* was there but stayed behind to train with Chevalier when the station ship sailed for Norfolk. Ellyson's friend, Lt. Kenneth Whiting, finally received his orders to aviation as well. He reported to Dayton in June 1914 for his preliminary course. While there, he accepted an offer from the Wright Co. for flight training and had already earned his Aero Club license when he arrived at Pensacola in September, though he still needed some additional training to qualify for the new "naval air pilot" designation. (As with the Army, the Navy had decided it needed something more than the F.A.I. test and created the naval air pilot qualification in 1914 along with the curriculum for the newly established school at Pensacola.) Whiting, though, outranked Chevalier, so he took over command of Pensacola until Mustin returned from Europe.[42] The last officers to arrive in Pensacola in 1914 were Lt. Louis Henry Maxfield, who reported in November, and Lt. Edward McDonnell, in December. McDonnell was the last officer to arrive as an individual; the next officers to report, in July 1915, reported as a group, as did all subsequent assignees. A few other officers also reported to aviation in 1914, but Bronson, Whiting, Maxfield, and McDonnell would soon play important roles in developing naval aviation.

The following year brought many changes to naval aviation. In November of 1914, the Naval Aeronautic Station had been formally established as a command at Pensacola. This solved many of the problems of the station ship being away, since it moved command responsibility from the ship to offices ashore, it gave the commander of Pensacola (formally the "commandant") more authority in dealing with the bureaus, and smoothed out problems with supply and capital improvements.[43] By the end of January 1915, all the aviators who had sailed to Europe in the *North Carolina* (with the exception of Smith and Herbster) had returned to Pensacola. Following a brief stint assisting Bristol in Washington, Mustin began putting the station back into shape and dealing with the chaos that had developed in his absence.[44] In March, Congress provided $1 million for aviation in the Navy's budget, which allowed Bristol immediately to order three new airplanes with more orders to follow.[45] The new planes were desperately needed, as Mustin reported only one aircraft in flying condition suitable for training.[46] Despite the lack of planes, experiments continued, with more tests using planes to find submarines and minefields taking place at Pensacola in June.[47]

Bristol's order for the three new planes provided another reason for the flyers' unhappiness with non-flyers (and Bristol in particular) in command. The three aircraft Bristol ordered were Burgess-Dunne pushers. The aviators had requested tractor machines, but Bristol believed that pushers were the better military design. Bristol's belief was just that: a belief ungrounded in evidence. He had no experience as a pilot. His knowledge came from a few flights as a passenger, observing flights from the ground, and consuming the limited and sometimes flawed aeronautical theory that appeared in print at the time. On the other hand, the aviators' desire for tractors was grounded in their empirical knowledge of aircraft design and practical experience with flying. Mustin, at the very least, had flown in a modern tractor design while in France, whereas Bristol may only have seen older American tractors. Nevertheless, Bristol felt his seniority, engineering knowledge, and/or greater Navy and administrative experience outweighed the wishes of those junior officers in Pensacola. Beyond the tractor/pusher issue, though, the purchased aircraft did not represent a significant advance in aircraft performance. There had been discussions between the Navy and U.S. airplane manufacturers about design specifications, but the aircraft being purchased were still manufacturers' standard models—nothing designed specifically for the Navy. The April 15 press release acknowledged that the Burgess-Dunne design did not meet all requirements for a Navy aircraft, but it came closer than any of the other designs the Navy considered. This did little, however, to assuage the frustrations of the aviators.[48]

REORGANIZATION (AGAIN)

In 1915, Congress caused yet another reorganization of naval aviation. The Navy Bill, which assigned the million dollars to naval aviation, also authorized the new position of Chief of Naval Operations (CNO), responsible for the operations of the fleet and war planning. The position absorbed the role of the aides for coordinating the activities of the various Navy Bureaus.[49] Secretary Daniels appointed William S. Benson to the position in May 1915 (he would serve as CNO until he retired in November 1919). Benson set about establishing and organizing his new office, and his order of July 8, 1915, placed the Office of Naval Aviation directly under the CNO.[50] Fiske had departed Washington a week earlier under orders to take command of the Naval War College in Newport, Rhode Island, a change of duty station apparently driven by his disagreements with Daniels.[51] The loss of the pro-aviation Fiske, even if his vision of naval aviation was not always shared by his aviator subordinates, weakened Bristol's influence with the bureaucracy. As CNO, Benson had more authority than Fiske to secure the cooperation of the bureaus, though not much more, initially.[52] However, he was neutral about aviation at best, whereas Fiske had been— and remained—a real advocate for the airplane in naval operations.

The increased funding for naval aviation also meant more students. July brought ten new officers to Pensacola for flight training—the largest number assigned to aviation at once up to that point. They were also the first to arrive together, and thus formed Pensacola's first true "class" of students. The students included Navy Lt. Alfred C. "Putty" Read, Alfred Cunningham (who had returned to aviation and was prepared to requalify under the new regulations), and Francis T. Evans, another Marine lieutenant.[53] This new group almost doubled the number of officers on flight duty in naval aviation. More officers arrived in smaller groups through the fall, including one destined for future fame: Marc A. Mitscher.[54]

With the influx of new students and new planes, and the return of the *North Carolina* as a station ship in September, naval aviation could begin more serious experiments. That fall, the flyers made more bombing tests (still with hand-dropped bombs) from greater altitude than the previous year.[55] With the return of the *North Carolina*, the aviators also resumed tests with Richardson's new catapult. It was installed on the ship and on September 28, 1915, Saufley, piloting the AB-2 flying boat, made the first Navy catapult launch since 1913. Redesignated from C-2 in the new scheme of 1914 (which was intended to avoid confusion between aircraft and submarine designations), the AB-2 was soon the assigned aircraft for catapult launches, perhaps because its boat construction was better able to withstand the stresses of catapult "shots" than the floatplanes with their extended floats.[56] Mustin made the first catapult launch from a ship under way in early November while Admiral Benson was conducting a two-day inspection of Pensacola.[57] However, the catapult broke down soon after and was taken off the ship. Richardson returned to Washington to make further refinements and redesign the catapult specifically for installation on the *North Carolina*.[58] The flyers also continued evaluating a variety of aviation instruments, especially compasses.[59] Their work paid dividends when, in November and December, the more experienced aviators began overwater flights out of sight of land for the first time. They proceeded carefully, flying up to sixty-five miles straight out to a destroyer and then straight back, but this simple flight track represented a huge leap in the ability of the airplane to scout for the Navy. All was not perfect, however, because it was necessary to have a boat near the shore steer the proper course for the destroyers so that the flyers could parallel the course and note the heading on their uncompensated compasses.[60] Still, the navigational accuracy was good enough that such flights became part of the curriculum at Pensacola. The aviators then began some preliminary work with destroyers in spotting fire—work that was expected to continue at the winter exercises in Guantanamo at the beginning of 1916.[61]

Perhaps as a result of these tests and the information coming back from Towers, Herbster, and Smith, naval aviation was ready to specify desired characteristics in new aircraft and not just take what the manufacturers offered. In July, Mustin proposed a "speed scout" type of seaplane, traveling 100 mph with a five-hour endurance for scouting ahead of the fleet. To make this speed, he was willing to give up the observer and limit armament to thirty pounds. However, he also wanted a second seat installed so that, with a reduced fuel load compensating for the passenger and extra ammunition, the plane could be used for spotting gunfire or attacking enemy scouting planes. As well, he proposed fitting it to carry heavy bombs to be dropped by a "detaching apparatus" operated by the pilot.[62] That same month, Bristol wrote to the Burgess Company to request its pricing for certain modifications to the Burgess-Dunne type of plane: tandem seating, greater horsepower, trussing for heavier loads, a fuselage with reinforced nose "to protect the pilot in case of a nose dive into the water," and wings folding either forward or back, "as may work out best."[63] (This was probably the "Gun" plane for which BuOrd began designing a bombsight and bomb racks later that fall.)[64] Clearly something more was needed in aircraft design to make the airplane usable to the Navy, as none of the thirteen planes then in the inventory deemed operable were considered suitable "service" airplanes. By August, there were twelve more planes on order (including the two from Europe), and Bristol hoped one or more of those would be suitable for a service type.[65]

LIGHTER THAN AIR

The Navy also began moving to develop its lighter-than-air assets in 1915, though it had been interested in airships for some time. In Chambers' August 8, 1913, letter to the General Board (describing the then-present status of naval aviation and what had been done to date), he explained that the Navy had done little with lighter-than-air to date because he had preferred to wait and see how the Army was progressing with dirigibles.

As we have seen, the Army LTA program was already moribund at that time. Perhaps this is the reason he closed by suggesting that "it is time to be doing something in this line as the development [of airships] and the education [of airship personnel] will take time."[66] When the General Board submitted its recommendations for naval aviation to Daniels on August 30, 1913, it concluded that a complete air fleet for the Navy should include floatplanes and flying boats for scouting from the fleet or naval bases, dirigibles for distant scouting and mining operations, and eventually "the largest class of rigid battle airships" based at strategic locations. These larger "rigid battle airships" would be capable of carrying several tons of explosives over long distances and could not only scout well ahead of the fleet, but could also directly attack "ships, arsenals, docks, etc."[67] As mentioned previously, the Chambers Board also came out cautiously in favor of dirigibles for the Navy in its November 25, 1913, report.[68] In 1914, Director of Naval Aviation Mark Bristol responded to a query from the Connecticut Aircraft Company regarding airships, saying, "the use of dirigibles in the Navy, at least, seems at the present time to be a necessity. This, however, is an opinion that may be changed in the light of future experience with them."[69]

Despite this certainty that naval aviation needed airships, at least to evaluate, the Navy did not act until 1915. A big reason for this was cost. The Chambers Board estimated that a single airplane, with all equipment and spare parts, could be had for $10,000. By contrast, a relatively small (roughly 350,000 cubic foot) dirigible[70] with necessary equipment and spare parts would cost $173,000. The costs for hangars and other support facilities were similarly proportional.[71] At those prices, the Navy could have purchased almost double the number of planes in its inventory on July 1, 1914, for the cost of one dirigible. Airplanes certainly seemed, if not more cost effective, then at least less of a financial risk than airships. In any case, Congress had only appropriated an initial $25,000 for naval aviation in FY 1912 and a mere $10,000 for the next three budget cycles. Not until the FY 1916 budget (passed March 3, 1915) did Congress provide enough money ($1 million) for the Navy to even consider purchasing an airship.[72]

Of course, the question must be asked: given the expense of building and operating an airship, the lack of a domestic airship industry, the progress made in airplane capabilities, and even the Army's apparent abandonment of LTA aviation, why did the Navy continue to be interested in airships? One reason was the importance that foreign governments placed on them. A July 1914 report from the Division of Naval Intelligence to the General Board on foreign aeronautical strength noted that Germany, France, Great Britain, Russia, Italy, and Austria-Hungary not only had several airships each (from Austria-Hungary and Russia with three each, to Germany's twenty), but also had even more under construction. Belgium and Spain had two dirigibles each and even Japan had one, though none of these last three countries had any more under construction or on order at the time of the report.[73] At least as important was the large airship's lifting capacity, great endurance, great range, and the ability to hover. These were capabilities that the airplane did not have and would not develop in the foreseeable future, if at all.

Endurance and range were important to the Navy in the scouting role. In 1914, Naval Constructor Richardson explained to Bristol the necessity for great endurance in airplanes. Given the relative speeds of planes in 1914 and the speed of the fleet, Richardson noted that an airplane capable of six hours' endurance (a stretch for that period), if it were to fly straight ahead of the fleet, spot an enemy fleet at the limit of its search pattern, and return to report the sighting, would give the fleet a mere two or three hours' notice before the two fleets could see each other, assuming they were on closing courses. If equipped with a wireless transmitter, the plane could report the enemy fleet as soon as it was sighted, rather than having to physically return to give the report. However, that would only add an hour or two at most.[74] Though the airship would be marginally slower than an airplane, its much greater endurance (potentially measured in days rather than hours) would allow an airship to scout considerably farther ahead of the fleet while its great lifting capacity would easily permit it to carry a long-distance wireless set. The General Board reiterated these arguments several times to Secretary of the Navy Daniels in 1916, noting clearly that the different characteristics of the dirigible (especially the large rigid type) and the airplane would make them useful in different situations.[75] This idea that the rigid airship and the airplane were complementary rather than competing technologies, would persist in the Navy (and to some extent, the Army) well into the post–World War I era. Yet despite the apparent importance of the type from the earliest days of military aviation, the United States would not get its first rigid airship (Army *or* Navy) until after World War I.

However, Congress' $1 million for aviation in the FY 1916 budget finally allowed the Navy to begin developing lighter-than-air aviation. The Navy ordered its first dirigible (a nonrigid) from the Connecticut Aircraft Company in July 1915 and a free balloon and kite balloon from the Goodyear Company later that fall. The Navy also initiated training of its first LTA aviators at this time. Lt. Louis Maxfield first completed training in airplanes, getting his license in July 1915 and was then sent to Akron, Ohio, where he inspected the construction of the Navy's first balloon.[76] Joined in Akron by Lt. Cdr. Frank McCrary (who had been helping Bristol in Washington), the two began lessons in ballooning from Goodyear and were the first naval officers to take any sort of LTA training.[77] (Though McCrary had not attended Pensacola, he had received aviation training from the British in 1914 while assigned to the staff of the naval attaché in London.)[78] The free balloon (necessary for training) was completed and delivered to the Navy in December 1915, but because Pensacola did not yet have a hydrogen gas generating plant to inflate the balloon, operations there had to wait.[79] Maxfield accepted the delivery of the kite balloon soon afterward.[80] Meanwhile, McCrary went to Connecticut to supervise construction of the Navy's first airship, the DN-1, and train to fly it.[81]

For naval aviation advocates things would get worse again before they got better. In March 1916, Bristol left Washington for sea duty, specifically to command the *North Carolina* (now attached to the fleet) and "the Air Service in the field" (i.e., with the fleet). Bristol vowed to "keep up supervision over the development of Aeronautics in the Navy the same as I have heretofore." He clearly thought he would be able to continue as

DNA despite being at sea instead of in Washington. With Bristol out of town, the responsibility for the aviation desk in Washington effectively fell to Bristol's assistant, Lt. (jg) Clarence Bronson (who had been Chevalier's lone student when the *North Carolina* left for Europe).[82] Bronson was far too junior to hold such responsibility alone, so Benson put the aviation desk under the control of Capt. Josiah McKean, Benson's aide for material. (Though the CNO replaced the older aide system, Benson created a similar organization within his office.) McKean was not enthusiastic about the change, expressing his opinion that aviation did not belong under him, but Benson and Daniels specifically wanted McKean (an experienced administrator) to take charge of aviation and get some results.[83]

In April, a month after McKean added aviation to his other duties, he noted that the organizational chart still had the Aeronautic Station at Pensacola reporting to Bristol, although the *North Carolina* was no longer assigned there. McKean condemned this as inefficient and recommended a reorganization of the "Aeronautic Branch of the Naval Service" that would bring it in line with the organization of similar specialties, such as the submarine service and the torpedo service. As things then stood, Bristol—though commanding a ship assigned to the fleet—had a shore station reporting to him and he in turn reported directly to the CNO. Under McKean's proposed reorganization, aviation assigned to the fleet (at that time consisting solely of the *North Carolina* and its attached aircraft) would report through Bristol to the appropriate fleet commander in chief like any other vessel. Furthermore, Pensacola would no longer report through Bristol, but rather through the CNO's Material Section (under McKean) to the CNO.[84] Benson approved these recommendations, and by July 1916, Bristol was responsible only for fleet aviation.[85]

On June 8, McKean recommended that Bronson be ordered back to sea on board the *North Carolina*. For Bronson's relief at the aviation desk, McKean wanted someone of the rank of commander; a more senior officer in that position could relieve McKean of some of his responsibilities for coordinating the aviation work of the bureaus. McKean proposed that this officer be selected for his "professional ability" and then given a short course in aeronautics to familiarize him with the work of the desk.[86] Whether McKean specifically wanted a nonflying officer for the position (like Bristol) or was simply aware of the dearth of available flyers with rank is unclear. (The only aviator with appropriate rank was Mustin, who was out of favor in Washington at that time. Ellyson and Rodgers might have been possibilities, but both were on sea duty and neither had asked to return to aviation.)[87] What he got was John Towers, now a lieutenant with much seniority in grade, recently returned from his tour in London. Towers reported as Bronson's relief in mid-October. Bronson was still turning over the aviation desk when he was killed on November 8 during a bombing test when a hand-thrown bomb hit the plane and exploded prematurely.[88] Towers, though knowledgeable and experienced, had been away from Washington for close to two years—much had changed in that time. Bronson's death, occurring as it did while Towers was still learning the ropes, was a real blow. Still, Towers' personal knowledge of British aircraft and doctrine, both further developed than the U.S. Navy's, gave him a significant head start on the job of preparing naval aviation for probable participation in the "European War," to the extent this was permitted.

In the first few months after Towers assumed the aviation desk in Washington, operational command of aviation at sea and ashore would revert to non-flyers. In December, Bristol departed naval aviation for good when he left the *North Carolina* and turned over the duties (but not the title, which disappeared) of commander of the Air Service to Rear Adm. Albert Gleaves, commander of the Destroyer Force, Atlantic Fleet. Mustin was essentially forced out as the commandant of the Pensacola Naval Aeronautic Station in January 1917. His relief at Pensacola was Capt. Joseph Jayne, a man who had no knowledge of or experience with airplanes when he arrived.[89] As it happened, Jayne was only in command for about two months before the United States joined the Allies as a cobelligerent and upended all plans.

MODERNIZATION OF THE AIR FLEET

In late May and early June 1916, three officers (two pilots and a passenger) died in airplane crashes in the old pusher hydroplanes, little changed from the first Curtiss and Wright designs, which were all the Navy had for training new aviators. One consequence of these deaths was the culmination of the tensions between Bristol and Mustin. Led by Mustin, the aviators who investigated these accidents concluded that the unfortunate men might not have died had they been flying planes with enclosed cockpits and tractor engines: the exposed seats on the front of the wing did nothing to protect the crew from impact with water or land, and the pusher configuration put the engine behind them where it was likely to break free from its mountings and crush them in a crash.[90] Still in charge of naval aviation at the time, Bristol had insisted on acquiring pushers, rather than the tractors the aviators wanted. Bristol continued to insist that the pusher style was the best plane for the Navy. This was based on his own mental model—placing himself as an observer in imaginary aircraft and thinking about the respective restrictions to his vision, while overlooking the need to compromise for safety and comfort; he ignored Mustin's firsthand experience in an enclosed fuselage tractor (an experience which changed Mustin's own opinion of the tractor design).[91] In 1915, Bristol had written Mustin, "I hope you will not use up too much time on arguments in regard to tractors and pushers, because arguments no[t] based on facts and evidence will waste your time and mine. As far as I can find out from all information abroad, the tractor is doomed for military purposes."[92] Bristol remained opposed to tractors to the end of his time with naval aviation. In December 1916, writing to Bernard Smith, he described the order grounding the pushers as "hasty and ill-advised" and implied that he could have prevented its issuance had he not been away from his office when it came down.[93] Bristol's intransigence on the pushers furnished yet another reason for flyers to oppose being led by non-flyers.[94]

The prejudice against tractors went back to the beginning of naval aviation. Chambers had been against them as well. He believed the tractor layout was only a fad, and that aircraft designers would naturally return to the pusher as the best design.[95] Bristol effectively continued Chambers' policy on this point. But in an echo of events in the Army almost two and a half years earlier, the three fatalities provided the catalyst that finally gave the Navy a large fleet of modern airplanes: the CNO grounded the push-ers as unsafe, and placed a large order (thirty airplanes) for Curtiss N-9s, the first really modern Navy aircraft design. A month later, a hurricane hit Pensacola, destroying most of the now-grounded pushers.[96] Broadly speaking, the N-9 was essentially a JN-4 Jenny fitted with floats, though there was considerable internal redesign to account for the different stresses on a floatplane as well as longer wings and enlarged control sur-faces to account for the greater weight. The differences were enough to jus-tify a different model designation.[97] It had the tractor layout and enclosed cockpit desired by the aviators and was the first Navy design delivered with Deperdussin-style controls, the new U.S. military standard. (The Army had adopted the "Dep" controls in 1915). The Dep is the same sys-tem used in civil and heavy military aircraft today: a wheel or yoke rolls the plane from side to side, and pushing it forward puts the plane into a dive while pulling back makes it climb; the rudder is controlled with a foot bar or pedals.[98] The N-9 was also the first Navy airplane to be ordered in significant numbers: thirty at once, whereas earlier aircraft had been ordered in small lots of one to three at a time. (The N-9 would remain in service as a primary trainer until at least 1926!)[99]

However, Mustin's fight with Bristol over the tractors (fueled, no doubt, by his more general frustrations with Bristol's administration of aviation) was probably responsible for his relief as commander of Pensacola.[100] Certainly, this was Mustin's view: writing to his wife about his removal, he said, "I don't know of any possible reason . . . [other than] my rows with Bristol and the Department; there is no other reason admissible."[101] He went back to sea as executive officer of the battleship USS *North Dakota* where he would spend much of the coming war. Though he would not return to aviation duty until after the war, he retained his strong interest in naval aviation.[102]

There were other significant, though perhaps less momentous, events in 1916 as well. Officers and enlisted men continued to arrive in Pensacola for training in greater numbers. Yet due to a shortage of officers in the Navy, Pensacola began an experiment of training eight enlisted men (including two Marines) as aviators. A January press release explained that these enlisted flyers would "be able to steer the aeroplanes under the direction of the officer in command and leave the officer to attend to the more important duty of handling the plane or scouting and fighting." The officer would still be a trained aviator himself, but the enlisted flyer could take the place of a second naval aviator on flights requiring two pilots. On completing this training, some of these enlisted men were promoted to officers and took the title "naval aviator," while others remained in the enlisted ranks as "quartermaster (aeroplane)."[103]

McCrary (now the executive officer of Pensacola) and Maxfield were both back in Pensacola by late spring and began training officers in static and free ballooning as a preliminary to airship training. Two officers from each incoming class were selected for this instruction (additional to HTA training), but certification as LTA pilots could not be completed since there was no dirigible suitable for training students there (or anywhere in the United States) until well into 1917.[104] Among those officers to arrive for training in this last year before the war was Marine Lt. Roy Geiger (no relation to the Army's Lt. Harold Geiger). Geiger's arrival in Pensacola roughly coincided with the beginning of LTA training there; he was among the first to train in balloons as well as airplanes.[105]

MAKING THE AIRPLANE MILITARILY USEFUL

As previously noted, John Towers, Bernard Smith, and Victor Herbster had been in London, Paris, and Berlin, respectively, since shortly after the outbreak of war in Europe. They kept a close eye on aviation developments, reporting to Washington every two weeks the "gossip, rumors, and unsubstantiated news" (in the words of their superior, Mark Bristol), along with information that was more official. Towers, as we have already seen, even managed to get an illicit ride over the front! As Bristol explained to a group of Marines at the Advance Base School in Philadelphia, the Navy was focused on three new technologies: "The dirigible, the aeroplane and the submarine are the unknown factors in this war that we are interested in the most. It is hoped the 'try out' will be so complete that both the capabilities and limitations of these craft will be demonstrated."[106]

While the war was seen as a great opportunity to observe what airplanes could do, the Navy Department did little about the fact that even by American standards none of the Navy's planes were suitable for war use in 1914.[107] Bristol attempted to change this, noting that the absolute need for naval aviation "has been forced upon us by the experiences in this European war." In 1915 he warned the Navy Department, "We must meet the present conditions at once. The mass of work required is a condition and not a theory that confronts the Department." Bristol followed this warning with a number of recommendations for purchasing more aircraft, assigning more personnel (both officers and enlisted), and making changes in the Navy organization to make the Office of Naval Aviation more efficient.[108] However, his recommendations went nowhere.

Woodrow Wilson's Secretary of the Navy, Josephus Daniels, had asked the General Board in late 1915 for a report on the "value and use" of aviation and submarines in light of the European war. With respect to aircraft, the board responded that they had proven very valuable in observation, reconnaissance, and spotting, but specified that this had mostly occurred over land with only a few instances of their use in naval warfare. While having only hearsay evidence of aircraft scouting "on the high seas" (by which they presumably meant aircraft based on ships rather than ashore), the board had "no doubt at all of their value for this purpose." However, the board concluded that airplanes had only a slight ability to "inflict positive damage" on ships, despite recognizing the airplane's "considerable effect in the bombardment of military establishments and places occupied by the enemy" in land warfare.[109]

Mustin, the highest-ranking naval aviator at the time, held a different view. In a March 1916 hearing, he told the General Board, "When we started off in [aviation], we thought the principal function of the aeroplane would be for scouting; now we think the principal function is offensive power." Asked to clarify, Mustin said, "I mean carrying torpedoes or high explosives and attacking [the] enemy's battleships before or during battle." Clearly, he did not see such aerial attack as being decisive by itself as he emphasized that spotting from aircraft remained "a good thing and a very necessary thing."[110] That fall, Mustin suggested to the board that more than two airplanes could be assigned to each battleship, noting that the armored cruiser *North Carolina* (the only ship then carrying aircraft) carried five completely assembled airplanes. He further reasoned that if recent tests with a towed kite balloon showed it to be useful for spotting, then ships would not have to carry a slow-speed spotting airplane. In that case, Mustin suggested each capital ship have at least one torpedo plane and four to six high-speed fighters that could also be used for scouting, spotting, and light bombing.[111] Mustin certainly proposed a more aggressive aviation program than the board was willing to accept or endorse, but he was not proposing that the airplane could replace the battleship; in his view, airplanes would continue to work *with* the battleships by attacking the enemy's screening forces and slowing down the enemy's battleships in order to allow the U.S. battle line to come to grips with them. Actual development of the torpedo and fighter planes proposed by Mustin were still years away, at least in the United States.

The fleet held its annual exercises in Guantanamo from March 25 to April 8, 1916, and the commander of the Atlantic Fleet, Adm. Frank F. Fletcher, planned a series of tests for naval aviation. Bristol had just left the Office of Naval Aviation in Washington and now commanded the *North Carolina*, attached to the fleet. Fletcher outlined eleven different exercises for Bristol's aviators ranging from simply landing and taking off from the open ocean or launching from a catapult at sea, to testing radio communications and practicing reconnaissance, scouting, and mock bomb attacks against different targets. Fletcher even wanted all aircraft to use machine guns to attack a kite flown from a battleship.

Unfortunately, Bristol's planes and the *North Carolina* were not up to even Fletcher's simple tests. The ship did not have a catapult fitted at this time, so the planes could not be launched from one. (Richardson was in the middle of redesigning it.) Of the four planes assigned to the

North Carolina, three were open-seat Curtiss pushers (AH-16, AH-17, and AH-18), shortly to be condemned as unsafe for training purposes, while the fourth (AH-19) was an as yet untried aircraft of new design (a "Model S" tractor floatplane) from a new manufacturer (the Glenn L. Martin Company). Bristol admitted to Fletcher that none of the planes was capable of taking off or landing safely in the open sea, and none was fitted with machine guns. In any case, he considered it inadvisable to attempt to fire machine guns from any of the Curtiss pushers for fear of empty shell casings falling back into the propeller (a problem inherent in the pusher layout). He might have been willing to attempt it with the Martin, but it had crashed early in the exercises and been damaged beyond what the ship could repair.

The four senior pilots (Patrick Bellinger, William McIlvain [a Marine], A. C. "Putty" Read, and Godfrey deC. Chevalier) and junior pilots (Harold Scofield, William Corry, Grattan C. Dichman, and Harold T. Bartlett) assigned to the *North Carolina* did the best they could with the remaining exercises, but the planes had to carry "imaginary" bombs because they lacked the lifting capacity to carry real ones. They also had trouble reaching an altitude of six thousand feet, a real problem when "the latest reports from abroad" indicated that reconnaissance and bombing needed to occur between eight thousand and ten thousand feet to be considered "safe" from ground fire. None of the planes were equipped with radios, though the *North Carolina*'s crew, with the assistance of the fleet radio officer, installed a radio on one plane, however it could only send and was heavy and unreliable. Fletcher saw promise in aerial spotting, but the lack of radio and the ineffectiveness of other attempted communications methods brought a quick end to those exercises. Some method of effective and rapid communication, he declared, was necessary before aerial spotting could be effective. Scouting of the bay went well enough, but the aviators had no cameras for aerial reconnaissance, so they had to sketch their observations. Fletcher doubted the accuracy and usefulness of such sketches, insisting that the airplanes needed cameras "so that the details of a country can quickly be obtained." The Navy had taken its first aerial photographs in March 1915 but had done little to develop a camera for photoreconnaissance work until Fletcher's report highlighted the need.[112]

In the end, while he praised the aviators for having done all they possibly could with their aircraft, Fletcher felt that "the present equipment is entirely inadequate for employment with the Fleet . . . [and] has little military value." This was not a blanket condemnation of naval aviation, but merely reflected the state of development of aircraft represented by those used in the exercises. Fletcher concluded with a recommendation for more experiments "at regular intervals" for the benefit of both the air service and the fleet, though this did not happen before the United States entered the war roughly a year later.[113]

Further thinking about American preparedness remained largely unrealized. A few days after the Guantanamo exercises concluded, Daniels directed the General Board "to make a study of the possible naval uses of aircraft" and to recommend numbers, types, and intended roles for them.[114] The board replied in June that naval aviation to date had concentrated on improving aircraft and flying technique; little had been done to study "the proper strategic and tactical employment" of naval aircraft, making it difficult to give specific recommendations. Given the rapid advances in aviation seen in the European war, the board said the U.S. Navy was "obliged for the present to follow the lessons of the war." The board noted that aircraft could carry only small loads, and so, "it follows that aeronautics does not offer a prospect of becoming the principal means of exercising compelling force against the enemy." In other words, the board was considering only the present capabilities of airplanes, and not the potential for improved performance in the future—an interesting position considering that the General Board gave due consideration to aviation's future possibilities at other times. From this more limited perspective, the board determined that the airplane was useful primarily in strategic scouting, tactical patrol, and spotting. Bombing, they said, would be possible only with command of the air. Given the danger posed by enemy aircraft, all Navy aircraft should be armed, but the board did not recommend dedicated fighters. "From the experience of the war," the board informed

Daniels, "it seems that aircraft are used for the following naval purposes: Reconnaissance, Patrolling in advance of the fleet, Fleet and ship fire control, Fighting other aircraft, Attacking submarines, Attacking surface craft, Coast patrol, [and] Raids upon hostile coasts." (A footnote to "Patrolling in advance of the fleet" specified that the term "aircraft" in this use included airships.) The board concluded that aviation would not be as important to the Navy as to the Army; thus, "there is no substantial reason apparent at the present time to yield to the clamor of extremists who assert the supremacy of aeronautics as a naval arm." [115] Nor was there any urgency to develop naval aviation.

This did not, however, mean that aviation could be overlooked, and the board recommended a standard ships' aviation division to consist of two planes and appropriate personnel. All battleships of the *Delaware* and later classes should have one such division, while all scout cruisers should have two each. To patrol the coast, each naval district in the United States (except the Great Lakes), as well as the Panama Canal Zone, should have an air division of three large flying boats and four smaller aircraft of the same types planned for shipboard use.[116] Including a 25 percent reserve of aircraft, the General Board called for a total of 177 large flying boats and 352 of the ship's plane type, 35 landplanes (for the Advance Base Force and for defense of certain naval stations), 19 kite balloons, 20 non-rigid dirigibles and one large, experimental rigid airship for the Navy.[117] Later in 1916, the board reiterated that the experience of the European war "bears out theoretical considerations before the war, that aircraft and naval water-borne vessels and particularly submarines, are complementary."[118] Aircraft might be limited in their abilities, but that did not mean they could be ignored.

The board's efforts were not in vain: three more ships, the armored cruisers *Huntington* (ex-*West Virginia*), *Seattle* (ex-*Washington*), and *Montana* were ordered to be fitted for carrying and operating aircraft. The *Seattle* was to be the new flagship for the Destroyer Force, Atlantic Fleet (Admiral Gleaves' command).[119] But their time as aviation cruisers was to be brief. Due to the United States' entry into the war and the desperate need for escort ships, on October 5, 1917, the Navy ordered all three aviation ships (*Seattle, Huntington,* and *North Carolina*—*Montana* was in the shipyard, awaiting its catapult) to offload the aviation gear and remove the catapults.[120]

The Navy was also considering its need for personnel as well as equipment. The 1916 Naval Appropriations Bill (signed into law August 29) greatly expanded the Navy, including establishing a Naval Flying Corps and extending aviation to the naval militias. On the one hand, this new corps would allow officers to specialize in aviation; they would no longer need sea time for promotion. On the other hand, those officers of the corps would also be a community outside the line, much like engineers had been prior to 1899. None of the naval aviators wanted that; they felt it was important that aviators be part of the line.

The bill set the total personnel of the Naval Flying Corps at 150 officers and 350 enlisted men—totals that would *not* count against the manpower totals Congress otherwise set for the Navy and Marine Corps. To help fill out these numbers, Congress also included provisions to appoint up to 15 acting ensigns or second lieutenants into the Naval Flying Corps for aviation duties only. These appointments could be made to warrant officers, enlisted men, or civilians, though in November 1916, the Navy was still considering the details of exactly how this would be done.[121] (The General Board was strongly against using any but "officers and men trained in the navy and fully acquainted with the peculiarities of naval duties in general.")[122] In the end, the Naval Flying Corps never came into existence, perhaps because its provisions were unacceptable to most in the Navy, flyers and non-flyers alike. But the bill's provisions for the Naval Militia and Naval Reserve were important. The following spring, when the United States joined World War I, these provisions would allow the Navy to expand naval aviation tremendously by signing up civilians for the limited-duty Naval Reserve Flying Corps.[123]

CREATING A SEPARATE MARINE AVIATION IDENTITY

In the summer of 1916, Marine Corps aviation took its first practical steps toward establishing an independent identity. Bronson (then in charge of the aviation desk in Washington) wrote to McKean on June 24, recommending that the aeronautic section of the First Advance Base Force in Philadelphia be established as soon as possible. Bronson's letter laid out an aviation section similar to Bernard Smith's recommendation after the 1914 Advance Base Exercises: two landplanes, two seaplanes, and two kite balloons, along with the necessary hangars and field repair equipment. For personnel, Bronson proposed seven Marine officers (all aviators) and five flying enlisted Marines, as well as twenty-six enlisted mechanics. This mix would provide one officer, one flying enlisted man, and four ground crew for each plane, one officer (aviator/observer) and one enlisted man (ground captain) for each balloon, with four enlisted men for miscellaneous duties as needed. Bronson explicitly stated that all Marine flyers should be qualified at Pensacola as either naval aviators for the officers, or quartermasters (aeroplane) for the enlisted men. Bronson further recommended an additional landplane at the Advance Base school for training. At that time, two Marines, Alfred Cunningham and William McIlvain, were already at the Army Signal Corps Aviation School at North Island, San Diego, to learn land flying.[124] Once qualified by the Army as junior military aviators (i.e., landplane flyers), they would be able to use the Advance Base's school plane to instruct other Marine aviators in land plane flying at the Philadelphia base. As soon as enough men were trained and enough money was available, Bronson expected that another aviation section would be created for the planned Second Advance Base Force on the West Coast.[125]

In addition to endorsing an independent role for Marine aviation, Bronson's letter also laid out the relationship between the Navy, naval aviation, and Marine Corps aviation that still holds true today. He wrote, "It is desired that the affairs of the Advance Base organization aeronautic section be administered by Marine Corps headquarters. Whatever organization for Aeronautics exists in the Navy Department will assume only general supervision over the aeronautic affairs in the Marine Corps." The various Navy bureaus having responsibility for aviation material would be directly responsible to the Corps for that material, albeit always "in accordance with plans approved by the [Navy] Department." Bronson also recognized that the Marine Corps did not have any congressional appropriations for aviation (and thus had neither money to spend, nor authority to spend any, on aviation). Therefore, the equipment for the Advance Base aviation section would have to be charged against the Navy's Aeronautic Appropriation and loaned to the Marine Corps "in the same way as other material lent by the Navy." This basic relationship—Navy bureaus supplying aviation equipment (paid for out of Navy appropriations) to the Marine Corps, which manages all Marine aviation with general guidance from the Office of Naval Aviation (now NAVAIR)—has remained essentially unchanged since Bronson wrote this letter in 1916.[126]

George Barnett, then–major general commandant, made similar recommendations to CNO Benson on July 3. In his letter, Barnett specifically requested that one out of every four Marine officers qualifying at Pensacola be sent to learn land flying with the Army, since Marine aviators would work over land as well as sea. His recommendation for the size and composition of the aviation unit was based on the belief that its mission would be "for reconnaissance work only"—to warn the Advance Base and any ships anchored there of impending attack and not otherwise to assist the ground and surface forces. The General Board agreed with Barnett's recommendations, and Benson approved the plan on August 18.[127] The major general commandant issued a letter on August 24 announcing the approval for establishing an aeronautic unit with the Advance Base Force in Philadelphia.

This pushed Cunningham to begin planning for establishing the new unit, even while he was still in training with the Army in San Diego and simultaneously studying for his promotional exams. He wrote to Barnett a mere five days later, giving preliminary recommendations to open the aeronautic section for duty on April 1, 1917. Cunningham gave two reasons for this particular date. First, even if orders were placed immediately, the first airplanes could not be delivered until January at the earliest. However, the weather in Philadelphia would likely allow few flying days from January until the end of March. Thus, by not starting until April, the

Marine Corps could effectively wait to observe the performance of experimental airplane designs then being tested by the Army and Navy before committing to acquiring airplanes for the new unit, yet would not lose any flying days thereby. Second, the men assigned to the new unit could be sent to Pensacola for training during those months when little productive flying could be done in Philadelphia anyway. In the meantime, Cunningham (in his spare time) would finish putting together an itemized list of equipment, machinery, and tools that the Marine aviators would need for the new airfield as well as submit his plans for a new wooden hangar design.[128]

While still in training with the Army, and in addition to his other work for the Marines, Cunningham in late 1916 was briefly assigned to the Helm Board (the Navy Commission on Navy Yards and Naval Stations, under Rear Adm. James Helm, established to recommend sites for new Naval Bases to accommodate the Navy's expansion, particularly new submarine bases and air stations) as the expert on aviation for that board's visits to potential sites on the West Coast.[129] By the end of January 1917, Barnett ordered Cunningham to inspect the grounds at the Philadelphia Navy Yard and make recommendations for the physical organization of the Advance Base Aeronautic Unit.[130] When he arrived in Philadelphia on March 3, Cunningham had additional orders to take command of that unit.[131] Aircraft and men began arriving soon afterward, though it would be some weeks before the facilities were completed. Even so, conditions in Philadelphia were not the best for flying, and after an inspection trip, Bernard Smith declared that the landplane field was too small for any but experienced pilots to use safely.[132] It is not clear from the records whether any flying was done there before Congress declared war on Germany one month later and upended all existing plans.

CONCLUSIONS

The period from the beginning of 1914 to the beginning of 1917 saw great ups and downs for naval aviation. On the one hand, at the beginning of 1914, it finally seemed to have a suitably positioned patron. Admiral Fiske, a great believer in the airplane's potential for the Navy, had succeeded in gaining direct control of naval aviation. Once he had direct authority over naval aviation, there were a slew of orders in quick succession establishing Pensacola, attaching the *Mississippi* as an aviation ship, and establishing a new organization for naval aviation. Admittedly, many of these are unsigned memos, but there can be little question that they represent Fiske's ideas for correcting what he saw as shortcomings hindering aviation's development under Chambers.

After this initial flurry, Fiske appears to have stepped back from such direct control and turned over further responsibility to Captain Bristol. Given Fiske's statement that he had Bristol working on the other side of Fiske's own desk, we might question just how many of Bristol's orders were really Fiske's in all but name. Yet the lack of any noticeable change in management after Fiske left Washington for the Naval War College suggests that Bristol was acting on his own throughout, albeit perhaps having fully absorbed Fiske's ideas. Bristol, like Chambers before him, knew nothing of aviation before reporting to the job, and he never became an aviation enthusiast to the degree that Chambers did. Regardless, any benefits that Fiske might have extended to naval aviation were lost when Admiral Benson reported as the first Chief of Naval Operations and Fiske in turn left Washington for Newport.

Naval aviation histories record Benson as one of those "battleship admirals" opposed to naval aviation and seeking to block it. But Benson's reputation may be overblown by authors or storytellers within the community seeking an enemy to unite the naval aviation community against— a scapegoat to explain why things did not go their way. Once Benson had authority over naval aviation, little changed until it was time for Bristol to return to sea. At that point, Benson turned responsibility over to Captain McKean, who clearly stated that he did not think he should have it. Nevertheless, Benson insisted, not so that McKean could kill aviation, but rather because he expected McKean to make something of it. Once again officers who were not aviation enthusiasts were in charge, though McKean seems to have been duty bound to make the best of the bad job he felt he had been given, trying to set it on a better path by getting

Samuel Langley's Aerodrome A collapsing on launch, December 8, 1903. The very public failure ended Langley's funding and heaped ridicule upon him and the Army's Board of Ordnance and Fortification for supporting him. *National Air and Space Museum*

Baldwin Airship trials at Fort Myer, 1908. The photo clearly shows the distance between the airship's two crewmembers, as well as the large crowds that attended both this and the Wright airplane trials. *National Air and Space Museum*

1908 Wright Military Flyer at Fort Myer. The photo shows only a single set of controls, meaning the airplane could only be flown from the left seat. It also shows the side-by-side levers used to control roll and yaw. *Air Force Historical Research Agency*

Wright Military Flyer at College Park, 1910, showing the catapult weight (resting on the ground within the tower) and rail needed to take off. The whole system needed to be oriented into the wind (including leveling the rail) for takeoff. *Air Force Historical Research Agency*

Eugene Ely lands on USS *Pennsylvania* as the ship's crew watches, January 11, 1911. The feat, along with Ely's takeoff from USS *Birmingham* a few months earlier, proved that aircraft could operate from ships, though both flights used platforms that were experimental and temporary. *National Air and Space Museum*

Glenn Curtiss and his tractor hydroaeroplane being hoisted aboard USS *Pennsylvania* in February 1911, an exercise closer to operational practice than either of Ely's flights. Curtiss is holding on to the hook in case the cables holding the airplane break. Notice how the relative positions of seat and engine almost completely block the pilot's view forward. *Courtesy Naval History and Heritage Command*

Navy officer Theodore Ellyson with Army officers G. E. M. Kelly, John Walker, and Paul Beck (l-r) at Curtiss' North Island school, 1911. *National Air and Space Museum*

The Navy's Wright B-1 and some of the enlisted support crew at Greenbury Point, Annapolis, in 1911. The Navy flew the B-1 as a landplane for a few months before converting it to a floatplane in December 1911. *U.S. Naval Institute photo archive*

Benjamin Foulois flies the Wright Military Flyer over a line of mules at Fort Sam Houston, 1911. Given his altitude and attitude, he may be on approach for landing rather than in the middle of one of his "indoctrination flights." *National Air and Space Museum*

Theodore Ellyson in the Curtiss A-1, in position to launch from an inclined wire at Hammondsport, NY in September 1911. *Courtesy Naval History and Heritage Command*

Lt. Riley Scott adjusts his bombsight before a flight with Thomas Milling at College Park in 1911. This marked the Army's first official bombing experiments. Note the prone position necessary to use Scott's bombsight and the two bombs suspended directly under the bombsight. *National Air and Space Museum*

Aerial view of the Signal Corps Aviation School at Augusta, Georgia, 1911–1912. This photo gives a good sense of the typical flight altitude of the time as well as the experience of aviators in these early airplanes (suggested by the front of the landing skid with flag visible at the side of the frame—in the same position as in the bottom photo on the previous page). *Courtesy Air Force Historical Research Agency*

College Park in 1912. Aircraft are (l-r) a Wright B (possibly S.C. no. 3), the Wright C (S.C. no. 10), the Curtiss D (S.C. no. 2) and a Curtiss E (no. 6 or 8). *Courtesy Air Force Historical Research Agency*

Carteé, Photo. 255

Lieutenant Kirtland and Captain Chandler (holding Lewis machine gun) in a Wright airplane at College Park, 1912. These were the Army's first official experiments in firing weapons from an airplane. *National Air and Space Museum*

Benjamin Foulois and radio transmitter, likely in S.C. no. 5, c. 1912. Note the telegraph key affixed to the top of the elevator lever and the hinged wing warp/rudder lever that was standard on Wright airplanes by this time. *Air Force Historical Support Division*

First successful Navy catapult launch of an aircraft (C-1), Washington Navy Yard, November 1912. This design incorporated devices to hold the plane on the launch cart, and the cart on the rail, until the catapult shot was completed. The cart had to be fished out of the water after a launch. *Courtesy Naval History and Heritage Command*

Georgia "Tiny" Broadwick in place for a parachute jump from a Martin T flown by Glenn Martin. The photo is likely from a 1913 air meet in Chicago, but they gave the same demonstration to the Army in January 1914. The object above her head contains the parachute, which pulled out of the container when she jumped. *National Air and Space Museum*

Pensacola Naval Aeronautical Station in 1914. The aircraft are a mix of Curtiss flying boats (Cs) and floatplanes (As), with one Wright (the B-3) fifth from the bottom. The planes would taxi close to the beach, where the engines would be stopped and the planes put on beaching trolleys and pushed up the ramps into the hangars, if necessary. The process was reversed for launching. *U.S. Naval Institute photo archive*

The A-3 on a beaching trolley at Veracruz, Mexico. Note the boat flags attached to the struts at each wingtip, added specifically for the Veracruz flights. *Courtesy Naval History and Heritage Command*

Herbert Dargue in the Burgess I (S.C. no. 17) with his ground crew in Manila, 1914. Though the airplane featured an enclosed fuselage, the wings and propellers were still of the Wright design. This is very noticeable in the shape of the propeller. *Courtesy Air Force Historical Research Agency*

John Towers, Glenn Curtiss, and British aviator Cyril Porte (l-r) in front of the *America* flying boat, 1914. When World War I ended the attempt to fly the Atlantic, Porte took the aircraft and the design back to the United Kingdom, where the *America* type flying boat saw use as a patrol aircraft around the British coast. *National Air and Space Museum*

AH-7, a tailless Burgess Dunne aircraft, fitted with bomb racks and a bomb under the lower port wing in September 1916. This marks the Navy's first experiments with a bomb rack. The object below the figure's knee may be either a compass or a bombsight. If the former, then the object on the float's nose might be the bombsight. Note that this airplane features a "ripple" camouflage pattern, most visible on the underside of the upper port wing and in the color bands on the struts and leading edges. The tapered shape amid the pontoon struts is an additional gas tank. *National Air and Space Museum.*

The AB-2 (the former C-2) is put into place on USS *North Carolina* for the first catapult launch from a ship. Henry Mustin made this launch in November 1915. The low height of the launch rail limits the length of the track. *Courtesy Naval History and Heritage Command*

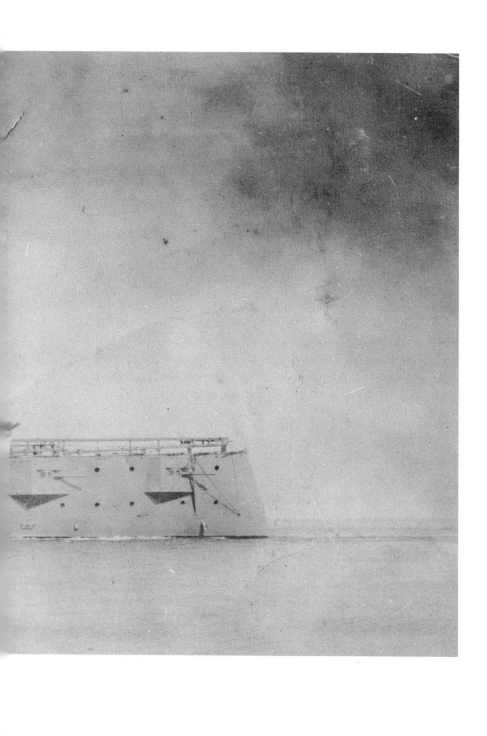

The permanent catapult installed on USS *North Carolina* in 1916. The aviators referred to it as the "scenic railway." The tracks on either side of the mast could store additional aircraft on launch carts. This design permits a longer acceleration length than the first design. The other aviation cruisers were also equipped with this design before all catapults were removed in 1917. *Courtesy Naval History and Heritage Command*

Herbert Dargue (in shadow at center) amid an unfriendly crowd outside Chihuahua City, 1916. The crowd was reportedly willing to leave the plane alone while pictures were being taken. The U.S. star marking in use at this time is visible on the tail, as is the Signal Corps number (43) on the side of the fuselage. *Air Force Historical Support Agency*

someone more senior to replace Lieutenant (junior grade) Bronson at the aviation desk and straightening out Bristol's attempt to keep hold of his prior job despite reassignment.

The reopening of Pensacola as a permanent Naval Aeronautical Station gave naval aviation a geographic stability that had been lacking up to that point. Increasing congressional appropriations also permitted the purchase of more aircraft and the training of more aviators. On the other hand, the aircraft being purchased by the nonflying Bristol continued to be pushers of a type that the aviators themselves had come to see as lethally dangerous, especially in the training role. The situation only changed with Benson's preliminary approval to ground the pushers in June 1916 (replicating the Army's decision more than two years earlier), followed by the fait accompli of a hurricane destroying most of them a month later. The result was the Navy's purchase of its first "modern" aircraft, the N-9. The Navy's initial order for thirty N-9s (of an eventual total of 560 by the end of 1918) represented a new stage in aeronautical procurement for the Navy; never again would it purchase only a handful of aircraft for operational purposes.

Much like the Army over the course of 1914, the Navy in 1916 had passed a tipping point in aircraft and personnel to permit a separation between the work of training new aviators and the experimental work aimed at making the airplane militarily useful. The annual fleet exercises in spring 1916 saw the first attempt to put naval aviation through its operational paces, although what it demonstrated was that the aircraft on hand were not up to the challenge. Newer, more capable aircraft designs were soon on the way, along with plans to create a squadron of catapult-equipped aviation cruisers to operate with the fleet and advance operational doctrine. Meanwhile, the massive expansion of the Navy authorized in the 1916 appropriations bill included more money for naval aviation and established a naval aviation reserve force. The latter was not significant at the time, but would have a huge impact on naval aviation in the coming war.

Finally, Marine Corps aviation had taken its first steps toward creating an identity independent of naval aviation. The creation of the aeronautic unit with the Advance Base Force in Philadelphia at the start of 1917 made real the idea Cunningham had proposed back in 1912. That said, it was quite small—in numbers, roughly equivalent to naval aviation in 1911 with only five qualified Marine aviators on hand and an authorized strength of four airplanes and a balloon. Nevertheless, this was the core around which the Marine Corps would build its aviation force in the coming war.

8

ARMY 1915–1917

The European War, Scandal, and a Deployment

The years of 1915 and 1916 were significant years for Army aviation. The growth from 1914 continued and the organization itself became more formalized and professional, though some of this was in reaction to a scandal. The Aviation Section of the Signal Corps would also learn a lot from watching the European war, even if (much like with the Navy) those lessons had little effect on training or the forces in the field. Indeed, when the 1st Aero Squadron deployed operationally with the Mexican Punitive Expedition, it brought little more than its own experiences while demonstrating the inadequacy of aircraft available to the U.S. Army at the time. The Aviation Section was thoroughly unprepared for Congress' sudden declaration of war in April 1917, but very receptive to the drastic changes that would be needed.

The Inspector General's January 1915 report on the aviation school set the Army searching for a permanent location for the school that the Army could own directly. But another significant recommendation from that report was for the Army to send aviators to the war in Europe as observers. Shortly after the fighting began in August 1914, both Scriven and Reber requested to have aviators included among the official U.S. Army observers assigned to the belligerents. Reber pointed out that none of the officers already assigned to observation duties had enough knowledge of aviation to make reports that would be of value to the Aviation Section. Nevertheless, the adjutant general refused the requests, saying that there were no vacancies with any of the belligerents to send additional officers. The isolationist Wilson administration wanted to keep the U.S. military observers of the war small in number, to minimize the chances of the United States being drawn into the war. Even if the Wilson administration had been of another mind, Great Britain, at least, had decided in September to prevent visits to the British front lines by observers from neutral countries.[1]

Fortunately for the Aviation Section, Squier was still on duty in London as the military attaché. Originally, he was not supposed to remain in London for more than two years. The war broke out before his time was up, however, and Squier's connections proved too beneficial for the Army to relinquish. Partly, these important connections stemmed from his own efforts and reputation as a scientist. While he concentrated on radio development, Squier also retained an interest in aviation. Prior to the war, he had sent back reports on the training, organization, and even doctrine being generated by the Royal Flying Corps (RFC), the Aviation Section's counterpart in the British Army. He also forwarded copies of official reports and publications on British aviation activities including, at one point, a set of confidential blueprints provided to him personally by the British Army's director general of Military Aeronautics. This access made Squier so valuable that the American ambassador in London, Walter Page, personally requested that his tour as attaché be extended to a full four years. Reluctantly, Secretary of War Garrison agreed to extend Squier's assignment in London until January 1915.[2]

The commencement of hostilities in what would eventually be called World War I only enhanced Squier's value as attaché. Both British Foreign Secretary Edward Grey and Secretary of State for War Lord Kitchener wanted to maintain American friendship in the hope of bringing the United States into the war. At a time when Britain was prohibiting access of neutral observers to the British Expeditionary Force (BEF) in France, and even dragging its feet at allowing observers from allied nations such as Russia and Japan to the front, Kitchener granted special permission to Squier. Kitchener had discussed his plan to send Squier to observe the BEF with General Joseph Joffre and General Sir John French, commanders of the French and British forces in France, respectively, but the offer came as a surprise to Squier. With the willing support of Ambassador Page, Kitchener spirited Squier out of London and granted him carte blanche to see whatever he wanted of the front lines. Since Squier's career had been almost entirely in technical services, he was ill-prepared to report on topics of interest to the combat arms, but he did bring back much information of interest to the technical branches of the U.S. Army. The importance of these connections and Squier's ability to maintain them meant that Squier would be kept on duty in London until 1916, when problems with the Aviation Section in the U.S. led the Army to recall him to straighten things out.[3]

During his visit to the front lines, Squier took special interest in aviation. On numerous visits to aviation squadrons, he observed the usefulness of aerial reconnaissance and the vital need for aerial artillery observation. The British and French forces had already demonstrated that pre-war estimates of ammunition usage and resupply rates were considerably lower than that actually experienced. This need led the British Army to establish large ammunition dumps and truck parks (for transporting supplies), while port facilities took on greater importance. Squier reported that German attacks on these targets through aerial bombardment could seriously affect the fighting capabilities of the Allied armies. In addition to talking with lower-echelon aviation commanders, Squier spent many hours discussing the changing role of aviation in the war with old friends such as General Sir David Henderson, commander of the RFC, and Colonel F. H. Sykes, Henderson's chief of staff. As a result of such efforts, Squier's official report to the War Department on this tour contained a great deal of information about the operation of aircraft themselves, as well as their influence on strategy and tactics, ranging from the obvious importance of aerial reconnaissance to the growing offensive uses of airplanes in bombardment. Included in the latter was his observation of the indirect effect of bombardment on field commanders' choice of headquarters. Whereas previously it was common for European generals to choose hotels or large villas where the military staff could live and work in some comfort, these same generals were now opting for locations less easily identified from the air! As well, he emphasized the great leaps in performance made by new airplane designs and stated that the European armies were finding it necessary to design military aircraft for specific combat roles. The fine-tuning of designs for reconnaissance, artillery observation, bombing, and pursuit roles stood in stark contrast to American belief that only a single airplane design (or perhaps two) was necessary for field work and that offensive uses of the airplane (that is, pursuit and bombing) were of only minimal importance.[4]

Squier's reports on aviation both in Britain and at the front in France likely contributed to a General Staff Corps document published in 1915 titled *Military Aviation*. The paper used information from the war in Europe to analyze "various aeronautical appliances in regard to their practical value in campaign." For the first time, the General Staff embraced offensive uses of the airplane, recommending one squadron of twelve aircraft (three companies of four planes each) with each field division. This larger squadron would add four planes to the previously prescribed reconnaissance and spotting aircraft: two high-speed aircraft for long-distance reconnaissance and for "fighting the enemy's aerial craft," and two "battle machines for the purpose of bomb dropping and offensive work against enemy material of all sorts." In other words, the General Staff wanted two fighters (or as they were known at the time, "pursuit planes") that could double as long-range reconnaissance craft and two bombers in each squadron. Similar composite squadrons would also be needed for mobile and fixed coast defense units and for garrisons stationed outside the United States (e.g., Hawaii, Panama, and the Philippines). Coastal and overseas locations would need, in addition, seaplanes for over-water operations.[5]

The paper also addressed lighter-than-air aviation, noting the great importance in Europe of captive kite balloons for spotting artillery and for constant observation of enemy movements. "In many cases," it said, "the captive balloons are used in conjunction with aeroplanes." The planes would locate targets invisible to the balloonist and mark their location for the balloon observer before continuing to other duties. The General Staff also examined the usefulness of dirigible balloons, describing and comparing nonrigid, semirigid, and rigid types. The General Staff made clear that it was not thinking of dirigibles as alternatives to airplanes, but as complements to airplanes and captive balloons, each assigned to the task best suited to it. Still, the staff paper hedged a bit, noting that dirigibles had not yet been a deciding factor in combat on either land or sea, but that all belligerents were nevertheless developing them "to the greatest extent possible."[6]

The General Staff paper went on to address the lessons of the European war to date in more detail, describing the advantages of aerial reconnaissance and spotting. In fact, these advantages were so great that the fighter (as a specialized type) had developed to attempt to deny those advantages to the enemy. "The only way enemy aeroplanes can be dealt with is by aeroplanes," stated the report, "because they are difficult targets [to hit] from the ground. To gain control of the air, a great preponderance in number and efficiency of aircraft is necessary." Aerial bombing had not yet achieved any great destruction, but a new type of plane, specifically designed "for dropping bombs and battle purposes," had considerable success in raids of thirty to sixty planes against "railways, roads, bridges, and hostile parks of various kinds." Organization of the planes was also important, and the General Staff noted that most belligerents assigned only one class (or type) of plane to a squadron—the typical squadron consisting of six planes and two spares—and attached all squadrons to field army headquarters. (The British were a notable exception, assigning twelve planes "of different classes" to squadrons.) Though aviation in Europe was assigned to army headquarters, which then distributed resources as and when needed, the staff expected that airplanes for artillery spotting would soon be assigned permanently to artillery regiments so as to make planes and crews immediately available to them at all times.[7]

The squadron personnel were also basically similar among the belligerents, with officers serving as pilots and observers while enlisted men mostly comprised the ground crews. With the increasing importance of aviation, however, all belligerents experienced difficulties training enough officers and had begun to train NCOs as pilots. The combatant nations were also training observers from relevant branches of the service to match the different missions: engineers to assess damage following a bombing attack, artillerists for artillery observation, and staff officers for reconnaissance of troop positions.[8]

Applying these lessons to the U.S. Army's Aviation Section, the General Staff noted that the development of its aviation units had been slow due to the considerably smaller amount of money spent on them compared to that in Europe. Restrictions on age, rank, and marital status also reduced the population from which the Army could draw potential aviators. The staff recommended legislation to allow the Army to obtain sufficient pilots, officer-observers, and planes equipped with better engines. In addition, it recommended the creation of captive balloon units and development of different types of dirigibles for the Army. Many of these recommendations also appeared in Scriven's annual report on the state of the Signal Corps issued later that fall.[9]

There is no direct evidence that Squier's reports from London and the front lines influenced the change in attitudes toward offensive airplanes or the renewed interest in LTA aviation. But Squier's reports went to several senior Army officers, including Scriven and the General Staff, and their opinions in 1915 had changed dramatically from just one or two years earlier. The Hay Committee hearings in August 1913 had revealed that neither Scriven nor the General Staff (according to its representative, Billy Mitchell) believed in an offensive role for aircraft, and Scriven had downplayed the potential importance of bombing in his 1914 annual report. The difference in attitude with respect to LTA development was not quite so extreme. Balloons and dirigibles were mentioned several times in the hearings but always rather tentatively, as a technology whose usefulness had not yet been demonstrated; the Army should keep an eye on them nonetheless. Scriven had made a similarly tentative case for renewed LTA development in his 1914 annual report and requested $500,000 in the FY 1915 budget to restart the Army's balloon and dirigible program. Secretary Garrison, however, removed the balloon funding before forwarding the Army's budget requests to Congress.[10] Still, the discussion of LTA aviation in both the General Staff paper and Scriven's annual report shows a greater sense of urgency in renewing Army development of balloons and dirigibles.

While Squier's reports may well have influenced changes in attitude toward LTA aviation and offensive uses of aircraft among the General Staff, the reports apparently did not reach much further down the chain of command than Scriven. Reber seems to have had access to them as well as to the Navy's assistant attachés' reports.[11] However, none of this information made it to the Aviation School. A student would later recall that, as late as 1916, there was little awareness of the role aviation was playing in the European war and even less discussion of it. What information that did make it to San Diego came through published accounts of the war, foreign officers who visited the school (such as a pair of Spanish flyers who inspected San Diego in June 1915), and Americans serving with relief agencies (such as the American Ambulance Service) and expatriate combat units (most famously the Lafayette Flying Corps).[12] In any event, both the Aviation School and the Aero Squadron had more immediate issues to occupy their attention.

One issue that finally dissipated over the course of 1915 was the rivalry between Curtiss and Wright aviators. The January report from the inspector general's office observed that the Aviation Section had no more Wright-made airplanes in inventory, and none of the Burgess-Wright planes had the original Wright lever controls. (In any case, Burgess had ceased making Wright designs under license toward the end of 1914, so there would be no more new Wright planes from Burgess.) Furthermore, the aviators had concluded that Curtiss' designs were best suited to service use. This meant that, regardless of which plane new students flew for primary training, they would have to learn the Curtiss yoke system before they could be useful in the field. In September, however, the Army finally began to transition to a standard control for all aircraft when the school installed a Deperdussin ("Dep") control system on a trainer and Curtiss began delivering new airplanes with the Dep controls. The Dep system finally answered Scriven's 1913 request for a single flight control system for all Army planes. Transition to the Dep also helped end the Wright/Curtiss rivalry that had occasionally proven detrimental to the smooth functioning of Army aviation.[13] (As described previously, the Navy made a similar transition to the Dep controls less than a year later.)

A Scandal

The easing of tensions between Wright and Curtiss pilots occurred at about the same time that tensions increased between Army flyers and their non-flying superiors. On November 5, 1914, Glenn Martin crashed while demonstrating a new airplane. His passenger, Capt. Lewis E. Goodier Jr., was seriously injured and spent a long recovery in the Army hospital in San Francisco where he was close to his father, Lt. Col. Lewis Goodier Sr., judge advocate for the Western Department. While in the hospital, the recovering pilot received letters from his fellow aviators complaining of irregularities involving Cowan. Goodier Jr. conferred with his father, who aided the group in bringing charges against Cowan on April 24, 1915, accusing him of fraudulently drawing flight pay, obtaining flying qualification for an unqualified officer, and dishonestly claiming credit for a flying achievement made by someone else. Tied up with the formal charges were accusations of favoritism and a disdain for the flyers' safety. Fundamentally, the charges reflected the aviators' unwillingness to be commanded by someone who was not a flyer, as well as their assessment of Cowan specifically. Though the charges were filed with the Western Department, Cowan, with Reber's assistance, succeeded in having the case transferred to the Judge Advocate General Corps (JAG) in Washington. The JAG investigated, eventually deciding that Cowan and Patterson were legally entitled to their flight pay and dismissed all charges as unsupported.[14]

This decision might have been the end of things, except that Cowan brought his own charges against Goodier Sr., essentially accusing him of inciting the flyers to rebel. Ironically, Goodier Sr.'s court-martial, which ran from October 18 to November 18, 1915, brought out many of the issues of Signal Corps mismanagement that the flyers had hoped to expose in accusing Cowan in the first place. In fact, the nature of Cowan's charges against Goodier Sr. allowed the defense to submit evidence that exposed Reber's complicity in many of Cowan's actions, including correspondence between Reber and Cowan that revealed favoritism in promotion and punishment, cover-ups, and indifference to safety issues. The letters also demonstrated Cowan's efforts to have officers whom he disliked removed from aviation. The court-martial found Lieutenant Colonel Goodier guilty, but the evidence submitted at trial led the Army to investigate Signal Corps control of the Aviation Section. Constituted by Chief of Staff Hugh Scott on February 12, 1916, the Garlington Board (led by the inspector general, Ernest A. Garlington, and also included the adjutant general and the president of the Army War College) investigated the issues and found enough evidence of wrongdoing that Secretary of War Newton Baker censured Scriven for failing to personally discipline his command. Baker also censured Reber for numerous things, including failure to keep Scriven informed. Consequently, Baker relieved Reber of command of the Aviation Section on May 5, 1916, and selected Squier as the new head of aviation. Mitchell had been acting head of the section since April—his first assignment to aviation—and continued in that role until Squier returned from London on May 20. Baker likewise relieved Cowan of command of the Signal Corps Aviation School on April 3 (and from aviation duty altogether in July), replacing him with Col. William Glassford. Following the turmoil, Senator Joseph Robinson (D-AR) introduced a resolution in January 1916 to create a joint House and Senate committee to investigate Army management of aviation, but the bill was defeated in the House. Still, the muck stirred up as part of the Goodier court-martial and subsequent investigations renewed congressional interest in separating aviation from

the Signal Corps. Moreover, the initial charges against Cowan only reinforced the growing perception of Army aviators as insubordinate junior
officers.[15] The whole episode also reveals a growing lack of consensus
within the Army aviation community, with fractures along flyer/non-flyer
lines as well as differences between headquarters in Washington and operators in the field.

The 1st Aviation Squadron also had concerns more immediate and
closer to home than what aviation was doing in the European war. Increased
tensions along the Mexican border in April 1915 led Gen. Frederick
Funston, commanding the border forces, to request a plane to provide aerial observation for his artillery.[16] Thus, the Army ordered Milling and 2nd
Lt. Byron Jones (a cavalry officer who had earned his JMA qualification in
August 1914) to Brownsville, Texas, on April 13, along with a detachment
of eight enlisted men, and S.C. No. 31, a Martin T. The detachment arrived
April 17, and Jones and Milling made their first flights three days later,
reconnoitering around the Mexican city of Matamoros, just across the Rio
Grande from Brownsville. Later that day, however, Jones hit a ditch while
taxiing the plane after landing, damaging the plane beyond repair. Milling
requested either a new fuselage or another plane, but Reber denied both
requests. On April 30, the adjutant general overruled Reber, ordering S.C.
No. 31 shipped back to San Diego. Cowan, still in command of the school,
sent S.C. No. 37 (another Martin T) to Texas as a replacement, and aerial reconnaissance resumed. Overall, the detachment did comparatively
little flying and would have been of limited use in spotting for the artillery, if needed, since the plane did not have a radio, and the local terrain
and foliage meant that messages dropped from the plane would be almost
impossible to find. Reber asked for the return of the detachment on May
18, pointing out that the field artillery unit it was intended to support had
been relieved of border duty. The detachment returned to San Diego on
May 27, having only scratched the surface of the needs and difficulties of
deploying to the field.[17]

Meanwhile, Foulois reorganized the 1st Aero Squadron into two
companies. Its division had introduced problems: because some officers

entered training as second lieutenants and others (prior to the act of July 18, 1914) entered as captains, there was no correlation between rank and flying experience, much less flying skill. Furthermore, assignment of aero company commanders had to follow Army rank (e.g., a second lieutenant could not command a captain), but the ongoing flight instructional duties of the company commanders required flying experience and skill. (The Army had been fortunate that Foulois' rank, experience, and skill all met the requirements for squadron command.) To address these problems, Foulois replaced the two companies with several sections: headquarters, shop, supply, training, and eight airplane sections. Each of the airplane sections consisted of two officers, one plane, and the necessary maintenance crew. Pilots and assistant pilots for each plane could be paired up so that relative rank matched relative skill and experience, and the best pilot—regardless of military rank—could be put in charge of training the squadron in field work.[18] The immediate problem of mismatch between rank and flying experience would eventually disappear as aviation matured and developed its own senior officers, but the "start-up" problems that resulted in these mismatches would persist for many years.

The reorganized squadron also began to receive new planes. In May, Curtiss delivered the first of eight new JN-2s (S.C. Nos. 41–48) that the Army had ordered to equip the squadron and in June delivered the remaining seven. The planes were supposed to embody the best of the Curtiss J and N models—hence the combined designator—but Curtiss considered these planes an extension of the J design and so gave it the suffix "2." The first eight planes were only enough to equip one Army squadron with the bare minimum needed for operations. That is, they were insufficient to supply the spare planes called for in the table of equipment. Still, the total order for fifteen planes represented the Army's largest single order of a single airplane design to date. Fortunately, the order was no larger, since experience would soon prove that these aircraft were far from a perfect design.[19]

On July 26, the entire 1st Aero Squadron left San Diego by rail for Fort Sill, Oklahoma, to participate in firing exercises with the field artillery. The fifteen officers, eighty-five enlisted men, and one civilian mechanic arrived at Fort Sill on July 29 along with their camp equipment and eight JN-2s. Through August 13, the squadron spent much of its time setting up camp and making needed improvements to the area, but flights commenced on August 10. Shortly thereafter, the Army ordered two plane sections (a total of two aircraft and four aviators) to Brownsville to work alongside artillery batteries also dispatched from Fort Sill. The plane sections left on August 14 and 15, leaving six aircraft in Oklahoma.[20]

Shortly after the squadron had taken possession of the first JN-2 in May, the pilots began to notice problems with the new design. Despite the squadron's attempts to alter the planes to address the shortcomings, things only got worse after arriving at Fort Sill. Six of the twelve engines delivered to San Diego with the planes were immediately condemned as unusable. Another required overhaul before installation, but it was not ready when the squadron left San Diego. Foulois' request that the Curtiss Company expedite delivery of new engines and other spare parts had no effect, and by September 1, all of the planes at Fort Sill were grounded. Following a crash on August 12 that seriously injured the pilot, Lt. R. B. Sutton, and killed his passenger, Capt. G. H. Knox of the Quartermaster Corps, the remaining pilots held an informal meeting about the JNs. The ten youngest officers believed the JN-2 was underpowered and unstable, possessed an overly sensitive rudder, and was shoddily constructed. In short, they felt these planes were unsafe to fly, especially with passengers. Foulois and Milling, the two senior officers, agreed that the planes had many shortcomings (Curtiss was, indeed, experiencing quality control problems connected to its sudden growth in order to meet large war-related European orders), but asserted that they were safe enough if flown within limits.[21]

The four pilots sent to Brownsville with the artillery batteries also experienced airplane problems. Under the command of 1st Lt. J. C. Morrow, the two sections arrived in Texas on August 18. Morrow immediately telegraphed Scriven to inform him that although the Brownsville airfield had been sufficient for Milling and Jones in their Martin T on their earlier deployment, it was too small for the underpowered JN-2s.

He requested permission to prepare another field a few miles away and also requested that the Signal Corps send two Martin Ts to replace the JN-2s. The response from Washington permitted Morrow's detachment to prepare the more distant field for use but specified that they still had to camp in or near the Army post. The CSO's office (possibly Reber as acting CSO)[22] was clearly perturbed at the request for different planes, replying, "You are equipped with service machines and none [sic] others will be furnished. If you cannot meet the incidents of active service you will be superseded." Thus, Morrow and his three pilots, all lieutenants—Jones, Arthur Christie, and H. W. Harms—tried their best to complete their missions with the JNs: a mix of artillery spotting practice and actual reconnaissance in search of Mexican "bandits" (a term broadly applied to any Mexican bands attacking on U.S. soil)[23] operating along the border. The pilots, however, were plagued with the same airplane problems as the group remaining at Fort Sill: poor handling and lack of power. On September 5, Morrow was injured in a crash attributed to the poor flying qualities of the JN-2. The Signal Corps ordered Capt. Townsend Dodd from the Aviation School to Brownsville to replace Morrow in command while the latter recovered, but Jones was in charge until Dodd could arrive. In the meantime, at the direction of the commanding officer at Brownsville, Jones issued a report declaring the JN-2s unfit for military service as they unnecessarily endangered the lives of anyone who flew in them.[24]

Reber claimed to be unaware of any problems with the JN-2s prior to receiving Jones' report. His claim is plausible: Carberry, who was inspecting their construction at the Curtiss plant, had expressed reservations about the climb rate of the planes but officially had recommended their acceptance. V. E. Clark, in San Diego, had inspected the planes following their delivery and recommended condemning them all, but apparently never made a formal report to that effect. Assistant Naval Constructor Jerome Hunsaker, the Navy's aeronautical design expert, had conducted wind tunnel tests on the JN-2 design in August and found numerous instabilities at high angles of attack (as when taking off, landing, or flying slowly), but his analysis did not reach the CSO's office until after Jones' report. When

Scriven eventually did read Hunsaker's report, he called Glenn Curtiss to Washington to discuss the issues, and Curtiss agreed to modify the Army's JN-2s, producing a plane almost identical to the new JN-3. (The Army had already ordered two JN-3s in August.) Curtiss sent one of his men and the necessary parts to Fort Sill to perform the necessary work on the 1st Aero Squadron's JN-2s.[25]

The Army's first two factory-built JN-3s arrived at Fort Sill in September, and the squadron tested them against both the original JN-2 and the upgraded JN-2. They determined that the JN-3 was an improvement but not a great one.[26] Foulois then sent two JN-3s (likely conversions rather than new-built) to Brownsville to replace the JN-2s.[27] By mid-January 1916, the Army had no more JN-2s in its inventory, because each had been either condemned or converted to the JN-3 standard. The danger was past, but Reber's and Cowan's actions (or inactions) in this matter emerged in the Goodier court-martial in October 1915 and contributed to the impression that the two men cared only for maintaining their own power, often at the expense of their subordinates' safety.[28]

The modification of JN-2s into JN-3s permitted the aviators at Fort Sill to resume work with the field artillery but only on a limited basis. One artillery commander reported that the few flights the aviators undertook in conjunction with artillery firing practice were of little benefit to the artillery. However, the flights did reveal that such aerial observation required observers trained in both artillery correction practices and aerial reconnaissance in order to recognize features from the air and provide the necessary corrections in a form the artillerists understood. The time at Fort Sill also gave the Aero Squadron experience with their new camp gear and trucks. In FY 1915, the Army had equipped the squadron with several heavy trucks, which, under Foulois' direction, the squadron converted into custom support vehicles, including one equipped as a portable machine shop; some fitted with tanks to carry oil and fuel; and others modified to carry tools, spare parts, ground crew, and other equipment. These trucks, along with a car and a few motorcycles, would play an important role in November when the squadron moved from Fort Sill to the new aeronautic center near Fort Sam Houston.[29]

ESTABLISHING THE 1ST AERO SQUADRON IN SAN ANTONIO

San Antonio was to be the new, permanent home of the 1st Aero Squadron. Scriven hoped that this would be the first of many aeronautic centers around the country. He and Foulois had inspected the land allotted to the aviators at Fort Sam Houston and had begun planning to convert it into a permanent aeronautic facility, later named Dodd Field.[30] By mid-November 1915, though much work remained to be done, enough buildings had been constructed to allow the squadron to move in. With the scheduled period of work at Fort Sill ending, Scriven ordered the squadron to San Antonio.[31]

Foulois saw the five-hundred-mile trip as an opportunity to practice the independent, cross-country movement necessary for field operations and received permission to make the move "by air." (The bulk of personnel and equipment would go by squadron vehicles.) He planned the airplanes' movement to match the speed of the ground elements, and thus expected to fly about one hundred miles per day (the distance he thought the trucks could travel in a day), taking five days to travel from Fort Sill to Fort Sam Houston. Each morning, Foulois sent out a small scouting detachment in vehicles to mark the intended landing field and arrange to keep the field clear while the planes landed. (Keeping the fields clear of sightseers and souvenir hunters was an important part of this trip: word of the squadron's planned movement and stops had leaked, and Foulois later recalled crowds of about ten thousand people at each of the daily stops when the planes arrived.)[32] He timed takeoff for the squadron's six planes (two were still in Brownsville) so that they would arrive over the designated landing field once the scouting detachment had everything prepared. Though the JN-3s were an improvement over the JN-2s, they still proved unable to carry two men plus full tanks of gas and oil, so the flights were made with a single pilot and full tanks. Once the planes were airborne, the mechanics sped off with their tools for the destination field so as to begin any needed repairs as soon as possible after landing. The rest of the squadron followed in the specialized trucks, two of them towing trailers. Anything that could not fit on the trucks either was shipped by rail to the next stop or else awaited a second trip by the trucks. Foulois had planned the route to follow the railroad tracks both to help with aerial navigation and also as a backup plan in case the movement by their own vehicles—planes, cars, motorcycles, and trucks—failed for any reason.[33]

The squadron began its movement from Fort Sill on November 19 and arrived in San Antonio on November 26. They were delayed two days in Austin due to poor weather, but otherwise the movement was a success. While they lost one of the trucks when it caught fire while traveling, none of the planes was forced down or crashed, and they needed only minor repairs along the way, though all were in bad shape by the time they completed the journey. The move had given Foulois a chance to test out how well the unit could move around on its own, and the squadron's ground personnel gained experience with their vehicles over a variety of terrain. Once the squadron arrived in San Antonio, it spent the winter of 1915 and early spring of 1916 settling into its new home and overhauling its planes. Though the ongoing border troubles with Mexico were not an issue in selecting San Antonio as the first aeronautic center, the 1st Aero Squadron's new home put the unit in excellent position to support any further Army activity along the border.[34]

As well as assigning the 1st Aero Squadron to its permanent home in Texas, the Signal Corps had, in April 1915, announced plans to establish aero squadrons in the Philippines, Hawaii, and the Canal Zone, in that order. (The schools in Hawaii and Manila had closed by this point.) By August, though, it was clear that the Signal Corps did not have the money, equipment, or personnel in the current fiscal year to send full squadrons to each location. Consequently, Scriven intended to send a single aero company (half a squadron) to each location instead of a full squadron to only one. The Philippines was to be first. In May, Reber had selected Patterson to command the 2nd Squadron, destined for Manila. Although Reber was aware that Patterson could not fly (a shortcoming that later came out during the Goodier court-martial in October–November), he wanted Patterson in command anyway, insisting that Patterson learn to fly before the squadron's first company left San Diego in January 1916. Apparently, Patterson did learn how to fly in time, as he was indeed named commander of the 1st Company, 2nd Aero Squadron on December 1, 1915, and shipped out with the majority of the company on January 5, 1916. Scriven, in his annual report for 1915, said that he hoped to send an aero company to Hawaii by April 1916 and, when funds were available, another aero company to the Canal Zone, after which the Signal Corps planned to bring Manila up to a full squadron. Brig. Gen. C. R. Edwards, commanding general of the Canal Zone, was particularly eager to get an aero squadron assigned. On August 12, 1915, he requested a squadron be sent as soon as possible, since airplanes were already considered an essential part of fortress defense. He would have to wait, though.[35]

THE PUNITIVE EXPEDITION

Late in the night of March 9, 1916, the Mexican revolutionary Gen. Francisco "Pancho" Villa led roughly five hundred of his men in an attack on the tiny town of Columbus, New Mexico. During the raid, the Villistas killed seventeen Americans, including some members of the 13th Cavalry stationed nearby, while losing over a hundred of their own force. Villa's reasons for this attack have never been definitively determined, but the result was clear: the Army ordered Funston to organize a force under Brig. Gen. John J. "Black Jack" Pershing to pursue and disperse the remainder of the band that attacked Columbus. The 1st Aero Squadron would be part of that force, taking U.S. Army aviation into combat for the first time.[36] Their inclusion meant the creation of additional aero companies for Hawaii and the Philippines would be delayed.

Reading newspaper articles about the Columbus raid and learning of the Army's orders, Foulois began preparations in case his squadron would be ordered to join the pursuit—orders that came March 12. Foulois' preparations meant that the squadron was ready to leave immediately when the orders came, arriving in Columbus on March 15. Pershing's ground forces stepped off in pursuit of Villa's band on March 15, but the squadron was not yet ready to join them because it had shipped its planes to Columbus by rail and needed time to reassemble them. The first plane was ready to fly on March 16, when Dodd, with Foulois as observer, made the squadron's first reconnaissance flight into Mexico. This flight illustrated the speed and range of aircraft in relation to marching troops. Although the flight covered only thirty miles and the squadron remained based a day behind the march, the aviators were nevertheless able to reconnoiter enough area to reassure Pershing that there were no armed bands within a day's march of his forces in any direction.[37]

The full squadron, such as it was, was ready to go on the morning of March 19: 11 pilot-officers (of 16 specified in the table of organization), 1 medical officer, 85 enlisted men (of 129 on the T/O), and 1 civilian engine expert. The officer personnel changed numerous times while the squadron was in Mexico, but it began the expedition with Foulois, Dodd, Carberry, Chapman, Dargue, Thomas S. Bowen, R. E. Willis, Walter G. Kilner, Arthur R. Christie, Ira A. Rader, and Edgar S. Gorrell as pilot/observers. Furthermore, although the squadron had its full complement of eight JN-3s, its twelve trucks and one car represented only half of the ground transport prescribed in the table of equipment. Thus, when Pershing sent orders on March 19 for the squadron to fly to Casas Grandes[38] where the ground troops were encamped (roughly one hundred miles from Columbus), half of the already-reduced enlisted strength had to remain behind, awaiting further transport. Those left behind were not idle; as part of the only unit assigned to the operation (and possibly in the entire Army) with motor vehicle experience, they were set to assembling trucks the Quartermaster Corps had shipped to Columbus to support the expedition.[39]

The squadron did not get off to a good start. Pershing's order only reached Foulois about 1:30 p.m. on March 19. Completing last-minute preparations took until shortly after 5 p.m. All eight planes took off at that time, headed for Casas Grandes, but Kilner's plane experienced motor trouble ten minutes later, and he had to turn back to Columbus. Four other planes traveled only as far as Ascensión, Mexico, before darkness fell; they remained there overnight with some of Pershing's expedition troops. (Foulois had arranged for troops at Ascensión to build fires around a landing area chosen by the troops.) Dargue, Willis, and Gorrell had each become separated from the squadron during the flight (there was no attempt at formation flying) and landed separately in Mexico. Willis crashed on landing, leaving him to walk to Casas Grandes; a detachment sent to recover the plane on March 22 came under fire from Mexicans but returned the next day and recovered salvageable parts. On March 20, the four planes in Ascensión completed their flight to Casas Grandes where they were soon joined by Dargue and Kilner. However, Thomas Bowen, one of the four pilots who had made the trip via Ascensión, crashed when a whirlwind caught his plane while landing at Colonia Dublán, leaving only five planes available for missions. Gorrell, who had gone astray on the first day, had run out of gas, and several days passed before he encountered an infantry truck convoy. He reunited with the squadron on March 23, though it would be two more days before he could retrieve his airplane.[40]

The operation also highlighted another problem arising from the lack of practice operating planes with ground troops in the field. The Army's ground forces had much to learn about the aviators' operational needs, and Pershing was lucky to have the planes arrive safely. For starters, the troops were not where the aviators expected. Pershing had ordered the squadron to join him at Casas Grandes, but his headquarters was actually several miles away at the small settlement of Colonia Dublán. The aviators had to land and query locals to discover this. Then when the aviators finally found Pershing's headquarters, they further discovered that the area set aside as a landing field was completely unsuitable—a dry marsh covered with stumps and high clumps of grass, which would have wrecked any plane that tried to land on it. The approaches were also dangerous, since the field was bordered on three sides by trees and on the fourth side by a river. Adding to the inherent dangers of the field in question, Foulois had arranged for marker fires at Pershing's headquarters just as at Ascensión, but the troops had set the marker fires under the trees. With all the obstacles hidden by darkness, if the pilots had pushed through to Pershing's headquarters in the dark on March 19, they would likely have wrecked all the planes and been lucky to escape with their lives.[41]

Nevertheless, now that the squadron had joined Pershing's column, it could begin operational flights. The pilots soon discovered that conditions in that part of Mexico were considerably more difficult than most anywhere else they had flown. Within just the first few days, three planes barely escaped crashing due to the swirling winds around the foothills and slopes of the Sierra Madre mountain range. A more pervasive problem, however, was altitude. Much of the Chihuahuan Desert, through which the expedition was marching, lies about five thousand feet above sea level, close to the JN-3's operational ceiling.[42] Matters worsened when Pershing ordered the pilots to reconnoiter among and over the Sierra Madres. Even though the mountains rise only a few thousand feet above the desert floor, their peaks reach between 10,000 and 12,000 feet above sea level—well above the ceiling of the planes. When it was discovered that the airplanes were unable to cross the mountains to perform the ordered reconnaissance, Foulois submitted a recommendation to Pershing for new airplanes, two each from five different makers: Martin (Model S), Curtiss (Model R-2), Sturtevant, Thomas, and Sloane. Each of the requested planes boasted engines with greater horsepower than those in the JN-3s. Reflecting the squadron's experience to date, Foulois also requested a spare engine for each pair of planes as well as numerous other spare parts including propellers, wings, landing gear, control surfaces, radiators, and magnetos.[43]

Foulois did not really expect that the Army would act on his request, and even if it did, it would be some time before new planes could reach the squadron. In the meantime, the squadron had to do its best with a dwindling supply of planes. Though the men had been able to do some refurbishment while the squadron was in San Antonio, the planes had still seen several months of hard use and exposure to the weather. The buffeting winds encountered in Mexico added to the problem, but the extreme dryness of the air presented the greatest challenge during the expedition; it was so dry that the wooden propellers delaminated when the glue dried out. The squadron tried removing propellers whenever a plane landed and storing them in a humidor until a plane needed to fly again, but this helped little in the long run. The squadron tested many propellers from different manufacturers, all with the same result. In the end, the Army arranged to establish a propeller plant in Columbus, to keep the squadron supplied with fresh props. On June 29, three Curtiss employees arrived to begin making propellers.[44]

Despite these problems, the 1st Aero Squadron did its best for Pershing's forces. On March 30, Foulois submitted to Pershing several plans for using the squadron. These contemplated that the planes would be used primarily for maintaining communications between the Army base at Columbus, Pershing's advance headquarters near Casas Grandes, and forward encampments of the widely separated troop columns. Pershing chose to use other methods for communications to the rear and send all airplanes to the expedition's forward base at Namiquipa. There, the planes would maintain field communications between Namiquipa and the various scouting columns.[45] Once the Americans found Villa's band, the aircraft would be relocated for use against the enemy. Before leaving for Mexico, Foulois had requested machine guns, bombsights, and bombs for the planes but received none. However, given that Pershing's forces never trapped Villa's band and only skirmished a few times, the 1st Aero Squadron probably would not have had opportunity to use the requested armament, even if the planes could have taken off with all the extra weight.[46] As it was, though the planes made some important reconnaissance flights, searching for enemy forces and locating friendly scouting columns (similar to what became known in World War I as "contact patrols"), the majority of flights were for carrying mail and dispatches.

In addition to equipment problems, the 1st Aero Squadron also faced political problems. The first, which the whole Pershing expedition shared, was that, although the Wilson administration had recognized Venustiano Carranza as head of the Mexican government and negotiated with him to allow Pershing's expedition into Mexico, Carranza was not happy with the U.S. Army's presence in Mexico. Carranza's government refused to aid Pershing's force, and, in fact, Carranzista troops attacked U.S. Army columns twice. With the typical Mexican citizen supporting either Carranza or Villa, the U.S. Army was effectively operating in a hostile country. For the aviators, this meant that landing anywhere away from friendly forces was risky.

On one occasion, Pershing asked the squadron to deliver messages to the American consul in the city of Chihuahua. After Foulois and Dargue landed outside the city, they were approached by a hostile-looking crowd. Before the locals arrived, Foulois ordered Dargue to take off and find a place of safety. Mexican federal police in the crowd fired on the retreating plane and jailed Foulois. The consul learned of Foulois' predicament and interceded with the military governor of Chihuahua, eventually securing Foulois' release. Meanwhile, Dargue had joined Carberry, who had landed on the other side of the city to deliver Dodd with duplicate messages for the consul. Dargue and Carberry were soon surrounded by another mob of locals. Though this group included Carranzista soldiers and officers, the army men did nothing to prevent the crowd from slashing the planes' fabric with knives, burning holes in the fabric with cigarettes, or loosening nuts and bolts. The mob caused enough damage to Dargue's plane that he was unable to take off when he and Carberry attempted to fly to safety. The situation was only resolved when Dodd and Foulois arrived with guards provided by the military governor.[47] On another occasion, Chapman, flying a reconnaissance mission by himself, landed near Santa Rosalia where Carranzista soldiers took him to their commander. Though Chapman was then allowed to leave, he discovered that the soldiers had looted his plane of his goggles, binoculars, and "considerable ammunition." Since the aircraft were unarmed, the ammunition was presumably for the sidearms the aviators carried, though it is not clear why Chapman would have had a large supply in the plane.

Other losses were only indirectly due to hostile locals. On April 14, Rader damaged his plane while landing on rough ground near a column of Army troops. More than a hundred miles from the nearest American base and in hostile country, he was forced to abandon the plane. Because it was so far away, the squadron made no attempt to recover the aircraft. Five days later, Dargue, with Willis as observer, experienced engine failure and crashed in the forced landing that followed. In this case, the two set fire to the plane to ensure that it could not be of use to anyone before hiking more than sixty miles back to base. Of course, not all of the airplane losses were the result of operating in hostile territory or accidents. By the time Dargue and Willis burned their plane, two other planes had been worn out through heavy use. When these two planes were condemned as unusable, the squadron stripped them of salvageable parts and destroyed what remained. This left the squadron with only two airplanes.[48]

Homegrown political problems caused other difficulties in the squadron's operations. Fallout from the Goodier court-martial had begun February 12, 1916, when the Army chief of staff appointed the Garlington Board. This board was still in session when the squadron flew into Mexico and concluded only on April 24. Though its findings came after the squadron's operations in Mexico had effectively ended, the board's investigation created distraction and unease throughout the Aviation Section. Then, just as the Garlington Board was wrapping up, the General Staff began its investigations. Simultaneously, Senator Robinson's bill for a joint House/Senate investigation into the Aviation Section's management was introduced in January and passed in the Senate without opposition on March 16, the day after the 1st Aero Squadron arrived in Columbus. The threat of congressional hearings remained a sword of Damocles over Army aviation until the bill died in the House in April.

The multiple investigations apparently led Scriven to effectively put Reber on administrative leave and assign Capt. George S. Gibbs as acting head of the Aviation Section on March 17. Mitchell, in turn, took over from Gibbs on April 3.[49] Mitchell's "acting head" role became even more official on May 5, when Secretary of War Baker officially removed Reber as head of the Aviation Section, leaving Mitchell to carry on until Squier returned from London on May 20. In Foulois' memoirs, he called Reber's removal "unfortunate," since it eliminated an officer he believed to be an excellent administrator, and one thoroughly conversant with the needs of the Aviation Section. In contrast, this was Mitchell's first assignment to aviation, and according to Foulois, he was "entirely inexperienced in solving the practical problems incident to flying." Mitchell, for instance, wrote a letter to Pershing during the Punitive Expedition complaining about Foulois' "unauthorized" purchases of gasoline for the airplanes from civilian sources. Responding to this missive, Pershing backed Foulois' purchases and informed Mitchell that he, Pershing, would continue to authorize such purchases as they were necessary to keep the planes flying. A by-the-book administrator was *not* what Foulois needed in Washington while he was scrambling to keep planes flying in hostile territory![50]

For all the other problems looming over it, the squadron's immediate concerns were with its aircraft. As already mentioned, by April 19, it was down to but two flyable airplanes. The next day, Pershing ordered the squadron's return to Columbus to reequip with new aircraft. Surprisingly, Foulois' March 22 memo to Pershing requesting more and better airplanes had borne fruit: Congress had passed an emergency appropriation on March 31 that included $500,000 for Army aviation. Yet when the aviators arrived in Columbus, they found four Curtiss N-8s waiting for them, rather than any of the types Foulois had specified in his memo. While the N-8s were new, their design was essentially the same as the JN-3.[51] Given that the squadron had already demonstrated the inadequacy of the JN-3 for field work in Mexico, it is not surprising that a few days' testing by the squadron in New Mexico rendered a similar decision on the N-8s; Foulois sent them to San Diego to be used as trainers. On May 1, the squadron took delivery of two Curtiss R-2s, one of the types Foulois had recommended in his March 22 memo. By May 25, ten more R-2s had been delivered, but the squadron found the R-2s lacking as well. Through August 28, when Foulois submitted his official report of the squadron's activities with Pershing's expedition, the squadron remained in Columbus, testing the R-2s and finding and fixing problems with both engines and airframes. By then, the squadron had also received twelve Lewis machine guns and one hundred bombs from the Ordnance Department, though their delivery did little good since the squadron was still trying to obtain suitable planes with which to use them.[52]

Though no one knew it at the time, the 1st Aero Squadron's flights in support of Pershing's troops effectively ended when the squadron returned to Columbus on April 20. Shortly afterward, a variety of incidents involving Pershing's troops and U.S.-Mexico border forces led Pershing to take a more cautious approach. By the beginning of August, before the aviators were ready to rejoin the expedition, Pershing's forces had withdrawn into their encampments, awaiting the outcome of diplomatic talks. Still lacking acceptable planes, the aero squadron, as a squadron, never rejoined Pershing in Mexico. By the end of August 1916, however, Foulois was maintaining a two-airplane section at Pershing's headquarters for communications. Foulois rotated pilots and planes through this assignment to give newer pilots experience with field operations.[53] But with the troops remaining in their encampments, the planes must have had relatively little to do. The Punitive Expedition finally received orders to return to the United States in January 1917, with the last troops crossing the border on February 5.

Foulois said many times that the 1st Aero Squadron's experiences in Mexico were important—"a vital milestone in the development of military aviation" in the United States. Though the planes were inadequate for the task, the squadron managed to make at least 134 flights in Mexico to support Pershing's expedition between March 26 and April 19, an average of slightly more than five-and-a-half flights per day despite a dwindling number of planes. Pershing was pleased with what the squadron was able to do for his force. Though his official report notes that "[aerial] missions were not always accomplished," he explained that this was due to problems with the planes and the conditions in Mexico, rather than untrained or unwilling personnel. He continued, "Many important reconnaissances have been made [by the aviators], and communication has often been maintained with distant columns, when no other means existed." He added: "Unstinted praise for the aviators . . . is universal throughout the Command." Pershing concluded his official report by quoting the final paragraph from Foulois' report as being "especially pertinent." In that paragraph, Foulois stated that "the knowledge gained by all concerned [in this operational assignment] should result in a more rapid and efficient development of the aviation service in the United States Army."[54]

Certainly there were immediate lessons to be learned. Existing airplanes were unsuited to field conditions; airplanes would need to be able to operate wherever the troops were. The Aviation Section needed a better organization for individual squadrons in the field, as well as additional test, evaluation, and repair units to support them.[55] Army administrators in Washington learned that maintaining an aviation squadron in the field could be up to two and a half times more expensive than previously thought.[56] The field army, too, learned significant lessons. Pershing and his subordinates gained valuable experience in what airplanes could do for the ground officer, at least from the point of view of reconnaissance and communications. As well, they learned much about the requirements and limitations of airplane operations.

RESERVE AVIATION

The Punitive Expedition caused ripples throughout the Army organization. At General Funston's request, the Wilson administration had federalized the National Guard forces of Arizona, New Mexico, and Texas on May 9, 1916.[57] These National Guard units, along with additional Regular Army units from elsewhere in the United States, were needed to beef up border security, especially as many of the Regular Army forces on border patrol had been assigned to the Punitive Expedition. On June 18, Wilson federalized the rest of the country's National Guard units, sending them to the Mexican border as well. Among the units in the latter call-up was the 1st Aero Company, New York National Guard.[58]

The New York 1st Aero Company had begun in 1915 when several wealthy members of the New York National Guard, led by U.S. Steel attorney Raynal C. Bolling, started taking flying lessons. The small group operated a single airplane during the "Business Men's Camp" at Plattsburgh, New York, in July 1915.[59] After the camp ended, Bolling and another member of the group, James E. Miller, began working with New York National Guard officials to organize themselves into an aero company, which came to pass on November 1, 1915. The Aero Club of America donated money to allow Bolling, commanding the company, to purchase two tractor planes. In the spring of 1916, the company replaced those planes with five new aircraft, including a Curtiss JN-4, a Thomas, a Sturtevant, and a Sloane—a list similar to that requested by Foulois in his March 22 memo to Pershing. The unit was mustered into federal service on July 13, 1916, but quickly mustered out again on November 2, having never deployed to the border. Meanwhile, on July 24, the New York National Guard began organizing a 2nd Aero Company, which was never mustered into federal service.[60]

Between the two National Guard call-ups, Congress had passed the National Defense Act of June 3, 1916. Among other provisions, the new law created the Officers' Reserve Corps and the Enlisted Reserve Corps, with a Signal Reserve Corps component of each, including aviation. These provisions cleared the way for the War Department to provide support for aviation in the organized militia (National Guard) in a way that would have been legally questionable (at best) in 1912 when Foulois, in the Division of Militia Affairs, had tried to encourage aviation in the National Guard units. In March 1916, the Aero Club of America donated money to give National Guard members flight training so that they could volunteer for service in support of the Punitive Expedition. Passage of the National Defense Act and the federalization of the remaining National Guard units led to the War Department's assuming the cost of training twenty-six Guard officers and twelve enlisted men in civilian flight schools. But the emergency on the Mexican border ended before any of these reservists could finish training.[61]

These two events—the call-up of a National Guard aeronautical unit and the establishment of an aviation component of the newly formed Reserve Corps—provided notice to the head of the Aviation Section, as well as to the chief signal officer, that they would have to expand their purview. The National Defense Act gave the Regular Army greater control over the training and organization of the National Guard in order to smooth the merger of the National Guard into the Army when called up. The Reserve Corps, of course, began under the complete control of the Army. These new relationships meant that the new head of the Aviation Section, George Squier, would exercise administration over National Guard and Reserve aviation in addition to aviation in the Regular Army.

Squier returned from London and took over from Mitchell on May 20, 1916, but Mitchell remained in the Aviation Section as Squier's assistant. Mitchell's assignment to the General Staff officially ended in June, at which point he was ordered to the Aviation Section for a full tour of duty. Although Mitchell had been the General Staff's aviation specialist, this was merely due to his status as the only Signal Corps officer on the General Staff. His assignment to the Aviation Section was his first serious involvement with aviation. Though he had brought in some junior aviators from the San Diego school to assist him when he took over from Gibbs in April, Mitchell was apparently sensitive to his own lack of flying experience. His concern may have stemmed from criticism directed at him by members of the Aero Club of America (including Henry Woodhouse) in the summer of 1916. Woodhouse and others accused Mitchell of inefficiency and general misconduct in his management of the Aviation Section and its finances, which, critics argued, impeded the development of military aviation. Baker personally investigated these charges and found no merit in them.

Nevertheless, the charges probably contributed to Mitchell's desire to learn to fly. In the fall of 1916, he succeeded in obtaining orders to weekend training at the Curtiss flight school in Newport News, Virginia, where several Signal Corps reservists were also training. The Army initially covered the costs, but later review determined that the funds used were only for training reservists. Mitchell, as Regular Army, had to repay the costs—the basis of his later statements that he had paid for his own training. According to several sources, Mitchell's flying, as a student, was erratic. Though he soloed at the school, events would take him to Europe before he could acquire any sort of license, whether civilian or military. He had wanted assignment to Europe as a military observer since the war began in 1914 and finally got his wish when the Army ordered him to France as an aeronautical observer in 1917. He left the United States on March 17.[62] By the time he arrived in Europe, the United States had entered the war on the Allied side. His assignment, and especially its timing, would have great significance for the development of aviation doctrine in the U.S. Army during World War I.

Foulois' presence in Washington was likely another goad leading to Mitchell's flying lessons. When Squier returned from London, he began an intense correspondence with Foulois, asking him for recommendations on improving the Aviation Section in the field based on his squadron's experiences in Mexico. Foulois was ordered to Washington at the end of September, where he detailed for Squier the 1st Aero Squadron's Mexican experiences that he could not put into official reports. Squier, in return, brought Foulois up to date on what was happening in European aviation. Foulois then returned to Texas on November 3 as Aviation Officer of the Southern Department. There, he laid out what would soon become Kelly Field near Fort Sam Houston, only to discover that the Army could not purchase the necessary land because the legislation that granted the Army money to buy land for airfields restricted such purchases to the northern and eastern parts of the country. Foulois again returned to Washington briefly to argue for a change in the law, since he felt the weather in the northern and eastern United States imposed far greater limitations on flying than in southern and western states. When the Army ordered Mitchell to Europe, it ordered Foulois, already in Washington, to replace Mitchell as Squier's assistant.[63]

ADMINISTRATIVE CHANGES IN 1916

The spring and summer of 1916 also brought other administrative changes to Army aviation, directly linked to neither the Goodier court-martial nor the Mexican Expedition. These changes had less obvious and/or immediate impact than those higher-profile events but would be of great significance in the near future when the United States entered the European war. The National Defense Act, for instance, was wide-ranging in its effects on

Army aviation beyond the creation of formal reserves and the strengthening of ties with the National Guard. It also included a provision that negated a troublesome clause in the Act of July 18,1914. Though the 1914 act had increased the number of officers who could be assigned to aviation and expanded the size of the Signal Corps accordingly, it had restricted assignments as student aviators to unmarried lieutenants under age thirty. Scriven and Reber immediately began working to have these limitations removed because they believed these rules significantly reduced the population from which they could recruit new aviators. Moreover, the 1914 law also specified that any officer promoted to captain in his basic service (i.e., in his parent branch) would have to return to troop duty. This provision threatened to push aviators out of aviation just at the point that they had become experienced flyers capable of holding leadership positions.[64]

As the Army's most senior flying officer, Foulois was at the greatest risk of having this rule force him out of aviation. Though he held the rank of captain in 1915, Foulois only held that rank in the Signal Corps. His permanent rank with the infantry (his basic service) remained lieutenant, but he was close to promotion in the infantry throughout 1915 and 1916. If he had been promoted during that time, he would have had to leave aviation again, depriving the Aviation Section of its most experienced aviator and best administrator who also held a pilot's license. The National Defense Act removed those restrictions on age, rank, and marital status for aviators, allowing Foulois to stay in aviation and broadening the population from which to recruit new flyers. It also allowed for an increase in the total number of officers, from 60 to 148, with allowances for higher ranks within the Aviation Section, including 1 colonel and 1 lieutenant colonel.[65]

In addition to the National Defense Act, Congress also voted to greatly increase appropriations for aviation during 1916. The urgent deficiency act passed on March 31 had provided $500,000 for Army aviation, almost double the FY 1916 allowance of $300,000. For the FY 1917 bill, the equipment problems of the 1st Aero Squadron in Mexico, combined with increasing worries about preparedness in case the United States was drawn into the European war, led Congress to allot nearly $13.3 million for aviation and another $600,000 to purchase land for airfields. With such expansion of personnel and equipment in the works, the Aviation Section began expanding training as well. On July 22, 1916, Lt. Joseph Carberry, who had served in Mexico with the 1st Aero Squadron, arrived in Mineola, New York, to establish the Signal Corps' second aviation school. The school's first plane arrived on August 1, and Carberry hired civilian flight instructors and mechanics to staff the school. Initially, the Signal Corps expected Mineola to quickly train civilian and militia aviators for duty on the Mexican border, but as the urgent need for such service faded, the Mineola school took on a more long-term role in training officers already in the National Guard. By September 25, Mineola had fourteen National Guard officers under instruction, many of whom were from New York. But the group also included students from North Carolina, New Hampshire, Colorado, Washington, Kentucky, Connecticut, Arkansas, and West Virginia. As winter approached, Scriven considered shifting the school to a southern location, just as had happened with the College Park facility. While flight instruction did, indeed, stop for the winter, Carberry convinced Scriven to leave the school in Mineola, where the more seasoned pilots could gain valuable experience flying in winter conditions. For the next several months, until American entry into World War I, Mineola was essentially a testing ground for equipment and accessories. Among these were extensive tests of "Barlow bombs" developed by civilian Lester P. Barlow and the Ordnance Department, as well as tests of new bomb racks.[66]

The Signal Corps opened another school intended for Guardsmen and Reservists at Ashburn Field near Chicago in July 1916. In December, when the weather there grew too cold, the Signal Corps transferred the Ashburn Field students to a new school outside of Memphis, Tennessee. On February 8, 1917, the Army approved Squier's request for another flying school at Essington, Pennsylvania, just south of Philadelphia.[67] The Essington station was to train pilots specifically for the 2nd Reserve Aero Squadron, which would form part of the coastal defenses of the Philadelphia area. Consequently, the station received seaplanes. These additional aviation schools were all considerably smaller than San Diego by any standard of measurement, but they did represent an intention to grow the Aviation Section. In Scriven's 1916 CSO report, he proposed that the Essington and Chicago/Memphis schools would eventually become full counterparts to San Diego, giving basic flight training to Regular Army officers and advanced training to both these and organized militia officers, with each school taking in students from three geographic departments: the Eastern, Central/Southern, and Western, respectively. (The militia officers would have to get their basic flight training in civilian schools before attending one of the Army schools.)[68]

The Aviation Section was also beginning to organize additional Regular Army aeronautic units in San Antonio in December 1916, led by the 2nd Company of the 2nd Aero Squadron. Once complete, it would be sent to the Philippines to reinforce the 1st Company sent out a year earlier. Three aero squadrons—the 3rd, 4th, and 5th—would also be organized in San Antonio. These units would initially remain there, but the intention was to relocate them to other geographic departments as experienced cadres once the Aviation Section expanded further at some future date. The Signal Corps also began forming companies for the 6th Squadron and the 7th Squadron, to be sent to Hawaii and Panama, respectively.[69] The establishment of these additional aero squadrons, even if they consisted of only a handful of personnel with no planes or other equipment yet, complemented the creation of additional aviation schools and provided a framework for significant expansion.

As previously mentioned, one of the long-term consequences of the Goodier court-martial was a General Staff investigation. On April 24, 1916, Secretary of War Baker ordered a General Staff committee, under the leadership of Col. Charles W. Kennedy, to consider whether changes were needed in the organization and administration of the Aviation Section, the Aviation School, and/or the 1st Aero Squadron. Responding to a committee request for information, Scriven wrote back on May 16, outlining the status of the Aviation Section and the reasoning behind its present organization. In this report, Scriven informed the committee that the Aviation Section needed two things: "one, to obtain suitable and sufficient personnel; two, to obtain suitable and sufficient materiel." Plenty of both would be needed for Scriven's proposed expansion of the Aviation Section.[70]

The Kennedy Committee heard from other sources as well. It considered reports on the organization and use of aviation among the European belligerents and invited testimony from aviators. At the committee's request, Scriven had ordered Milling to serve as a consultant on aviation, but the committee ultimately heard from all twenty-three qualified, active aviators. In a turnaround from the Hay Committee hearings in 1913, twenty-one of the aviators now favored the separation of aviation from the Signal Corps—Milling and Patterson were the only two opposed. Dargue brought before the Kennedy Committee the idea that the commander of an aviation unit should be a flyer himself—an idea that would resurface many times in the future. In the end, the Kennedy Committee took a middle course, concluding that aviation could only be fully developed as a new, separate arm of the Army, but that "the time of its separation" from the Signal Corps could wait until the Army had incorporated and assessed the committee's other recommended changes. The committee further acknowledged that creating a new aviation branch would likely require changes in the laws governing the Army, as well as additional personnel and equipment to support it, but it said the specifics could wait until the Army determined the right time for separation.[71]

The assistant chief of staff, Maj. Gen. Tasker Bliss, felt that the young aviators had shown a "spirit of insubordination" many times, including in their testimony before the Kennedy Committee, and that the committee should therefore have discounted their testimony in favor of aviation's independence. Baker, presumably, agreed with Bliss' opinions about the flyers, since he stated in congressional hearings on April 8, 1916, that he felt the aviators were young and impatient. What the Aviation Section really needed, Baker said, was not independence from the Signal Corps but rather a leader who was "a man of mature yet severe judgment and trained disciplinary ideas to restrain the exuberance of youth." Baker agreed with the Kennedy Committee that the time had not yet come for separation. On July 10, he approved Bliss' recommendations on the Kennedy Committee's report. Perhaps the most significant of these for the long term was that the head of the Aviation Section, while still under administrative control of the CSO, should nevertheless have absolute control over aviation, with "his recommendations to be disapproved only by the Secretary of War or the Chief of Staff." This potentially provided Squier, head of the Aviation Section since May 20, a great deal of independence, but it is not clear that he took advantage of this opportunity. Scriven also remained opposed to separation. In his annual report later that fall, he agreed that the aviation service should eventually be separated from the Signal Corps, but that "the separation of this service from any technical corps should take place when the air service is capable of standing alone. This time has not yet come."[72]

When Scriven responded to the Kennedy Committee's request for information on May 16, he seems to have been aware that it contemplated separation for the air service. He explained to the committee that regardless of whether aviation separated from the Signal Corps or remained part of it, there should be some sort of dedicated executive and administrative headquarters to manage all aspects of Army aviation. He said that the officers assigned to head up the various parts of this headquarters, to say nothing of the overall commander, would need to be "well versed in organization, with the initiative necessary for the creation of new and untried agencies, and the ability to make the wants of the service clearly understood to those above and below them." This headquarters, he suggested, would oversee the aviation schools, an Army Aviation experiment and testing station (to test existing designs of airplanes and equipment and to experiment with new designs), and many tactical aircraft units. The tactical units were to be stationed "right along with the troops to which they are attached," so that aviation could be integrated with ground forces.[73]

Even before the Kennedy Committee met, however, Scriven was already making changes in the Aviation Section, including the establishment of the Technical Aero Advisory and Inspection Board of the Signal Corps. Consisting of three Army aviators and two consulting engineers—one an expert on engines and the other an expert in aerodynamics—Scriven created the board to determine the best planes for military use currently available in the United States and to draw up specifications for the purchase of new planes. This board, as he told the Kennedy Committee, was necessary to deal with the increased workload of a growing Aviation Section. The board would become even more important in the coming months as Congress first increased the Aviation Section's allowance of personnel and then voted to allot more than $13 million to Army aviation. By the fall of 1916, in his annual report to Congress, Baker noted that the Aviation Section had placed orders for 34 new primary training planes, 120 advanced training planes, 91 two-seat reconnaissance planes, 13 single-seat pursuit planes, 6 two-seat "land combat" planes (probably bombers), and 155 two-seat reconnaissance floatplanes. The primary trainers would go to San Diego while the advanced training planes would be distributed between there and the newly established schools at Mineola and Chicago. (Memphis had not yet been established, but it was merely a winter location for the Chicago school.) The floatplanes were intended for the aero squadrons in the Philippines, Hawaii, and the Canal Zone, as well as for reserve squadrons (like the one in Philadelphia) intended to work with the coastal defenses.[74]

ARMY BALLOONING REVIVAL

Scriven had also decided to revive lighter-than-air aviation in the Army, which had taken a distinct second place to airplanes ever since the Army purchased the Wright Military Flyer. The Army acquired the Wright plane just a few months after the first classes convened at the ballooning school in Fort Omaha, Nebraska, on May 3, 1909. Though the Army purchased a handful of spherical balloons in the next few years, it bought no more dirigibles beyond Baldwin's. By the end of 1911, the Baldwin airship's envelope had become so porous that it could make only short flights and those with only one crewman on board; the Signal Corps condemned it in 1912. By that time, the Army had concluded that airplane performance would soon surpass that of dirigibles and concluded that the Army no longer needed LTA aviation, whether spherical or dirigible balloons. The personnel shortage within the Signal Corps that limited the number of men assigned to airplane training also meant that no one could be spared for LTA training, even if Army policy with respect to balloons had not changed. Similarly, the minimal funding Congress allotted to Army aviation was barely enough to keep the airplane side going, leaving nothing to spare for a new dirigible that would cost considerably more than a new plane. The Signal Corps moved the ballooning school from Fort Omaha to Fort Leavenworth in 1913, but the school became defunct soon thereafter due to lack of funding and interest.[75]

Interest in LTA flight never completely went away, however, and by 1916 the Army was seeing a resurgence at a time when the Navy was also seriously considering dirigibles. This growing interest in both services was spurred by the widespread use of kite balloons and dirigibles in the European war—particularly the German rigid airships. Secretary Baker told a congressional committee in April 1916 that "the dirigible balloon has been regarded as a failure, except in the case of the Zeppelins" and that the Germans kept rigid airship design and construction (by both the Zeppelin and Schütte-Lanz companies) a closely held military secret, so there was little use in the U.S. Army's building one. Less than a month later, however, Scriven's letter to the Kennedy Committee made it clear that he expected the tactical units of an enlarged and reorganized Aviation Section would include "observation balloons and possibly dirigibles" in addition to squadrons of airplanes. In the CSO's annual report that year, Scriven noted that he had already established an "aerostatic division" within the Aviation Section and recommended reopening the balloon school at Fort Omaha, which still had its hydrogen generating plant. Scriven also announced his intentions that "captive balloon organizations will be equipped as soon as practicable and instruction with training dirigibles will be inaugurated." Five captive balloons were already on order for use with the field artillery. In this, the Signal Corps was following the recommendations of Capt. Frederick Hennessy, a junior military aviator who had been returned to the field artillery.[76] Hennessy, though he had no ballooning experience himself, had observed testing of a new Goodyear Rubber Company kite balloon on May 19, 1916, at Cleveland, Ohio. He recommended that the Army purchase two of these new balloons for experimental purposes and that each field artillery battalion should eventually have at least one such balloon assigned to it.

Due to the situation along the Mexican border, the Field Artillery School at Fort Sill had been suspended, so Scriven intended to send the balloons to Fort Sam Houston to work with the field artillery's 3rd Regiment, stationed there. Scriven ordered Lahm to take charge of the balloons in Texas and sent Hennessy there as Lahm's assistant, though there is no evidence any balloons were ever sent. On November 11, 1916, Scriven ordered Chandler to turn over command of the Signal Corps School at Fort Leavenworth to a replacement and proceed to Fort Omaha to reestablish the balloon school. By the end of January 1917, the school had ninety-three enlisted men and six officers assigned to it, though apparently only Lt. Lewis C. Davidson was a student, the other officers occupying staff positions.[77]

In hindsight, another important event of 1916 was the return of Henry "Hap" Arnold to aviation. Shortly after the 1913 Hay Committee hearings, Arnold had married and left both aviation and Washington to return to the field. He and his wife had spent most of the intervening years in the Philippines where Arnold served with the 13th Infantry. He had watched the attempt to establish the Philippines Aero School through January 1915, but made no effort to join them in flying, even informally. Arnold had regularly corresponded with Milling, who kept him abreast of aviation developments. Although interested in Milling's updates, Arnold showed no interest in returning to aviation. However, while returning from his Philippine tour of duty in February 1916, he received a telegram from Mitchell inviting him back into aviation. Arnold accepted, and was assigned in May as supply officer at the San Diego Aviation School during the shake-up in the Aviation Section that replaced Cowan with Glassford as commander of the school. This was not a flying position, though the Army granted Arnold the JMA rating based on his earlier qualifications, making him eligible to fly if he wished. Initially he did not, but he eventually overcame his fears, got his wife's permission to resume flying, and refreshed his qualifications by the end of 1916. Now returned to aviation duty, Arnold was then assigned to command the 7th Aero Squadron in the Canal Zone. He left San Diego on January 30, 1917, bound for Washington and New York before taking ship for Panama on February 28.[78]

Arnold left San Diego while the school was under yet another investigation. On January 10, 1917, Lt. W. A. Robertson had taken off in a plane with Lt. Col. H. G. Bishop of the field officers aviation course as observer. While flying to Yuma, Arizona, they got lost and ran out of gas on the shores of the Gulf of California in Mexico. Aviators at the school, including Arnold and Dargue, eventually gained Glassford's permission to mount what proved to be an unsuccessful aerial search: volunteer searchers on the ground eventually rescued the missing aviators. Regardless, Glassford, who had taken over the school after Cowan's censure for mismanagement, now came under scrutiny himself. Many of the junior flyers felt Glassford had waited too long to mount a search and had done so half-heartedly. He was eventually censured by the Army and replaced on April 11. In the meantime, though, Glassford wrote scathing performance reports for those junior flyers, including Arnold, who had criticized his actions, though the negative reports do not seem to have had any long-term effects on any of their careers.[79]

Following these latest events at the San Diego school were more personnel changes in Washington. On February 14, 1917, Scriven voluntarily retired from a long career in the Army. His decision to retire probably had more to do with his age (sixty-three) and Baker's censure of him the previous summer, but Glassford's behavior regarding the search and the subsequent investigation may have accelerated the date. Baker tapped Squier as Scriven's replacement as CSO. While Foulois might have been an excellent replacement for Squier as chief of the Aviation Section, he was too junior. Instead, he remained as assistant to the new head of the Aviation Section, Lt. Col. John Bennet. Though a nonflying Signal Officer, Bennet was at least a recent graduate of the field officers' course in aviation that had been inaugurated at San Diego not long before (the same school Bishop had been attending when he had his unfortunate flight). This, then, was the organization in Washington governing Army aviation when the United States declared war on Germany on April 6, 1917.[80]

CONCLUSIONS

The treatment of observers' reports from Europe during this period illustrates the duality of U.S. Army aviation. While Army leadership in Washington was keeping an eye on aviation developments during the war, getting reports from Squier in London as well as additional information from the U.S. Navy's assistant attachés in London, Paris, and Berlin, none of that information was affecting the development of aviation out west, whether at the school or with the 1st Aero Squadron. Officials in Washington, whether the CSO's office or the head of the Aviation Section, disseminated no information regarding overseas aviation developments, did not issue any orders reflecting influence of those developments, and did not change acquisition or development of material (modifying new aircraft requirements or ordering development of aerial ordnance, for instance) in response to the information received. As for those officers actually working with aircraft, their ignorance of the information in Washington meant that they had nothing to guide or even initiate any efforts to respond to events overseas on their own. When Foulois finally requested that the Army send machine guns for the aircraft and bombs and bomb racks that the 1st Aero might start testing, it was not in reaction to European developments, but rather to the squadron's own participation in the Mexican Punitive Expedition.

The physical and mental distance between flyers out west and their superiors in Washington were highlighted in the stories that emerged from the Goodier court-martial and the investigations that followed. The combined result forced the Army to realize that it had paid too little attention to the development of this new arm. The new regulations that came out of these investigations, as well as the formal censures of Scriven and Reber and relief of both Reber and Cowan from their respective command positions, put everyone on notice that Army leadership would be paying more attention to aviation in the future. The new regulations made Army aviation more professional, and new leadership was, if nothing else, more friendly to aviation.

This period also saw Army aviation moving decisively to become part of the Army's fighting forces via the exercises at Fort Sill and the subsequent deployment with the Mexican Punitive Expedition. These experiences both gave the aviators (and the Army) a better sense of what qualities were needed in an operationally useful airplane and revealed the shortcomings of those airplanes already in the inventory or available on the market. U.S. participation in World War I came before these material problems could be rectified, but the experiences may have eased the way for congressional acceptance of the situation when the first allied missions to the United States made clear the inadequacies of the U.S. aviation industry. On the flip side, even proposed solutions to the Army's aircraft problems were very limited and did practically nothing to prepare either the aviators or the Army for the kinds of missions that aviation would soon be called on to perform in Europe.

9

INTERSERVICE ORGANIZATION II
Joint Boards

Chapter 5 explored the largely informal connections between aviation in the Army and Navy departments (with Marine aviation falling under the latter). This chapter explores the more formally constituted interactions between the services in the form of joint boards and committees.

THE NATIONAL ADVISORY COMMITTEE FOR AERONAUTICS

Shortly after buying their first aircraft, both the War Department and the Navy Department considered the usefulness of a government laboratory to pursue research of interest to military aviation. The Army purchased its first plane two years before the Navy, but the first push for a national aeronautical lab came from the Navy. There are two likely reasons for this. The first is that naval officers like Chambers, the first military officer to lobby for a national lab, recognized that many of the problems faced by naval aviation were largely unique to naval aviation. The private market would probably not have many buyers looking for a plane that could operate from a ship at sea, while Navy purchases of such a design would likely remain but a small part of the total airplane market. Consequently, private manufacturers would be unlikely to address problems that the Navy wanted solved. By contrast, fewer of the Army's concerns with aircraft design were unique to the Army, at least at that time. So Army leaders were likely more confident that their concerns would eventually be met by manufacturers without resorting to a government lab that might compete with and/or discourage private research.

The second likely reason for the Navy's pushing a national aeronautical lab is that the Navy already had similar labs for engine research (in the Bureau of Engineering) and ships' hydrodynamics (Bureau of Construction and Repair). In other words, the Navy was already familiar with the benefits of government labs and was used to running them, so establishing another for aeronautical research was a logical next step. The Army, on the other hand, did not have the same tradition of "in-house" labs. The one exception was in the Ordnance Department, which conducted basic research into weapons design and explosives at its proving grounds. The Navy's BuOrd had similar facilities and purposes. However, the Army did not have (and up until this point, did not need) the organization or facilities for doing research like that performed by the Navy's BuEng or BuC&R.[1]

Whatever his driving impulse(s) may have been, Chambers was lobbying for a national lab for aeronautical research before anyone in the Army—even before the Navy had any money to buy planes! Just a few weeks after Eugene Ely's successful flights in January 1911, Chambers wrote to congratulate him on the feat. In that letter, Chambers also explained his thoughts on what a Navy aviation program ought to look like and how it should be organized. He seemed to discount the immediate need for a new Navy research facility when he told Ely that "We [the Navy] don't expect to do any independent experimental work for a long time except, perhaps, with small models or laboratory work." Chambers felt it more important for the Navy to establish stations for instruction first, and his phrasing implies that he thought the "small models or laboratory work" could be performed in extant Navy facilities. But he obviously foresaw a time when the Navy might get into "experimental work" in a large way.[2]

Chambers soon joined forces with Charles Walcott, who had become secretary of the Smithsonian in 1907, after Samuel Langley's death. By 1911, Walcott had also conceived of the need for a national aeronautical laboratory and proposed reopening Langley's laboratory for this purpose. In April 1911, the press reported (erroneously) that an aeronautical research center would soon be established under the Smithsonian and operated by the Bureau of Standards.[3]

Though Chambers was an enthusiastic supporter of a Smithsonian aeronautical lab (and may even have been the author of the initiative), others in the Navy opposed the idea. Capt. David Taylor, who oversaw the Navy's Experimental Model Basin in BuC&R,[4] felt that the proposed aeronautical lab would duplicate the work done by his model basin. The Bureau of Steam Engineering also opposed the national lab on the basis that their experimental engine testing station at Annapolis could very easily be adapted to test aviation motors and propellers. President William Taft's Committee on Economy and Efficiency found merit in Taylor's arguments and in the interest of efficiency drafted an executive order declaring that the Navy's model basin should conduct national aerodynamic research. Secretary of the Navy George Meyer subsequently contacted Secretary of War Jacob Dickinson about a plan to coordinate Navy and Army research in aviation, but Dickinson replied that it was probably better for the two services to conduct their own experiments. The Army and Navy proposals went to Taft's Committee but apparently petered out there.[5]

By early 1912, Albert F. Zahm had joined Chambers and Walcott in supporting a national aerodynamic laboratory. At this point, Zahm, a respected aeronautical researcher, was professor of physics and mechanics at Catholic University. He was also well connected within the Aero Club of Washington and the Aero Club of America. He used his position as consulting editor of the *Aero Club of America Bulletin* to publish articles (by both himself and others) in the newsletter favoring a national laboratory. Chambers contributed an article to the May 1912 issue of the *Bulletin* suggesting once again that the Smithsonian reactivate Langley's laboratory as a national aeronautical lab. Following Wilbur Wright's death on May 30,

1912, Chambers began earnestly suggesting that an appropriate memorial would be naming a research building after him (at a facility named for Langley!).[6]

Chambers also pushed a national lab in his official report on aviation to the chief of BuNav in September 1912. (Secretary Meyer included this document, without comment, as "Appendix No. 1" in his 1912 annual report.) Chambers' report explained, "Important experiments involving physical research" should not be conducted at any of his proposed regular aeronautical stations, but "should be relegated to an aerodynamic laboratory and its aerodrome annex." He went on to give seven pages of recommendations for a "National Aerodynamic Laboratory." Some of these were quite broad. For instance, his proposal that the lab should be devoted to experimental verification of manufacturers' claims (horsepower of engines or thrust of propellers, for instance) but also to basic research (such as discovering and refining laws and formulas for aeronautical design). Other proposals were quite specific, such as placing the laboratory in Potomac Park, in Washington, where the lab could conduct research on both land and water flying in close proximity to both Navy and Army facilities. His lengthy recommendations notwithstanding, Chambers concluded with the idea that such an important facility should not be based on the proposals of one man. Instead, "a commission or board [should] be appointed to consider and report to the President, for recommendation to Congress, on the necessity or desirability for the establishment of a national aerodynamic laboratory, and on its scope, its organization, the most suitable location for it, and the cost of its installation."[7]

Chambers' report for the Navy seems to have borne fruit. On December 16, 1912, Secretary Meyer formally passed Chambers' commission proposal on to President Taft. Taft acted quickly, naming a nineteen-member National Aerodynamical Laboratory Commission, better known for its chairman, Dr. R. S. Woodward, president of the Carnegie Institution of Washington. Chambers and Taylor were the two Navy members, while General Allen (chief signal officer) and Major Reber (at that time, chief signal officer of the Eastern District) represented the Army. Charles

Walcott was on the committee, as was Albert Zahm. Other members of note included Henry A. Wise Wood, vice president of the Aero Club of America; Prof. William Humphreys of the U.S. Weather Bureau; Dr. S. W. Stratton, director of the National Bureau of Standards; Prof. William F. Durand of Stanford University; Prof. Richard Maclaurin, president of MIT; and Charles Manly, who had been Langley's chief mechanic. Taft's charge to the commission was almost exactly what Chambers had proposed: to consider the need for a national aeronautic lab and, if necessary, to make recommendations to Congress for its establishment.[8]

The Woodward Commission immediately ran into trouble. For starters, Congress, concerned that President Theodore Roosevelt's use of presidential commissions infringed on Congressional authority, had passed a law in 1910 requiring congressional sanction of any such commissions. Without Congress' approval, presidential commissions could not use public funds to support their work, nor could government employees serve on unapproved presidential commissions. Friendly congressmen introduced bills in both chambers to authorize the Woodward Commission, but although the Senate bill passed, the one presented in the House did not.[9]

While the Woodward Commission could probably have covered its own meeting expenses, the prohibition against government employees was a problem for Humphreys, Stratton, and the commission's four military members. Nevertheless, the commission met on January 23, 1913, at the Carnegie Institute's building in Washington. Two days later, they had agreed that a national aeronautical lab was necessary, preferably located in Washington. The proposal largely followed Chambers' 1912 outline with one exception: the commission recommended that the lab be independent, attached to neither the Smithsonian nor the National Bureau of Standards. However, the draft legislation circulated to the commission members on January 29 omitted the independence wording. When a quorum of ten members met on February 5 to approve the draft bill, seven of them wanted to add language that would place the laboratory under the Smithsonian. Taylor, of course, opposed the idea, but abstained from voting. General Allen, who had written the original independence wording, likewise abstained. Smithsonian Secretary Walcott also abstained, though as historian Alex Roland says, this was probably just for decorum's sake. With seven in favor and three abstentions, the quorum approved the draft bill with the Smithsonian wording.[10]

Then the Woodward Commission fell apart. Taylor and Stratton vigorously opposed the bill over the Smithsonian connection, and Maclaurin also withdrew his support on that basis. Stratton wanted the lab within the Bureau of Standards, while Maclaurin thought it would be better placed near a college or university (such as his own MIT) where it could take advantage of the school's staff and their knowledge. Chambers, Walcott, and Zahm all shared the idea that the national lab should be at the Smithsonian. Taylor succeeded in forcing a second vote on the bill by the full commission, and they passed it with a vote of 13–3 with three abstentions. In the meantime, supporters of the Smithsonian plan had given copies of the bill discussed on February 5 (with the Smithsonian wording in place) to friends in Congress, where opinions were even more splintered than in the Woodward Commission. The 62nd Congress ended on March 4, 1913, without bills coming before the full membership of either chamber. The bills were reintroduced early in the 63rd Congress, but both died in committee.[11]

As Roland has pointed out, the Woodward Commission disagreed not only about who should oversee the laboratory, but also about what kind of work the lab would do. Many of those behind the Smithsonian proposal saw aeronautics in scientific terms and envisioned that the national lab would perform fundamental scientific research, like discovering the laws of aerodynamics and refining the physical constants necessary to their application. Many of those opposed to placing the lab within the Smithsonian believed that aeronautics was primarily an engineering problem, and so considered the lab as a place for engineering research: discovering more efficient airfoil shapes, reducing drag, and similar projects. While the Smithsonian was an excellent home for scientific investigation, placing the lab at the Navy's Model Basin or at MIT would be more conducive to engineering research.[12]

With the 63rd Congress' rejection of the bills, a few members of the Woodward Commission took matters into their own hands. Early in 1913, Walcott began efforts to get the Smithsonian Board of Regents to reopen Langley's Aerodynamical Laboratory. As approved by the Board of Regents on May 5, the lab's new organization resembled that proposed in Chambers' 1912 report, though it was more limited in scope. With only minimal funding available from the Smithsonian, the Langley lab would necessarily be constrained in the research it could undertake, though Walcott hoped Congress would eventually underwrite its funding at increased levels. To make the Langley lab palatable to the Progressives of the incoming Wilson administration and a Democratic Congress, the Board of Regents authorized the lab to work only for the benefit of the U.S. government (both military and civilian departments), eschewing research that would benefit private individuals or industry unless it was funded by the private sector. The eleven-member board overseeing the work of the Langley lab included two representatives each from the Army and Navy: George Scriven (now chief signal officer) and Maj. Edgar Russel (head of the Aeronautical Division) from the Army, and Chambers and Naval Constructor Holden Richardson from the Navy. The Langley Advisory Committee devoted its initial meetings to determining the state of aeronautical research and identifying topics in need of attention. To that end, the committee voted to send their recorder, Zahm, on an information-gathering tour of European aeronautical labs in the company of Assistant Naval Constructor Jerome Hunsaker.[13]

Also in early 1913, Maclaurin resumed his own plans for aeronautical research at MIT. The school already had a graduate program in naval architecture, which included the study and analysis of hydrodynamic forces. With hydrodynamics so similar to aerodynamics (this was also Taylor's argument for attaching an aerodynamic lab to his model basin), Maclaurin had already been considering an equivalent program of aeronautical engineering even before joining the Woodward Commission. He had put these plans on hold pending the outcome of the commission, but with its failure, Maclaurin returned to the idea of establishing aeronautical engineering (with associated laboratories) at MIT. Hunsaker had just completed a master's degree in naval architecture at MIT and had become interested in aerodynamics toward the end of his program. This burgeoning interest led him to translate a French article on the topic for the U.S. Naval Institute's *Proceedings*, followed soon afterward by a translation of Gustave Eiffel's *The Resistance of the Air and Aviation*. Consequently, Maclaurin saw this up-and-coming engineer as an ideal candidate to guide MIT's new program. He approached Hunsaker in April 1913 to see if he was willing to stay at MIT and help develop the aeronautics curriculum. Hunsaker quickly agreed and in June, Secretary of the Navy Daniels approved Hunsaker's three-year detail to MIT for this purpose. Hunsaker's first task would be a survey of aeronautical laboratories in Europe. It was in response to Maclaurin's plan to send Hunsaker on this trip that the Langley Advisory Committee voted to have Zahm accompany Hunsaker. The two men returned to the United States in December, and Hunsaker immediately started work on a curriculum for MIT.[14]

At the end of 1913, Walcott discovered that the law against government workers serving on committees without congressional approval also applied to the Langley Advisory Committee. In spring 1914, he went before Congress to get their approval, but the Progressives in Congress were looking to streamline government and were unwilling to authorize something that might grow into an independent Bureau of Aeronautics. When Walcott received confirmation from the comptroller general in May that the Langley Advisory Committee was, in fact, illegal, Walcott disbanded it and again closed down the Langley Aerodynamical Laboratory.[15] As already discussed, Chambers had been "plucked" in the summer of 1913, but remained on active duty nevertheless. While he continued to push for some sort of national aeronautic lab, his influence was waning. It waned further when Fiske took control of naval aviation in January 1914 and appointed Bristol as the director of naval aviation, relegating Chambers to lesser duties. This left Walcott more or less alone in pushing for a lab.

At the end of 1914, Walcott made another effort, feeling that the advent of World War I in Europe and the subsequent preparedness movement in the United States would make the idea of a national aeronautic lab more palatable to Congress. In December, he once again proposed a national lab to the Smithsonian Regents, who authorized him to head a subcommittee that would assemble a proposal for Congress. In January 1915, the full Board of Regents approved the subcommittee's draft bill, which emphasized an advisory committee (along the lines of 1913's Langley Advisory Committee, the committee in Chambers' 1912 report, or the inspiration for both: Britain's Advisory Committee for Aeronautics) while pushing the lab to the background. Playing to the Progressivists' desire for efficiency, the proposed advisory committee would be a central clearinghouse for information and would thereby prevent duplication of effort among existing government and private aeronautical labs. Friendly congressmen quickly introduced the bill in the Naval Affairs Committees in the House and the Senate, which passed them on to the full chambers with little change. In order to beat the close of the 63rd Congress on March 4, Congress attached the joint proposal for an advisory committee for aeronautics to the annual naval appropriations bill, which passed on March 3, 1915.[16]

With the Advisory Committee for Aeronautics now authorized, the Army began playing a greater role. The committee met for the first time in the office of the secretary of war on April 15 and in Walcott's absence elected Scriven as its temporary chairman. This first meeting was taken up with self-organization. The committee's first action was to rename itself the *National* Advisory Committee for Aeronautics (NACA) to distinguish the American group from the Advisory Committee for Aeronautics (ACA) in Great Britain. Scriven then presented a long letter describing his proposed organization for the NACA, in which he also suggested that the new organization use its influence to support increased military aviation budgets. He was opposed to a great proliferation of subcommittees, believing that too many would cause the NACA to lose focus and effectiveness. Instead, he wanted to see the main committee (i.e., the full membership of the NACA as approved by Congress) subdivided into three boards: an administrative board of government representatives, a science board of the members from private life (all of whom had science and/or engineering backgrounds), and a three-man executive council for the day-to-day operations of the NACA. Scriven got his wish for an executive committee, though the Main Committee created it with seven members. The executive committee then met, elected the absent Walcott as its chair, and adjourned until Walcott could join them. Scriven succeeded in getting the main committee to remove from its draft rules and regulations (sent to President Wilson for his approval) a suggestion by Walcott for subcommittees chaired by a member of the main committee, but open to outside experts as needed. Walcott, however, learned of this omission and successfully appealed directly to the President to restore this provision.[17]

Historian Samuel Huntington has argued that interservice rivalry only became a serious political problem when the Army and Navy began competing with each other directly for money.[18] Though he had the services' 1947 unification in the National Military Establishment in mind, the events of 1915–1916 support his argument. In September 1915, Secretary of the Navy Daniels wrote to the newly created Naval Consulting Board for its recommendations for setting up an experimental research lab.[19] Scriven saw a copy of this letter, citing it in his own proposal to the NACA in October that the committee should make its own appeal to Congress for money to establish an NACA aeronautical lab. Historian Alex Roland notes that it is difficult to tell whether Scriven's proposal was in support of Daniels' impulse or a political move to block the Navy. Whatever the case, the NACA had been authorized in a naval appropriations bill, and its funding continued to come through the Navy Department. Therefore, when a special meeting of the NACA approved an FY 1917 budget request of $85,000, including more than $53,000 for an aeronautical lab, the request was forwarded to Daniels for inclusion in the Navy requests. Daniels opposed the addition of the NACA's expanded budget for two reasons. First, because the Navy was already requesting a significantly larger budget for FY 1917, including funding for the Naval Consulting Board, and Daniels was afraid that Congress would balk at funding both the NCB and the NACA. Second, Daniels pointed out that the NACA had been established for the good of aviation generally, not just for the Navy, implying that the Navy ought not to be responsible for the NACA's funding. When

Daniels rejected the NACA's requested budget, Walcott and Stratton (head of the National Bureau of Standards) met with Daniels and subsequently testified before the House Naval Affairs Committee. On August 26, 1916, President Wilson signed the naval appropriations bill for FY 1917 into law, including $85,000 for the NACA.[20]

The NACA provided a framework for Army-Navy cooperation on aircraft, both formally as a mediating body between the two services and informally through the presence of both Army and Navy officers on the main committee and the many subcommittees. In the Annual Report of the Secretary of the Navy for 1916, Daniels told Congress, "The Advisory Committee for Aeronautics, authorized under and appropriated for in the naval bill, is working in hearty cooperation with the aviation corps of both the Army and Navy, and it is hoped and believed this spirit of cooperation and the results of the study of this scientific body and the Naval Consulting Board will aid in a more rapidly increasing and efficient aviation branch of the service." Furthermore, the NACA promised to be a central authority that could perform (or at least guide) the sort of research that both Army and Navy air services felt they needed to progress. However, the committee was still finding its way. It did not yet have a master plan for research, instead addressing problems in an ad hoc manner. Congress had approved the creation of an NACA aeronautical lab, and Squier was instrumental in selecting Langley Field (in Hampton, Virginia) as a site where the Aviation Section of the Signal Corps could work side by side with the NACA lab. However, it would take several years for the NACA to turn Congress' funding into a laboratory facility ready to undertake aeronautical studies.[21] Yet even after it had a laboratory and a clear master plan, it was anticipated that the NACA would still not be able to take on all of the research desired by the Army and Navy; Squier's desire for the Army and the NACA to work at the same location is proof of that.

JOINT ARMY-NAVY BOARDS

The many opportunities for interservice interaction in the various attempts to set up a national aerodynamics laboratory (culminating in the NACA) may have contributed to a realization that the Army and Navy had more to discuss regarding aviation than basic scientific and engineering research. Under President Theodore Roosevelt, the two services had established the Joint Army and Navy Board (frequently called simply the Joint Board) in 1903 to coordinate their actions in defense of the United States and its possessions.[22] On September 7, 1916, Secretary of the Navy Daniels wrote the president of the Joint Board requesting that it define "the respective duties of the Army and the Navy, in connection with defense of the coast against aircraft attacks." Daniels directed special attention to the Canal Zone, "where the duties of the Army and Navy . . . are so intimately related." Traditionally, Army responsibility for coastal defense against approaching enemy fleets began at the furthest extent of its reach (i.e., the limit of coastal artillery), but with both services now operating aircraft, this line of demarcation was becoming blurry: were airplanes an extension of artillery (thus increasing the Army's responsibilities), or merely a tool of artillery (leaving the line unchanged)? Daniels wanted the Joint Board to clarify the responsibilities for defending shore stations in general, and Navy stations in particular, against aerial attack and to outline how the two departments should coordinate and cooperate in such defense. Daniels also asked the Joint Board to consider whether it was advisable to standardize equipment for aerial defense against aircraft between Army and Navy. The wording of these questions indicates that Daniels was not thinking about defensive fighter planes (even the Army was not yet equipping its aircraft with machine guns); rather, he was contemplating antiaircraft guns and other ground-based protective measures.[23]

Meanwhile, on October 11, 1916, in response to questions raised by Squier, Acting Secretary of War William Ingraham proposed a joint board to consider interservice coordination in developing airships for the Army and Navy.[24] The Navy agreed and initially named to this board Capt. Hugh Rodman (from the Navy's General Board), Capt. Josiah McKean (the CNO's aide for material), and Lt. John Towers. Then–Lieutenant Colonel Squier, Maj. Stanley D. Embick (Coast Artillery Corps), and Maj. D. T. Moore (Field Artillery and member of the Army's General Staff) represented the Army. However, this board not only suffered from a vague mandate, but also lacked formal identification. CNO Benson referred to it as the "Joint Board, Army and Navy re Division of Aeronautic Cognizance," and in a letter of March 1917 it called itself the "Board of Army and Navy Officers relative development aeronautical service," but it was more often referred to as the "Joint Board on Aeronautic Cognizance" or simply the "Cognizance Board." (Only in 1919 was it officially named the "Joint Army and Navy Board on Aeronautics," more commonly known as the "Aeronautical Board.")[25] The lack of a formal precept contributed to the multiplicity of names, and the Cognizance Board was not so much *established* as it *evolved* into its final purpose.

The initial impulse for the Cognizance Board (as proposed by Ingraham) was to address questions of airship development. But before it met for the first time, its purpose began expanding to broader issues of interservice cooperation regarding the air services and to some of the questions Daniels had directed toward the Joint Board in September. On October 27, Benson recommended to Daniels that he name an officer from the General Board, one from the CNO's office, and a naval aviator as the Navy members of the Cognizance Board (recommendations Daniels apparently followed in Rodman, McKean, and Towers). Benson then outlined what he thought should be the responsibilities of Army and Navy aircraft in defending the country and its possessions. The Army, he said, should be responsible for all aircraft operating with the mobile army, those spotting for coastal artillery, and those protecting other Army fortifications. The Navy should similarly be responsible for all aircraft operating with fleets and those operating from shore bases for scouting over the water, and for protecting other Navy shore establishments not close enough to any Army responsibilities to benefit from Army aerial defenses. (Having said this, Benson listed the Navy yards, magazines, radio stations, ship and submarine bases, and Marine Barracks deserving of aerial defense. Of twenty-five entries, he only marked one—the Darien Radio Station in the Canal Zone—as being an Army responsibility.) Benson concluded his memorandum with the statement that it was debatable whether dirigibles would be

needed for overland work or be useful in the defense of cities or fortifications. He proposed that the joint board should address this question and,
if it decided that dirigibles were needed, consider whether they should be
supplied by the Army or by the Navy, which had a clear use for dirigibles
in scouting at sea.[26]

Benson had asked his office staff for their comments on the questions
raised by Daniels in the secretary's September 7 letter to the Joint Board.
As a member of the Joint Board, Benson wanted to be prepared in case the
board agreed to take up discussion of the issues. The three responses (dated
November 20–22) all concurred that some sort of joint board was desirable
to address the issue of Army and Navy responsibility for air defense and
to establish doctrine to coordinate such defense. Perhaps because Benson's
October 27 letter to Daniels had spoken only of the need to coordinate
aircraft used in defense, the replies from the office staff emphasized the
need to establish responsibility for other, ground-based defense against
enemy aerial attack, such as antiaircraft guns. Benson's respondents were
also in agreement that some joint body should formally study coordination of other aspects of the services' aviation programs, with an eye toward
standardization of parts and equipment. Towers, one of the office respondents, was emphatic that a "Permanent Joint Technical Board" was needed
to "draw up definite plans for cooperation of the two services." He said
such standardization was "essential," and that "immediate action is necessary" to resolve questions of interservice coordination.[27] These responses
backed up Benson's idea that the proposed joint board needed to address
more than just airships.

Benson's desire for a broader mandate seems to have informed Daniels'
expectation of the work of the Cognizance Board. In the secretary's annual
report to Congress (submitted December 1, 1916), Daniels explained,
"A joint Army and Navy board will shortly convene to decide upon the
division of responsibility between these services for the air forces of the
Nation." Daniels was particularly interested in clearly defining who was
responsible for each aspect of continental defense, since the Navy was
planning to establish coastal air patrol stations. He did not want to spend

Navy resources on these stations if they were going to be made superflu-
ous by Army plans or, perhaps worse, if they would have to be turned over
to the Army. Daniels wanted "a complete understanding between the two
services" before committing to any new air stations.[28]

The Army seemed to be having similar discussions at about the same
time. On December 29, 1916, Secretary of War Newton Baker forwarded
to Daniels several documents from the Army War College "pertaining to
the question of defense against air attack and the proper joint relations
between the Army and Navy in connection with this subject." He proposed
submitting the questions to the joint board discussing airship development. On January 12, 1917, Franklin Roosevelt (as Acting Secretary of the
Navy) not only "heartily agreed" with Baker's proposal, but also proposed
further expanding the purview of this board to include "the whole subject
of cooperation" between Army and Navy forces assigned to local defense
of the coast. Roosevelt then outlined a series of additional questions for
the board to consider, starting with the four points Daniels had asked the
General Board about on September 7, and adding further questions raised
in the staff responses to Benson's October 27 missive. Given this increase
in the Cognizance Board's purpose, Roosevelt told Baker that he would
replace Towers with a more senior Navy officer: Capt. George Marvel.
Marvel was the director of Naval Districts, the officer most responsible for
managing the Navy's shore-based defense on a national level.[29]

While the two secretaries were discussing expanded responsibilities for
the Cognizance Board, the board itself finally met to address its original
mandate, the development of "Zeppelins or other mobile lighter-than-air
craft for military and naval purposes."[30] On January 6, the board (identifying itself merely as a "Board of Army and Navy Officers") submitted its
recommendations on airships. The report was little more than a brief letter and stated, "The Board is convinced that airships of the 'Zeppelin' type
will prove a valuable element in the national defense." Noting that no one
in the United States had a design for such a craft, much less the facilities to
construct one, the board recommended that the Army and Navy cooperate to design and build a rigid airship. Only two of the board's six members

(Towers and Squier) were involved in aviation, so it recommended the creation of a new joint board to coordinate and oversee the project. This new board was to have seven members: the chief constructor of the Navy would preside over three additional Navy and three Army officers, each having appropriate technical expertise.[31]

Daniels and Baker quickly organized the Joint Army and Navy Airship Board (known simply as the "Airship Board" or sometimes the "Zeppelin Board") sometime in January 1917 with David Taylor (rear admiral and chief constructor since December 14, 1914) as its head.[32] Hunsaker and Towers were founding members along with newly minted naval aviator Lt. W. G. Child, while the Army contingent consisted of Squier, Capt. Virginius Clark and Capt. Charles deForest Chandler.[33] The United States' declaration of war against Germany on April 6, 1917, quickly changed the nature of this board from overseeing design and construction of an airship to addressing the more pressing question of whether either service needed airships for the war. The Airship Board's final report, submitted July 1918, reflects the changed priorities of the U.S. military with the advent of participation in World War I. It recommended that if either Army or Navy wanted rigid airships for use in Europe or over European waters, those airships should be purchased in England. Any airships wanted for use in the United States, its territories, or possessions should be constructed in the United States. The Airship Board echoed the Cognizance Board's recommendations in stating that, since the Navy had a clear need for large rigid airships for ocean patrol, it should take the lead in airship construction while providing full information to the Army. It also recommended that the Navy make a long-term plan to build four airships and the necessary infrastructure for their construction and operation. Finally, the Airship Board recommended its own dissolution because its members were now busy with other wartime duties and not in a position to supervise overseas purchase or domestic construction of airships. Instead, it suggested that such work could best be completed by existing construction organizations in the respective services. The service secretaries accepted this recommendation and formally dissolved the Airship Board on September 21, 1918.[34]

While the Airship Board was being organized, the Cognizance Board took up its new, expanded duties: determining the "proper joint relations" between Army and Navy on the subject of aircraft and the "whole subject of cooperation" of the services with respect to aircraft and coastal defense. The Cognizance Board wasted no time, issuing a report on March 12, 1917, that addressed the several questions Roosevelt had asked in his January 12 letter to Baker.[35]

The Cognizance Board's report declared that "a war with a first class power will find the two services constantly operating together" along the coastline. As a result, the two air services should plan for "joint development, organization, and operation," rather than allowing each air arm to develop independently "within delimited exact areas of responsibility." While agreeing that the coastline should be a general line of demarcation between Army and Navy, the board decided that being too specific about where Navy responsibility stopped and Army responsibility started would be "neither practicable nor desirable." The report did, however, present general definitions of Army and Navy responsibilities. These followed very closely the division of responsibilities proposed by Benson in his letter to Daniels on October 27, 1916. The Army would be responsible for aircraft operating with the mobile army and those spotting for coastal artillery, while the Navy retained aircraft operating with the fleets and those operating from land bases for scouting over the sea. The only difference was Benson's proposal that each service retain control over aircraft protecting their own shore establishments, whereas the Cognizance Board recommended that the Navy retain control over only those planes under the command of naval districts and Advance Base Forces while the Army would command all other shore-based aircraft.[36]

The board reasoned that any battle against an invading force was likely to be a fluid situation, with the Army and Navy each taking the lead role at different points, and it thus felt that the aviators from both services should get used to working together. To this end, the board proposed joint training stations for pilots and observers from both services "so that each service may effectively supplement the other in time of need." Furthermore, the board stated that the aircraft in use by both services should be as similar as possible, with standard motors and controls, and that if either service established its own aircraft plant, the other should have use of it as well. In order to standardize the equipment, the board wanted both services to cooperate in the design and purchase of new aircraft, with the Navy taking the lead in developing seaplanes and the Army in developing landplanes.[37]

The Cognizance Board's report essentially codified the existing tacit understanding of the responsibilities of the Army and Navy air services in terms of their respective duties and areas of operation. The notion that the Navy should develop seaplanes and the Army landplanes was nothing new either. Though the broad wording would lead to some interservice friction once the United States entered World War I, the delineation of responsibility would guide the Army and Navy well into the interwar period. Establishing joint training stations for combined training of aviators from both services was new and forward thinking, but neither service moved to establish these before the United States entered the war not quite a month after the board submitted this report. Meanwhile, the United States' sudden shift from neutral to combatant status generated all sorts of joint issues, and the Cognizance Board was kept busy addressing most of those related to aviation.[38]

One more joint board deserves mention here, though it did not come into existence until after the United States entered World War I. On May 5, the secretaries of the War Department and the Navy Department established the Joint Army and Navy Technical Board (the "Technical Board") largely in response to requests from the United States' new allies for aircraft in numbers well beyond anything the U.S. military had considered. The main purpose of this new board was to establish what types of planes (bombers, fighters, reconnaissance, etc.) and engines the U.S. military would purchase to meet its greatly increased need for aircraft. The Technical Board also addressed issues of standardization between Army and Navy aircraft, the need for which had been noted by Towers a few months earlier. However, it was not to be the "Permanent Joint Technical

Board" that Towers had called for, since—like the Airship Board—the Technical Board would not outlast the war. Once the Technical Board had decided what kinds of planes were needed and in what numbers, its purpose began to drift, and it became less and less important to the conduct of the war. The Technical Board met for the last time on July 24, 1918.[39]

CONCLUSIONS

Even as the flyers had to negotiate relations with their parent services, the services found they needed to negotiate relations with each other in ways they previously had not. Aviation provided a greater area of common ground and thus the potential for greater interservice conflict than any previous development. The gradual shift of each service's control over its aviators from loose informality to a more rigid and defined managerial structure mirrored the development of increasingly formalized interservice contacts—the various joint boards—necessary to ensure coordination, if not cooperation, between the War Department and the Navy Department with respect to aviation. These contacts, however, focused on issues of common scientific, technical, and (eventually) production of aircraft. Other than trying to work out responsibility for aerial defense (both air- and ground-based) of the nation and its territories, there was no attempt to create any sort of common aviation doctrine.

CONCLUSION

This was the status of aviation at the beginning of 1917: both the Army and the Navy had sufficient airplanes and aviators that they were not merely "self-sustaining" (training only as many new aviators as were lost to all causes and barely able to replace aircraft lost) but capable of real growth while simultaneously having enough planes and experienced aviators to allow some to concentrate on testing equipment and techniques necessary to making the airplane militarily useful as well as beginning operational deployments. The Marines were not far behind—the training and basic testing of hardware were, of course, primarily Navy responsibilities, but the establishment of the Advance Base Aeronautic Unit in Philadelphia meant they would soon field an operational aviation force that would also be able to do the testing and evaluation necessary for the Marine-specific missions. Doctrinally, the Marines were the most advanced, if only because Cunningham had established such a clear vision for Marine aviation at the beginning and hewed closely to it throughout. The Philadelphia force, once complete, would fulfill his initial idea for how the Marines would use aircraft. In both the Army and the Navy, doctrine was much less settled.

In the Navy, doctrine remained largely tacit, and there was a huge gap between the ideas about how the Navy would use airplanes and the ability of the planes and aviators to actually do those things. Winter fleet maneuvers had demonstrated a primitive ability for airplanes to spot vessels approaching a coast (though not too far from the coast) while events at Veracruz had demonstrated aviation's ability to reconnoiter over land (something of interest to the Marines but not the Navy) and quickly survey harbors and anchorages for underwater obstructions and mines. But in 1917, the Navy had only just gained enough confidence in airplane compasses to permit the most experienced aviators to fly from Pensacola to a point miles offshore (and well out of sight of land) and back, and only under carefully controlled conditions. Naval aviators had yet to show that they could take off at sea, fly a search, and then navigate back to a ship that had moved in the meantime. Nor had the Navy yet developed (much less adopted as standard equipment) an aerial radio that would make such searches more efficient. The radio was also necessary for the other mission for which the Navy had wanted airplanes: spotting for ship's guns. Naval theorists had considered the usefulness of arming Navy planes with machine guns (to deny the enemy the benefits of aerial spotting and reconnaissance) as well as bombs and torpedoes, but the Navy had done only preliminary experiments with bombs and bombsights and nothing at all with respect to torpedoes or machine guns. Of course, Navy airplanes had gotten to the point of being able to carry the extra weight of small bombs or machine guns only by about 1916, and a full-sized torpedo was out of the question. Plans to test a machine gun in the air were scuttled in the 1916 maneuvers when the one airplane present that was deemed capable of safely carrying a machine gun was damaged and unable to be repaired in time. The exercises also showed naval aviation's inability to perform reconnaissance effectively at even the most conservative estimates of an altitude considered "safe" from ground fire (based on observations of the war in Europe).

Things were not much better in the Army. As with the Navy, aviation doctrine was largely tacit, and plans for aircraft deployment and use far outstripped capabilities—of Army aviation as a whole and of the state of aircraft technology as well. Army aviation had performed some important reconnaissance at the beginning of the 1916 Punitive Expedition and had served well in the liaison role. But the expedition had also brutally demonstrated that the Army did not yet have airplanes capable of operating effectively in the high desert of northern Mexico, nor was the

Army prepared to maintain them in the harsh, dry conditions there. The Army had actually done testing of aerial machine guns and bombing, but Foulois' unfulfilled requests for aircraft armament show that the Army was no closer to fielding such capabilities than the Navy at this time. Because closing speeds of land forces were relatively slow, the Army's need for reconnaissance reports was not as time sensitive as in the Navy (where an instantaneous radio report of an enemy fleet might give two hours' warning instead of only one), but like the Navy, the Army needed radio to make aerial artillery spotting viable. Yet the Army was only marginally closer than the Navy to fielding an airplane radio.

Taken in isolation, this was merely the state of the respective services' development of aviation. The only surprising comparison between the services may be that the Navy was not significantly further behind the Army in developing aviation despite starting two years later and facing more organizational difficulties. The U.S. services only seem to be "behind" in development when compared to military aviation in Europe in 1917. Having described the historical events, what patterns emerge from studying them, and do those patterns explain the state of development in 1917?

First and foremost are the networks that developed. In the Army, we see senior people (successive chiefs of the Signal Corps) acting as technology patrons: initiating discussion of how aviation could be useful to the service, and actively creating an organization to establish and maintain Army aviation. That said, individual interest in (and patronage of) aviation varied somewhat among successive chiefs. Adolphus Greely fought long and hard to reestablish and maintain a military ballooning program within the Signal Corps and was a strong supporter of Samuel Langley's experiments. His successor, James Allen, carried Greely's ideas forward, but seemed less personally invested in aviation, leaving much of its management to his subordinates at the Aviation Desk. Following acquisition of the first dirigible airship and airplane, even that level of interest seems to have disappeared for a time, leaving the junior officers in charge of the respective aircraft on their own. The attitude of the office of the Signal Corps could be characterized as somewhere between, "We've got one, now what?" and "We've given you one, now stop bothering me." This neglect seems to have killed off the dirigible program (and the Army's dirigible itself), even as it ceded initiative (without any responsibility or authority) to junior officer Benjamin Foulois for the airplane.

Signal Corps interest in aviation revived in 1911, as seen by the assignment of new officers to aviation training and the purchase of new aircraft. This strengthened the bottom end of the network (the likely advocates) by the addition of people and resources, but also weakened that part of the network since it introduced divisions between the officers trained in one type of aircraft control system vs. those trained in the other, and confused the lines of authority and seniority among the aviators. These internal divisions among the junior officers actually using the technology soon became less significant, though it would take some time for the mismatch between rank and flying experience to entirely disappear. However, the division between the junior officers actively using the technology "in the field" (the technology advocates) versus the more senior officers in bureaucratic roles in Washington (technology patrons) remained, with each side convinced the other did not have the "full picture."

This disconnect was ameliorated in different ways, none of them permanent. Initially, the proximity of College Park to Washington (especially when aviators were commuting from offices downtown) kept problems from growing too large. But once the Army elected to leave College Park, the aviators became much more isolated from headquarters. Having an aviator in Washington to help "translate" between the two groups helped, as when Arnold requested relief from flying duties and was reassigned to Washington, first in the Aeronautical Division and then as assistant to Chief of Signal James Allen. But Arnold's time in Washington was brief. Though Reber was an aviator, he was a balloonist and does not appear to have understood airplanes. At the very least, he apparently did not provide the bridge between practical experience and purely intellectual understanding of heavier-than-air flight that he might have. Foulois' return to Washington in late 1916 to advise and assist Squier (a very engaged patron of aviation) held promise of being a very fruitful pairing, but the U.S. declaration of war soon afterward meant that this, too, was a very brief period.

The Navy's network formed differently but had similar problems connecting advocates and potential patrons. In 1909 and 1910, the chiefs of three separate Navy bureaus (all holding flag rank) expressed a desire to acquire (and presumably take control of) airplanes for the Navy. For some reason, the Navy secretary, presented with two of these requests simultaneously, chose not to put either bureau in charge, but instead to assign responsibility to a captain (Washington I. Chambers) who was essentially an aide to an aide. Junior to the admirals in charge and with no clear mandate to direct aviation, only "coordinate" it, he had no way to compel cooperation from the bureaus. He briefly acquired a patron in the form of Admiral of the Navy George Dewey, who outranked every other uniformed Navy officer, but whose position as head of the General Board was merely advisory. Congress created further confusion by voting money for naval aviation but putting it in the budget of yet a fourth bureau whose chief had neither asked for nor was interested in control of aviation.

Chambers nevertheless became as much of a patron to aviation as he could be, developing into a committed advocate for his vision of aviation. Unfortunately, the same division between headquarters and the aviators in the field seen in Army aviation soon emerged in the Navy as well; the advocates came to believe that headquarters neither understood nor listened to them while headquarters interpreted their repeated attempts to explain their concerns as insubordination. Meanwhile, another aviation supporter, Rear Adm. Bradley Fiske, believed Chambers was deliberately holding naval aviation back. Though Fiske was assigned to Washington as an aide to the Navy secretary, he had the rank and political skill to take over responsibility for aviation from BuNav and sideline Chambers. Having achieved this goal, Fiske seems to have lost interest in aviation, leaving its future to his hand-picked man, Capt. Mark Bristol. Whether Fiske exercised control entirely through verbal instructions to Bristol or his subordinate was indeed acting on his own, Bristol had Fiske's authority backing him up and was thereby able to act as a patron where Chambers could not, despite holding the same rank.

Fiske provided naval aviation some stability in the form of a permanent home in Pensacola and a formally constituted Office of Naval Aviation (ONA). However, whatever stability Fiske's patronage provided was not to last. Less than two years after taking over aviation, Fiske was shipped off to the Naval War College and the Office of Naval Aviation was moved again, this time into the office of the newly created Chief of Naval Operations (CNO). Since the ONA had only been created under Fiske's authority as an aide, the office's transfer to a new boss in a different office (with no requirement from higher authority to maintain the ONA) once again put naval aviation's organization in question. Bristol's continuation for a time as director of naval aviation under the CNO provided some stability, but his eventual reassignment to sea duty (and failure of his efforts to retain the directorship while at sea) led to aviation once again being under an officer who did not want the responsibility (Captain McKean).

As with the Army, there were moments when having an experienced aviator in Washington could have bridged the intellectual gap between practitioners in the field and theorists in leadership. Mustin explicitly identified the gap in a letter to Bristol in 1914, expressing his frustration that Bristol refused to listen to him on points regarding the aircraft and their equipment: "I have not been able to convince you that my ideas in these two features carry more weight than the ideas you get from sources that are unsupported by practical flying knowledge."[1] Indeed, the gap between Bristol and Mustin was so great that it was likely a major cause of Mustin's removal from aviation at the beginning of 1917. As with Army aviation, the Navy seldom had a qualified and experienced aviator in Washington to bridge the two perspectives. Chambers briefly had the assistance in his office of Ellyson, but only for a few months in 1913. Bristol also had an aviator, but only a relatively inexperienced lieutenant (junior grade), Bronson. Towers, Bronson's replacement under McKean, was a much more knowledgeable and experienced advocate for naval aviation in

Washington. He also brought more rank to the position, as a full lieutenant who was close to promotion. Yet he remained a very junior officer in Washington; it was his knowledge and aviation experience that earned the respect of his superiors, not his rank. As with Foulois' similar assignment, though, Towers had little opportunity to make a difference in Washington before the United States' declaration of war changed everything.

The Marine aviation network was much smaller than those of the Army or the Navy, and this was both its strength and its weakness. Strength because the smaller numbers of aviators (no more than two or three for much of the period up to 1917) meant there was less opportunity for division among the advocates. Since the entire Marine officer corps was also much smaller than that of the other two services, there were fewer bureaucratic layers between Cunningham and the major general commandant. It is also possible (though I encountered no direct evidence) that a more personal familiarity among the Marines' smaller officer corps helped ameliorate the physical and experiential distance between headquarters and the field. Though Cunningham left flying for a time (at his wife's insistence), he remained active in promoting aviation, effectively serving as the director of Marine aviation as a member of the major general commandant's staff from 1913 to 1915. Thus, he was the aviation commander in Washington with actual flying experience that the other two services' aviators desired. Yet while Marine aviation's small size helped in these ways, the small size also made it more difficult for Marine aviation to develop its own independent identity through testing and experiments based on its own needs (rather than those of the Navy) and creation of its own operational forces.

All three services faced a problem with technology: both the abilities of the aircraft available to the services as well as the aviators' ability to effectively use the aircraft they did have. On the hardware side, aircraft remained a weak link in all the services' networks. Aside from inherently unstable designs (such as the Wright Model C and the Curtiss JN-2) and the dangers posed by pusher designs in not-infrequent crashes, aircraft of the time were, by later standards, underpowered. While later pre-war designs did not require carefully managing aircrew weight (with the heaviest pilots able to carry only the lightest companions) as was necessary with the first airplanes, they still had little lifting ability to spare for heavy equipment such as radios or ordnance. On top of this, engines remained unreliable. Certainly they failed less in 1916 than they had even in 1911, but they were still prone to unexpected stoppage during flight requiring the aviators to drop everything else and search for a safe place to make an emergency landing.

Thus, for much of the pre–World War I era covered here, the operators were concentrating on survival rather than development of doctrine. Even setting aside technical problems with the aircraft, these flyers, once qualified as aviators (by whichever standard existed at the time), still needed to build up experience and confidence to allow them to live to fly again without devoting 100 percent of their effort into not dying! On a more metaphorical level, their numbers for much of this period remained too small to be a self-sustaining community. New officers were assigned to training, but the additions only slightly outpaced losses due to death, reassignment, and the occasional withdrawal for personal reasons. The aviators were able to test arming aircraft with machine guns and bombs but did not have the support from headquarters to move beyond limited experiments to developing tactics and doctrine for using these weapons.

Still, how these networks did or did not form is not the only factor shaping military aviation's development. Differences in organizational structure and how each service tried to fit aviation into that structure also influenced the development of military aviation. In this period, Army structure centered on its three combat arms: infantry, cavalry, and artillery. These were supported by specialty organizations (corps and smaller departments) that prepared the combat arms for war (Ordnance Department, Quartermaster Corps), provided administrative support (Judge Advocate General Corps, Pay Department[2]), or directly supported the Army in the field (Medical Corps, Signal Corps). The Signal Corps' responsibilities centered on the collection and dissemination of information. Since these were the simplest and easiest functions for balloons, dirigibles, and airplanes to fulfill, the Signal Corps claimed responsibility for all aircraft. Other Signal Corps responsibilities such as the newer technologies of the telegraph, telephone, and radio for battlefield communications meant that the Signal Corps also hosted officers trained in science and technology. Since the Army had not yet embraced motorized ground vehicles, only the Ordnance Department, among the Army's other organizations, offered officers who might have had the relevant technical knowledge and training to have supported aviation, but it apparently had no desire to try to take aviation away from the Signal Corps. This provided military aviation a "protected space" in which to grow but, as demonstrated by testimony in various Congressional hearings, meant that it was harder for aviation to develop in areas that were not Signal Corps responsibilities.

The Navy had no specific organization to handle its one combat arm: ships. Until the 1915 creation of the position of Chief of Naval Operations, all ships and squadrons at sea reported directly to the Navy secretary, advised (during the earlier part of the period covered by this book) by an aide for operations. All of the Navy's bureaus prior to 1915 were focused on supporting the ships at sea, such as the Bureau of Construction and Repair (C&R) to build and maintain the ships themselves, the Bureau of Equipment to provide most everything not an integral part of the hull, a Bureau of Steam Engineering for engines of all types (not just steam engines) as well as electrical systems and radio, and a Bureau of Ordnance to deal with everything related to weapons. As in the Army, other bureaus existed for things like legal support, medical support, and handling consumables and pay accounts. This more decentralized system did not offer an obvious place for aviation to reside. Yet almost any of the "material" bureaus (C&R, Equipment, or Steam Engineering) would have been a better choice for aviation than the Bureau of Navigation (which combined technical and administrative functions), where Congress put it for reasons unknown. No one seems to have objected when Fiske, then the aide for operations, moved aviation from BuNav to his own office, effectively putting it on the same level as commands at sea. When Congress created the position and office of the Chief of Naval Operations as a new organization on the same level as the bureaus, it made sense to put aviation under this new operational command. But it did not naturally "belong" there, any more than it had "belonged" in BuNav. Naval aviation was the proverbial "red-headed stepchild," neither liked nor wanted by many of the Navy's leaders. Thus, it did not have the same "protected space" in which to grow that Army aviation had in the Signal Corps, hindering its growth.

The situation for Marine aviation was complicated by its relationship with the Navy. The Marine Corps relied on the Navy for much of its administrative needs and was small enough up to 1917 not to require the sort of organization that existed in either the Army or the Navy. The major general commandant's staff served those functions to the extent the Corps needed them. Marine aviation had the approval (and possibly the active patronage) of the two commanders of the Marine Corps during this era: William Biddle and George Barnett. Their approval of Cunningham's ideas provided a protected space within the Marine Corps without the restrictions imposed by Army aviation's dependence on the Signal Corps. On the other hand, Marine aviation's dependence on the Navy for equipment and training meant that the Marines shared the Navy's problems with these— to say nothing of the difficulty of getting aircraft out of the Navy for strictly Marine Corps purposes.

Culture undoubtedly played a role in shaping military aviation as well, though one harder to tease out than organizational structure. Aviation was the Army's first experiment with the internal combustion engine and mechanization generally—recall that the trucks ordered for the Punitive Expedition had to be assembled by the aviation squadron's mechanics because they were the only ones with the relevant experience. Thus, not only was the airplane itself outside the Army's experience, so was its propulsion method, likely leading many outside the aviation network to look askance at this noisy, dirty technology. This sort of prejudice no doubt led to Foulois' "buzzing" of the troops gathering in Texas in 1911—what he excused as "indoctrination flights"—that likely only made things worse. Army aviation, and those involved with it, faced an uphill battle against culture in getting the rest of the Army to accept that aviation was a useful and necessary addition to the service.

Unlike the Army, the Navy had a long experience of mechanical power. It first used steam engines to power ships during the Civil War, and internal combustion engines were introduced with the first submarine in 1900, which was powered by a gasoline engine. In fact, the Navy was much more used to large machines (even sailing ships are a type of machine) than the Army (whose largest machines were the breech-loading horse-drawn field artillery and larger fixed coastal artillery pieces which began coming into use in the 1880s). The Navy's bureau system reflected this culture, dividing the responsibility for the complex machinery of ships into several different bureaus. This contributed to naval aviation's problems before the First World War, but arguably put it in a better position than the Army for the massive increase in aviation's scale that came with participation in the war. Dealing with a new, noisy, dirty technology was also not new in the Navy: airplanes were proceeded by about a decade by the first submarines, whose on-board conditions soon earned them the nickname "pig-boats." Indeed, quite a number of the early naval aviators transferred from submarine service. It seems likely that naval aviation faced less cultural resistance from its parent service than did Army aviation, at least from the perspective of mechanization; prospective aviators in both services were told by fellow officers and superiors that aviation seemed like a fast way of killing yourself.

The important parts of Marine Corps culture for this narrative were the extremely small size of its officer corps and the fact that the Marine Corps had just reinvented itself to avoid the threat of elimination (something the Corps had done numerous times over its history). The small size was important because it meant that most (if not all) officers had served with each other at some point: senior officers could draw on personal knowledge when selecting juniors for an assignment or, in the case of the airplane, when considering a junior's suggestion. In the larger Navy or Army officer communities, there was a better chance that something like Cunningham's suggestion for using aircraft would have reached someone in the bureaucracy to whom the originator was nothing more than a name, increasing the chances that the correspondence would get no special attention and languish in the files. The second aspect—that the Marine Corps had a history of periodically reinventing itself to remain viable and had just recently done so again—gave the Corps a bias toward flexibility not present in the other two services.[3] As such, it was likely more willing as an organization to seriously consider proposals that might increase its fighting effectiveness, even if they might seem odd or outlandish at first glance, such as using airplanes in place of nonexistent cavalry.

However, while culture and organizational structure of the three services likely played a part in shaping each services' aviation arm and aviation doctrine, they are secondary to the networks (and selected people within those networks) that emerged. In both Army and Navy there were effectively two different networks in each service: one of the advocates and potential advocates in the field, and the other of each service's leadership in Washington, including patrons and potential patrons. In the period covered in this book, these two networks sometimes operated at cross-purposes but could never completely agree on how to develop aviation equipment and doctrine, thus making it harder to advance either. The Marine Corps network was much smaller and less divided, meaning fewer competing theories about doctrine, but its extremely small size and dependence on the Navy for equipment meant that it was no more able to test those theories than the Army or Navy. And in all three services, the airplanes themselves remained a weak link.

Despite these problems, the air services of the Army, Navy, and Marine Corps were on relatively solid ground by the beginning of 1917. They appeared to be set for a slow but steady growth in numbers of planes and personnel assigned to each. Moreover, each service had established (or had plans to establish) operational units to begin learning to integrate aviation with the respective services' traditional forces. Absent some unexpected shake-up, each air service seems to have been on a path of steady progress:

increasing numbers of personnel and aircraft assigned, improvements in the quality of men and material, and the organic development of doctrine.

The United States' declaration of war against Germany on April 6, 1917, finally brought the country into the war that President Wilson had been trying to stay out of (and had forbidden the military to prepare for). The sudden shift from peace to war completely upended aviation planning in all three U.S. services. For starters, while the U.S. military had been following technological development of aircraft among the belligerents from 1914, this had had little effect on the state of the art in the United States, where only the Curtiss JN-4 Jenny and the Model H flying boats had any military worth: the Jenny as a training aircraft, and the increasingly larger Curtiss flying boats as anti-submarine patrol craft. Neither the services nor the manufacturers in the United States had an aircraft even on the drawing board that could hold its own in aerial combat as it existed on the Western Front. Moreover, neither the services nor industry was prepared for the sheer number of aircraft (along with the accompanying requirements for aircrew, ground crew, logistics, and manufacturing necessary to make, operate, and support the aircraft) needed to fight in the war alongside the United Kingdom, France, and Italy.

Yet even had the United States been prepared to produce equipment and trained personnel on the scale needed for the war, its aviation services had failed to absorb enough of the lessons of aerial warfare over Europe and its coastal waters into their own doctrine. At the beginning of 1917, aviation doctrine in each of the U.S. services existed only in the broadest sense. While the services were beginning to move toward integrating aviation with their traditional forces, this process was only starting in early 1917. Even in the absence of the United States' declaration of war against Germany, it remained to be seen whether such integration would work, whether the numbers of aircraft and aviation units proposed was adequate, or any number of similar details regarding how aircraft would (or could) be used on a daily basis. Furthermore, any aviation doctrine remained tacit: passed on to new aviation cadets in training or (theoretically) once reaching their operational assignments, but nothing written down for dissemination. Nor is there evidence that each service's traditional forces knew how to work with (or, in the case of their commanders, how to use) airplanes.

Of course, since each of the aviation services ended up performing missions during the war that were significantly different from what each *thought* it would be doing in the event of war, perhaps it was a benefit that no one beyond a few dozen aviators had to unlearn doctrine that would likely only have confused them as they worked to learn new doctrines taught by their new allies. On the other hand, if the services had been able to establish effective networks, putting advocates and patrons in complete agreement on how best to develop and use the airplane, it is possible that the United States' military aviation services might have faced combat in Europe with airplanes and doctrine better suited to the task. The services might still not have been able to operate effectively without at least some help and guidance from their new allies, but at least, perhaps, they might have been caught less flat-footed at suddenly finding themselves in a shooting war against enemies having more than three years' hard-won experience in using the airplane against their opponents—which now included the Americans.

NOTES

PROLOGUE

1. Information in this and the preceding paragraphs is drawn from John David Anderson, *Inventing Flight: The Wright Brothers & their Predecessors* (Baltimore, MD: Johns Hopkins University Press, 2004), particularly 6–59; and Jeremy R. Kinney, *Airplanes: The Life Story of a Technology*, Greenwood Technographies (Westport, CT: Greenwood Press, 2006), 2–8. For more information on Chanute and the growing group of aeronautical researchers/inventors active in the United States from roughly 1880 to 1903, see Tom D. Crouch, *A Dream of Wings: Americans and the Airplane, 1875–1905* (New York: W. W. Norton, 1981; repr., 2002).

2. 50,000 in 1898 dollars is the equivalent of between 1.6 million and almost 60 million in 2021 dollars, depending on method of comparison; see, for example, "How much is a dollar from the past worth today?," MeasuringWorth, 2021, www.measuringworth.com/dollarvaluetoday/.

3. Secretary of War, Special Order 259, in BOF Minutes, v. 1, 5 (meeting of Oct. 30, 1888); and *Congressional Record*, 1904, 1364 (Jan. 27). Many inventions tested and purchased by the Army were developed by Army officers, and civilian inventors complained to Congress that there was a bias toward a military source for such improvements. Congress intended the civilian member of the BOF to represent the interests of nonmilitary inventors. Secretary of War, Special Order 259; Russell Jay Parkinson, "Politics, Patents, and Planes: Military Aeronautics in the United States, 1863–1907" (PhD diss., Duke University, 1963), 164.

4. BOF Minutes, v. 13, 67 (meeting of Aug. 30, 1901).

5. In 1901, the board would report its purpose as "the development and test of war material with a view to its adoption in service." BOF Minutes, v. 13, 77 (meeting of Oct. 3, 1901). For more on the development of the BOF, see Parkinson, "Politics, Patents, and Planes," Chap. 7.

6. The word "dirigible" was in common use at the time, meaning "steerable." Later on, the term would become a synonym for a lighter-than-air "airship."

7. For these aerial proposals, at least, referral of a letter to one of the Army's bureaus was the end; I did not find a single reference to such a referred letter coming back to the board for further action.

8. Wallace Rundell Beardsley, "Samuel Pierpont Langley: His Early Academic Years at the Western University of Pennsylvania" (PhD diss., University of Pittsburgh, 1978), vii-viii.

9. Langley wanted a Greek term for his craft, but they were somewhat inaccurately named; "aerodrome" was soon more properly used to denote airfields, rather than airplanes. See Crouch, *Dream*, 133. For the complicated Aerodrome numbering, see S. P. Langley and Charles M. Manly, *Langley Memoir on Mechanical Flight*, Smithsonian Contributions to Knowledge (Washington: Smithsonian Institution, 1911), 92–109.

10. Frank G. Carpenter, "How We Shall Fly," *Evening Star* (Washington, DC), December 12, 1896.

11. S. P. Langley, "The Flying Machine," *McClure's Magazine* 9, no. 2 (1897), 660.

12. Langley and Manly, *Memoir*, 123; Crouch, *Dream*, 255.

13. 54th Congress, 1st session, S302. The bill's author may have had in mind members of the Board of Ordnance and Fortification.

14. 54th Congress, 1st session, S3246/HR9288.

15. 54th Congress, 2nd session, HR9805. Cowdon, from Vienna, Virginia, not far from Washington, seems to have been a politically active person in addition to his interest in flight. "The New House Members," *New York Times*, December 4, 1900. If Cowdon was the original author, then HR9805 was probably an attempt to ride the coattails of Langley's success. Cowdon also tried the BOF, writing and even appearing before the board in late 1897. The board declared his airship in too undeveloped a state to warrant testing. BOF Minutes, v. 9, 106 (meeting of Dec. 20, 1897).

16. Parkinson, "Politics, Patents, and Planes," 171.

17. Parkinson, 172; Crouch, *Dream*, 256–57.

18. Stephen B. Goddard, *Race to the Sky: The Wright Brothers versus the United States Government* (Jefferson, NC: McFarland, 2003), 47–48. Goddard says that Bell's salon chose Walcott to make the approach to McKinley because of

his many government connections and his demonstrated ability to get what he wanted out of the government.

19. Ellis Yochelson, *Charles Doolittle Walcott, 1850–1927, A Biographical Memoir* (New York: Columbia University Press for the National Academy of Sciences, 1967), 495. Parkinson says that Walcott arranged his own meeting with Meiklejohn and that it was Meiklejohn who recommended visiting the Navy secretary. Parkinson, "Politics, Patents, and Planes," 179–81. In fact, Roosevelt was another friend of Langley, through their common lodging at the Cosmos Club in DC and had seen at least one of Langley's unsuccessful Aerodrome launches with Rudyard Kipling. Edmund Morris, *The Rise of Theodore Roosevelt*, revised and updated ed. (New York: Modern Library, 2001), 868n77; Rudyard Kipling, *Something of Myself* (1937), Chap. V, http://www.telelib.com/authors/K/KiplingRudyard/prose/SomethingOfMyself/myself_chap_5.html.

20. Crouch, *Dream*, 257.

21. Roosevelt to John D. Long, March 25, 1898, in Theodore Roosevelt, *Letters and Speeches*, Library of America (New York: Literary Classics of the United States, 2004), 142. Roosevelt's letter is often cited as evidence for his role in initiating military interest in the airplane; see, for instance, Stephen K. Stein, *From Torpedoes to Aviation: Washington Irving Chambers and Technological Innovation in the New Navy, 1876–1913* (Tuscaloosa, AL: University of Alabama Press, 2007), 158. Walcott and Manly credit President McKinley for getting the BOF to support Langley's further experiments.

22. 3896 (April 29, 1898), BOF Correspondence.

23. 7998 Davis to Long, April 30, 1898, and 1st Endorsement, June 16, 1898, SecNavGC. Interestingly, the British Admiralty declined to buy an airplane from the Wright brothers in 1907 using similar wording, saying that their invention would be "of no practical use to the Naval Service." Quoted in Norman Polmar and Minoru Genda, *Aircraft Carriers: A History of Carrier Aviation and Its Influence on World Events*, 2nd ed., 2 vols. (Washington, DC: Potomac Books, 2006): v. 1, 9.

24. 3896, Greeley to Secretary of War, May 25, 1898, BOF Correspondence.

25. Charles Manly's account says that all of this happened due to President McKinley's interest, and that McKinley ordered the BOF to provide Langley the money (Langley and Manly, *Memoir*, 123–4). Walcott also attributed the joint board and the BOF's actions to McKinley's interest (Yochelson, *Walcott*, 495). However, there is no reference to any communication with McKinley in the BOF files, nor in Langley's papers at NASM.

26. BOF Minutes, v. 10, 109 (meeting of Nov. 9, 1898). Parkinson says that getting the BOF to fund Langley was Secretary of War Russell A. Alger's idea as Congress was overwhelmed with emergency war spending and had never been particularly interested in funding experiments. BOF funding would also free Langley from congressional oversight: something Langley wished to avoid. Parkinson, "Politics, Patents, and Planes," 183–4.

27. *Congressional Record*, Jan. 27, 1904, 1364.

28. Parkinson, "Politics, Patents, and Planes," 185.

29. Robert Edward Tayler, "A Historical Study of Samuel Langley and his Contribution Toward the Development of the Airplane" (Master's thesis, American University, 1964), 103–11, 115–16.

30. By 1903, the membership of the BOF was completely different than it had been in 1898. The concern was that the BOF as an organization had that much discretion over that much money with, apparently, no oversight.

31. *Congressional Record* Jan. 27, 1904, 1364–7.

32. Lorenzo P. J. Auriti, "Aeroelastic Analysis of the Langley Aerodrome" (Master's thesis, University of Toronto, 1998), 91.

33. BOF Minutes v. 17, 40 (meeting of Oct. 24, 1905).

34. BOF Minutes v. 10, 14–15 (meeting of Feb. 16, 1898) response to Charles Fiesse and 25 (meeting of March 15, 1898) response to William Auberlin.

35. BOF Minutes v. 20, 7 (meeting of Feb. 6, 1908).

36. Orville Wright, *How We Invented the Airplane*, ed. Fred C. Kelly (New York: David McKay Company, 1953), 64–65.

INTRODUCTION

1. For an example of the former, see Lori A. Henning, *Harnessing the Airplane: American and British Cavalry Responses to a New Technology, 1903–1939* (Norman, OK: University of Oklahoma Press, 2019). For the latter, see Geoffrey Till, "Adopting the Aircraft Carrier: The British, American, and Japanese Cases," in *Military Innovation in the Interwar Period*, ed. Williamson Murray and Allan Reed Millett (New York: Cambridge University Press, 1996).

2. Carl John Horn, "Military Innovation and the Helicopter: A Comparison of Development in the United States Army and Marine Corps, 1945–1965" (PhD diss., Ohio State University, 2003).

3. Stephen Budiansky, *Air Power: The Men, Machines, and Ideas that Revolutionized War, From Kitty Hawk to Gulf War II* (New York: Viking Penguin, 2004).

4. Herbert A. Johnson, *Wingless Eagle: U.S. Army Aviation through World War I* (Chapel Hill, NC: University of North Carolina Press, 2001).

5. Martin Van Creveld is one of the latter, devoting roughly 10 pages to the carrier war in the Pacific, a few more to naval aviation in the Battle of the Atlantic, and 20 to the post-war "Twilight of Naval Aviation" out of 441 pages in his book, *The Age of Airpower* (New York: Public Affairs, 2011).

6. See, for instance, Geoffrey Till, *Air Power and the Royal Navy, 1914–1945 : A Historical Survey* (London: Macdonald and Jane's, 1979).

7. Peter B. Mersky, *U.S. Marine Corps Aviation: 1912 to the Present*, Third ed. (Baltimore: Nautical and Aviation Publishing, 1997).

8. Barry Posen, *The Sources of Military Doctrine: France, Britain, and Germany Between the World Wars* (Ithaca, NY: Cornell University Press, 1984).

9. For a bibliographic treatment of these models and their sources, see Laurence M. Burke II, "Methodologies and Models in Military Innovation Studies," *International Journal of Military History and Historiography* 40, no. 1 (2020), 110–34.

10. See, for instance, Bruno Latour, *Science in Action: How to Follow Scientists and Engineers Through Society* (Cambridge, MA: Harvard University Press, 1987). Latour expands and refines these ideas in his later article, "On Recalling ANT," *Sociological Review* 47, no. 1 supplement (1999), 15–25.

11. For a deeper dive into ANT and its usefulness in examining military innovation, see Burke, "Methodologies and Models."

12. Monte A. Calvert, *The Mechanical Engineer in America, 1830–1910; Professional Cultures in Conflict* (Baltimore: Johns Hopkins Press, 1967).

13. Henry Woodhouse, for instance, set himself up as an expert in aeronautics and as such, his "expert" opinion was sought by many decision-makers. However, it later came out that he had lied about the basis for his expertise, though it must be admitted that much of what he published by whatever means was (and remains) valuable. See historian Clark Reynolds' biography of Woodhouse in the introduction to Henry Woodhouse, *Textbook of Naval Aeronautics* (New York: Century, 1917; repr., Naval Institute Press, 1991).

CHAPTER 1. ARMY 1907–1910

1. Juliette A. Hennessy, *The United States Army Air Arm, April 1861 to April 1917*, General Histories (Washington, DC: Office of Air Force History, U.S. Air Force, 1985), 1–11; Charles de Forest Chandler and Frank Purdy Lahm,

How Our Army Grew Wings: Airmen and Aircraft before 1914 (New York: Ronald Press, 1943), Chap. 2.

2. Hennessy, *AAA*, 11–12; Rebecca Robbins Raines, *Getting the Message Through: A Branch History of the U. S. Army Signal Corps* (Washington, DC: Center for Military History, 1996), 45–64, 69, 84–86; Chandler and Lahm, *HOAGW*, 40–44.

3. Hennessy, *AAA*, 12–13; Raines, *Message*, 93–94; Chandler and Lahm, *HOAGW*, 45–50. Information on Squier and his work for Greely may be found in Arthur E. Kennelly, "Biographical Memoir of George Owen Squier, 1865–1934," in *Biographical Memoirs* (National Academy of Sciences, 1938), 151–52. See also the finding aid for the Squier Papers as well as the contents of Box 2, Folder 2, Squier Papers. Clark discusses Squier's transfer to the Signal Corps and his selection as one of Greely's assistants in Washington, but only in connection with Squier's work on improving telegraphic transmission over wire. Paul Wilson Clark, "Major General George Owen Squier: Military Scientist" (PhD diss., Case Western Reserve University, 1974), 67–69.

4. Fort Sam Houston Museum, *Maneuver Camp, 1911: Transformation of the Army at Fort Sam Houston* (Fort Sam Houston, TX: Fort Sam Houston Museum, 2009), 3–10.

5. Hennessy, *AAA*, 13–14; Chandler and Lahm, *HOAGW*, 50–52; Raines, *Message*, 127–28.

6. Hennessy, *AAA*, 13–14; Chandler and Lahm, *HOAGW*, 58–71; Raines, *Message*, 127–28.

7. Clark, "Squier," 110–11, 120–21, 124–25; Alfred F. Hurley, *Billy Mitchell, Crusader for Air Power*, new ed. (Bloomington: Indiana University Press, 1975), 10.

8. Clark, "Squier," 114–16; Raines, *Message*, 123.

9. *Message*, 123. Clark claims that Allen was not so interested in aviation and that Squier was behind Signal Corps interest in aviation. Clark, "Squier," 122–23.

10. Hennessy, *AAA*, 14–19; Chandler and Lahm, *HOAGW*, 139–46; Raines, *Message*, 127. Allen's order is reprinted in Hennessy as "Appendix 1" and a copy may also be found in DMA-Letters.

11. See, for example, Hennessy, *AAA*, 25–26; Chandler and Lahm, *HOAGW*, 141–44; Raines, *Message*, 128; Tom D. Crouch, *The Bishop's Boys: A Life of Wilbur and Orville Wright* (New York: W. W. Norton, 1989), 292–94, 330–32, 346–47.

12. The Aero Club of America was founded in 1905. It was established primarily to oversee the sport of ballooning, but it also sponsored contests and encouraged scientific study of aviation. Based in New York City, the Aero Club's early membership consisted of wealthy businessmen. The ACA eventually became a national organization and a leading voice in what historian Herbert Johnson has called "the aeronaut constituency." Herbert A. Johnson, *Wingless Eagle: U.S. Army Aviation through World War I* (Chapel Hill, NC: University of North Carolina Press, 2001), 11–19.

13. Clark, "Squier," 127, 130; Crouch, *Bishop's Boys*, 341; BOF Minutes v. 19: 36, 38 (Meeting of October 3, 1907).

14. Clark, "Squier," 132–33.

15. BOF Minutes v. 19: 41–42, 45 (Meeting of November 7, 1907).

16. BOF Minutes v. 19: 53 (Meeting of December 5, 1907) and v. 20: 4 (Meeting of January 2, 1908); Chandler and Lahm, *HOAGW*, 143–44; Crouch, *Bishop's Boys*, 346–47; Hennessy, *AAA*, 25–26. The specification is dated December 23, 1907, but it may not have been published until after the BOF gave its approval in January.

17. "Signal Corps Specification No. 486"; Clark, "Squier," 136–38; Hennessy, *AAA*, 26–27. Clark gives evidence that, in addition to the Wright brothers, the Signal Corps mailed the specifications to Alexander Graham Bell, Augustus Herring, and four other engineers prominent in the study of heavier-than-air aviation for their feedback before forwarding the specifications to the BOF.

18. *AAA*, 26–27; Chandler and Lahm, *HOAGW*, 147–49; Crouch, *Bishop's Boys*, 346–47; BOF Minutes, v. 20: 7 (Meeting of February 6, 1908).

19. Chandler and Lahm, *HOAGW*, 147–50; BOF Minutes, v. 20: 35 (Meeting of October 1, 1908); BOF Index Cards, "Wright Bros. aeroplane." The cited index card notes that the initial decision was that the Wright airplane was "to be procured with funds allotted from another appropriation." This has been crossed out in red ink with the notation: "Superseded by action of Oct. 1, 1908."

20. The Army as a whole was undergoing significant changes in the years between 1898 and 1916. Within the Signal Corps, Allen was trying to incorporate advances in wired and wireless communication while facing increased demands from a growing Army for both. See Allan Reed Millett and Peter Maslowski, *For the Common Defense: A Military History of the United States of America*, revised and expanded ed. (New York: Free Press,

1994), Chap. Ten: "Building the Military Forces of a World Power, 1899–1917"; and Fort Sam Houston Museum, *Maneuver Camp*, 3–10.

21. For Curtiss' relation to Baldwin, see William F. Trimble, *Hero of the Air: Glenn Curtiss and the Birth of Naval Aviation* (Annapolis, MD: Naval Institute Press, 2010), 11–15.

22. Maj. Edgar Russel was originally named to this board, but in July, Allen ordered him to Fort Leavenworth in relief of Saltzman as head of the Signal Corps School. Once the turnover was complete, Saltzman reported for duty in Washington in September, including taking Russel's place on the aeronautical board. Chandler and Lahm, *HOAGW*, 113n5.

23. *HOAGW*, 112–15, 100–101; Trimble, *Hero*, 37–38; Draft of "Chronology of the Army Air Service" by Ernest Jones (hereafter "Jones, 'Chronology'"). Entries for 1908: May 1 and "Official Airship Trials," Box 7, Folder 3, Foulois Papers-AFAL.

24. Foulois' memoirs do not mention seeing any aircraft prior to the 1908 trials at Fort Myer. Benjamin Delahauf Foulois and Carroll V. Glines, *From the Wright Brothers to the Astronauts: The Memoirs of Benjamin D. Foulois*, 1st ed. (New York: McGraw-Hill, 1968).

25. Foulois, *Memoirs*, Chapters 2 and 3 *passim*, and 42–46; Benjamin D. Foulois, "The Tactical and Strategical Value of Dirigible Balloons and Dynamical Flying Machines" (hereafter "Foulois Thesis"). Copies of Foulois' thesis may be found in: Box 39, Folder 1, Foulois Papers-LC; and in Box 5, Folder 3, Foulois Papers-AFAL.

26. "Foulois Thesis."

27. "Foulois Thesis"; Foulois, *Memoirs*, 49–50.

28. Crouch, *Bishop's Boys*, 349–53, 362–64; Trimble, *Hero*, 19–35.

29. Crouch, *Bishop's Boys*, 363.

30. *Bishop's Boys*, 362–64; Trimble, *Hero*, 26, 29–30, 32–36.

31. *Hero*, 37–38; Chandler and Lahm, *HOAGW*, 113–18 and Appendices 3 and 4; Foulois, *Memoirs*, 48–52, 54; Jones, "Chronology," entry for 1908: "Official Airship Trials," Foulois-AFAL.

32. *Memoirs*, 12, 50–52; Crouch, *Bishop's Boys*, 371–73; Trimble, *Hero*, 37–39.

33. Fred Howard describes Creecy as Selfridge's friend. Fred Howard, *Wilbur and Orville: A Biography of the Wright Brothers* (Mineola, NY: Dover Publications, 1998), 265.

34. Newspaper accounts say that Lahm's was the first flight of a military officer. Clark points out that Selfridge had flown earlier that year in an AEA plane.

So Lahm's claim is more accurately the first military officer as a passenger. However, Squier maintained throughout his life that he, not Lahm, was the first military passenger, claiming to have flown secretly with Orville Wright prior to Lahm's flight. Clark is inclined to believe that Wright would not have made such a breach of protocol as to give a junior officer the opportunity to be first but offers no evidence as to when Squier's earlier flight might have taken place. Of course, the airplane was so new, there could be no military protocol to breach. More likely than a "secret flight" is an error of memory: Squier later forgot that Lahm had flown first, and made the claim for himself, then attempted to defend his claim when challenged. See Clark, "Squier," 141n48. Against Squier's claim to primacy, James Cooke's official history of the Air Service in WWI says Orville Wright invited Squier to ride with him on September 12, but "Squier responded with an obvious lack of enthusiasm for getting into the air himself." James J. Cooke, *The U.S. Air Service in the Great War, 1917–1919* (Westport, CT: Praeger, 1996), 3.

35. The historiography disagrees on just how Selfridge ended up being the passenger on that fateful flight. Crouch and Trimble say it was Selfridge's turn to fly as a member of the trial board. Crouch, *Bishop's Boys*, 375; Trimble, *Hero*, 39. Foulois gives secondhand information that Selfridge volunteered for the flight, but Foulois questions whether Selfridge would have done so, citing Selfridge's apparent nervousness at flying during the balloon training. Foulois, *Memoirs*, 56. Chandler and Lahm say Orville invited Selfridge to be the passenger that day. Chandler and Lahm, *HOAGW*, 154. Turnbull and Lord relate that Sweet was scheduled to go up that day (and that since Sweet was a heavy man, the larger propellers were installed to account for his greater weight), but that Bell and others convinced him to yield his turn to Selfridge since this was Selfridge's last opportunity to fly before leaving for St. Joseph. Archibald D. Turnbull and Clifford L. Lord, *History of United States Naval Aviation*, 1st ed. (London: Oxford University Press, 1949), 4. Sweet himself recalled that he had lost a coin toss to Selfridge, which is interesting because a newspaper story written at the time of Creecy's death in 1930 also mentions the coin toss, but says Creecy is the one who lost to Selfridge. Transcript: "Narrative by: Commander George C. Sweet, USN (Ret.), Early Aeronautics in the Navy," recorded May 9, 1945; Biographical Notebooks—Chronological—1910 (1); Towers Papers; Arlington National Cemetery Website, "Richard B. Creecy," http://www.arlingtoncemetery.net/rbcreecy.htm. This and the previous note highlight the malleable nature of memory, particularly years after the fact, as

well as the needs of individual and institutional history. See, for instance, Lynn Abrams, *Oral History Theory* (New York: Routledge, 2010), especially 18–25 and the chapter entitled "Memory" (78–105).

36. For technical details of what led to the crash, see Crouch, *Bishop's Boys*, 377–78.

37. *Bishop's Boys*, 375–378; Chandler and Lahm, *HOAGW*, 154; Trimble, *Hero*, 39–41; Foulois, *Memoirs*, 55–58; Turnbull and Lord, *History*, 4; Clark, "Squier," 143–47.

38. Shock claims the airship made only five flights. James R. Shock, *U.S. Army Airships, 1908–1942* (Edgewater, FL: Atlantis Productions, 2002), 18.

39. Chandler and Lahm, *HOAGW*, 117–22; Foulois, *Memoirs*, 57–59.

40. Crouch, *Bishop's Boys*, 254–55, 295, 395–96; Chandler and Lahm, *HOAGW*, 155–56; Foulois, *Memoirs*, 60–61.

41. Crouch, *Bishop's Boys*, 396–99; Chandler and Lahm, *HOAGW*, 156–162; Foulois, *Memoirs*, 62–65; 8796 "Proceedings of the board of officers convened . . . for the purpose of observing trials of aeronautical devices, etc." (Aug. 2, 1909), BOF Correspondence.

42. Hennessy, *AAA*, 34; Crouch, *Bishop's Boys*, 408; Chandler and Lahm, *HOAGW*, 162–63; Foulois, *Memoirs*, 65–66. There is some disagreement over the date Wilbur arrived in College Park. Crouch says it was October 6, while Chandler and Lahm say October 5. Foulois says Wilbur returned to *Washington* on the fifth, so he may have spent the night of the fifth in Washington and shifted to College Park the next day.

43. *Memoirs*, 59, 66–67. In a speech Foulois gave in 1950, he said he did not learn that the trip was a reprimand until six or eight months later. "Transcript of speech given by Foulois at the Dining-in, USAF Hospital, Andrews AFB, 22 Nov. 1950," Box 10, Folder 4, Foulois Papers-AFAL.

44. The CSO did not have a large staff. It is probable that the staff officer behind Foulois' European trip was Chandler, assuming he was back from Fort Omaha: Chandler's authorship of Allen's October 1907 letter is evidence that Chandler preferred dirigibles over airplanes. Moreover, just after the 1909 trials, Allen had assigned Squier to oversee a research project involving radio experiments—something that occupied Squier's full attention and kept him occupied at a research facility just outside Washington. Clark, "Squier," 132, 177–78. If, as I suspect, Allen was relying on Squier and Chandler for advice on handling aviation, then Foulois' orders came at a time when Chandler had the upper hand. The notion of sending Foulois on a useless trip, thereby

preventing him from getting flight training or being the first Army officer to solo in an airplane solely for disagreeing with the "official" line of thought seems exceedingly petty. Sadly, that does not necessarily put it outside the realm of possibility.

45. Chandler and Lahm, *HOAGW*, 162–65; Hennessy, *AAA*, 34–37; Foulois, *Memoirs*, 67–69; Crouch, *Bishop's Boys*, 408–09. For the changes in control systems, see the many letters from Ernest Jones to Foulois on the topic in Box 41, folder 9, Foulois Papers, LC. While Crouch says that Wilbur was in New York City to meet Orville and Katherine on their return from Europe on November 4 (the day before the crash) and that all three Wrights went directly from New York to Dayton (making no mention of a return to College Park or the repairs of the Army plane), Foulois says Wilbur assessed the damage and ordered parts to repair it from Dayton. A letter from Wilbur Wright to Charles Walcott (at that time, Secretary of the Smithsonian Institution) dated November 29, 1909, indicates that Wilbur was in Washington "last week." Marvin W. McFarland, *The Papers of Wilbur and Orville Wright*, vol. 2: 1906–1948 (New York: McGraw-Hill, 1953), 970. Though Wilbur does not specify why he was in Washington, he may well have been bringing parts from Dayton and overseeing repair of the Army's plane.

46. Hennessy, *AAA*, 47–50; Dik Alan Daso, *Hap Arnold and the Evolution of American Airpower*, Smithsonian History of Aviation Series (Washington, DC: Smithsonian Institution Press, 2000), 46–47.

47. Henry Harley Arnold, *Global Mission*, 1st ed. (New York: Harper, 1949), 31; Rebecca Hancock Cameron, *Training to Fly: Military Flight Training, 1907–1945* (Washington: Air Force History and Museums Program, 1999), 45.

48. Foulois, *Memoirs*, 63.

49. Johnson dates this law to 1901: Johnson, *Wingless Eagle*, 137. The term "Manchu Law" seems to have been borrowed from popular culture following the Boxer Rebellion in China. One example of the reasoning may be found in H.R.H. [Howard R. Hickok], "The Manchus," *Journal of the United States Cavalry Association* 23, no. 94 (1913).

50. Hennessy, *AAA*, 39; Chandler and Lahm, *HOAGW*, 166–67; Foulois, *Memoirs*, 69. Footnotes in all three sources say that Humphreys was so upset at not being allowed to continue aviation work that he resigned his commission a few months later. He returned to serve with the Aviation Section for a few months during the First World War.

51. *Secretary of War Annual Report, 1910*, Report of the Chief Signal Officer, 654; Foulois, *Memoirs*, 68–70, 73–82; Chandler and Lahm, *HOAGW*, 180–84; Hennessy, *AAA*, 39–40.

52. Foulois, *Memoirs*, 73–82; Chandler and Lahm, *HOAGW*, 180–184; Hennessy, *AAA*, 39–40; Meghan Cunningham and Air Force History and Museums Program (U.S.), *The Logbook of Signal Corps No. 1: The U.S. Army's First Airplane* (Washington, DC: Air Force History and Museums Program, 2004), 19–20, 24–27; Transcript of Foulois interview (Tape #3), 1964, 6–7, 9–10, Box 10, Folder 4; Transcript of Foulois interview (Tape #20), December 12, 1961, 4–5, Box 7, Folder 6; Partial transcript of speech given at USAF Hospital, Andrews AFB, November 22, 1950, 5–6, Box 10, Folder 4, all transcripts Foulois Papers, AFAL.

CHAPTER 2. NAVY/MARINES 1909–1912

1. Portions of this chapter are drawn from Laurence M. Burke II, "Water Wings: The Early Years of Navy and Marine Corps Aviation," in *New Interpretations in Naval History: Selected Papers from the Sixteenth Naval History Symposium Held at the United States Naval Academy 10–11 September 2009*, ed. Craig C. Felker and Marcus O. Jones (Newport, RI: Naval War College Press, 2012).

2. Roger W. Barnett, *Navy Strategic Culture: Why the Navy Thinks Differently* (Annapolis, MD: Naval Institute Press, 2009), 17.

3. Transcript: "Narrative by: Commander George C. Sweet, USN (Ret.), Early Aeronautics in the Navy," recorded May 9, 1945, *Biographical Notebooks—Chronological—1910 (1)*, Towers Papers.

4. 26983–20, Cowles, "Memorandum for the Secretary of the Navy," Dec. 2, 1908, SecNavGC.

5. Sweet transcript, Towers Papers.

6. 26983–20:1, BuEquip to SecNav, Aug. 19, 1909, SecNavGC.

7. Cone to SecNav, Oct. 7, 1910, *Corresp.: Aviation Progress*, Chambers Papers.

8. Paolo Enrico Coletta, *American Secretaries of the Navy*, 2 vols. (Annapolis, MD: Naval Institute Press, 1980), 495–500.

9. Potter to Aide for Operations, Oct. 1, 1910, *Corresp.: Aviation Progress*, Chambers Papers.

10. Wainwright to Aide for Material, Oct. 12, 1910, *Corresp.: Aviation Progress*, Chambers Papers.

11. For more on the General Board, see John Trost Kuehn, "The Influence of Naval Arms Limitation on U.S. Naval Innovation During the Interwar Period,

1921–1937" (PhD diss., Kansas State University, 2007), Chap. 3, especially 45–51.

12. Archibald D. Turnbull and Clifford L. Lord, *History of United States Naval Aviation*, 1st ed. (London: Oxford University Press, 1949), 8; President of the General Board to Secretary of the Navy, Oct. 14, 1910, GB-449.

13. The assigned officers were Naval Constructor William McEntee for BuC&R and Lt. Nathaniel Wright for BuEng. Acting SecNav [Winthrop] to BuC&R, BuEng, Oct. 13, 1910; BuC&R [Watt] to SecNav, Oct. 11, 1910; BuEng [Cone] to SecNav, Oct. 13, 1910, all in *Corresp.: Aviation Progress*, Chambers Papers.

14. Swift to Chambers, Nov. 24 and Dec. 1, 1909, *Official Correspondence*, Chambers Papers; Stephen K. Stein, *From Torpedoes to Aviation: Washington Irving Chambers and Technological Innovation in the New Navy, 1876–1913* (Tuscaloosa, AL: University of Alabama Press, 2007), 157.

15. For naval officers' technical training at the time, see Brendan Patrick Foley, "Fighting Engineers: The U.S. Navy and Mechanical Engineering, 1840–1905" PhD diss., Massachusetts Institute of Technology, 2003), 204–22.

16. Stein, *Chambers*. For recognition of Chambers' technical expertise, see Stein, Chap. 11. Chambers' assignment to the aviation correspondence is on 159–60.

17. *Chambers*, 159.

18. Chambers to SecNav, Nov. 23, 1910, *Official Correspondence—First Orders & Paper on Aviation*, Chambers' Papers. Ely's was actually the second attempt to launch from a ship; about two months before, a plane was to be launched from a German passenger liner, but on the day of the attempt, the plane was damaged, and the liner sailed before the plane could be repaired. The Navy was to have two destroyers nearby to observe and assist in the attempt, with orders to report on the possibilities of scouting with airplanes at sea. Winthrop to Commander, Atlantic Torpedo Fleet, Nov. 2, 1910, *Official Corresp.*, Chambers Papers. Chambers had also approached the Wright Brothers, but they refused to participate in such an experiment. Chambers, "The Development of Naval Aviation" lecture to the Aeronautical Society [undated, but between April and July 1911]; and Chambers, "Brief Summary of the First Steps in the Development of Naval Aeronautics" (2129–17), May 24, 1917, both in *Corresp.: Naval Aeronautic Progress*, Chambers Papers.

19. The historiography is divided as to when and whether Curtiss' hydroplane flew at all on this excursion. See accounts in Turnbull and Lord, *History*, 13;

Elretta Sudsbury and North Island Historical Committee, *Jackrabbits to Jets: The History of North Island, San Diego, California*, 1st ed. (San Diego, CA: Neyenesch Printers, 1967), 13–15, 18–19; William F. Trimble, *Hero of the Air: Glenn Curtiss and the Birth of Naval Aviation* (Annapolis, MD: Naval Institute Press, 2010), 111–14; Glenn H. Curtiss and Augustus Post, *The Curtiss Aviation Book* (New York: Frederick A. Stokes, 1912), 133–35. 2nd Lt. Paul Walker, one of Curtiss' Army students, unequivocally states Curtiss flew both legs of the trip. Walker to Adjutant General, California District, March 1, 1911, copy in 167.401–3, Lahm Papers.

20. "The Development of Naval Aviation," Text of speech to the Aeronautical Society [undated, but between March 9 and July 1, 1911], *Corresp.: Aviation Progress*, Chambers Papers.

21. Chambers to SecNav, Nov. 23, 1910, and April 3, 1911, *Corresp: Aviation Progress*, Chambers Papers.

22. 26983–52 Acting SecNav [Beekman Winthrop] to U.S. Representative R. C. Hobson, July 28, 1910, SecNavGC.

23. 26983–105, CINCPACFLT to SecNav, Feb. 4, 1911; 26983–105:5, CO *CHESTER* to SecNav, April 11, 1911, all in SecNav GC. With increasing distance, even small angular errors in reading a compass would have great effect. Interestingly, Schroeder thought the best use for such kites would be as targets for training antiaircraft gunners. 26983–105:2, CINCLANTFLT to SecNav April 3, 1911; and 26983–105:4 CO *MAYFLOWER* to SecNav April 12, 1911, all in SecNavGC.

24. SecNav [Meyer] to Chambers, March 13, 1911, *Official Corresp.*, Chambers Papers.

25. Winthrop to Chambers, March 30, 1911, *Official Corresp.*, Chambers Papers.

26. Winthrop to Chambers, April 13, 1911, *Official Corresp.*, Chambers Papers.

27. Chambers to General Board, "Memorandum RE 'Aeronautics,'" August 8, 1913, GB-449; Chambers, "Brief Summary of the First Steps in the Development of Naval Aviation" May 24, 1917, 8; *Corresp.: Naval Aviation Progress*; Chambers Papers, Stein, *Chambers*, 164–5. "Memorandum" [n.d.], *Corresp.: Naval Aviation Progress*, Chambers Papers. Chambers was almost evicted from this poor space as well: a retirement board intended to meet in the space, but even after Chambers had the room repainted and a new floor laid down, the board refused to meet there because "it was not regarded as sufficiently sanitary."

28. Ellyson to SecNav, February 17, 1911, *Corresp: Ellyson, T. G.*, Chambers Papers.

29. Today, aircraft speed is measured in nautical miles per hour, or "knots," but figures for these early airplanes are probably statute miles per hour. Neither of the sources consulted gave range or endurance figures for any of the Navy's early Wright or Curtiss aircraft. George Van Deurs, *Wings for the Fleet: A Narrative of Naval Aviation's Early Development, 1910–1916* (Annapolis, MD: Naval Institute Press, 1966); Gordon Swanborough and Peter M. Bowers, *United States Navy Aircraft since 1911* (New York: Funk & Wagnalls, 1968). In the Navy, aircraft speed was standardized in knots in 1916: 1955–16, SecNav to [various], May 9, 1916, ONA.

30. BuNav [written by Chambers] to Rodgers, Nov. 28, 1911, *Corresp.: Aviation Camps—Establishment*, Chambers Papers, and SecNav Report, 1911, 59.

31. Chambers' biographer, Stein, believes that Chambers felt torpedoes had been "quarantined" at the Torpedo Experiment Station on its island in Narragansett Bay, and that this had allowed them to be forgotten about by the rest of the Navy. Chambers' push for integration may have been an effort to keep the same thing from happening to aviation. Stein, personal conversation with author, April 2009.

32. Memorandum, "Aeroplanes in Warfare" October 10, 1910, *Corresp.: Aviation Progress*, Chambers Papers.

33. "Speech of Hon. Richmond P. Hobson, of Alabama, in the House of Representatives, Tuesday, January 17, 1911" *Congressional Record*, Feb. 4, 1911, 2017–19.

34. Fiske to General Board, April 7, 1911, GB-449.

35. Baker to Daniels, April 30, 1913, *Corresp.: Aviation Warfare*, Chambers Papers.

36. Turnbull and Lord, *History*, 20. Chambers to BuNav, "Aeroplane experiments on the SAN MARCOS," Oct. 7, 1911, *Corresp.: Aviation Warfare*, Chambers Papers. The point about "defensive airplanes" (what we now call "fighter planes") is an interesting point for 1911, given that, despite much thinking on the subject, and experiments with firing various guns from aircraft, the first "defensive airplanes" do not appear in the skies until World War I. Kennett identifies the Fokker Eindecker (first deliveries, May 1915) as the first true fighter plane. Lee B. Kennett, *The First Air War, 1914–1918* (New York: Free Press, 1991), 69.

37. 26983-72, Winthrop (Acting SecNav—letter prepared by Chambers) to Glenn Curtiss, December 13, 1910, SecNavGC; Stein, *Chambers*, 163; George Van Deurs, *Anchors in the Sky: Spuds Ellyson, the First Naval Aviator* (San Rafael, CA: Presidio Press, 1978), 37, 53–5.

38. Ellyson to Chambers, Feb. 1, 1911, *Corresp.: Ellyson, T. G.*, Chambers Papers. Ellyson's is not the only claim to the idea of using the ropes and sandbags, see Van Deurs, *Wings*, 26.
39. Ellyson to Chambers, Feb. 14 and 17, 1911, *Corresp.: Ellyson, T.G.*, Chambers Papers.
40. Curtiss and Post, *The Curtiss Aviation Book*, 126–39.
41. F. H. Russell, Manager, The Wright Company, to Chambers, March 9, 1911, *Corresp.: Wright Company*, Chambers Papers. Chambers, "Brief Summary of the First Steps in the Development of Naval Aeronautics" (2129–17), 5, in *Corresp.: Naval Aeronautic Progress*, Chambers Papers. Curtiss may have harbored the same expectations, but his offer was not explicitly linked to purchases.
42. 26983–109 Telegram, Winthrop (prepared by Chambers) to the Wright Company, March 13, 1911, SecNavGC; Stein, *Chambers*, 163.
43. Though the Navy had previously used spotters in turrets and on individual guns, ship's spotter was a relatively new job in the U.S. Navy. From an armored housing near the top of a ship's mast (which both increased his range of vision and put him above the ship's own gun smoke), the spotter's role was to identify targets, establish range and distance to those targets, and pass the information to the ship's battery. After each shot (or salvo), he was to provide corrections in order to keep the guns on target.
44. BuNav to Towers, 28NOV1910, *Biographical Notebooks—Chronological, 1910 (1)*, Towers Papers.
45. Fanciulli [Curtiss' Agent] to Chambers, 14FEB1911, *Biographical Notebooks—Chronological, 1911 (1)*, Towers Papers. Detailers are officers in (at this time) BuNav responsible for matching personnel due for rotation to a new assignment with available assignments and writing up the necessary orders. Officers and enlisted men may contact their detailer with specific requests for their next duty, such as Towers' request for assignment to aviation. As it was, Towers almost missed out again: Ensign Charles Pousland had orders to report to Ellyson for flight training, but instead he chose alternative orders to command a destroyer; Towers was sent in Pousland's place. Chambers to Ellyson, Feb. 16, 1911, and Pousland to Towers, Jan. 9, 1961, *Biographical Notebooks—Chronological, 1911 (1)*, Towers Papers.
46. General narrative for this paragraph: Transcript of Towers' taped reminiscences [n.d.], *Biographical Notebooks—Chronological, 1910 (1)*, Towers Papers; and Clark G. Reynolds, *Admiral John Towers: The Struggle for Naval Air Supremacy* (Annapolis, MD: Naval Institute Press, 1991), 25–33.

47. Ellyson, in fact, was also responsible for much of Towers' flight training. Reynolds, 33–44.
48. Ellyson to Chambers, Feb. 14, 1911, *Corresp.: Ellyson, T. G.*, Chambers Papers.
49. Ellyson to Chambers, Feb. 22, 1911, *Corresp.: Ellyson, T. G.*, Chambers Papers. It seems likely the Army officers' disdain of the mechanical side of things was behind Benjamin Foulois' accusations of faulty repairs and poor training in Kelly's death in May 1911, described in chapter 3.
50. In 1911, the only airplane pilot's licenses were those granted by the Aero Club of America on behalf of the France-based *Federation Aeronautique International* (F.A.I.) or International Aeronautic Federation. The Aero Club of America was the F.A.I. affiliate in the United States and, as such, supervised airplane, balloon, and dirigible pilot tests as well as certifying international aviation record-setting attempts in the United States. The F.A.I. licenses were more a certification of skill than a legal requirement to operate an airplane, but both the Army and the Navy used them as an unofficial qualification before establishing their own, more stringent requirements for aviators. Even then, the F.A.I. license persisted as a basic flight qualification before military aviators could move on to more advanced training for the service license. Henry Harley Arnold, *Global Mission*, 1st ed. (New York: Harper, 1949), 33.
51. Chambers to Ellyson, March 11, 1911, *Corresp.: Ellyson, T. G.*, Chambers Papers.
52. Ellyson to Chambers, Sept. 7, 1911, *Corresp.: Ellyson, T. G.*, Chambers Papers.
53. Chambers to Chief, BuNav, May 1, 1911, *Corresp.: Aviation Camps—Establishment*, Chambers Papers.
54. Van Deurs, *Wings*, 49.
55. Van Deurs, *Ellyson*, 133–4.
56. Trimble, *Hero*, 109. For more on the difficulties in developing compasses for aircraft use, see Monte Duane Wright, *Most Probable Position: A History of Aerial Navigation to 1941* (Manhattan, KS: University Press of Kansas, 1972), esp. 43–7.
57. Later that year, McCurdy and Curtiss tested an aerial wireless set at a meet at Bridgeport, CT. Ellyson to Chief, BuNav, May 17, 1911, *Corresp.: Ellyson, T. G.*, Chambers Papers.
58. 26983-72, various letters and telegrams, SecNavGC; Turnbull and Lord, *History*, 13–4. See also Trimble, *Hero*, 109–11.

59. Chief, BuNav to Commandant, Navy Yard, Washington, Sept. 20, 1911, *Corresp.: Airplane Instruments*, Chambers Papers. For a deeper discussion of the unique physical problems in designing aircraft instruments, see John K. Bradley, "Putting the Wind up the Pilot: Cloud Flying with Early Aircraft Instruments," *History of Technology* 18 (1996).

60. Ellyson to Chambers, Dec. 4, 1911, *Corresp.: Ellyson, T. G.*, Chambers Papers.

61. Towers, "Aviation Commandery," speech given Oct. 24, 1952, *Personal File: Speeches*, Towers Papers.

62. Wireless telegraphy was still in its infancy in 1911, but the U.S. Navy was a major player in its development and a primary user, see Susan J. Douglas, "The Navy Adopts the Radio, 1899–1919," in *Military Enterprise and Technological Change*, ed. Merritt Roe Smith (Cambridge, MA: MIT Press, 1985).

63. 30120–736, BuEng Corresp.

64. Mark L. Evans and Roy A. Grossnick, *United States Naval Aviation 1910–2010*, 2 vols. (Washington, DC: GPO, 2015), 1:8; Chief, BuNav [prepared by Chambers] to Rodgers, Nov. 28, 1911, *Corresp.: Aviation Camps Establishment*, Chambers Papers.

65. Curtiss was apparently more businesslike about the situation, whereas the Wrights seem to have taken it more personally. Frank Coffyn, one of the Wrights' exhibition pilots, helped Towers disguise himself for a flight in a Wright plane at a Chicago meet in August 1910. The Wrights eventually found out and considered Coffyn a "traitor" for having knowingly taken up a Curtiss student. Van Deurs, *Ellyson*, 105; Reynolds, *Towers*, 41–2, 47–8.

66. Towers, partial manuscript for autobiography [n.p.], 23, in *Personal File: Speeches and Writings*, Towers Papers.

67. Benjamin Delahauf Foulois and Carroll V. Glines, *From the Wright Brothers to the Astronauts: The Memoirs of Benjamin D. Foulois*, 1st ed. (New York: McGraw-Hill, 1968), 91; Juliette A. Hennessy, *The United States Army Air Arm, April 1861 to April 1917*, General Histories (Washington, DC: Office of Air Force History, U.S. Air Force, 1985), 42; Rebecca Hancock Cameron, *Training to Fly: Military Flight Training, 1907–1945* (Washington, DC: Air Force History and Museums Program, 1999), 45–46.

68. Officers Detailed to Aviation to BuNav, 1st endorsement (Rodgers), June 25, 1912, *Corresp.: Naval Specifications*, Chambers Papers; Van Deurs, *Ellyson*, 105.

69. *Ellyson*, 130–31, 148–49. Chambers Memorandum, "Concerning Participation of Government Aviators in Public Meets and Celebrations," May 24, 1913, and

handwritten note, "Policy—Safe & Sane—Conservative," [n.d. possibly early 1911], both in *Corresp.: Aviation Progress*, Chambers Papers.

70. Reynolds, *Towers*, 52.

71. Van Deurs, *Wings*, 94.

72. Towers to SecNav, October 17, 1913, and endorsements, *Corresp.: Naval Architecture*, Chambers papers; Reynolds, *Towers*, 70–72.

73. Towers, partial manuscript for autobiography [n.d.], *Personal File: Speeches and Writings*, 25–26, Towers Papers; Van Deurs, *Wings*, 60–63. Richardson had not accounted for the different center of thrust and center of gravity on an airplane as compared to a ship, nor had he yet considered that the airplane float needed to break the suction of the water flowing over a smooth hull in order to take off.

74. Chambers to Chief, BuNav, Dec. 18, 1911, *Corresp.: Aviation Progress*, Chambers Papers. Curtiss was already wintering over in San Diego, but at this time had lost control of his Hammondsport factory to creditors as a result of the financial pressures of the legal battle with the Wrights. In San Diego, the Navy was as close as it could be to a supply of Curtiss replacement parts.

75. Chief, BuNav [prepared by Chambers] to Ellyson, Dec. 28, 1911, and to Rodgers, same date, *Corresp.: Aviation Camps—Establishment*, Chambers Papers.

76. Handwritten draft, Chambers to Kinkaid [CO of Experiment Station], May 25, 1912, *Corresp.: Aviation Camps—Establishment*, Chambers Papers.

77. Van Deurs, *Wings*, Appendix A.

78. Towers, "Tapes" 4, *Biographical Notebooks—Chronological: 1911 (2)*, Towers Papers.

79. Ellyson to Chambers, Feb. 27, 1912; Chambers to Ellyson, Jan. 11, 1912, both in *Corresp.: Aviation Camps—San Diego*, Chambers Papers.

80. Herbster to Chambers, Jan. 29, 1912, *Corresp.: Aviation Camps—Organization*, Chambers Papers. Ellyson to Chambers, Feb. 3, 1912, *Corresp: Ellyson, T. G.*, Chambers Papers. Van Deurs, *Ellyson*, 117.

81. Towers to Chambers, Feb. 17, 1912; Ellyson to Chambers, Feb. 27, 1912; Towers to Chambers, April 5, 1912; Towers to Chambers, April 24, 1912; Towers to Chambers, March 12, 1912, all in *Corresp.: Aviation Camps—San Diego*, Chambers Papers.

82. Van Deurs, *Ellyson*, 118–24; Richardson to Chambers, March 22, 1912, *Corresp.: Richardson, H. C.*, Chambers Papers. Towers to Chambers, April 24, 1912; Rodgers to Ellyson, April 20, 1912, both in *Corresp.: Aviation Camps—San Diego*, Chambers Papers.

83. Towers to Chambers, March 21, 1912, *Corresp.: Aviation Camps—San Diego,* Chambers Papers.

84. Towers, "Tapes" 4, *Biographical Notebooks—Chronological: 1911 (2),* Towers Papers; Ellyson to Chambers, Jan. 31, 1911, *Corresp.: Ellyson, T. G.,* Chambers Papers.

85. Herbster to Chambers, Jan. 29, 1912, *Corresp.: Aviation Camps—San Diego,* Chambers Papers. Cunningham to Chambers, July 25, 1913, *Biographical Notebooks—Chronological: 1913 (1),* Towers Papers; Van Deurs, *Wings,* 65.

86. Richardson to Chambers, March 16, 1912, *Corresp.: Richardson, H. C.,* Chambers Papers. Curtiss to Chambers, March 18, 1912, *Corresp.: Aviation Camps—San Diego,* Chambers Papers.

87. Towers, "Tapes" 5, *Biographical Notebooks—Chronological: 1911 (2),* Towers Papers.

CHAPTER 3. ARMY 1911–1912

1. Benjamin Delahauf Foulois and Carroll V. Glines, *From the Wright Brothers to the Astronauts: The Memoirs of Benjamin D. Foulois,* 1st ed. (New York: McGraw-Hill, 1968), 89. Another possibility of the "new" control system may have involved a wheel. Some pictures of the Wright B (SC no. 3) appear to show a wheel on a yoke, similar to the Curtiss controls, though this may be a later experiment. See, for instance, Juliette A. Hennessy, *The United States Army Air Arm, April 1861 to April 1917,* General Histories (Washington, DC: Office of Air Force History, U.S. Air Force, 1985), 44.

2. For the history of the 1911 Maneuver Division and the reasons for it, see Thomas A. Bruscino Jr., "A Troubled Past: The Army and Security on the Mexican Border, 1915–1917," *Military Review,* July–August 2008 (2008): 31; Richard D. Challener, *Admirals, Generals, and American Foreign Policy, 1898–1914* (Princeton, NJ: Princeton University Press, 1973), 344–50; Fort Sam Houston Museum, *Maneuver Camp, 1911: Transformation of the Army at Fort Sam Houston* (Fort Sam Houston, TX: Fort Sam Houston Museum, 2009).

3. Foulois, *Memoirs,* 82–85; Charles de Forest Chandler and Frank Purdy Lahm, *How Our Army Grew Wings: Airmen and Aircraft before 1914* (New York: Ronald Press, 1943), 184–86; Hennessy, *AAA,* 40; Transcript of Foulois interview, December 12, 1961, 6, 8–11, Box 7, Folder 6, Foulois Papers-AFAL.

4. SecWarAR, 1909, 50–51; Chandler and Lahm, *HOAGW,* 183n6; Herbert A. Johnson, *Wingless Eagle: U.S. Army Aviation through World War I* (Chapel Hill, NC: University of North Carolina Press, 2001), 56.

5. Throughout the time period covered in this book, the government fiscal year ran from July 1 to the following June 30 and was identified by the year in which it ended. Thus, FY 1912 ran from July 1, 1911, to June 30, 1912. The annual reports from the secretaries of the Army and the Navy would likewise address the fiscal year, so that the 1912 annual report would be sent to Congress in the fall of 1912.

6. For the beginnings of the Wright-Curtiss legal struggle, see William F. Trimble, *Hero of the Air: Glenn Curtiss and the Birth of Naval Aviation* (Annapolis, MD: Naval Institute Press, 2010), 51–55, 57, 63–64, 72–74, 76–77, 79–82, 87, 102–103; and Tom D. Crouch, *The Bishop's Boys: A Life of Wilbur and Orville Wright* (New York: W. W. Norton, 1989), 412–23. Crouch's book addresses the Wrights' legal battles against several accused infringers, not just Curtiss. Clark notes that in 1909, Allen had gotten permission from the BOF to use $16,000 that the board had allotted to the Signal Corps for aviation (but not yet spent) in order to purchase other types of planes. However, the initiation of the Wrights' patent suit against Curtiss made Allen unwilling to risk buying a Curtiss plane at that time. Paul Wilson Clark, "Major General George Owen Squier: Military Scientist" (PhD diss., Case Western Reserve University, 1974), 163–64.

7. Hennessy, *AAA*, 40–42; Chandler and Lahm, *HOAGW*, 182–83, 187, 193–94; Foulois, *Memoirs*, 85–86. The airplane remains in the collection of the National Air and Space Museum. Hennessy, *AAA*, 42; Clark, "Squier," 165n128.

8. Foulois, *Memoirs*, 86; Hennessy, *AAA*, 42, 45–47, 86; Chandler and Lahm, *HOAGW*, 260; U.S. Congress, House Committee on Military Affairs, *Aeronautics in the Army*, 63rd Congress, First Session, August 12, 14–16, 1913, 37–38; Ernest Jones notes for aviation chronology, *Miscellany—Aviation Chronology, Notes and Writings*, Foulois Papers-LC. Hennessy says Beck's collaborator, Lt. Myron Crissy of the Coast Artillery Corps, also flew with Parmelee at the 1911 meet, testing their improved bombsight by dropping live bombs. In a footnote, however, she notes that Crissy later said that neither he nor Beck had made any tests of the bombsight at the San Francisco meet.

9. For Ellyson's attendance, see George Van Deurs, *Anchors in the Sky: Spuds Ellyson, the First Naval Aviator* (San Rafael, CA: Presidio Press, 1978), 57–59.

10. Stephen K. Stein, *From Torpedoes to Aviation: Washington Irving Chambers and Technological Innovation in the New Navy, 1876–1913* (Tuscaloosa, AL: University of Alabama Press, 2007), 163; Chandler and Lahm, *HOAGW*, 260–61; Foulois, *Memoirs*, 86; Hennessy, *AAA*, 42–45, 86; Trimble, *Hero*, 115–17.

11. Chandler and Lahm, *HOAGW*, 187–89; Hennessy, *AAA*, 42–45; Henry Harley Arnold, *Global Mission*, 1st ed. (New York: Harper, 1949), 23; Foulois, *Memoirs*, 86–91; "Provisional Aeroplane Regulations for the Signal Corps, United States Army, 1911," Box 7, Folder 6, Foulois Papers-AFAL.

12. Foulois to the Wright Company, May 5, 1911, Box 22, Folder 4, Foulois Papers-LC.

13. Foulois, *Memoirs*, 91; Chandler and Lahm, *HOAGW*, 189–90. It does not appear that Orville and Wilbur Wright knew about Ely and Coffyn riding in each other's planes. Later that year, Coffyn would get in trouble with the brothers for knowingly taking Navy Lt. John Towers, a Curtiss student, on a flight in a Wright plane. See chap. 2, note 65.

14. Foulois, *Memoirs*, 91–92; Chandler and Lahm, *HOAGW*, 190; Hennessy, *AAA*, 45; Fort Sam Houston Museum, *Maneuver Camp*, 70.

15. *Maneuver Camp*, 70; Hennessy, *AAA*, 45; Chandler and Lahm, *HOAGW*, 190–91; Foulois, *Memoirs*, 92–94; *A History of Military Aviation in San Antonio* ([San Antonio, TX?]: U.S. Dept. of Defense, 2000), 5; Partial transcript of speech given by Foulois at USAF Hospital, Andrews AFB, November 22, 1950, 1–7, Box 10, Folder 4, Foulois Papers-AFAL.

16. Foulois, *Memoirs*, 93–94; Chandler and Lahm, *HOAGW*, 191; *A History of Military Aviation in San Antonio*, 5; Partial transcript of speech given by Foulois at USAF Hospital, Andrews AFB, November 22, 1950, 1–7, Box 10, Folder 4, Foulois Papers-AFAL. Daniel Deemers says it was Beck's elevation over Foulois as commander of the Provisional Aero Squadron that drove a wedge between the two, but Foulois' accusations over Kelly's death certainly could not have improved matters. Daniel J. Demers, "Pioneer Airman's Tragic Destiny," *Aviation History*, July 2012, 18.

17. Hennessy, *AAA*, 47; Chandler and Lahm, *HOAGW*, 194–96; Arnold, *Global Mission*, 15–17, 23.

18. Arnold, *Global Mission*, 15–17; Dik Alan Daso, *Hap Arnold and the Evolution of American Airpower*, Smithsonian History of Aviation Series (Washington, DC: Smithsonian Institution Press, 2000), 44.

19. Daso, *Arnold*, 47–49; Chandler and Lahm, *HOAGW*, 194–96; Hennessy, *AAA*, 47; Arnold, *Global Mission*, 25–30.

20. The published sources differ as to exactly when these planes showed up in Maryland. Chandler and Lahm say simply that No. 3 arrived first, and No. 4 was delivered on July 1. Hennessy also gives no specific date for the delivery of No. 3 but agrees that it was at College Park before No. 4 arrived on June 19.

21. Hennessy, *AAA*, 47–50; Rebecca Hancock Cameron, *Training to Fly: Military Flight Training, 1907–1945* (Washington, DC: Air Force History and Museums Program, 1999), 43–45; Chandler and Lahm, *HOAGW*, 194–97, 198–99, 201; Arnold, *Global Mission*, 30–31; Daso, *Arnold*, 49. None of the sources gives a date for exactly when Beck or the enlisted men on aviation duty at Fort Sam Houston reported to College Park, but it makes sense that they would have remained in Texas, completing the rebuilding of S.C. No. 2. Hennessy (50) cites Chandler and Lahm (203) in saying that S.C. No. 2 had been rebuilt in Texas before arriving in College Park. Arnold (*Global Mission*, 30–31), however, says Beck rebuilt the plane in College Park. Cameron (44) agrees that the "partially repaired Curtiss" was shipped back to College Park where repairs were completed.

22. Chandler and Lahm, *HOAGW*, 198–99, 201–02; Hennessy, *AAA*, 47–53; Daso, *Arnold*, 49; Arnold, *Global Mission*, 30–31; Foulois, *Memoirs*, 95. Arnold makes clear that in addition to instructing other pilots, he and Milling were concerned about instructing their ground crew in the proper care and maintenance of the planes: Arnold, *Global Mission*, 33–34.

23. Paul Beck, "The Aeroplane as Applied to the Army," in *The Curtiss Aviation Book* (New York: Frederick A. Stokes, 1912), 205–18.

24. Chandler and Lahm, *HOAGW*, 199–201, 206–07; Hennessy, *AAA*, 53–54; Daso, *Arnold*, 51; Arnold, *Global Mission*, 33–34; Foulois, *Memoirs*, 95–96; *Aeronautics in the Army*, 102–03.

25. Chandler and Lahm, *HOAGW*, 197–99, 200, 202–05; Hennessy, *AAA*, 53–54; Arnold, *Global Mission*, 31–35; Daso, *Arnold*, 50.

26. Cameron, *Training*, 41, 47–48; Hennessy, *AAA*, 54–57; Chandler and Lahm, *HOAGW*, 210–211; Daso, *Arnold*, 52–53; Foulois, *Memoirs*, 97. Beck remained behind on account of his father's death, while Kennedy was receiving treatment at Walter Reed Army Hospital. None of the sources consulted specify what Kennedy was being treated for.

27. Chandler and Lahm, *HOAGW*, 210–17; Hennessy, *AAA*, 57–58; Cameron, *Training*, 47–50; Arnold, *Global Mission*, 36–37; Daso, *Arnold*, 52–54; Foulois, *Memoirs*, 97, 99–100.

28. Arnold, *Global Mission*, 34; Chandler and Lahm, *HOAGW*, 206, 209–10; Hennessy, *AAA*, 54; Daso, *Arnold*, 51; Foulois, *Memoirs*, 97.

29. "Requirements for a Weight Carrying Aeroplane," February 8, 1912, *Corresp.: Naval Specifications*, Chambers Papers.

30. "Specifications for a Light Scouting Machine," March 9, 1912, *Corresp.: Naval Specifications*, Chambers Papers.

31. Cameron, *Training*, 50–52; Beck, "The Aeroplane as Applied to the Army," 214–15; Chandler and Lahm, *HOAGW*, 209–10; Hennessy, *AAA*, 58.

32. Daso, *Arnold*, 52; Hennessy, *AAA*, 59; Chandler and Lahm, *HOAGW*, 216–17; Cameron, *Training*, 52–53.

33. Chandler and Lahm, *HOAGW*, 219, 228–29, 240–42; Hennessy, *AAA*, 60–61.

34. As already noted, Curtiss' Scout had been delivered to Augusta, but finished its acceptance qualifications in College Park.

35. Chandler and Lahm, *HOAGW*, 220–222; Hennessy, *AAA*, 62; Arnold, *Global Mission*, 37; Daso, *Arnold*, 55; Cameron, *Training*, 54. Hennessy says the Wright Co. delivered another Model C as a replacement for the one that crashed (since the crashed plane had not yet been accepted by the Army); however she is not clear as to when this plane was delivered. She does specify that the replacement plane was designated S.C. No. 10, which would have been the designation of the crashed plane had it been accepted, and that the Model C accepted in October was designated S.C. No. 11. This seems to imply that the Wright Co. delivered the replacement aircraft sometime that summer, but this is not necessarily true. The Army assigned S.C. numbers according to purchase, so the plane accepted in October already had No. 11 attached to it. The Army might have found it easier to reuse No. 10 for the next plane, rather than cause confusion by redesignating No. 11. Swanborough and Bowers report that the Army eventually bought seven Wright Model Cs with serial numbers 7, 10–14, and 16, but Chandler and Lahm state that No.7 was a Model B ordered in December 1911 for delivery to the Philippine Islands. Gordon Swanborough and Peter M. Bowers, *United States Military Aircraft since 1909* (Washington, DC: Smithsonian Institution Press, 1989), 609; Chandler and Lahm, *HOAGW*, 244.

36. *HOAGW*, Appendix 10. Hennessy reproduces these same requirements as Appendix 8, but an undated list in Chambers' papers adds a requirement for an additional cross-country flight of at least twenty miles (ten miles out and ten miles back) at a minimum height of a thousand feet. Given the similarity to the "military reconnaissance flight," the specific requirements of the cross-country flight were likely just folded into the military reconnaissance flight with the understanding that the twenty miles of that flight were to be cross-country rather than multiple laps around a closed course. "Qualifications for Military Aviators," *Corresp: Naval Specifications*, Chambers Papers.

37. Foulois, *Memoirs*, 99–100; Chandler and Lahm, *HOAGW*, 228–9, 239–42.

38. Chandler and Lahm, *HOAGW*, 222–25; Hennessy, *AAA*, 61–62; Arnold, *Global Mission*, 48; Daso, *Arnold*, 51. Arnold, in *Global Mission*, implies that talk of aerial combat came from the journalists themselves.

39. Ralph S. Cooper, "Beckwith Havens," http://earlyaviators.com/ehavens. htm. Accessed January 13, 2021; Hennessy, *AAA*, 62; Chandler and Lahm, *HOAGW*, 229; Johnson, *Wingless Eagle*, 51; Foulois, *Memoirs*, 99–100.

40. Hennessy, *AAA*, 62; Chandler and Lahm, *HOAGW*, 229–32; Arnold, *Global Mission*, 39–40; Daso, *Arnold*, 55–56; SecWarAR, 1913, 782.

41. SecWarAR, 1912, 968.

42. SecWarAR, 1912, 968; SecWarAR, 1913, 782, 788; Hennessy, *AAA*, 62, 71; Chandler and Lahm, *HOAGW*, 229–30; Foulois, *Memoirs*, 101; Johnson, *Wingless Eagle*, 51.

43. *Aeronautics in the Army*, 27. Reber expressed the opinion that, of the 247 licensed civilian pilots in the United States at that time, fewer than 10 could make a cross-country flight of two hundred miles. For more on pre-war flying exhibitions, see David T. Courtwright, *Sky as Frontier: Adventure, Aviation, and Empire*, 1st ed., Centennial of Flight Series (College Station, TX: Texas A&M University Press, 2005), 27–37; Crouch, *Bishop's Boys*, 424–39; Trimble, *Hero*, 75–96.

44. *Aeronautics in the Army*, 95.

45. Chandler and Lahm, *HOAGW*, 236–37; Hennessy, *AAA*, 71–72; Daso, *Arnold*, 57; SecWarAR, 1913, 782–83.

46. For more on the history of indirect fire in the U.S. Army prior to World War I, see John R. Walker, "Bracketing the Enemy: Forward Observers and Combined Arms Effectiveness During the Second World War" (PhD diss., Kent State University, 2009), 22–37.

47. Arnold, *Global Mission*, 40–41; Daso, *Arnold*, 57–58; Chandler and Lahm, *HOAGW*, 237–38; Hennessy, *AAA*, 72; Johnson, *Wingless Eagle*, 57–58.

48. Daso's biography of Arnold contains a detailed analysis of what is known and what might have happened to cause the loss of control and subsequent recovery.

49. Scriven, "Requirements for Military Aviator Rating 1914, War Department" October 27, 1913. Reproduced in Hennessy, *AAA*, Appendix 11; and Chandler and Lahm, *HOAGW*, Appendix 14.

50. Hennessy, *AAA*, 57, 60, 71, 72; Chandler and Lahm, *HOAGW*, 215, 232–33, 238; Daso, *Arnold*, 56–60; Arnold, *Global Mission*, 40–41; Foulois, *Memoirs*, 102; *Aeronautics in the Army*, 31–32; Lt. J. O. Mauborgne to Allen, November 10 and 14, 1912, *Subject File—Aviation Duty, Signal Corps: Wireless Radio*

Experiments, Foulois Papers LC. For accounts of Beck's death, see Michael Robert Patterson, "Paul Ward Beck," http://www.arlingtoncemetery.net/pwbeck.htm; and Demers, "Pioneer Airman's Tragic Destiny."

51. Foulois to Adjutant General, September 1, 1912; Wood to Reber, September 3, 1912; 2nd Indorsement, Scriven (Acting CSO) to Adjutant General, September 23, 1912; all in *Subject File—Aviation Duty, Signal Corps: Miscellany, 1912*, Foulois Papers LC.

52. Ronald G. Machoian, "Looking Skyward: The Emergence of an Air-Minded Culture in the US Army," (Maxwell AFB, AL: Air University Press, 2004), 2–3.

53. Chandler and Lahm, *HOAGW*, 244; Hennessy, *AAA*, 79; Cameron, *Training*, 83. Fort William McKinley is now known as Fort Bonifacio and lies within the modern Manila metropolitan area.

54. It is not clear whether Burge continued to fly in the Philippines, though Hennessy indicates that the Army gave him formal orders to flying status on October 6, 1914. Cameron notes that Burge later became an officer and retired as a lieutenant colonel. Hennessy, *AAA*, Appendix 15; Cameron, *Training*, 579n29.

55. Chandler and Lahm, *HOAGW*, 244–46; Hennessy, *AAA*, 79–80; Cameron, *Training*, 83–84.

56. Chandler and Lahm, *HOAGW*, 72–73; Foulois, *Memoirs*, 102–103; Foulois to Orville Wright, November 16, 1912, *Subject File—Aviation Duty, Signal Corps: Wright "C" Aircraft*, Foulois Papers LC.

CHAPTER 4. NAVY/MARINES 1912–1913

1. George Van Deurs, *Wings for the Fleet: A Narrative of Naval Aviation's Early Development, 1910–1916* (Annapolis, MD: Naval Institute Press, 1966), 75, 161.

2. "History of Advanced Base," May 15, 1913, compiled by Cdr. R. H. Jackson, USN, GB-408 [Advance Base].

3. Excerpts from American Hydro-Aeroplane Co. [C. R. Brown] to Chambers, March 27, 1912, and C. R. Brown to Chambers, April 1, 1912, *Biographical Notebooks—Chronological: 1910 (1)*, Towers Papers.

4. Cunningham to Officer in Charge, Advanced Base School, February 12, 1912, *Corresp.: Naval Airplanes*, Chambers Papers.

5. Memorandum: Chambers to Aide for Personnel, February 29, 1912, and SecNav to Major General Commandant, U.S. Marine Corps [hereafter MGC], March 4, 1912, both in *Corresp.: Naval Airplanes*, Chambers Papers.

6. Edward C. Johnson, *Marine Corps Aviation: The Early Years, 1912–1940*, ed. Graham A. Cosmas (Washington, DC: History and Museums Division, Headquarters, USMC, 1977), 4–5; J. W. Kinkaid [in charge of the Experiment Station at Annapolis] to Chambers, May 22, 1912, *Corresp.: Aviation Camps Establishment*, Chambers Papers.

7. Cunningham held the former view, whereas Smith was more in tune with the latter. Johnson, *Marine Aviation*, 4(fn), 11(fn). See also Cunningham to Mims, October 30, 1918, *Cunningham Letters*, Cunningham Papers.

8. Chambers to Chief, BuNav, Dec. 14, 1912, *Corresp.: Aviation Appropriations*, Chambers Papers.

9. Chambers to Chief, BuNav, May 22, 1912, and Chambers to Senator Perkins [Chair, Sen. Comm. on Naval Affairs], both in *Corresp.: Aviation Appropriations*, Chambers Papers.

10. Morin to Lieutenant Commander Ziegemeier, April 1, 1912, and April 15, 1912, *Corresp.: Aviation—Radio Developments*; Rodgers to Head, Naval Engineering Experiment Station, July 20, 1912, and July 27, 1912, *Corresp.: Aviation Camps— Annapolis*; Ensign Maddox to Head of Engineering Experiment Station, Aug. 2, 1912, *Corresp.: Aviation—Radio Developments*, all in Chambers Papers.

11. Van Deurs, *Wings*, 65.

12. Rodgers to Chambers, July 21, 1912, *Biographical Notebooks—Chronological: 1912*, Towers Papers; Van Deurs, *Wings*, 76.

13. 14 Bristol to Lt. Maxfield, Aug. 8, 1914, ONA.

14. Rodgers to Chambers, Jan. 30, 1912 [marked "1911"] and April 10, 1912, *Corresp.: Aviation Camps—San Diego, CA*, Chambers Papers.

15. Chambers "Brief Memorandum Concerning the Advance of Aviation and its Bearing on the Foregoing Recommendations" [undated, probably early 1913], *Corresp.: Aviation Progress*, Chambers Papers. See also 26983–556, Daniels to Congressman William S. Greene, Sept. 30, 1915, SecNavGC.

16. Van Deurs, *Wings*, 95.

17. Dewey to SecNav, June 26, 1912, GB-449.

18. Chambers to Navy Dept., June 28, 1912, GB-449.

19. This first experimental catapult was built using old parts from torpedo launching systems. Chambers to G. L. Smith, July 12, 1917, *Official Corresp.*, Chambers Papers; Van Deurs, *Wings*, 67; *Anchors in the Sky: Spuds Ellyson, the First Naval Aviator* (San Rafael, CA: Presidio Press, 1978), 133–35.

20. Chambers to G. L. Smith, July 12, 1917, *Official Corresp.*, Chambers Papers; Van Deurs, *Wings*, 69–70; *Ellyson*, Chap. 14.

21. 26983–20, Cowles, "Memorandum for the Secretary of the Navy," Dec. 2, 1908, SecNavGC.

22. Ellyson to Chambers, Feb. 22, 1911, *Corresp.: Ellyson, T. G.*, Chambers Papers.

23. Commander, Atlantic Submarine Flotilla to SecNav (Division of Operations), Oct. 21, 1912, *Corresp.; Submarines*, Chambers Papers.

24. Senior Aviation Officer [Towers] to SecNav (Bureau of Operations), Dec. 18, 1912, GB-418.

25. Paolo Enrico Coletta, *Patrick N. L. Bellinger and U.S. Naval Aviation* (Lanham, MD: University Press of America, 1987), 47–8; Van Deurs, *Ellyson*, 147–48.

26. Senior Aviation Officer [Towers] to SecNav, March 5, 1913; Senior Aviation Officer to SecNav, March 7, 1913; and Towers to Ellyson, March 4, 1913, all in *Corresp.: Aviation Reports, Guantanamo Bay*, Chambers Papers; Clark G. Reynolds, *Admiral John Towers: The Struggle for Naval Air Supremacy* (Annapolis, MD: Naval Institute Press, 1991), 57–62.

27. Chambers [?] "The Development of Naval Aviation," [n.d., probably early 1911], *Corresp.: Aviation Progress*; "Navy Aviation at Guantanamo Bay," March 20, 1913, *Corresp: Aviation Camps—Annapolis*, both Chambers Papers; Reynolds, *Towers*, 56–63; Van Deurs, *Wings*, 79–82; John Fass Morton, *Mustin: A Naval Family of the 20th Century* (Annapolis, MD: Naval Institute Press, 2003), 65–81, passim. Like Cunningham, Mustin was concerned about how his wife would react to his flying. He asked Towers to keep his Guantanamo training quiet, "on account of domestic reasons." Towers to Ellyson, March 4, 1913, *Corresp.: Aviation Reports, Guantanamo Bay*, Chambers Papers.

28. Mustin to SecNav, Nov. 18, 1913, *Corresp.: Naval Aviation*, Chambers Papers.

29. "List of Officers Who Have Taken Flights" undated [probably mid- to late-1913], *Corresp.: Aviation Camps Establishment*, Chambers Papers; Reynolds, *Towers*, 59.

30. "Navy Aviation at Guantanamo Bay" March 20, 1913, *Corresp.: Aviation Camps—Annapolis*, Chambers Papers.

31. Towers to Ellyson [assisting Chambers in Washington], Feb. 20, 1913, *Subj. Files: Aviation Reports, Guantanamo Bay*, Chambers Papers.

32. Chambers, "Brief Summary" (2129–17), 17, *Corresp.: Naval Aviation Progress*, Chambers Papers.

33. Senior Aviation Officer [Towers] to Officer in Charge of Aviation, "Weekly Report on Aviation, ending Saturday, March 15, 1913," *Subj. Files: Aviation*

Reports, Guantanamo Bay, Chambers Papers; Van Deurs, *Wings*, 82–87, 93–4, 103–104.

34. *Wings*, 82–87, 93–4, 103–104; Van Deurs, *Ellyson*, 130–51, passim.

35. William F. Trimble, *Jerome C. Hunsaker and the Rise of American Aeronautics*, Smithsonian History of Aviation and Spaceflight Series (Washington, DC: Smithsonian Institution Press, 2002), 17–18, 21, Chap. 2.

36. "Findings of the Board Appointed to Investigate the Circumstances Attending the Death of Ensign Wm. D. Billingsley, U.S.N." [n.d.], *Corresp.: Aeronautics Magazine*, Chambers Papers; Reynolds, *Towers*, 65–70; Van Deurs, *Wings*, 83–87.

37. At that point, the remaining airplanes consisted of the A-2 and A-3, the B-1, "nearing the end of its usefulness," the C-1, and the Burgess flying boat, the D-1. The A-1 was only good for parts; however, another Curtiss flying boat, the C-2, was then undergoing testing, and another Wright, the B-3, was going to be built from spare parts and the remains of the B-2. Chambers, "Memorandum RE 'Aeronautics,'" August 8, 1913, GB-449.

38. Reynolds, *Towers*, 65–68; Van Deurs, *Wings*, 84–87. Van Deurs says the aviators, rather than being worried about drowning, avoided wearing the seatbelts because they wanted to be able to get clear of the engine (behind them) in a crash.

39. Chambers to SecNav, May 28, 1913 (and attached items), *Official Corresp.*, Chambers Papers; Chambers, "Brief Summary of the First Steps in the Development of Naval Aeronautics" (2129–17) May 24, 1917, *Corresp: Naval Aviation—Progress*, Chambers Papers.

40. Chambers, "Brief Summary," 15, *Corresp.: Naval Aviation—Progress*; and Chambers to BuNav, July 8, 1913, *Official Corresp.*, both in Chambers Papers; Morton, *Mustin*, 76–79.

41. Stephen K. Stein, *From Torpedoes to Aviation: Washington Irving Chambers and Technological Innovation in the New Navy, 1876–1913* (Tuscaloosa, AL: University of Alabama Press, 2007), 186–88.

42. Many letters from Chambers to hopeful inventors emphasize his desire to make airplanes safe before dealing with aerial ordnance. One that explains his position in some detail is Chambers to Chief of BuNav, May [?] 1912, "Subject: John W. Currell Re his aerial torpedo," *Corresp.: Aviation Bombing*, Chambers Papers.

43. Chambers, "Memorandum on Naval Aviation," attached to Chambers to SecNav, June 28, 1912, GB-449.

44. Fiske to President, General Board, April 7, 1911, GB-449, Bradley A. Fiske, *From Midshipman to Rear-Admiral* (New York: Century, 1919), 503–6.

45. Fiske, *From Midshipman*, 538.

46. The events surrounding Chambers' "plucking" in this and the previous paragraphs are taken from Stein, *Chambers*, 181–98.
47. Cunningham to Chambers, Sept. 3, 1913, *Corresp.: Naval Airplanes*, Chambers Papers.
48. 1740-14, Cunningham to Bristol, Dec. 3, 1914, ONA; MGC to Commandant, Navy Yard, Washington, DC, February 10, 1914, *First Marine Aviation Force*, Cunningham Papers; Johnson, *Marine Aviation*, 8; Van Deurs, *Wings*, 128; Reginald Wright Arthur, *Contact! Careers of US Naval Aviators Assigned Numbers 1 to 2000*, 1st ed. (Washington: Naval Aviator Register, 1967), 4–5.
49. Roosevelt to Chambers, Oct. 9, 1913, *Official Corresp.*, Chambers Papers.
50. "Report of the Board on Aeronautics," 1–2. A copy of this report may be found in *Corresp.: Naval Aeronautic Progress*, Chambers Papers.
51. "Report of the Board on Aeronautics," 2–3, 9–15.
52. "Report," 4–5.
53. "Report," 2, 5–8.
54. "Report," 17–20.
55. "Report," 12–14.
56. "Report," 15–17.
57. "Report," Appendix B, "Minutes of the Proceedings of the Board on Aeronautics," "Sixth Day."
58. 26983–184½, "Hearings of Secretary of the Navy before House Naval Committee, 1914," SecNavGC.

CHAPTER 5. INTERSERVICE ORGANIZATION I

1. See, for instance, John H. Morrow Jr., *The Great War in the Air: Military Aviation from 1909 to 1921* (Washington, DC: Smithsonian Institution Press, 1993).
2. For a brief history of Army-Navy interactions up to the adoption of the airplane, see Robert Greenhalgh Albion, *Makers of Naval Policy, 1798–1947*, ed. Rowena Reed (Annapolis, MD: Naval Institute Press, 1980), 347–58.
3. Samuel P. Huntington, "Interservice Competition and the Political Roles of the Armed Services," *The American Political Science Review* 55, no. 1 (1961): 40.
4. "Aero Lost in Clouds," unidentified newspaper clipping [probably Baltimore] n.d. [probably September 21, 1911]; *Corresp.: Aviation Safety*, Chambers Papers.
5. George Van Deurs, *Wings for the Fleet: A Narrative of Naval Aviation's Early Development, 1910–1916* (Annapolis, MD: Naval Institute Press, 1966), 49; SecNavAR 1913, 141.

6. Charles de Forest Chandler and Frank Purdy Lahm, *How Our Army Grew Wings: Airmen and Aircraft before 1914* (New York: Ronald Press, 1943), 225–26; Van Deurs, *Wings*, 51.

7. Clark G. Reynolds, *Admiral John Towers: The Struggle for Naval Aviation* (Annapolis, MD: Naval Institute Press, 1991), 41, 44.

8. Cunningham to Chambers [n.d., 1913], *Correspondence: "C" Miscellany*, Chambers Papers.

9. Theodore Taylor, *The Magnificent Mitscher* (New York: W. W. Norton, 1954; repr., Naval Institute Press, 1991), 33; Dik Alan Daso, *Hap Arnold and the Evolution of American Airpower*, Smithsonian History of Aviation Series (Washington, DC: Smithsonian Institution Press, 2000), 64–65; Van Deurs, *Wings*, 51.

10. Ellyson to Chambers, March 5 and 31, 1911, and Chambers to Ellyson, March 11, 1911; *Biographical Notebooks: 1911(1)*; Towers Papers.

11. Ellyson to Chambers, July 13, 1911; *Corresp.: Ellyson, T. G.*; Chambers Papers.

12. Ellyson to Chambers, March 17 and March 31, 1911; *Corresp.: Ellyson, T. G.*; Chambers Papers.

13. Ellyson to Chambers, Aug. 31, 1912; *Corresp.: Ellyson, T. G.*; Chambers Papers.

14. 1354–14, Bristol to Herbster, Oct. 5, 1914, ONA.

15. Chambers, "Memorandum RE 'Aeronautics,'" August 8, 1913, GB-449.

16. Milling to Reber, November 23, December 15, 1913, and Milling to CSO, December 6, 1913, *Official Corresp. 1913*, Chambers Papers.

17. R[obert]. S. Griffin [chief, BuEng] to Officer in Charge of Aviation Camp, August 5, 1913, and Chambers to BuEng, November 24, 1913, *Corresp.: Aviation—Radio Developments*, Chambers Papers.

18. Chambers to Aide for Operations, September 15, 1913, *Official Corresp. 1913*, Chambers Papers.

19. 26983–332, Asst. SecWar to SecNav, Oct. 12, 1914, and reply, SecNavGC.

20. 26983–253:1, Daniels to Lambert, Feb. 17, 1915, SecNavGC.

21. Many military attaché reports are in the ONA files, and the arrangement is specifically mentioned in 2430–15, [Bristol] to Reber, July 7, 1915, ONA.

22. Chambers to General Board, August 8, 1913, GB-449.

23. 1039–14, Daniels to Mr. R. L. Matteson, Aug. 18, 1914, ONA.

24. Bristol to Secretary, Naval War College, Oct. 21, 1916; *GC*; Bristol Papers.

25. Chambers to General Board, August 8, 1913, GB-449.

26. Chambers, "Brief Summary," 17; *Corresp: Naval Aviation—Progress*; Chambers Papers.

27. Juliette A. Hennessy, *The United States Army Air Arm, April 1861 to April 1917*, General Histories (Washington, DC: Office of Air Force History, U.S. Air Force, 1985), 62, 71; Chandler and Lahm, *HOAGW*, 230–31, 233.

28. 26983–159, Acting SecWar [Robert Oliver] to SecNav, Sept. 21, 1912, SecNavGC.

29. Chambers to Smith, October 23, 1913; *Official Corresp.*; Chambers Papers.

30. Herbster and Stolz to Reber, December 18, 1913, *Biographical Notebooks— Chronological—1913 (3)*, Towers Papers; Hennessy, *AAA*, 96.

31. SecWarAR, 1914 (CSO report) 522; Hennessy, *AAA*, 101; Benjamin Delahauf Foulois and Carroll V. Glines, *From the Wright Brothers to the Astronauts: The Memoirs of Benjamin D. Foulois*, 1st ed. (New York: McGraw-Hill, 1968), 113. Hennessy reports that naval aviators also participated in these tests, carrying CAC officers as observers, but I can find no evidence that any naval aviators were in San Diego during January 1914.

32. Reynolds, *Towers*, 59.

33. 2467–14, SecWar to SecNav, July 7, 1915, ONA.

34. 3397–15, SecNav to Commandant, PNAS, Sept. 4, 1915, ONA.

35. Mark L. Evans and Roy A. Grossnick, *United States Naval Aviation 1910– 2010*, 2 vols. (Washington, DC: GPO, 2015), 20; Archibald D. Turnbull and Clifford L. Lord, *History of United States Naval Aviation*, 1st ed. (London: Oxford University Press, 1949), 53–54.

36. 701–14, McIlvain to Bristol, June 3, 1914, and 5168–15, 1st Endorsement: CNO to BuNav, Dec. 18, 1915, ONA.

37. At this time, it may have been expected that all Marine aviators would attend the Army school at some point; however, in a July letter to Benson, Barnett recommended that only one out of every four Marine aviators should be sent on to the Army school. 2883–16, MGC to CNO, July 3, 1916, ONA.

38. 26983–38,3 Curtiss to Alan Hawley, President of ACA, Jan. 24, 1915, and Daniels to Hawley, March 29, 1915, SecNav GC.

39. Mustin to Corinne, Jan. 23, 1914; *Family Corresp.*; Mustin Papers.

40. 1596–15, Bristol, lecture, "Aircraft and Advanced Bases," delivered May 12, 1915, ONA.

41. See, for instance, Cunningham to Mims, August 1 and August 30, 1918, *Cunningham Letters*, Cunningham Papers.

CHAPTER 6. ARMY 1912–1914

1. Charles de Forest Chandler and Frank Purdy Lahm, *How Our Army Grew Wings: Airmen and Aircraft before 1914* (New York: Ronald Press, 1943), 242–43, 251, 261–62; Juliette A. Hennessy, *The United States Army Air Arm, April 1861 to April 1917*, General Histories (Washington, DC: Office of Air Force History, U.S. Air Force, 1985), 73–74, 86, 102; Rebecca Hancock Cameron, *Training to Fly: Military Flight Training, 1907–1945* (Washington, DC: Air Force History and Museums Program, 1999), 55, 57.

2. Rebecca Robbins Raines, *Getting the Message Through: A Branch History of the U. S. Army Signal Corps* (Washington, DC: Center for Military History, 1996), 133.

3. Cameron, *Training*, 55; Chandler and Lahm, *HOAGW*, 251–53; Hennessy, *AAA*, 73–74.

4. Richard D. Challener, *Admirals, Generals, and American Foreign Policy, 1898–1914* (Princeton, NJ: Princeton University Press, 1973), 354–63, 381–85; Benjamin Delahauf Foulois and Carroll V. Glines, *From the Wright Brothers to the Astronauts: The Memoirs of Benjamin D. Foulois*, 1st ed. (New York: McGraw-Hill, 1968), 107–8; Hennessy, *AAA*, 74; Thomas A. Bruscino Jr., "A Troubled Past: The Army and Security on the Mexican Border, 1915–1917," *Military Review*, July–August 2008 (2008): 32.

5. U.S. Congress, House Committee on Military Affairs, *Aeronautics in the Army*, 63rd Congress, First Session, August 12, 14–16, 1913, 106–7.

6. *Aeronautics in the Army*, 106–7; Chandler and Lahm, *HOAGW*, 255.

7. This Burgess Model I was a one-off design that used the Wright wings and twin-pusher propellers but mounted a 60 hp Sturtevant engine and placed the two crewmen within an enclosed fuselage. Like the Burgess Model H, the Model I was designed with tandem (fore-and-aft) seating instead of side-by-side. *HOAGW*, 241–42.

8. Foulois, *Memoirs*, 108–9; Chandler and Lahm, *HOAGW*, 254.

9. Foulois, *Memoirs*, 109–10.

10. Chandler and Lahm, *HOAGW*, 254–55; Hennessy, *AAA*, 76–78; *Aeronautics in the Army*, 107–8.

11. *AAA*, 76; Chandler and Lahm, *HOAGW*, 256.

12. Officially, Chandler remained in charge of the Aeronautical Division, but clearly, he could not handle the day-to-day requirements from Georgia, much less Texas. Still, he remained the official commander. Even his assignment to the Philippines was not cause to replace him in this role. See "The

Nation's Air Army and Its Early Leaders," *Air Force Magazine* 94, no. 5 (2011): 103. Compare Mark Bristol's efforts to remain in charge of naval aviation after his assignment to the fleet in Chap. 7.

13. Dik Alan Daso, *Hap Arnold and the Evolution of American Airpower*, Smithsonian History of Aviation Series (Washington, DC: Smithsonian Institution Press, 2000), 59–60, 63, 73–74; Henry Harley Arnold, *Global Mission*, 1st ed. (New York: Harper, 1949), 41–42; Hennessy, *AAA*, 72.

14. Chandler and Lahm, *HOAGW*, 256, 258; Hennessy, *AAA*, 73, 79, 88; Cameron, *Training*, 56–57; *Aeronautics in the Army*, 35.

15. Hennessy, on 74, says that the Wright D assigned to Texas City was S.C. No. 19, while in a note on 79, she says it was No. 20. Hennessy, *AAA*. The Wright D does not even rate a mention by Swanborough and Bowers, though they do have an entry for the single Wright Model F built for the Army. Gordon Swanborough and Peter M. Bowers, *United States Military Aircraft since 1909* (Washington, DC: Smithsonian Institution Press, 1989), 609–10.

16. Chandler and Lahm, *HOAGW*, 256–57; Hennessy, *AAA*, 79.

17. Chandler and Lahm, *HOAGW*, 261–62; Hennessy, *AAA*, 86; Cameron, *Training*, 57.

18. *Training*, 59.

19. Chandler and Lahm, *HOAGW*, 255, 262; Hennessy, *AAA*, 87.

20. Chandler and Lahm, *HOAGW*, 262–63; Hennessy, *AAA*, 87. Chandler and Lahm say that both Brereton's accidents took place on April 9, but Hennessy says Signal Corps records date the fatal crash to April 8 and the subsequent crash to May 21.

21. Chandler and Lahm say McLeary left in April 1914 (*HOAGW*, 272) but the date in Appendix 1 says April 17, 1913 (283). This latter date agrees with Hennessy (*AAA*, 88).

22. Hennessy, *AAA*, 88; Chandler and Lahm, *HOAGW*, 264.

23. *HOAGW*, 266; *AAA*, 88, 91.

24. *HOAGW*, 265; *AAA*, 91. These sources disagree on what the cost of the lease was as well as exactly what the payment was for.

25. Different secondary sources identify the owner of the land as either the Spreckels Company or the Coronado Beach Company. Trimble identifies John D. Spreckels as a representative of the Coronado Beach Company with whom Curtiss negotiated, which may be the source of the confusion: William F. Trimble, *Hero of the Air: Glenn Curtiss and the Birth of Naval Aviation* (Annapolis, MD: Naval Institute Press, 2010), 105.

26. Chandler and Lahm, *HOAGW*, 259, 261–62, 265–66; Hennessy, *AAA*, 86, 91; Elretta Sudsbury and North Island Historical Committee. *Jackrabbits to Jets: The History of North Island, San Diego, California*. 1st ed. (San Diego, CA: Neyenesch Printers, 1967), 9–10; Trimble, *Hero*, 105–6.

27. Chandler and Lahm, *HOAGW*, 265; Hennessy, *AAA*, 84–85, 91; Cameron, *Training*, 86; SecWarAR, 1914, 524.

28. Chandler and Lahm, *HOAGW*, 246; Hennessy, *AAA*, 80; Cameron, *Training*, 84.

29. Chandler and Lahm say that both Wright Cs were shipped to Manila in May (*HOAGW*, 246), but Hennessy cites Signal Corps records showing that the Corps did not ship No. 12 until the fall (*AAA*, 81 fn). Given the shipping time to the Philippines, the plane likely began its trip to Manila in June, when Scriven ordered most of the 1st Provisional Aero Squadron from Texas City to San Diego.

30. Chandler and Lahm, *HOAGW*, 247–49; Hennessy, *AAA*, 80–81; Cameron, *Training*, 84; Daso, *Arnold*, 61; Foulois, *Memoirs*, 103; SecWarAR, 1914, 517, 524.

31. Chandler and Lahm, *HOAGW*, 248–50; Hennessy, *AAA*, 81; Cameron, *Training*, 84; SecWarAR, 1914, 524.

32. Chandler and Lahm, *HOAGW*, 248–50; Hennessy, *AAA*, 81–84; Cameron, *Training*, 84–86; SecWarAR, 1914, 524. Cameron says that Lt. Henry Post crashed S.C. No. 17 in Manila Bay in January 1914, but in fact, Post was never in the Philippines and crashed into San Diego Bay that month.

33. Chandler and Lahm, *HOAGW*, 249.

34. *HOAGW*, 257; Hennessy, *AAA*, 108.

35. Foulois to Scriven, February 17, 1913, Box 7, Folder 7, Foulois Papers-AFAL; Chandler and Lahm, *HOAGW*, 257; Arnold, *Global Mission*, 42; Herbert A. Johnson, *Wingless Eagle: U.S. Army Aviation through World War I* (Chapel Hill, NC: University of North Carolina Press, 2001), 61.

36. Foulois to Scriven, February 17, 1913, Box 7, Folder 7, Foulois Papers-AFAL.

37. Hennessy, *AAA*, 108; Foulois, *Memoirs*, 103–7.

38. Hennessy, *AAA*, 109.

39. *Aeronautics in the Army*.

40. Alfred F. Hurley, *Billy Mitchell, Crusader for Air Power*, New ed. (Bloomington: Indiana University Press, 1975), 17; *Aeronautics in the Army*, 76–78.

41. *Aeronautics in the Army*, 7–11.

42. Raines, *Message*, 133.

43. Johnson, *Wingless Eagle*, 64, 140–41; *Aeronautics in the Army*, 90–91.

44. Foulois was still with his infantry regiment, and Hennessy had been relieved from aviation duty just a few weeks earlier after a board declared he was "temperamentally unfit to become an aviator." Arnold was technically still on aviation duty but had not flown in nearly a year. He had already requested relief from aviation duty due to his pending marriage.

45. *Aeronautics in the Army*, Testimony of Foulois (50–62), Arnold (88–93), Milling (93–99), and Hennessy (99–102).

46. *Aeronautics in the Army*, 38, 40, 44–45. Beck did not name the officers he felt were "thoroughly competent," though he likely meant himself, and possibly Foulois and Lahm, both of whom had been "manchu'd" out of aviation. Arnold and McLeary are also possibilities as they had requested their own relief from aviation and had (or in Arnold's case, soon would be) returned to their line regiments.

47. *Aeronautics in the Army*, 39–40, 42.

48. *Aeronautics in the Army*, 38–39.

49. *Aeronautics in the Army*, 34–35, 45.

50. The Army only began using tables of organization and equipment in 1914: Raines, *Message*, 142.

51. *Aeronautics in the Army*, 78, 110–12, 114–16, 120–22, 129–30.

52. See Scriven's testimony: *Aeronautics in the Army*, 9–10. Scriven does not identify which legislation nullified the Manchu Law for aviators. However, it was probably a provision of the FY 1914 appropriations bill, passed March 3, 1913.

53. The FY 1914 appropriations bill limited to thirty the number of officers who could be assigned to aviation. See Hennessy, *AAA*, 109.

54. *Aeronautics in the Army*, 8–12, 47–48, 50–56, 64, 66–69, 73–74, 79, 83, 84–85, 89, 96, 120, 122, 257, 267.

55. Hurley, *Mitchell*, 17; *Aeronautics in the Army*, 65, 84, 88, 120. The bill (H.R. 5304, as passed) is reproduced in Hennessy, *AAA*, Appendix 13 and Chandler and Lahm, *HOAGW*, Appendix 16.

56. See Hennessy, *AAA*, Appendix 14.

57. H.R. 5304, as passed. The FY 1914 appropriations bill, passed March 2, 1913, had granted the first pay increase to pilots and aviation mechanicians.

58. For more on the qualifications of U.S. military attachés, see Paul Wilson Clark, "Major General George Owen Squier: Military Scientist" (PhD diss., Case Western Reserve University, 1974), 196–98. Though Squier was soon sending reports on aviation (among other topics) back to Washington, and

Scriven was receiving copies, it seems the aviation reports were not reaching the head of the Aviation Section: Clark, 242–43.

59. Chandler and Lahm, *HOAGW*, 265; Hennessy, *AAA*, 95.
60. Foulois, *Memoirs*, 111–12; Chandler and Lahm, *HOAGW*, 282.
61. *HOAGW*, Appendix 14.
62. Hennessy, *AAA*, 96, 99; Chandler and Lahm, *HOAGW*, 270; Cameron, *Training*, 59–61.
63. Data compiled from Chandler and Lahm, *HOAGW*, Appendix 1.
64. *Aeronautics in the Army*, 68–69, 92–93, 96–97.
65. Chandler and Lahm, *HOAGW*, 268; Hennessy, *AAA*, 99.
66. Chandler and Lahm, *HOAGW*, 267–68; Hennessy, *AAA*, 79,81, 99, 100–01; Foulois, *Memoirs*, 112–13; Johnson, *Wingless Eagle*, 38.
67. Hennessy, *AAA*, 102–04; Cameron, *Training*, 63; Foulois and Glines, *Memoirs*, 114; Johnson, *Wingless Eagle*, 40–41, 127–28; John C. Fredriksen, *The United States Air Force: A Chronology* (Santa Barbara, CA: ABC-CLIO, 2011), 14; SecWarAR, 1914, 517, 522.
68. Hennessy, *AAA*, 105; Cameron, *Training*, 64–65.
69. Chandler and Lahm, *HOAGW*, 271 and Appendix 15; Hennessy, *AAA*, 99, 103.
70. Chandler and Lahm, *HOAGW*, 277; Hennessy, *AAA*, 102; Sudsbury, *Jackrabbits*, 29; Lisa Ritter, "Pack Man," *Air & Space/Smithsonian*, May 2010; SecWarAR, 1914, 522.
71. Chandler and Lahm, *HOAGW*, 272, 276; Hennessy, *AAA*, 101–02, 105; Foulois, *Memoirs*, 113–14; SecWarAR, 1914, 522.
72. At the time, the town's name was written as two words: "Vera Cruz." The modern spelling is "Veracruz."
73. Challener, *Admirals, Generals, and American Foreign Policy, 1898–1914*, 344–63, 379–97.
74. Chandler and Lahm, *HOAGW*, 276; Hennessy, *AAA*, 105–06, 117–20; Foulois, *Memoirs*, 115; SecWarAR, 1914, 517, 522. Scriven's report (522) says the 1st Aero Squadron was organized in September, rather than August. The September date may indicate when Scriven approved Cowan's order.
75. Hennessy, *AAA*, 117; Foulois, *Memoirs*, 115–16; SecWarAR, 1914, 518–21.
76. Hennessy, *AAA*, 117; Foulois and Glines, *Memoirs*, 116; "It's a Sad Story, Mates," *Aeronautics* XV, no. 6 (1914): 84; "Navy to Have Aeroplane Competition," *Aeronautics* XV, no. 8 (1914): 74; SecWarAR, 1914, 509, 518; Peter M. Bowers, *Curtiss Aircraft: 1907–1947* (London: Putnam, 1979), 63–66.

77. See 110–14, Wright Company [Grover Loening] to Captain Mark Bristol [Director of Naval Aviation], February 11, 1914, ONA.

78. Swanborough and Bowers, *Military Aircraft*, 606; "Martin, Martin-Willard," Aerofiles, http://aerofiles.com/_martin.html. There is some disagreement among sources as to whether S.C. No. 33 was a Martin TT and No. 37 a Martin T, or vice-versa.

79. Hennessy, *AAA*, 112–13; Cameron, *Training*, 62–63.

80. Hennessy, *AAA*, 103–04, 122; Cameron, *Training*, 62–63; Bowers, *Curtiss Aircraft*, 67.

81. Hennessy, *AAA*, 122; Cameron, *Training*, 62; SecWarAR, 1914, 522. Cameron cites the identical quotation from an earlier message from Cowan to Scriven, implying that Cowan was the source of this policy and that Scriven may have just copied the phrasing into his report.

82. William F. Trimble, *Wings for the Navy: A History of the Naval Aircraft Factory, 1917–1956* (Annapolis, MD: Naval Institute Press, 1990), 35.

83. Hennessy, *AAA*, 125–27; Foulois, *Memoirs*, 117.

84. Hennessy, *AAA*, 124–25; Foulois, *Memoirs*, 116–17.

85. The Quartermaster Corps was responsible for building and maintaining the physical plant of a base.

86. Hennessy, *AAA*, 128, 137; SecWarAR, 1914, 523–24

87. Hennessy, *AAA*, 128, 137–39, 145, 149; Cameron, *Training*, 77–78; *Aeronautics in the Army*, Appendix 7; SecWarAR, 1914, 523–24

CHAPTER 7. NAVY/MARINES 1914–1917

1. Bradley A. Fiske, *From Midshipman to Rear-Admiral* (New York: Century, 1919), 538–39.

2. 1–14-½, Memorandum for the Aide for Operations "Development of Aeronautics," [n.d., but probably Dec. 1913]; [1–14–1?], Memorandum "Development of an Aeronautic Service in the Navy," Dec. 30, 1913; 1–14–3 [Fiske?] Press release "Naval Aeronautics: air craft [sic] will take their place in the Fleet," Dec. 31, 1913, all ONA.

3. These responsibilities were codified by Daniels in 26983–170:1, Daniels, "NAVAL AEROPLANES—Division of cognizance of parts of" June 5, 1913, SecNavGC.

4. 2–14–1, Daniels to Towers, Jan. 3, 1914, ONA.

5. 10–14, Bristol to CO *Mississippi* [Mustin] Jan. 7, 1914, ONA.

6. Mustin to SecNav, Nov. 18, 1913, *Corresp.: Naval Aviation*, Chambers Papers.

7. 13–14, Bristol to Towers (via Mustin), Jan. 6, 1913, ONA.

8. John Fass Morton, *Mustin: A Naval Family of the 20th Century* (Annapolis, MD: Naval Institute Press, 2003), 81–101, passim.

9. Mustin to wife [n.d., between January 23 and April 21, 1914, letters], *Family Corresp.*, Mustin Papers.

10. Clark G. Reynolds, *Admiral John Towers: The Struggle for Naval Air Supremacy* (Annapolis, MD: Naval Institute Press, 1991), 72; George Van Deurs, *Wings for the Fleet: A Narrative of Naval Aviation's Early Development, 1910–1916* (Annapolis, MD: Naval Institute Press, 1966), 99–100. See also letters from Bristol to Chambers, Feb. 6, 13, and 19, 1914, *Corresp.: "B" Miscellany*, Chambers Papers.

11. Bristol to Chambers, Feb. 19, 1914, *Corresp.: "B" Miscellany*, Chambers Papers.

12. Bristol to Mustin, April 3, 1915, *Board of Inquest, 1915*, Mustin Papers.

13. 8–14, [Bristol] to Aide for Personnel, Jan. 6, 1913, plus 5 enclosures, ONA.

14. 255–14, Smith to CO, Flying School [Towers], March 10, 1914, ONA.

15. 16721–86:1, Barnett to CINCLANTFLT, Feb. 3, 1914, and CINCLANTFLT to Aide for Operations, Feb. 14, 1914, SecNavGC.

16. 1037–14, CO *Mississippi* to CINCLANTFLT, May 19, 1914, ONA.

17. Chambers, "Brief Summary," 17, *Corresp: Naval Aviation—Progress*, Chambers Papers.

18. Bristol to Mustin, 11JUN1914 [typed copy], *Biographical Notebooks: Chronological—1914 (1)*, Towers Papers.

19. 611–14, Mustin to Bristol, May 14, 1914, and 693–14 [Bristol?] "Memorandum for Secretary," May 29, 1914, both in ONA. For further details of the events at Veracruz and Tampico and naval aviation's role, see Mark L. Evans and Roy A. Grossnick, *United States Naval Aviation 1910–2010*, 2 vols. (Washington, DC: GPO, 2015), v. 1:15–16; Frank L. Owlsley Jr. and Wesley Phillips Newton, "Eyes in the Skies," *Proceedings of the United States Naval Institute* 112, no. 4 (Supplement) (1986); Jack Sweetman, *American Naval History*, 3rd ed. (Annapolis, MD: Naval Institute Press, 2002), 116–17.

20. 1037–14, Badger to Fiske, May 20, 1914, ONA.

21. 611–14, Mustin to Bristol, May 14, 1914, ONA.

22. 1028–14, Towers to Bristol, Aug. 3, 1914, ONA, Reynolds, *Towers*, 84, 89.

23. Reynolds, *Towers*, 80–84, 89; Peter M. Bowers, *Curtiss Aircraft: 1907–1947* (London: Putnam, 1979), 57–60.

24. Reynolds, *Towers*, 89–95.

25. Reynolds, *Towers*, 98–99, 101–105; Transcript of Towers' taped reminiscences [n.d.], *Biographical Notebooks—Chronological, 1916(1)*, Towers Papers.

26. Morton, *Mustin*, 96. 904–14, Mustin to Bristol, July 11, 1914, ONA.

27. 1027–14, Bristol to Mustin, August 1, 1914 (and Bristol's reply, August 6, 1914); 1049–14, Telegram, Mustin to Bristol, August 6, 1914 (and Bristol's reply of same date); 1051–14, Mustin to Bristol, August 5, 1914 (and Bristol's reply, August 17); 1060–14 Telegram, Herbster to Bristol August 6, 1914 (and Bristol's reply, August 8, 1914), all ONA; Archibald D. Turnbull and Clifford L. Lord, *History of United States Naval Aviation*, 1st ed. (London: Oxford University Press, 1949), 44; Van Deurs, *Wings*, 115–17.

28. *Wings*, 115–17; Morton, *Mustin*, 96–101.

29. *Mustin*, 103.

30. 1082–14, Bristol to Oman, August 13, 1914, and 1460–14, [Bristol?] to Fiske, October 16, 1914, both ONA.

31. 1106–14, Telegram, Oman to SecNav, August 19, 1914, ONA.

32. Mustin to Bristol, August 24, 1914, GB-449.

33. 1189–14, Office of Naval Aeronautics to Office of Naval Intelligence, Sept. 4, 1914, ONA.

34. 659–14 1st Endorsement, Fiske to [SecNav?] June 24, 1914, ONA.

35. 974–14 Herbster to Bristol, July 28, 1914, ONA.

36. All of the flyers got some practice dropping small "missiles" onto targets while in Guantanamo in 1913, and Towers and Smith practiced dropping bombs in late May 1914 while in Veracruz. Reynolds, *Towers*, 59, 79.

37. 1316–14, Fiske to BuOrd, Sept. 30, 1914, ONA.

38. 4407–15, BuOrd to ONA, October 30, 1915.

39. 999–14, Herbster to Bristol, July 29, 1914, ONA.

40. 709–14, Fiske to SecNav, June 9, 1914, ONA.

41. 1298–14, Fiske to SecNav, Sept. 26, 1914, *and* 1578–14, Bristol to Smith, Nov. 18, 1914, ONA.

42. Van Deurs, *Wings*, 115–20, Appendix A; 1308–14, Whiting to Bristol, Sept. 25, 1914, ONA.

43. 1460–14, Fiske to Navy Dept., Oct. 16, 1914, and 1596–15 Bristol, Lecture: "Aircraft and Advanced Bases," May 12, 1915, ONA.

44. Mustin to Bristol, Feb. 19, 1915, *General Corresp.*, Bristol Papers; Van Deurs, *Wings*, 125.

45. 1222–15, Press release, April 15, 1915, ONA; 1697–15, Press release, April 26, 1915, ONA; 995–16, Bristol to Daniels, March 4, 1916, ONA.

46. 764–15, Telegram, Mustin to Bristol, March 11, 1915, ONA.

47. 2261–15, Mustin to Bristol, June 15, 1915, and 2337–15, Mustin to Bristol, June 30, 1915, ONA.

48. 1222–15, Press release, April 15, 1915, ONA; 1697–15, Press release, April 26, 1915, ONA; 995–16, Bristol to Daniels, March 4, 1916, ONA.

49. Naval Historical Center, Department of the Navy, "Terms of the Office of the Chief of Naval Operations," https://www.history.navy.mil/content/history/ nhhc/research/library/research-guides/lists-of-senior-officers-and-civilian- officials-of-the-us-navy/chiefs-of-naval-operations/terms-for-the-chiefs- of-naval-operations.html.

50. 2434–15, [Benson?] July 8, 1915, ONA. The reorganization was made offi- cial by Daniels in 26983–566 ½ , Daniels, Memorandum, Oct. 12, 1915, SecNavGC.

51. Turnbull and Lord, *History*, 51–2.

52. The position of CNO was considerably weaker when it was established than it is now. Robert William Love Jr., ed. *The Chiefs of Naval Operations* (Annapolis, MD: Naval Institute Press, 1980), 4–7.

53. 2557–15, Navy Department Press Notice, July 1, 1915, ONA.

54. Van Deurs, *Wings*, 129–30.

55. 2296–15 2nd Endorsement, Whiting to BuOrd, Sept. 29, 1915, ONA.

56. For more on the new designation scheme, see Gordon Swanborough and Peter M. Bowers, *United States Navy Aircraft since 1911* (New York: Funk & Wagnalls, 1968), 4–5.

57. 4500–15, Navy Dept., Press Notice, Nov. 10, 1915, ONA.

58. Van Deurs, *Wings*, 139–40.

59. 3126–15, Mustin to BuNav, Aug. 16, 1915, ONA.

60. "Marines Take Wing," 4, *Organization, 1914–1939*, Cunningham Papers.

61. 4870–15, Mustin to Bristol, Nov. 27, 1915; 5015–15, LTJG Edwards to ONA, Dec. 4, 1915; and 800–16, CinCLANTFLT [Fletcher] to CNO, Feb. 9, 1916, all in ONA.

62. 2578–15, Mustin to ONA, July 13, 1915, ONA.

63. 2730–15, Bristol to The Burgess Co., July 24, 1915, ONA. I found no response from Burgess in these files.

64. 4407–15, BuOrd to ONA, Oct. 30, 1915; and 4478–15, ONA to BuOrd, Nov. 9, 1915, both in ONA.

65. 3076–15, [Bristol] to CNO, Aug. 14, 1915, ONA.

66. Chambers to General Board, August 8, 1913, GB-449.

67. General Board to Daniels, August 30, 1913, GB-449.

68. "Report of the Board on Aeronautics," 5–8.

69. 284–14, Bristol to Mr. E. A. Mulliken, Connecticut Air Craft Co., May 6, 1914, ONA.

70. By comparison, the Baldwin airship purchased by the Army in 1908 was only 20,000 cubic feet, while Germany's *Luftschiffbau Zeppelin* was already making Zeppelins almost 800,000 cubic feet in size in 1913. Their Zeppelins would approach 2 million cubic feet in size by 1918. The Goodyear Airship Company had already built a nonrigid airship (a "blimp," though the term was not yet in use) of 346,000 cubic feet in 1912, whereas the current Goodyear blimps used for advertising in the United States (as of this writing) are just over 202,000 cubic feet. Charles de Forest Chandler and Frank Purdy Lahm, *How Our Army Grew Wings: Airmen and Aircraft before 1914* (New York: Ronald Press, 1943), 291; Tom D. Crouch, *Lighter Than Air: An Illustrated History of Balloons and Airships* (Baltimore: Johns Hopkins University Press, in association with the Smithsonian National Air and Space Museum, 2009), 181.

71. "Report of the Board on Aeronautics," 21.

72. Senate Naval Affairs Committee, *Naval Investigation: Hearings before the Subcommittee of the Committee on Naval Affairs*, 66th Congress, 2nd Session, 1921, 2678.

73. "Report by Captain I. [?] H. Oliver, Director of Naval Intelligence for General Board on the aeronautical strength of all nations." July 14, 1914, GB-449.

74. 1563–14, Richardson to Bristol, November 3, 1914, ONA.

75. "Necessity for Dirigibles," Serial 486, General Board to Daniels, March 1, 1916; General Board to Daniels, June 24, 1916, both GB-449.

76. Van Deurs, *Wings*, Appendix A.

77. Roy A. Grossnick, *Kite Balloons to Airships: The Navy's Lighter-Than-Air Experience* (Washington, DC: Deputy Chief of Naval Operations (Air Warfare): Naval Air Systems Command, 1987), 3–4.

78. 1025–14, 3rd Endorsement, Aide for Operations to BuNav, August 5, 1914; ONA.

79. 5168–15 1st Endorsement, CNO to BuNav, Dec. 18, 1915, ONA.

80. 708–16 report from Maxfield on test of Goodyear kite balloon [date-stamped February 16, 1916], document is filed with 773–16 CNO to BuC&R, February 25, 1916, ONA. Grossnick says the free balloon was accepted December 14 and the kite balloon December 22: Grossnick, *Kite Balloons to Airships*, 4.

81. "DN" stood for "dirigible, nonrigid," though it was the only airship to carry the designation. The next generation of Navy airships was designated "B–class airships," effectively making the DN-1, the only one of its design, the "A–class," though it remained known as the DN. Grossnick, *Kite Balloons to Airships*, 4–5.
82. 938–16, Bristol to Herbster, March 2, 1916, ONA; Van Deurs, *Wings*, 136.
83. Turnbull and Lord, *History*, 59.
84. 4156–16, McKean to CNO, April 10, 1916, ONA.
85. Van Deurs, *Wings*, 151–52.
86. 2382–16, Aide for Material (McKean) to CNO, June 8, 1916, ONA.
87. Morton, *Mustin*, 105–9; Van Deurs, *Wings*, 147–53.
88. Reynolds, *Towers*, 106–7.
89. Van Deurs, *Wings*, 142, 155–56.
90. Mustin to Bristol, May 14, 1915, and Mustin to Bristol, Nov. 8, 1915, *Corresp.*, Mustin Papers.
91. Mustin to Bristol, August 24, 1914, GB-449.
92. Bristol to Mustin, April 16, 1915, *General Corresp.*, Bristol Papers.
93. Bristol to Smith, December 13, 1916, *General Corresp.*, Bristol Papers.
94. Van Deurs, *Wings*, 150–52. 2320–15, Bristol to Mustin, June 30, 1915, ONA.
95. Chambers to Smith, Oct. 25, 1913, *Official Corresp.*, Chambers Papers.
96. 2505–16, radiogram, Mustin to CNO, June 12, 1916, ONA; "Marines Take Wing," [n.d., but text indicates sometime between 1931 and 1935. Handwritten note on document indicates "From pamphlet, 'Marine Corps Aviation.'"], loose pages, Cunningham Papers; Roger Willock, *Unaccustomed to Fear: A Biography of the Late General Roy S. Geiger, U.S.M.C*, MCA Heritage Library (Quantico, VA: Marine Corps Association, 1983), 72.
97. Swanborough and Bowers, *Navy Aircraft*, 93; Bowers, *Curtiss Aircraft*, 111–12.
98. Armand Jean Auguste Deperdussin. Aeroplane. USA Patent 1,049,820, filed January 7, 1913.
99. Swanborough and Bowers, *Navy Aircraft*, 92; Van Deurs, *Wings*, 153–55.
100. SecNav to CNO July 1, 1916, and CNO to Mustin July 6, 1916, both *Subject Files: Board of Inquest, 1916*, Mustin Papers, both show a level of irritation with Mustin. Mustin's reply to the secretary's questions (Mustin to CNO, July 23, 1916, *Subject Files: Board of Inquest, 1916*, Mustin Papers) is an eleven-page response that clearly expresses Mustin's frustrations with Bristol's poor management of naval aviation, and borders on insubordination.

101. Mustin to Corinne [his wife], July 18, 1917, *Family Corresp.*, Mustin Papers.

102. Reginald Wright Arthur, *Contact! Careers of US Naval Aviators Assigned Numbers 1 to 2000*, 1st ed. (Washington, DC: Naval Aviator Register, 1967), 9.

103. 5341–15, Bristol to Mustin, December 29, 1915, ONA; 176–16, "Press Notice," January 14, 1916, ONA; George F. Pearce, *The U.S. Navy in Pensacola: From Sailing Ships to Naval Aviation, 1825–1930* (Pensacola, FL: University Press of Florida, 1980), 143; Roy A. Grossnick and William J. Armstrong, *United States Naval Aviation, 1910–1995* (Washington, DC: Naval Historical Center Dept. of the Navy, 1997), 407–408. For discussion of the various titles used to denote officer and enlisted pilots of varying skill levels, see Evans and Grossnick, v. 2: Chap. 8. I have chosen to use "naval aviator" consistently for all naval officers qualified to fly aircraft.

104. Grossnick, *Kite Balloons to Airships*, 9.

105. Willock, *Unaccustomed to Fear*, 68–76.

106. 1596–15, [Mark Bristol], "Lecture: Aircraft and Advanced Bases," May 12, 1915, 3, 4, ONA.

107. Bristol to Fiske, Sept, 25, 1914, GB-449.

108. 2350–15, [Bristol], "Suggestion of Plans for Future Development of Aeronautics," June 30, 1915, ONA.

109. General Board to Daniels, September 27, 1915, GB-420.

110. "Comment by Lieutenant Commander Mustin before Executive Committee of the General Board, March 7, 1916," GB-449.

111. "Hearing of Lieutenant Commander Mustin, U.S.N. before the Executive Committee of the General Board, on the subject of aviation." October 12, 1916, GB-449.

112. 1638–16, Fletcher to Benson, April 13, 1916 (and attachments), ONA; *Flying Officers of the United States Navy, 1917–1919* (Atglen, PA: Schiffer Military History, 1997), 59–60. Though not mentioned in the official report, *North Carolina* also carried at least one student aviator, Marc Mitscher. Theodore Taylor, *The Magnificent Mitscher* (New York: W. W. Norton, 1954; repr., Naval Institute Press, 1991), 38–39.

113. 1638–16, Fletcher to Benson, April 13, 1916 (and attachments), ONA.

114. Daniels to General Board, April 12, 1916, GB-449.

115. General Board to Daniels, June 24, 1916, GB-449.

116. General Board to Daniels, June 24, 1916, GB-449.

117. General Board, "Building Program: 1918, October 16, 1916," Serial No. 589(t), GB-420.

118. General Board to Daniels, August 25, 1916, GB-449.
119. 1421–16, [Bronson?] to Mustin, April 1, 1916, ONA; Van Deurs, *Wings*, 142; "Seattle—I," "Huntington—I," Naval History and Heritage Command, "Dictionary of American Naval Fighting Ships," https://www.history.navy.mil/research/histories/ship-histories/danfs.html.
120. 5271–17, Commander Cruiser Force, Atlantic Fleet to BuNav, September 25, 1917, ONA; 5477–17, N. E. Irwin to USS *Seattle*, October 5, 1917, ONA.
121. Henry Woodhouse, *Textbook of Naval Aeronautics* (New York: Century, 1917; repr., Naval Institute Press, 1991), 145–48; 4143–16, Bronson to SecNav, November 13, 1916, ONA.
122. General Board to Daniels, June 24, 1916, GB-449.
123. Turnbull and Lord, *History*, 86–92.
124. Cunningham to [Charles J.] Miller, January 22, 1931, *Northern Bombing Group*, Cunningham Papers. Another copy is in *Personal Papers*, Cunningham Papers.
125. Bronson to McKean, June 24, 1916 (2458–16), *Capt. Cunningham—Personal Folder*, Cunningham Papers. Though Bronson originated this memo, its contents were likely written by (or at least with the input of) Cunningham.
126. Bronson to McKean, June 24, 1916 (2458–16). For the current relationship between naval aviation and Marine Corps aviation, see John P. Condon, *U.S. Marine Corps Aviation* (Washington, DC: Deputy Chief of Naval Operations [Air Warfare], 1987), 1.
127. 2883–16, MGC to CNO, July 3, 1916 (and endorsements), ONA.
128. 3552–16, Cunningham to Bronson, Cunningham to MGC, August 29, 1916, ONA.
129. United States Marine Corps History Division, "Lieutenant Colonel Alfred Austell Cunningham, USMC," https://www.usmcu.edu/Research/Marine-Corps-History-Division/People/Whos-Who-in-Marine-Corps-History/Abrell-Cushman/Lieutenant-Colonel-Alfred-Austell-Cunningham/; SecNavAR, 1917, 51; Turnbull and Lord, *History*, 74–75.
130. 205–17, CNO to Commandant, Navy Yard, Philadelphia, January 30, 1917, ONA.
131. Edward C. Johnson, *Marine Corps Aviation: The Early Years, 1912–1940*, ed. Graham A. Cosmas (Washington, DC: History and Museums Division, Headquarters, USMC, 1977), 10; Edwin North McClellan, manuscript, "Flying Leathernecks" [n.d., not earlier than 1928], *Northern Bombing Group*, Cunningham Papers.

132. 669–17, Benson to BuEng, March 12, 1917, ONA; 3421–17, Smith, "Report of visit to the Aeronautical Company, Marine Corps Advance Base, Navy Yard, Philadelphia" [n.d., but must be late July/early August 1917], ONA.

CHAPTER 8. ARMY 1915–1917

1. Juliette A. Hennessy, *The United States Army Air Arm, April 1861 to April 1917*, General Histories (Washington, DC: Office of Air Force History, U.S. Air Force, 1985), 128, 137; Rebecca Hancock Cameron, *Training to Fly: Military Flight Training, 1907–1945* (Washington, DC: Air Force History and Museums Program, 1999), 88; Alfred F. Hurley, *Billy Mitchell, Crusader for Air Power*, new ed. (Bloomington: Indiana University Press, 1975), 18; Paul Wilson Clark, "Major General George Owen Squier: Military Scientist" (PhD diss., Case Western Reserve University, 1974), 221–24.
2. Clark, "Squier," 198, 205–7, 221.
3. Clark, "Squier," 219–21, 223–28, 245; Kitchener to French, November 14, 1914, Squier Papers.
4. Clark, "Squier," 228–32, 240–41.
5. General Staff Corps of the Army War College, *Military Aviation* (Washington, DC: Army War College, 1915), 5–7. Hurley notes that Mitchell may have written this report. See Hurley, *Mitchell*, 19–20 and 155n40.
6. General Staff Corps of the Army War College, *Military Aviation*, 8–9.
7. *Military Aviation*, 12–16.
8. *Military Aviation*, 16.
9. *Military Aviation*, 17–18; SecWarAR, 1915, 742–44.
10. SecWarAR, 1914, 507–9; Hennessy, *AAA*, 128; Clark, "Squier," 243.
11. 2430–15, [Bristol] to Reber, July 7, 1915, ONA.
12. Clark, "Squier," 242; Hennessy, *AAA*, 140; Cameron, *Training*, 87–89.
13. Hennessy, *AAA*, 137–38, 144; Cameron, *Training*, 45–46, 65, 67–68.
14. Hennessy, *AAA*, 123, 144; Herbert A. Johnson, *Wingless Eagle: U.S. Army Aviation through World War I* (Chapel Hill, NC: University of North Carolina Press, 2001), 117–29; Cameron, *Training*, 68–69.
15. Johnson, *Wingless Eagle*, 123–29, 131–32, 174; Hennessy, *AAA*, 144–45, 153–54; Cameron, *Training*, 68–69; Rebecca Robbins Raines, *Getting the Message Through: A Branch History of the U. S. Army Signal Corps* (Washington, DC: Center for Military History, 1996), 165–67; Hurley, *Mitchell*, 20.

16. Thomas A. Bruscino Jr., "A Troubled Past: The Army and Security on the Mexican Border, 1915–1917," *Military Review*, July–August 2008 (2008): 32–33.

17. Hennessy, *AAA*, 145, 238; Charles de Forest Chandler and Frank Purdy Lahm, *How Our Army Grew Wings: Airmen and Aircraft Before 1914* (New York: Ronald Press, 1943), 285.

18. Hennessy, *AAA*, 146.

19. Hennessy, *AAA*, 135; Cameron, *Training*, 64; Peter M. Bowers, *Curtiss Aircraft: 1907–1947* (London: Putnam, 1979), 143; Gordon Swanborough and Peter M. Bowers, *United States Military Aircraft Since 1909* (Washington, DC: Smithsonian Institution Press, 1989), 601.

20. Hennessy, *AAA*, 147–48; Benjamin Delahauf Foulois and Carroll V. Glines, *From the Wright Brothers to the Astronauts: The Memoirs of Benjamin D. Foulois*, 1st ed. (New York: McGraw-Hill, 1968), 119; Transcript of Foulois interview (Tape #15), September 15, 1965, 2–3, Box 10, Folder 4 [hereafter simply "Tape #15"], Foulois Papers-AFAL.

21. Hennessy, *AAA*, 147; Foulois, *Memoirs*, 120–21. Johnson, *Wingless Eagle*, 165. Interestingly, Foulois later claimed that the first time he piloted one of these planes was in mid-November 1915, when he had Milling take him up to get used to the Curtiss yoke control system that all the planes were equipped with. Tape # 15, 4, Foulois Papers-AFAL.

22. See Hennessy, *AAA*, 148–49.

23. For more on the reasons for unrest along the U.S.-Mexican border and the U.S. military responses, see Alan Knight, *The Mexican Revolution*, 2 vols., Cambridge Latin American studies (New York: Cambridge University Press, 1986), 2: 392–406; Bruscino, "Troubled Past," 32–34.

24. Hennessy, *AAA*, 147–49; Foulois, *Memoirs*, 119–20.

25. Hennessy, *AAA*, 135–36, 148; Foulois, *Memoirs*, 120–21; Johnson, *Wingless Eagle*, 127–28.

26. These new-built JN-3s were the first planes delivered to the Army with the Dep control. The JN-2s had the Curtiss shoulder yoke and retained these controls after conversion to the JN-3 standard. Bowers, *Curtiss Aircraft*, 150–51.

27. Hennessy, *AAA*, 149. Foulois' account implies that Curtiss sent men and materials to Brownsville to upgrade the planes there in situ. Foulois, *Memoirs*, 121.

28. Hennessy, *AAA*, 136, 148–49; Foulois, *Memoirs*, 120–21; Johnson, *Wingless Eagle*, 127–28, 131.

29. Hennessy, *AAA*, 137, 147; Tape # 15, 1, Foulois Papers-AFAL.

30. *A History of Military Aviation in San Antonio* (n.p.: U.S. Dept. of Defense, 2000), 5–6.

31. Tape # 15, 3–4, Foulois Papers-AFAL; Foulois, *Memoirs*, 121; Hennessy, *AAA*, 149.

32. Tape # 15, 5–6, Foulois Papers-AFAL; Foulois, *Memoirs*, 121; Hennessy, *AAA*, 149.

33. Tape # 15, 5–6, 16, Foulois Papers-AFAL; *AAA*, 149–50; Foulois, *Memoirs*, 121–22.

34. Tape # 15, 1–4, 6–7, Foulois Papers-AFAL; Hennessy, *AAA*, 149–50; Foulois, *Memoirs*, 121–22; Bruscino, "Troubled Past," 33–38.

35. Hennessy, *AAA*, 150–52; Johnson, *Wingless Eagle*, 122–23, 130; SecWarAR, 1916, 746.

36. Bruscino, "Troubled Past," 31, 38–39, 44n53; Hennessy, *AAA*, 167; Foulois, *Memoirs*, 122–26.

37. Bruscino, "Troubled Past," 39; Foulois, *Memoirs*, 122–26; Hennessy, *AAA*, 167–68; "Report of the Operations of the First Aero Squadron, Signal Corps, With Punitive Expedition, U.S.A., For Period March 15 to August 15, 1916," Box 8, Folder 5 [hereafter simply "Foulois report, 1916"], 1, Foulois Papers-AFAL.

38. Even in contemporary, official reports, the location is sometimes given as "Nuevo Casas Grandes." The confusion may arise from the fact that the two are just a few miles from each other, and Nuevo Casas Grandes is closer to where Pershing initially encamped at Colonia Dublán.

39. "Foulois Report, 1916," 1, Foulois Papers-AFAL; Foulois, *Memoirs*, 126; Hennessy, *AAA*, 167–68. Roger G. Miller, *A Preliminary to War: The 1st Aero Squadron and the Mexican Punitive Expedition of 1916* (Washington, DC: Air Force History and Museums Program, 2003), 17–19. On the Army's lack of motor vehicles in general, and trucks for the expedition in particular, see James W. Hurst, *Pancho Villa and Black Jack Pershing: the Punitive Expedition in Mexico* (Westport, CT: Praeger, 2008), 130–33.

40. "Foulois Report—1916," 1–2, Foulois Papers-AFAL; Hennessy, *AAA*, 167–68; Foulois, *Memoirs*, 126–27; Miller, *Preliminary to War*, 20–22, 24–25, 27–28.

41. Foulois, *Memoirs*, 127–28; Miller, *Preliminary to War*, 21.

42. Bowers does not provide any performance information on the JN-3 but lists a service ceiling of only 6,500 feet for the later JN-4D. Bowers, *Curtiss Aircraft*, 156.

43. "Foulois Report—1916," 2–3, 4, Foulois Papers-AFAL; SecWarAR, 1916, 882–83; Hennessy, *AAA*, 168–69; Foulois, *Memoirs*, 128–29; Miller, *Preliminary to War*, 25–27.

44. "Foulois Report—1916," 4, 8, Foulois Papers-AFAL; Hennessy, *AAA*, 168, 169; Foulois, *Memoirs*, 134; Johnson, *Wingless Eagle*, 166; Raines, *Message*, 148; Miller, *Preliminary to War*, 44–45.

45. Johnson, *Wingless Eagle*, 168.

46. John J. Pershing, "Punitive Expedition Report," (Colonia Dublán, Mexico, 1916), Appendix J (A copy may be found online at https://cgsc.contentdm .oclc.org/digital/collection/p4013coll7/id/702/); "Foulois Report—1916," 5–8, Foulois Papers-AFAL; Hennessy, *AAA*, 168–72; Foulois, *Memoirs*, 126, 128–33.

47. Bruscino, "Troubled Past," 37, 39–41; "Foulois Report—1916," 5–6, Foulois Papers-AFAL; Hennessy, *AAA*, 170; Foulois, *Memoirs*, 129–33; Miller, *Preliminary to War*, 35–36.

48. "Foulois Report—1916," 6–8, Foulois Papers-AFAL; Hennessy, *AAA*, 170–72; Foulois, *Memoirs*, 133; Miller, *Preliminary to War*, 39–41.

49. Hennessy's footnote with the dates of Gibbs' and Mitchell's "acting" status (Hennessy, *AAA*, 156 fn.) says simply that Gibbs "had assumed charge . . . during the temporary absence of Lt. Col. Reber" with no explanation for Reber's absence.

50. Hennessy, *AAA*, 153–54, 156 fn; Johnson, *Wingless Eagle*, 131–32; Raines, *Message*, 165–67; Foulois, *Memoirs*, 124–25, 141; Miller, *Preliminary to War*, 48–49.

51. Both Foulois and Hennessy say that the N-8 was virtually the same as the JN-4, but Bowers says it was a copy of the JN-3 with a different engine, airfoil, and the Curtiss shoulder yoke controls rather than the Dep. Foulois, *Memoirs*, 134; Hennessy, *AAA*, 174 fn; Bowers, *Curtiss Aircraft*, 111.

52. "Foulois Report—1916," 8, 9, 11; Foulois, *Memoirs*, 134; Hennessy, *AAA*, 172–73; Bowers, *Curtiss Aircraft*, 150–51; Bruscino, "Troubled Past," 41.

53. Hurst, *Villa and Pershing*, 89–110, 117–18; Foulois, *Memoirs*, 135; Miller, *Preliminary to War*, 46–48; Hennessy, *AAA*, 174; "Foulois Report—1916," 8, 9, 11.

54. Foulois, *Memoirs*, 136; "Foulois Report—1916," 4–9; Pershing, "Punitive Expedition Report," 44–45.

55. "Foulois Report—1916," 9–10.

56. Scriven to Chief, War College Division, General Staff, May 16, 1916, 2, Aeronautical Division, 1907–1916, RG18.

57. Technically, the ability to "federalize" National Guard units was not possible until passage of the National Defense Act of June 3, 1916, so what the president had done was to "call up" the organized militia of the three border states. However, the effect was the same. See the discussion in Hurst, *Villa and Pershing*, 106.

58. Bruscino, "Troubled Past," 40; Hennessy, *AAA*, 133. By the end of August, there were nearly 112,000 U.S. troops guarding the Mexican border, see Hurst, *Villa and Pershing*, 100.

59. For more on these camps, see Allan Reed Millett and Peter Maslowski, *For the Common Defense: A Military History of the United States of America*, Revised and expanded ed. (New York: Free Press, 1994), 340–41.

60. Hennessy, *AAA*, 133–34, 177; Raines, *Message*, 152.

61. Hennessy, *AAA*, 182–83.

62. Hennessy, *AAA*, 154, 185–86; Hurley, *Mitchell*, 21; Foulois, *Memoirs*, 140.

63. Hennessy, *AAA*, 175–76; Foulois, *Memoirs*, 135, 138–41. Curiously, Foulois, on 135, agrees with Hennessy that his movements were the result of orders, but on 138–41, Foulois implies that the trips to Washington were his own idea and occurred while he was on leave.

64. SecWarAR, 1915, 742–44; Scriven to Adjutant General of the Army, April 5, 1916 (This document is filed as Appendix H of Scriven to Chief, War College Division, General Staff, May 16, 1916), Aeronautical Division, 1907–1916, RG18; *Memoirs*, 118–19; Hennessy, *AAA*, 154–55; Johnson, *Wingless Eagle*, 179.

65. SecWarAR, 1915, 744; Foulois, *Memoirs*, 119; Hennessy, *AAA*, 154–55; Johnson, *Wingless Eagle*, 179.

66. Hennessy, *AAA*, 154, 177–81; Cameron, *Training*, 94–95; SecWarAR, 1916, 40–42, 884.

67. Essington is next to the present-day Philadelphia International Airport.

68. Hennessy, *AAA*, 181–82; Cameron, *Training*, 95; SecWarAR, 1916, 41–42, 884.

69. SecWarAR, 1916, 861–62; Hennessy, *AAA*, 165, 191–92.

70. Johnson, *Wingless Eagle*, 132; Raines, *Message*, 166; Hennessy, *AAA*, 154, 157; Scriven to Chief, War College Division, General Staff, May 16, 1916, 8–10, Aeronautical Division, 1907–1916, RG18.

71. Hennessy, *AAA*, 157; Raines, *Message*, 166; Johnson, *Wingless Eagle*, 132–35; Clark, "Squier," 253–54; "Report of Committee on Aviation," April 25, 1916, 11–12, copy in Foulois Papers-LC, Box 23, Folder 4.

72. Bliss to Baker, July 7, 1916, copy in Foulois Papers-LC, Box 23, Folder 4; U.S. Congress, House Committee on Military Affairs, *Army Appropriation Bill, 1917*, 64th Congress, First Session, March 28—April 11, 1916, Statement of Newton D. Baker, April 8, 838, 840, 846; Clark, "Squier," 253–54; SecWarAR, 1916, 891.

73. Scriven to Chief, War College Division, General Staff, May 16, 1916, 9–10, Aeronautical Division, 1907–1916, RG18.
74. Scriven to Chief, War College Division, General Staff, May 16, 1916, 1–2, Appendix I, Aeronautical Division, 1907–1916, RG18; SecWarAR, 1916, 41–42.
75. Chandler and Lahm, HOAGW, 103–05, 122–23; Hennessy, *AAA*, 19.
76. Chandler and Lahm, HOAGW, 283.
77. *Army Appropriation Bill, 1917*, 853; Scriven to Chief, War College Division, General Staff, May 16, 1916, 10, Aeronautical Division, 1907–1916, RG18; SecWarAR, 1916, 41, 883; Hennessy, *AAA*, 162–63.
78. Henry Harley Arnold, *Global Mission*, 1st ed. (New York: Harper, 1949), 43–46; Dik Alan Daso, *Hap Arnold and the Evolution of American Airpower*, Smithsonian History of Aviation Series (Washington, DC: Smithsonian Institution Press, 2000), 75–83.
79. Hennessy, *AAA*, 188–91; Raines, *Message*, 167; Arnold, *Global Mission*, 45–46; Daso, *Arnold*, 82–85.
80. Hennessy, *AAA*, 191; Raines, *Message*, 167; Foulois, *Memoirs*, 141.

CHAPTER 9. INTERSERVICE ORGANIZATION II

1. See Towers' comment that the Army "had nothing corresponding to [BuEng], or officers well trained in gas engines." 1006–17, Towers to Benson, April 9, 1917, ONA.
2. Chambers to Ely, February 9, 1911, *Corresp. 1910–1919—Eugene Ely*, Chambers Papers.
3. Archibald D. Turnbull and Clifford L. Lord, *History of United States Naval Aviation*, 1st ed. (London: Oxford University Press, 1949), 16; William F. Trimble, *Jerome C. Hunsaker and the Rise of American Aeronautics*, Smithsonian History of Aviation and Spaceflight Series (Washington, DC: Smithsonian Institution Press, 2002), 26; Herbert A. Johnson, *Wingless Eagle: U.S. Army Aviation through World War I* (Chapel Hill, NC: University of North Carolina Press, 2001), 108; Alex Roland, *Model Research: The National Advisory Committee for Aeronautics, 1915–1958*, 2 vols. (Washington, DC: NASA, 1985), v. 1:4–7.
4. See: Naval Sea Systems Command, "David W. Taylor," https://www.navsea.navy.mil/Home/Warfare-Centers/NSWC-Carderock/Who-We-Are/Rear-Adm-David-W-Taylor/.
5. Turnbull and Lord, *History*, 16–17; Roland, *Model Research*, 4–6.

6. Tom D. Crouch, *A Dream of Wings: Americans and the Airplane, 1875–1905* (New York: W. W. Norton, 1981; reprint, 2002), 78–84, 130–31; Roland, *Model Research*, 6–8; Stephen K. Stein, *From Torpedoes to Aviation: Washington Irving Chambers and Technological Innovation in the New Navy, 1876–1913* (Tuscaloosa, AL: University of Alabama Press, 2007), 177–78; Chambers, Untitled document beginning "(In Connection with the idea that we ought to lead the world in Aeronautical Progress," [n.d., but likely Summer 1912], *Corresp.: Aviation Progress*, Chambers Papers.

7. SecNavAR 1912, 159, 163–70.

8. Stein, *Chambers*, 178; Roland, *Model Research*, 10; Rudolph Forster to SecNav, December 20, 1912, *Official Correspondence 1912*, Chambers Papers; Acting SecNav to Chambers, December 23, 1912, *Corresp.: Aviation Progress*, Chambers Papers. Stein says Taft created the commission on December 12, but Roland and the letters in the Chambers Papers all say it was December 19.

9. Roland, *Model Research*, 10–11; Stein, *Chambers*, 178.

10. Acting SecNav to Chambers, December 23, 1912, *Corresp.: Aviation Progress*, Chambers Papers; Roland, *Model Research*, 11–13.

11. Roland, 13–15; Trimble, *Hunsaker*, 26–27; Stein, *Chambers*, 178–79.

12. Roland, *Model Research*, 11–13.

13. Roland, 16–18, 18n41; Trimble, *Hunsaker*, 27; Stein, *Chambers*, 183.

14. Trimble, *Hunsaker*, 18, 21–27, 31–32; Roland, *Model Research*, 18, 18n43. Zahm had the reputation as an aeronautical researcher, but Hunsaker had corresponded extensively with Eiffel, who gave them access to French research. Zahm and Hunsaker issued separate reports: the Smithsonian published Zahm's "Report of European Aeronautical Laboratories," dated July 27, 1914, while Hunsaker's "Europe's Facilities for Aeronautical Research" appeared in *Flying*, v. III, nos. 3 and 4 (April and May 1914).

15. Roland, *Model Research*, 19–20.

16. Roland, 20–25; Stein, *Chambers*, 183–84.

17. Roland, *Model Research*, 27–30.

18. Samuel P. Huntington, "Interservice Competition and the Political Roles of the Armed Services," *American Political Science Review* 55, no. 1 (1961).

19. On the origins of the NCB and its own laboratory facilities, see Lloyd N. Scott, *Naval Consulting Board of the United States* (Washington, DC: GPO, 1920), 7–13, 109–13. For a more critical assessment of the Naval Consulting Board,

see Daniel J. Kevles, *The Physicists: The History of a Scientific Community in Modern America* (Cambridge, MA: Harvard University Press, 1987), 105–7.

20. Roland, *Model Research*, 30–32.

21. SecNavAR 1916, 26–27; Roland, *Model Research*, 27, 32–33; Paul Wilson Clark, "Major General George Owen Squier: Military Scientist" (PhD diss., Case Western Reserve University, 1974), 269–72.

22. Russell Frank Weigley, *The American Way of War: A History of United States Military Strategy and Policy*, The Wars of the United States (New York: Macmillan, 1973), 200–201.

23. 4218–16, Daniels to President, Joint Board, September 7, 1916, ONA.

24. Copies of Squier's letter to the Adjutant General (October 2, 1916) and Ingraham's letter to Daniels (October 11, 1916) are attached to G.B. No.449 (Serial 615), Dewey to Daniels, October 19, 1916, GB-449. Ingraham's letter is also reproduced as Appendix I in Adrian O. Van Wyen, *The Aeronautical Board: 1916–1947* (Washington, DC: GPO, 1947).

25. Turnbull and Lord, *History*, 75; Clark G. Reynolds, *Admiral John Towers: The Struggle for Naval Air Supremacy* (Annapolis, MD: Naval Institute Press, 1991), 109; 3967–16, Benson to Daniels, October 27, 1916, ONA; Board of Army and Navy officers . . . to SecNav, March 12, 1917, Box 33, Folder 7, Foulois Papers-LC; Van Wyen, *Aeronautical Board*, 2–3.

26. 3967–16 Benson to Daniels, October 27, 1916, ONA. Van Wyen's history of this board also recounts an alternate version of the board's establishment (recorded by the secretary of the Aeronautical Board in 1920) wherein Ingraham's suggestion created the "Zeppelin Board," while Benson's letter caused the establishment of a second board. According to this version, the two boards merged sometime after the scope of the Zeppelin Board expanded on January 31, 1917. Van Wyen, *Aeronautical Board*, 2, n5.

27. Memorandum for CNO, November 20, 1916; Memorandum for CNO, November 21, 1916; Towers, Memorandum for McKean, November 22, 1916; all 4218–16, ONA.

28. SecNavAR 1916, 26.

29. Van Wyen, *Aeronautical Board*, 2–3. The two letters quoted are reproduced in Van Wyen as Appendices II and III. A copy of Roosevelt's letter is at 26983–633:3, Roosevelt to Baker, January 12, 1917, SecNavGC.

30. Ingraham to Daniels, October 11, 1916, see note 24 for locations.

314 | Notes to Pages 242–244

31. 25–17, Board of Army and Navy Officers to SecNav and SecWar, January 6, 1917, ONA.

32. Grossnick and Armstrong date the establishment of the Airship Board to January 6, but this is the same date as the Cognizance Board report recommending its creation. Roy A. Grossnick and William J. Armstrong, *United States Naval Aviation, 1910–1995* (Washington, DC: Naval Historical Center Dept. of the Navy, 1997), 23.

33. The Cognizance Board report recommending this Airship Board suggested that it should consist of six officers *in addition to* Chief Constructor Taylor. An Army informational "Stencil" from July 1917 lists seven members of this board: Taylor, Towers, Child, and Hunsaker for the Navy, with Squier joining Chandler and Clark as the third Army member: Intelligence Section, Airplane Division, U.S. Army Air Service, July 19, 1917, "Stencil 241: U.S. Army Air Service," 10, Folder "[???] & Army Air Service," File 1–2c, DMA-Information Section. The Airship Board's final report in 1918, however, is signed by only six officers in total: Joint Army and Navy Airship Board to Secretaries of War and Navy, [n.d., copy in Foulois Papers hand-dated July 19, 1918]. A copy of this document is appended to Serial 859, August 21, 1918, GB-449; another is in Box 33, Folder 7, Foulois Papers-LC.

34. William F. Althoff, *USS Los Angeles: The Navy's Venerable Airship and Aviation Technology* (Washington, DC: Brassey's, 2004), xviii, xxii–xxiii; Douglas Hill Robinson and Charles L. Keller, *"Up Ship!": A History of the U.S. Navy's Rigid Airships 1919–1935* (Annapolis, MD: Naval Institute Press, 1982), 8–10; Joint Army and Navy Airship Board to Secretaries of War and Navy, (copy in Foulois Papers hand-dated July 19, 1918), see n33 for locations.

35. 26983–633:3, Roosevelt to Baker, January 12, 1917, SecNavGC. Robert Greenhalgh Albion, *Makers of Naval Policy, 1798–1947*, ed. Rowena Reed (Annapolis, MD: Naval Institute Press, 1980), 367–68; Van Wyen, *Aeronautical Board*, 29–31.

36. 3697–16, Benson to Daniels, October 27, 1916, ONA; Board of Army and Navy Officers relative development aeronautical service to SecNav, March 12, 1917. Copies of the Board's report may be found in GB-449; Box 33, Folder 7, Foulois Papers-LC; and reproduced in Van Wyen, *Aeronautical Board*, as Appendix XVIII.

37. Board . . . to SecNav, March 12, 1917.

38. Albion, *Makers of Naval Policy*, 366–68; Van Wyen, *Aeronautical Board*, 31–32.
39. W. H. Sitz, *A History of U.S. Naval Aviation* (Washington, DC: United States Navy Department, Bureau of Aeronautics, 1930), 13–14; I. B. Holley Jr., *Ideas and Weapons* (New York: Yale University Press, 1953), 40–46, 70–74; 4218–16, Towers, Memorandum for McKean, November 22, 1916, ONA.

CONCLUSION
1. Mustin to Bristol, August 29, 1914, *Corresp.*, Mustin Papers.
2. The Quartermaster and Pay Departments merged along with the Subsistence Department in 1912 to form the Quartermaster Corps.
3. Allan Reed Millett, *Semper Fidelis: The History of the United States Marine Corps*, rev. and expanded ed., *The Macmillan Wars of the United States* (New York: Free Press, 1991), 142–44.

SOURCES CITED

ARCHIVAL COLLECTIONS

Air Force Historical Research Agency, Document Collections
　Lahm, Frank Purdy Papers (1894–1967)
General Alfred M. Gray Marine Corps Research Center, Marine Corps Archives
　and Special Collections, PC 459—A. A. Cunningham Papers
Library of Congress, Manuscript Division
　Henry Croskey Mustin Papers
　John H. Towers Papers
　Mark L. Bristol Papers
　Rodgers Family Papers
　Washington Irving Chambers Papers
National Air and Space Museum Archives
　XXXX-0494—Samuel P. Langley Collection
　Technical Files
National Archives and Records Administration
　RG18—Records of the Army Air Forces
　RG72—Records of the Bureau of Aeronautics
　RG80—General Records of the Department of the Navy, 1798–1947
　RG165—Records of the War Department General and Special Staffs
United States Air Force Academy Library, Special Collections
　MS 11—George Owen Squier Papers
　MS 17—Benjamin D. Foulois Papers

GOVERNMENT DOCUMENTS

Deperdussin, Armand Jean Auguste. "Aeroplane." United States Patent Office, 1913.
General Staff Corps of the Army War College. *Military Aviation*. Washington:
　Army War College, 1915.

Machoian, Ronald G. "Looking Skyward: The Emergence of an Air-Minded Culture in the US Army." Wright Flyer Paper No. 17. Maxwell AFB, AL: Air University Press, 2004.

Mooney, Chase C., and Martha E. Laymen. "Organization of Military Aeronautics, 1907–1935." 1944.

Pershing, John J. "Punitive Expedition Report." Colonia Dublán, Mexico, 1916.

Secretary of the Army, Annual Reports, 1898–1917

Secretary of the Navy, Annual Reports, 1911–1917

U.S. Congress. *Congressional Record*. 1904, 1911.

U.S. Congress. House. Committee on Military Affairs.

Aeronautics in the Army, 63rd Congress, First Session, August 12, 14–16, 1913.

Army Appropriation Bill, 1917, 64th Congress, First Session, March 28–April 11, 1916.

U.S. Congress. Senate. Committee on Naval Affairs.

Naval Investigation: Hearings Before the Subcommittee of the Committee on Naval Affairs, 66th Congress, 2nd Session, 1921.

BOOKS

Abrams, Lynn. *Oral History Theory*. New York: Routledge, 2010.

Albion, Robert Greenhalgh. *Makers of Naval Policy, 1798–1947*. Edited by Rowena Reed. Annapolis, MD: Naval Institute Press, 1980.

Althoff, William F. *USS Los Angeles: The Navy's Venerable Airship and Aviation Technology*. Washington, DC: Brassey's, 2004.

Anderson, John David. *Inventing Flight: The Wright Brothers & their Predecessors*. Baltimore, MD: Johns Hopkins University Press, 2004.

Arnold, Henry Harley. *Global Mission*. 1st ed. New York: Harper, 1949.

Arthur, Reginald Wright. *Contact! Careers of US Naval Aviators Assigned Numbers 1 to 2000*. 1st ed. Washington: Naval Aviator Register, 1967.

Barnett, Roger W. *Navy Strategic Culture: Why the Navy Thinks Differently*. Annapolis, MD: Naval Institute Press, 2009.

Bowers, Peter M. *Curtiss Aircraft: 1907–1947*. London: Putnam & Company, Ltd., 1979.

Budiansky, Stephen. *Air Power: The Men, Machines, and Ideas that Revolutionized War, From Kitty Hawk to Gulf War II*. New York: Viking Penguin, 2004.

Calvert, Monte A. *The Mechanical Engineer in America, 1830–1910; Professional Cultures in Conflict*. Baltimore: Johns Hopkins Press, 1967.

Cameron, Rebecca Hancock. *Training to Fly: Military Flight Training, 1907–1945*. Washington: Air Force History and Museums Program, 1999.

Challener, Richard D. *Admirals, Generals, and American Foreign Policy, 1898–1914*. Princeton, NJ: Princeton University Press, 1973.

Chandler, Charles de Forest, and Frank Purdy Lahm. *How Our Army Grew Wings: Airmen and Aircraft Before 1914*. New York: Ronald Press, 1943.

Coletta, Paolo Enrico. *American Secretaries of the Navy*. 2 vols Annapolis, Md.: Naval Institute Press, 1980.

———. *Patrick Bellinger and U.S. Naval Aviation*. University Press of America, 1987.

Condon, John P. *U.S. Marine Corps Aviation*. Washington: Deputy Chief of Naval Operations (Air Warfare), 1987.

Cooke, James J. *The U.S. Air Service in the Great War, 1917–1919*. Westport, CT: Praeger, 1996.

Courtwright, David T. *Sky as Frontier: Adventure, Aviation, and Empire*. Centennial of Flight series. 1st ed. College Station, TX: Texas A&M University Press, 2005.

Crouch, Tom D. *The Bishop's Boys: A Life of Wilbur and Orville Wright*. New York: W. W. Norton, 1989.

———. *A Dream of Wings: Americans and the Airplane, 1875–1905*. New York: W. W. Norton, 1981. 2002. 1981.

———. *Lighter Than Air: An Illustrated History of Balloons and Airships*. Baltimore: Johns Hopkins University Press, in association with the Smithsonian National Air and Space Museum, 2009.

Cunningham, Meghan, and Air Force History and Museums Program (U.S.). *The Logbook of Signal Corps No. 1: The U.S. Army's First Airplane*. Washington, DC: Air Force History and Museums Program, 2004.

Curtiss, Glenn H., and Augustus Post. *The Curtiss Aviation Book*. New York: Frederick A. Stokes, 1912.

Daso, Dik Alan. *Hap Arnold and the Evolution of American Airpower*. Smithsonian History of Aviation Series. Washington, DC: Smithsonian Institution Press, 2000.

Evans, Mark L., and Roy A. Grossnick. *United States Naval Aviation 1910–2010*. 2 vols. Washington, DC: GPO, 2015.

Fiske, Bradley A. *From Midshipman to Rear-Admiral*. New York: Century, 1919.

Flying Officers of the United States Navy, 1917–1919. Atglen, PA: Schiffer Military History, 1997.

Fort Sam Houston Museum. *Maneuver Camp, 1911: Transformation of the Army at Fort Sam Houston*. Fort Sam Houston, TX: Fort Sam Houston Museum, 2009.

Foulois, Benjamin Delahauf, and Carroll V. Glines. *From the Wright Brothers to the Astronauts: The Memoirs of Benjamin D. Foulois.* 1st ed. New York: McGraw-Hill, 1968.

Fredriksen, John C. *The United States Air Force: A Chronology.* Santa Barbara, CA: ABC-CLIO, 2011.

Goddard, Stephen B. *Race to the Sky: The Wright Brothers versus the United States Government.* Jefferson, NC: McFarland, 2003.

Grossnick, Roy A. *Kite Balloons to Airships: The Navy's Lighter-Than-Air Experience.* Washington, DC: Deputy Chief of Naval Operations (Air Warfare): Naval Air Systems Command, 1987.

Grossnick, Roy A., and William J. Armstrong. *United States Naval Aviation, 1910–1995.* Washington, DC: Naval Historical Center Dept. of the Navy, 1997.

Hennessy, Juliette A. *The United States Army Air Arm, April 1861 to April 1917.* General Histories. Washington, DC: Office of Air Force History, U.S. Air Force, 1985.

Henning, Lori A. *Harnessing the Airplane: American and British Cavalry Responses to a New Technology, 1903–1939.* Norman, OK: University of Oklahoma Press, 2019.

A History of Military Aviation in San Antonio. [San Antonio, TX?]: U.S. Dept. of Defense, 2000.

Holley, I. B., Jr. *Ideas and Weapons.* New York: Yale University Press, 1953.

Howard, Fred. *Wilbur and Orville: A Biography of the Wright Brothers.* Mineola, NY: Dover Publications, 1998.

Hurley, Alfred F. *Billy Mitchell, Crusader for Air Power.* New ed. Bloomington: Indiana University Press, 1975.

Hurst, James W. *Pancho Villa and Black Jack Pershing: the Punitive Expedition in Mexico.* Westport, CT: Praeger, 2008.

Johnson, Edward C. *Marine Corps Aviation: The Early Years, 1912–1940.* edited by Graham A. Cosmas Washington, DC: History and Museums Division, Headquarters, USMC, 1977.

Johnson, Herbert A. *Wingless Eagle: U.S. Army Aviation through World War I.* Chapel Hill, NC: University of North Carolina Press, 2001.

Kennett, Lee B. *The First Air War, 1914–1918.* New York: Free Press, 1991.

Kevles, Daniel J. *The Physicists: The History of a Scientific Community in Modern America.* Cambridge, MA: Harvard University Press, 1987. 1971.

Kinney, Jeremy R. *Airplanes: The Life Story of a Technology.* Greenwood Technographies. Westport, CT: Greenwood Press, 2006.

Kipling, Rudyard. *Something of Myself*. 1937. http://www.telelib.com/authors/K/
KiplingRudyard/prose/SomethingOfMyself/myself_chap_5.html.

Knight, Alan. *The Mexican Revolution*. Cambridge Latin American studies. 2
vols. New York: Cambridge University Press, 1986.

Langley, S. P., and Charles M. Manly. *Langley Memoir on Mechanical Flight*.
Smithsonian Contributions to Knowledge. Washington: Smithsonian
Institution, 1911.

Latour, Bruno. *Science in Action: How to Follow Scientists and Engineers
Through Society*. Cambridge, MA: Harvard University Press, 1987.

Love, Robert William, Jr., ed. *The Chiefs of Naval Operations*. Annapolis, MD:
Naval Institute Press, 1980.

McFarland, Marvin W. *The Papers of Wilbur and Orville Wright*. Vol. 2: 1906–
1948, New York: McGraw-Hill, 1953.

Mersky, Peter B. *U.S. Marine Corps Aviation: 1912 to the Present*. Third ed.
Baltimore: Nautical and Aviation Publishing, 1997.

Miller, Roger G. *A Preliminary to War: The 1st Aero Squadron and the Mexican
Punitive Expedition of 1916*. Washington, DC: Air Force History and
Museums Program, 2003.

Millett, Allan Reed. *Semper Fidelis: The History of the United States Marine
Corps*. The Macmillan Wars of the United States. Rev. and expanded ed.
New York: Free Press, 1991.

Millett, Allan Reed, and Peter Maslowski. *For the Common Defense: A Military
History of the United States of America*. Revised and expanded ed. New
York: Free Press, 1994.

Morris, Edmund. *The Rise of Theodore Roosevelt*. Revised and updated ed. New
York: Modern Library, 2001. 1979.

Morton, John Fass. *Mustin: A Naval Family of the 20th Century*. Annapolis,
MD: Naval Institute Press, 2003.

Pearce, George F. *The U.S. Navy in Pensacola: From Sailing Ships to Naval
Aviation, 1825–1930*. Gainesville, FL: University Press of Florida, 1980.

Polmar, Norman, and Minoru Genda. *Aircraft Carriers: A History of Carrier
Aviation and Its Influence on World Events*. 2nd ed. 2 vols. Washington, DC:
Potomac Books, 2006.

Posen, Barry. *The Sources of Military Doctrine: France, Britain, and Germany
Between the World Wars*. Ithaca: Cornell University Press, 1984.

Raines, Rebecca Robbins. *Getting the Message Through: A Branch History of the
U. S. Army Signal Corps*. Washington, DC: Center for Military History, 1996.

Reynolds, Clark G. *Admiral John Towers: The Struggle for Naval Air Supremacy.* Annapolis, MD: Naval Institute Press, 1991.

Robinson, Douglas Hill, and Charles L. Keller. *"Up Ship!": A History of the U.S. Navy's Rigid Airships 1919–1935.* Annapolis, MD: Naval Institute Press, 1982.

Roland, Alex. *Model Research: The National Advisory Committee for Aeronautics, 1915–1958.* 2 vols. Vol. 1. Washington, DC: NASA, 1985.

Scott, Lloyd N. *Naval Consulting Board of the United States.* Washington: GPO, 1920.

Shock, James R. *U.S. Army Airships, 1908–1942.* Edgewater, FL: Atlantis, 2002.

Sitz, W. H. *A History of U.S. Naval Aviation.* Washington, DC: United States Navy Department, Bureau of Aeronautics, 1930.

Stein, Stephen K. *From Torpedoes to Aviation: Washington Irving Chambers and Technological Innovation in the New Navy, 1876–1913.* Tuscaloosa, AL: University of Alabama Press, 2007.

Sudsbury, Elretta, and North Island Historical Committee. *Jackrabbits to Jets: The History of North Island, San Diego, California.* 1st ed. San Diego, CA: Neyenesch Printers, 1967.

Swanborough, Gordon, and Peter M. Bowers. *United States Military Aircraft Since 1909.* Washington, DC: Smithsonian Institution Press, 1989.

———. *United States Navy Aircraft Since 1911.* New York: Funk & Wagnalls, 1968.

Sweetman, Jack. *American Naval History.* 3rd ed. Annapolis, MD: Naval Institute Press, 2002.

Taylor, Theodore. *The Magnificent Mitscher.* New York: W. W. Norton, 1954. Naval Institute Press, 1991.

Till, Geoffrey. *Air Power and the Royal Navy, 1914–1945: A Historical Survey.* London: Macdonald and Jane's, 1979.

Trimble, William F. *Hero of the Air: Glenn Curtiss and the Birth of Naval Aviation.* Annapolis, MD: Naval Institute Press, 2010.

———. *Jerome C. Hunsaker and the Rise of American Aeronautics.* Smithsonian History of Aviation and Spaceflight Series. Washington, DC: Smithsonian Institution Press, 2002.

———. *Wings for the Navy: A History of the Naval Aircraft Factory, 1917–1956.* Annapolis, MD: Naval Institute Press, 1990.

Turnbull, Archibald D., and Clifford L. Lord. *History of United States Naval Aviation.* 1st ed. London: Oxford University Press, 1949.

Van Creveld, Martin. *The Age of Airpower.* New York: Public Affairs, 2011.

Van Deurs, George. *Anchors in the Sky: Spuds Ellyson, the First Naval Aviator.* San Rafael, CA: Presidio Press, 1978.

————. *Wings for the Fleet: A Narrative of Naval Aviation's Early Development, 1910–1916*. Annapolis, MD: Naval Institute Press, 1966.

Van Wyen, Adrian O. *The Aeronautical Board: 1916–1947*. Washington: GPO, 1947.

Weigley, Russell Frank. *The American Way of War: A History of United States Military Strategy and Policy*. The Wars of the United States. New York: Macmillan, 1973.

Willock, Roger. *Unaccustomed to Fear: A Biography of the Late General Roy S. Geiger, U.S.M.C.* MCA Heritage Library. Quantico, VA: Marine Corps Association, 1983.

Woodhouse, Henry. *Textbook of Naval Aeronautics*. New York: Century, 1917. Naval Institute Press, 1991.

Wright, Monte Duane. *Most Probable Position: A History of Aerial Navigation to 1941*. Lawrence, KS: University Press of Kansas, 1972.

Wright, Orville. *How We Invented the Airplane*. Edited by Fred C. Kelly. New York: David McKay, 1953.

Yochelson, Ellis. *Charles Doolittle Walcott, 1850–1927, A Biographical Memoir*. Reprinted from the National Academy of Sciences, Washington, DC, Biographical Memoirs, Vol. 39. New York: Columbia University Press for the National Academy of Sciences, 1967.

ARTICLES AND CHAPTERS

Beck, Paul. "The Aeroplane as Applied to the Army." Chap. V in *The Curtiss Aviation Book*, edited by Glenn H. Curtiss. New York: Frederick A. Stokes Company, 1912.

Bradley, John K. "Putting the Wind up the Pilot: Cloud Flying with Early Aircraft Instruments." *History of Technology* 18 (1996): 95–111.

Bruscino, Thomas A., Jr. "A Troubled Past: The Army and Security on the Mexican Border, 1915–1917." *Military Review*, July–August 2008 (2008): 31–44.

Burke, Laurence M., II. "Methodologies and Models in Military Innovation Studies." *International Journal of Military History and Historiography* 40, no. 1 (May 2020): 110–34.

————. "Water Wings: The Early Years of Navy and Marine Corps Aviation." Chap. 3 in *New Interpretations in Naval History: Selected Papers from the Sixteenth Naval History Symposium Held at the United States Naval Academy 10–11 September 2009*. Edited by Craig C. Felker and Marcus O. Jones, 23–34. Newport, RI: Naval War College Press, 2012.

Carpenter, Frank G. "How We Shall Fly." (Washington, DC) *Evening Star*, December 12, 1896, 21.

Cooper, Ralph S. "Beckwith Havens." http://earlyaviators.com/ehavens.htm.

Demers, Daniel J. "Pioneer Airman's Tragic Destiny." *Aviation History*, July 2012, 18–19.

Douglas, Susan J. "The Navy Adopts the Radio, 1899–1919." Chap. 3 in *Military Enterprise and Technological Change*. Edited by Merritt Roe Smith, 117–74. Cambridge, MA: MIT Press, 1985.

H.R.H. [Howard R. Hickok]. "The Manchus." *Journal of the United States Cavalry Association* 23, no. 94 (January 1913): 697–98.

History Division, United States Marine Corps. "Lieutenant Colonel Alfred Austell Cunningham, USMC (Deceased)." https://www.usmcu.edu/Research /Marine-Corps-History-Division/People/Whos-Who-in-Marine-Corps -History/Abrell-Cushman/Lieutenant-Colonel-Alfred-Austell-Cunningham/.

Huntington, Samuel P. "Interservice Competition and the Political Roles of the Armed Services." *The American Political Science Review* 55, no. 1 (March 1961): 12.

"It's a Sad Story, Mates." *Aeronautics* XV, no. 6 (September 30, 1914): 84.

Kennelly, Arthur E. "Biographical Memoir of George Owen Squier, 1865–1934." In *Biographical Memoirs*, 151–59: National Academy of Sciences, 1938.

Langley, S. P. "The Flying Machine." *McClure's Magazine* 9, no. 2 (June 1897): 647–60.

Latour, Bruno. "On Recalling ANT." *The Sociological Review* 47, no. 1 supplement (1999): 15–25.

Machoian, Ronald G. "Looking Skyward: The Emergence of an Air-Minded Culture in the US Army." Maxwell AFB, AL: Air University Press, 2004.

"Martin, Martin-Willard." Aerofiles. http://aerofiles.com/_martin.html.

"The Nation's Air Army and Its Early Leaders." *Air Force Magazine* 94, no. 5 (May 2011): 103.

Naval Historical Center, Department of the Navy. "Terms of the Office of the Chief of Naval Operations." https://www.history.navy.mil/content/history /nhhc/research/library/research-guides/lists-of-senior-officers-and-civilian -officials-of-the-us-navy/chiefs-of-naval-operations/terms-for-the-chiefs-of -naval-operations.html.

Naval History and Heritage Command. "Dictionary of American Naval Fighting Ships." https://www.history.navy.mil/content/history/nhhc/research/histories /ship-histories/danfs.html.

Naval Sea Systems Command. "David W. Taylor." https://www.navsea.navy.mil /Home/Warfare-Centers/NSWC-Carderock/Who-We-Are/Rear-Adm -David-W-Taylor/.

"Navy to have Aeroplane Competition." *Aeronautics* XV, no. 8 (1914): 118.

Owsley, Frank L., Jr., and Wesley Phillips Newton. "Eyes in the Skies." *Proceedings of the United States Naval Institute* 112, no. 4 (Supplement) (1986): 17–25.

Patterson, Michael Robert. "Paul Ward Beck." http://www.arlingtoncemetery.net/pwbeck.htm.

Ritter, Lisa. "Pack Man." *Air & Space/Smithsonian*, May 2010, 68–72.

Till, Geoffrey. "Adopting the Aircraft Carrier: The British, American, and Japanese Cases." Chap. 5 in *Military Innovation in the Interwar Period*. Edited by Williamson Murray and Allan Reed Millett, 191–226. New York: Cambridge University Press, 1996.

DISSERTATIONS

Auriti, Lorenzo P. J. "Aeroelastic Analysis of the Langley Aerodrome." MS thesis. University of Toronto, 1998.

Beardsley, Wallace Rundell. "Samuel Pierpont Langley: His Early Academic Years at the Western University of Pennsylvania." PhD diss. University of Pittsburgh, 1978.

Clark, Paul Wilson. "Major General George Owen Squier: Military Scientist." PhD diss. Case Western Reserve University, 1974.

Foley, Brendan Patrick. "Fighting Engineers: The U.S. Navy and Mechanical Engineering, 1840–1905." PhD diss. Massachusetts Institute of Technology, 2003.

Horn, Carl John. "Military Innovation and the Helicopter: A Comparison of Development in the United States Army and Marine Corps, 1945–1965." PhD diss. Ohio State University, 2003.

Kuehn, John Trost. "The Influence of Naval Arms Limitation on U.S. Naval Innovation During the Interwar Period, 1921–1937." PhD diss. Kansas State University, 2007.

Parkinson, Russell Jay. "Politics, Patents, and Planes: Military Aeronautics in the United States, 1863–1907." PhD diss. Duke University, 1963.

Walker, John R. "Bracketing the Enemy: Forward Observers and Combined Arms Effectiveness During the Second World War." PhD diss. Kent State University, 2009.

INDEX

Actor/Network Theory (ANT), 4–9, 249–51, 253–54, 258, 260

ad hoc joint board re: Langley, xxi–xxii, 13

Adjutant general, 188, 195

Advance Base Aeronautic Unit, 183, 247

Advance Base Force, 83, 96, 99, 155–56, 179, 186, 243; aeronautic section, 181–82; maneuvers, 154, 181

Advance Base School, 82, 111, 174, 181

advocates and patrons, 7–8, 17, 34, 39, 42, 62–63, 92, 99–100, 128, 134, 151–52, 153, 165, 170, 183, 184, 215, 225–26, 249, 250, 251–2, 253, 256, 258, 260

Aerial Experiment Association (AEA), 22–24, 26

aerial navigation, 48, 49, 65–66, 86–87, 114, 115, 120, 165, 201, 248; proficiency in: 135

Aero Club of America (ACA), 16, 23, 24, 39, 76, 111, 213, 214, 229, 231; *Bulletin*, 229

Aero Club of Philadelphia, 83

Aero Club of Washington, 229

Aerodromes, xx, xxiv–xxv, 5

aeronautical centers (Army), 131, 147, 148, 201

Aeronautical Division (Army), 15, 16, 20, 64, 116–17, 134, 149–50

aeronautical engineers, 91; civilian, 144, 150, 220

Aeronautics, 143

aides (aids), 38, 39, 165, 251, 255; for material, 38, 170; for operations, 38; for personnel, 38, 83

air compass, 86, 165, 248

Air Department (Navy), proposed, 97

air/ground cooperation, 115, 131, 205–6, 212, 220, 226, 258

air/ground communications (alternate), 65, 77, 110, 177, 196

aircraft; "Noisy Nan", 83; A-1 Triad (Curtiss E); 42–43, 88, 89; A-2 (Curtiss pusher), 42–43, 54, 89; A-3 (Curtiss pusher), 84, 88, 155, 156; A-4 (Curtiss pusher), 156; AH-10 (Burgess-Dunne), 110; AH-16 through -18 (Curtiss pusher), 177; AH-19 (Martin S), 177; B-1 (Wright), 42–43, 49, 53, 89, 103, 104; B-2 (Wright), 54, 89, 91–92; B-3 (Wright design), 92; Baldwin Airship, 20, 24, 116, 221, 249–50; balloon, free, 169; balloon, kite, 169; Bleriot tractor, 160; Burgess H, 109, 136, 144; Burgess-Dunne, 161–64, 166; Burgess-Wright, 64; C-1 (Curtiss F), 94, 88, 89, 91; C-2 (Curtiss F) redesignated AB-2, 165; C-3 through -5 (Curtiss F), 155; Collier Wright B, 114; Curtiss, 48, 59, 172; Curtiss flying boat, 84; Curtiss JN-2, 197–98, 202; JN-2 unsafe, 199–200, 253; JN-2s

Bureau of Navigation (BuNav), 41, 44, 46, 53, 84, 95, 152, 251, 255–56

Bureau of Ordnance (BuOrd) (Navy), 39, 95, 161, 166, 228, 255

Bureau of Steam Engineering (BuEng), 37, 47, 95, 106, 228–29, 255

Burge, Vernon, 80, 123

Burgess Company (and Curtiss), 64, 69–70, 92, 139, 143, 166, 194

Business Men's Camp, 212

California; Coronado Heights, 147; Los Angeles, 146; San Diego Bay, 147; San Diego, 40, 45, 49, 52–54, 82, 84, 88, 109–11, 115, 116–21, 124, 134–36, 139, 142, 146–49, 181–82, 196–97, 217–18, 224; San Francisco, 147, 194

Call, Loren H., 70, 115, 117–18; death of, 118, 136

Capehart, Wadleigh, 159

Carberry, Joseph, 110, 119–20, 138, 141, 199, 204, 208, 217

Carter, William H., 62, 66, 116

Chamberlain, John, 138, 140, 144

Chambers Board, 94–100, 152, 162, 167

Chambers, Washington Irving, 38, 40–42, 44, 52–53, 61, 83–84, 86, 88–89, 91, 97, 104–7, 111–12, 152–53, 156, 166, 172, 184, 227–33, 251–52; plucked, 92–93, 98, 234; active duty, retired, 94–95; airplanes in fleet only, 43; and safety, 48–49, 51; and aero. lab, 230; designs O.W.L., 52

Chandler, Charles deForest, 14, 17, 19–20, 28, 30, 61, 63, 66, 72, 78, 103, 113–14, 116, 122, 124–25, 134, 223, 242

Chandler, Rex, 119; death of, 119, 143

Chanute, Octave, xvii–xviii, xxii, 27

Chapman, Carleton, 121–23, 138, 204, 208; orders away from aviation, 123

Chester, 37

Chevalier, Godfrey de Courcelles, 89, 91, 155, 162, 170, 177; commanding Pensacola, 161

Chief of Naval Operations (CNO), 36, 165, 172, 182, 184, 239, 252, 255–56

Chief of Staff (Army), 209

Chief Signal Officer (CSO), xxi, xxiii, 12, 14–16, 68, 80, 117, 126, 199, 213, 220, 225, 230, 233; acting, 114; of Eastern District, 230; of Philippines, 79, 122; of 2nd Division, 116

Child, Warren Gerald, 242

Christie, Arthur, 199, 204

Clark, Virginius E., 120, 199

Coast Artillery Corps (Army), 65, 70, 74, 110, 124, 238

coastal defense responsibilities, 238–39, 241, 243. *See also* land/sea boundary; interservice cooperation

coastal patrol, 95, 179, 240

Coffyn, Frank, 60–61, 70

Collier, Robert J., 57–58, 114

comparisons, interservice, 1, 35, 55–56, 99–100, 104–8, 111–12, 130, 186, 228, 247–49, 252–53, 255–58

competition for flight time (training/experiments/practice), 53–54, 81, 85, 110, 145, 149, 247

competitions, 66, 72, 76, 111; fly-off, 106, 142–43; Mackay trophy, 76, 146

Cone, Hutch I. 39, as chief of BuEng, 37

Congress, U.S., xxiv–xxv, 12, 19, 43, 55, 84, 98, 102, 114, 180, 209, 230, 235, 232–33, 235, 237; Act of July 18, 1914, 133, 145, 197; aviation bills, 117, 124–33, 149; aviation funding, 58, 132, 148, 163, 165, 167, 169, 185, 193, 210, 216, 221, 251; declares war, 183, 187, 215, 217, 225, 242, 251, 259; hearings, 124–34, 149, 192, 219, 222–23, 234–35, 237, 255; limits Presidential Commissions, 231, 234

About the Author

LAURENCE M. BURKE II is the aviation curator at the National Museum of the Marine Corps in Virginia. He earned an undergraduate degree from Rensselaer Polytechnic Institute, a master's degree in museum studies from George Washington University, and, in 2014, a PhD in history and public policy from Carnegie Mellon University. After that, he taught history at the U.S. Naval Academy as a postdoctoral fellow and served as curator of naval aviation at the National Air and Space Museum for several years before transitioning to his current position in Virginia.

The Naval Institute Press is the book-publishing arm of the U.S. Naval Institute, a private, nonprofit, membership society for sea service professionals and others who share an interest in naval and maritime affairs. Established in 1873 at the U.S. Naval Academy in Annapolis, Maryland, where its offices remain today, the Naval Institute has members worldwide.

Members of the Naval Institute support the education programs of the society and receive the influential monthly magazine *Proceedings* or the colorful bimonthly magazine *Naval History* and discounts on fine nautical prints and on ship and aircraft photos. They also have access to the transcripts of the Institute's Oral History Program and get discounted admission to any of the Institute-sponsored seminars offered around the country.

The Naval Institute's book-publishing program, begun in 1898 with basic guides to naval practices, has broadened its scope to include books of more general interest. Now the Naval Institute Press publishes about seventy titles each year, ranging from how-to books on boating and navigation to battle histories, biographies, ship and aircraft guides, and novels. Institute members receive significant discounts on the Press' more than eight hundred books in print.

Full-time students are eligible for special half-price membership rates. Life memberships are also available.

For a free catalog describing Naval Institute Press books currently available, and for further information about joining the U.S. Naval Institute, please write to:

Member Services
U.S. Naval Institute
291 Wood Road
Annapolis, MD 21402-5034
Telephone: (800) 233-8764
Fax: (410) 571-1703
Web address: www.usni.org